THE SELLING
BIBLE

THE
SELLING
BIBLE

For People in the Business of Selling

BY JOHN F. LAWHON

COUNCIL OAK BOOKS ~ TULSA

ISBN Number 1-57178-007-6
Library of Congress Catalog Card Number 94-79522
Manufactured in the United States of America

DESIGN AND PRODUCTION, Carol Haralson
EDITING, Sherwood Harris, Charles Neighbors
TEXT MANAGEMENT, Pamela S. Reynolds

EXCLUSIVE DISTRIBUTOR TO THE TRADE:

COUNCIL OAK BOOKS
Tulsa, Oklahoma

For ordering information, please see the final page of this book.

C O N T E N T S

Section II

THE BOOK OF REVELATIONS

INTRODUCTION TO THE BOOK OF REVELATIONS

The "whys" of selling revealed ~ Why it is in your best interest to do only those things that will make you more productive ~ Insights to make sales easier

9. THE SECRET OF SELF MOTIVATION REVEALED FOR THE FIRST TIME   144

Doing what you want to do—not what someone orders or tells you to ~ How people become goal oriented ~ Personal goals can be achieved when you have career goals ~ Your Personal Action Plan

10. HABITS: "THAT WON'T WORK FOR ME"   155

There is no ineffective skill ~ Skills are habits, habits are skills ~ Productive selling skills/habits vs. counterproductive selling skills/habits

11. THE FOUR ADVANCED EDUCATIONAL SCIENCES: HOW WE LEARN   162

Spaced repetition ~ Interactive learning ~ You can't learn to swim in a classroom ~ Learning by objective, cause and effect ~ Focused repetition: all productive skills/habits are developed using this science

12. THE 9-DOT PUZZLE   169

Solving the 9-Dot Puzzle and what it means ~ The difference between stupidity and ignorance ~ The difference between general and specialized knowledge ~ Jack of all trades, master of none?

13. THE PRINCIPLE OF REFLECTION   184

Magic works because the eye sees what the mind tells it to see ~ "They have ears but they hear not..." ~ The value of the benefits of what you sell is created by those who understand and use this principle

Section III

THE BOOK OF KNOWLEDGE

INTRODUCTION TO THE BOOK OF KNOWLEDGE

The only reason salespeople are needed ~ The knowledge and information needed by prospective customers has never before been identified or fully defined ~ The five basic groups of knowledge

20. LEARNING HOW THINGS GET DONE IN YOUR COMPANY 263

Before you start selling, learn how things get done in your company: who does what, why they do it and who gets them to do it—in the front office, credit, inventory, warehousing, delivery or shipping, and advertising ~ Professionals don't promise things their products and companies can't do ~ Knowledge can help you avoid grief and aggravation ~ When the buyer needs services your company doesn't provide

21. KNOWING YOUR PRODUCT 270

Knowing what you need to know and why you need to know ~ A learning plan to follow~ Raw materials ~ Plastic and synthetics ~ Design ~ Details ~ Function

22. KNOWING YOUR INVENTORIES 279

Knowing what you have, what you can get, and when you can get it ~ Inventory and availability information needed to complete a sale every time and make you an expert

23. ADVERTISING BASICS 282

Ignorance of company and competitor advertising is a major source of salesperson incompetence in the eyes of the customer ~ Two case histories

Section V

The Book of Trade Secrets

INTRODUCTION TO TRADE SECRETS

Why "how-to" books never get read ~ No knowledge or skills required to acquire counterproductive skills

40. You Have No Bad Competitors 433

41. Choosing the Best Sales Career for You 437

42. People Bond with People 445

43. Selling Standards 450

THE SELLING
BIBLE

SECTION 1

1 / *The Business of Selling*

THE GREAT AMERICAN DREAM IS TO OWN YOUR

OWN BUSINESS AND BE YOUR OWN BOSS.

A COMPELLING PART OF THE GREAT AMERICAN DREAM has always been to own your own business. Be your own boss. Achieve a stage in your life where no one can tell you what to do. The problem with that dream is that no one in business has *ever* achieved that goal.

The first thing you discover about owning your own business is that a lot of people have the power or the authority to tell *you* what to do. The most obvious of these is the government. Your bosses will come from every bureaucratic agency, from the IRS to OSHA, and they will have absolute authority over certain areas of your business. And after them, state and local bureaucrats will impose their authority any place and every place overlooked by Washington.

The second thing you discover is that the *customer* is your boss. Period. The absolute authority in your company. The customer owns the key to your door.

Only to the degree that the customer buys what you have to sell and pays you what you need in order to make a profit after expenses, interest on debt, and taxes, etc., will you succeed. But even then only on one condition: What the customer buys from you must live up to what he or she was led to expect. It will be how well your customers' purchases meets their needs that will determine how satisfied they are with what they have bought. The more satisfied, the more likely that customer is to do more business with your company. If really satisfied, this customer will recommend others to do business with you.

But if the products or services fail to live up to what your customers had been led to expect, they *will* become dissatisfied with the purchase. And, as it fails to meet more and more of their needs, these customers will become more and more dissatisfied. Dissatisfied customers will *not* return to do business with your company and will tell others *not* to do business with you.

Here is a critical point that every business owner and executive should understand. Fewer than four percent of dissatisfied customers ever complain to the seller, but they will tell many, many times more people about that dissatisfaction than a satisfied customer will tell others of their satisfaction.

I have talked to thousands of business people who have told me they were only in business to make money. They will all fail. It may be sooner or later, but they will fail. The laws of nature guarantee their failure: Bottom line profit is an effect. And we know there can be no effect without a cause. What is it that causes bottom line profit in business? Satisfied customers!

Therefore, the only goal that will guarantee success and bottom line profit for any business in the long run is turning its prospective customers into satisfied customers. Either you are in "the business of selling" or you are not in business.

The failure rate of first-time business start-ups is staggering—fewer than twenty percent survive for more than five years. On the other hand, the fastest-growing area of business start-ups all over the world are franchises, which offer a systematic way for you to run your own business. All you do is administer the system and if it is a good franchise you will succeed.

Currently, over 94 percent of all those buying business franchises are successful. Who determines their success? The customers. If they are satisfied, the franchises succeed. If not, they fail. You can be fired. By whom? Your customers.

Of the hundreds of franchises I have studied, one is far and away the best. When I tell you about this franchise you are going to find it absolutely impossible to believe, but every word you read is true.

All franchises ask the buyer to have some money. This must be unencumbered money to buy the franchise, the operating capital needed, and enough for you to live on until the franchise starts making enough money for you to take out a salary or profits. This investment can amount to as little as $50,000 or be well up in the millions. Whatever the amount, if you fail, you lose it.

For all that money and effort, those buying a franchise that requires under $100,000 can usually hope to earn for themselves on the average $25,000 to $35,000 a year. A few will earn more, most a lot less, and that is usually with the owners working long hours, but of course, they *can* say they own their own business.

If you really want to own your own business, provided you realize that its only goal will be satisfied customers, then I would like to tell you about the most lucrative franchise that ever has or ever will be offered to anyone.

If you own one of these franchises here is what will be included:

• It pays all expenses except personal expenses, including office supplies and rent, telephone, utilities, taxes, permits, licenses, and equipment, including computers, furnishings, even advertising!

• This is the only franchise I know of that pays for your medical insurance, vacations, and sick pay.

• All your state, local, and federal taxes are paid, including corporate taxes. You are only responsible for filing your personal returns.

• All legal expenses are paid, including anything that leads to litigation. That alone is one of the fastest-growing causes of business failure.

• All inventories are supplied by the franchise at no cost to you. You have complete use of all the company facilities, including all selling facilities. You may request help from anyone in the company at any time, even the president if you need it. You can ask for help from all your company's suppliers.

• The franchiser furnishes and administers a full-line credit program for your customers. All deliveries and services will be handled for you.

• The huge truckloads of state, local, and federal red tape are handled for you. You never even see it.

• When you consider the hours of most franchise owners like doughnut shops, fast food, fast printers, and such, the working hours required by this franchise are really quite short.

I said you might find much of this hard to believe, but I have not told you the most important thing about this franchise: You are guaranteed a net profit on every penny's worth of business you do, whether the franchiser makes a profit or not.

How much can you expect to earn with this franchise? As in all businesses, your earnings are in direct proportion to the amount of specialized knowledge you need for the franchise you chose and the productive skills you need to develop in order to operate your business successfully. If you follow the systematic procedures with the franchises that require less specialized knowledge and simpler skills, your business will actually be profitable from its first day of operations, even as you are gaining the specialized knowledge and developing the productive skills you need to run it successfully.

But, there *is* a catch. In any start-up, including this one, every ounce of energy and every waking moment must be used productively. I have started many businesses and opened many new operations. Even after I had my own jet airplane and over a thousand employees, I had to knuckle down and do what had to be done until every new operation was off and running.

In the simplest start-up of one of these franchises, to succeed you will be working harder than you ever have while you're learning, but even then you should be producing profits of $2,000 a month or more within 90 days. When you consider the fringe benefits the franchiser pays for, you can add another $600 or more to that number. By the end of the first year, your profits should be running about $30,000 a year plus benefits. By the end of your second year, you should be averaging over $40,000 plus benefits and after three years, over $50,000. From then on you simply follow your systematic way of running your business and it should continue to grow steadily.

And that's just the base-level franchise. Others are based on even higher levels of specialized knowledge and skills. In those cases, your commitment in time and effort must be even greater. Your sacrifices will be more demanding and your income will not start as soon, but once it does, I promise you that everyone who makes the commitment to administer their franchise systematically and keeps that commitment will succeed beyond their wildest dreams.

Many of the wealthiest people in the world started with one of these franchises I have been describing, and many of them started on a very basic level. That's how I started and I can assure you that in my wildest dreams, I never imagined myself riding in my own jet airplane with luxurious homes in some of the world's most exciting cities. But more than anything else I would not be able to do what I want to do. Today, I am my own boss, but it was my satisfied customers who promoted me to that position.

Okay! Okay! What is this incredible franchise that permits you to own your own business and succeed beyond your wildest dreams? What business could it possible be? Surely even the base-level franchise must cost a fortune.

It's "the business of selling" franchise.

This book will give you every bit of the information you need to acquire a "business of selling" franchise and to succeed beyond your wildest dreams. In reality, all business is "the business of selling." The owner of a commissioned sales position who runs it like his own business has the best of all business franchises. Because it is the only business that guarantees its owner a profit on every bit of business while someone else puts up the money and takes all the risk.

Until this book was published, there was no systematic format that told you how to operate successfully your own "business of selling." So your investment in the cost of this book is the full cost of the most valuable franchise ever offered. With this book you own the franchise. But it will be your commitment to "the business of selling" that will guarantee your success beyond your wildest dreams.

2 / *Who Can Succeed in Selling?*

EVERY GREAT AND COMMANDING MOMENT IN THE ANNALS
OF THE WORLD IS THE TRIUMPH OF SOME ENTHUSIASM.
Ralph Waldo Emerson

IT IS TRUE THAT ENTHUSIASM HAS SOLD MORE THAN ALL OTHER
THINGS COMBINED, BUT IT WAS CONFIDENCE THAT CAUSED THE
SALESPERSON TO REACT WITH ENTHUSIASM AND IT WAS
COMPETENCE THAT GAVE HIM THE CONFIDENCE. TRUTH IS THAT
COMPETENCE HAS SOLD MORE THAN ALL OTHER THINGS COMBINED,
BUT IT IS "ENTHUSIASM" THAT GETS THE CREDIT.
John F. Lawhon

WHEN IT COMES TO WHO CAN SELL, there is only one thing on which everyone agrees: Enthusiasm has made more sales than all other things combined.

Major companies and business associations constantly ask me to visit their companies and conventions to "pump up" their salespeople and fill them with enthusiasm. These people are willing to pay almost any fee to anyone they think can do that. Owners and management alike know there is nothing that can do more good for a company than an enthusiastic sales organization.

Now, here is the rub: I *can't* pump up anyone's sales force and fill it with enthusiasm; neither can anybody else. Anyone who thinks he can doesn't know what enthusiasm is or what causes it. There is a natural law called The Law of Cause and Effect: There can be no effect if there has been no cause.

Enthusiasm is a reaction, an "effect." Before a salesperson can react with enthusiasm, something must cause that to happen. Find out what *causes* a salesperson to react enthusiastically and you will have the answer to "Who can succeed in selling?"

Another great truth in selling is that everyone who really succeeds has "empathy" for their customers. Because of that, most of these experts say, "Salespeople must be able to put themselves in their prospective customers' shoes, feel as they feel." Sorry, but empathy is a reaction too, just like enthusiasm. But if you can discover what *causes* a salesperson to react to prospective customers with empathy you will have the answer to "Who can succeed in selling?"

Want to see someone react with enthusiasm in its purest and most exciting form? Go to any grade school and sit in the back of a first-grade class. When the teacher asks a question, little Mary, who knows the answer, will jump up and down waving her arms. "Teacher! Teacher! I know! I know! Ask me. Ask me." Little Johnny, who doesn't have the answer, will try to slide under his desk, hoping against hope the teacher doesn't call on him.

What caused little Mary to react with such wild enthusiasm? Confidence. What gave her that confidence? Competence. She felt competent because she had the answer. She also *knew* she had it. That gave her confidence and in turn caused her to react with the purest form of enthusiasm.

What caused little Johnny to react with so much fear and trepidation? Lack of confidence. Why did he lack confidence? Because he was incompetent. He didn't have the answer and knew he didn't. That lack of competence destroyed his confidence and *caused* him to *react* with fear and trepidation.

Before class started, you could have gotten little Johnny all pumped up. You could have made him believe he had the answers to the questions the teacher would ask, but when she asked a question for which he didn't know the answer, that artificially induced enthusiasm, along with his false sense of confidence, would turn instantly into fear and trepidation. All the king's horses and all the king's men couldn't put little Johnny back together again.

Little Mary wanted all the approval, praise, and recognition she could get, while little Johnny was only trying to avoid the ridicule, humiliation, disapproval, and reprimand he knew he would get if the teacher called on him.

What is the basis of selling competence?

The first breakthrough I made in my research for this book was discovering the technical basis of all selling. Most salespeople will be reading this definition for the first time:

THE TECHNICAL BASIS OF SELLING IS SUPPLYING THE INFORMATION THE PROSPECTIVE CUSTOMER NEEDS TO MAKE THE BEST BUYING DECISION.

You will come to realize the key word is "best." If the prospective customer needs no further information in order to buy what is being sold, then he or she does not need a salesperson—an order taker can get the job done. On the other hand, if the prospective customer needs more information to make the *best* buying decision and the salesperson doesn't have it, then it can't be supplied. In fact, that salesperson could be nothing more than an order taker masquerading as a salesperson who *can't* do the only job he or she was hired to do.

In its simplest form, selling can be experienced when a complete stranger asks a person the best route to the nearest hospital. It is the most natural thing in the world for one to want to provide that information. We can all relate to this situation. Our competence makes us happy to help, but if we don't know, we apologize for our incompetence and say, "I am sorry. I am a stranger here myself. Let me see if I can find out for you." Now, this is not our job and we don't get paid for doing it, yet it is the natural thing for us to do. We will feel better for having done it.

But what if you know there are two hospitals and the stranger asks you for directions to the hospital? You ask, "Which one?" Obviously, you cannot tell someone the best way to get to the hospital if you do not know which one is their destination. Besides, you would still not be able to tell them the best way to get there if you didn't know the best route. Notice: That question "which one?" made that person aware of the fact that there were two or more hospitals. That person now has a bigger problem.

This example shows you the two basic elements of any sale:

1. The salesperson's job is to learn enough about a prospective customer's needs to determine what will best meet those needs, while making the prospective customer consciously aware of those needs. The salesperson does that by asking questions as we understood when the question "Which one?" was asked.

2. The salesperson also has to know enough about what he or she is selling to be able to demonstrate to the prospective customer how a particular product or service will best meet their needs.

Not one in a thousand commissioned salespeople has the basic productive skills needed to accomplish that first objective nor does the average salesperson usually have the basic knowledge and information needed to achieve the second.

Consequently, the main reason sales are lost is because the salesperson did not learn enough about the prospective customer and his or her needs. The second biggest reason for lost sales is that the salesperson did not know enough about what he or she was selling. Almost every lost sale can be traced to one or both of these factors.

No one was ever born with the knowledge and information he or she needs to help a prospective customer make the best buying decision, any more than they were born knowing the best way to get to a hospital. If they do have that information, they learned it.

No one was ever born with the effective productive selling skills they need to use that knowledge and information any more than they were born with the skills needed to play the piano. We may well have been born with a lot of talent, but if we have productive playing skills, they were developed *after* we were born. There is no such thing as a *born salesperson* anymore than there is a born piano player.

Now we can see how having knowledge and information can cause a salesperson to react with enthusiasm, just like little Mary in the first-grade. But what would cause that salesperson to react with empathy? To show how this happens at the most basic level, let me tell you about an experience I once had when I was staying in a Detroit hotel at 8-Mile Road and Telegraph Road.

I had to visit a company on 14-Mile Road in Warren, Michigan. I had been there many times and knew the freeway was the quickest and best route. But no sooner had I entered the freeway than I came to a barricade. The road was closed and all traffic had to exit. That created a massive traffic jam that made me over an hour late.

That evening when I got ready to return to the hotel, I went down to 12-Mile Road because I knew it had six lanes. I had gone only two miles when the road was reduced to two lanes. This was during the rush hour, and I began to think I would never get back to my hotel. The next day, I had to go to Warren again, so this time I went north on Telegraph to 14-Mile Road. I had gone only one mile when I came to a dead end and had to go right or left. I went left and wound up in Neverneverland. Again, I was late.

Like all men and prospective customers, I will go to any length to keep from having to stop for directions, but that evening I stopped in a convenience store to ask. When I entered, a young man was going in, too. He went over to the cold drink cases and I went to see the clerk.

When I asked the clerk if he could tell me the best way to get to 8-Mile Road and Telegraph Road, out of the corner of my eyes, I noticed the young man straighten up. The clerk said, "Take the freeway." When I told the clerk about the barricade, I saw the young man getting fidgety. Then the clerk said, "Take 14-Mile Road." As I started telling him about my problem with that, the young man at the cold drink case couldn't stand it any longer.

Just like little Mary in the first-grade class, he was almost hopping as he came up to me. "Mister, Mister! I know! I drive that way every day. You are right, the freeway is closed. If you want to know the best way to go, get on the freeway south and get off at 7-Mile Road. Take that to Telegraph and cut back to 8-Mile. I have tried them all and that's the best way." I thanked him profusely, followed his advice, and found he was right.

That young man had reacted with *empathy* when he said, "I know, I know! I drive that way every day—the freeway is closed." *Empathy* is the quality that allows you to put yourself in another person's place. That young man had reacted with empathy that put him in my shoes. He said, "I know, because I have been there myself and you are right." He reacted with so much enthusiasm and empathy I was sold for sure. Had he been trying to sell me something, that is all the convincing I would have needed. He could have just gone ahead and written the order. I would gladly have signed it.

And I will bet you that after I left, that young man said to the clerk, "He sure was a nice man, wasn't he?" and the clerk's response was, "Kid, you wouldn't think so if you worked here and every other fool who comes in the door doesn't intend to buy a thing, they just waste your time asking questions."

The clerk would have been reacting with *antipathy*, a feeling of abhorrence or distaste, the opposite of empathy, just as fear and trepidation are the opposites of *enthusiasm*. I sensed that when I first asked him for directions. When the clerk said, "Take the freeway," and I said it was closed, he got visibly testy. Then, when I started to refute his 14-Mile Road recommendation, I could actually feel the heat of his antipathy toward me.

Here are two other things the clerk might have done:

• When I told him what I wanted to know, he could have said, "There is a map on the wall over there, why don't you just make yourself at home, grab a cup of our fresh-brewed coffee, look at all the different ways to go. Pick out the one you think you like the best. I will stop over in a minute to see if you have any questions I might answer."

• He could have gone even further. He could have said, "Let me take you over to our map and show you all the different ways you can go so you can pick out the one you like best."

That would have been awfully nice of him and I sure would have appreciated it, but it would not have helped me one bit. The map would not have shown that the freeway was blockaded and it would not have told me the best route to take.

Variations on these two responses are what most salespeople use when they come in contact with a prospective customer. These responses will actually cause most of their prospective customers not to buy.

On the other hand, what the young man did was exactly what a professionally competent salesperson would have done. He listened to the conversation until he had learned enough about my problem or need and realized he knew the best way. Because he knew that he knew, that made *him* competent to supply me with the information I needed to find the best solution to *my* need. That feeling of competence gave him confidence and caused him to react with complete empathy and to almost explode with enthusiasm. He *made* that sale and all he was paid for his hard-gained knowledge and information was my gratitude and heartfelt thanks.

It is often taught that selling is either the hardest, high-paying work there is or the easiest, low-paid work. Nothing could be further from the truth. Incompetent salespeople feel the same antipathy toward their customers and their jobs as the clerk in that convenience store. It is no fun and they are not being paid a fraction of what they think they should get for doing such a rotten, laborious, debasing job. There is no harder work than that.

The professionally competent salesperson sets out to turn every prospective customer into a *satisfied* customer. Because these salespeople are competent to do just that, they react to every prospective customer with all the empathy and enthusiasm of the young man in the convenience store or little Mary in the classroom. And they succeed most of the time. Furthermore, they get all the satisfaction and the good feelings as the young man and the little girl. Just getting the chance to succeed was enough reward for those two, but in selling, the successful salesperson gets paid, too, and paid very, very well. Imagine getting a huge cash reward—even becoming *rich*—for doing something you enjoyed doing so much you would have done it for nothing! There is no easier work than that.

These examples demonstrate the extreme cases in selling: those who are *incompetent* and those who are *competent*. It has long been known that most people who try selling don't succeed, turning to some other career, while very few of those who remain in selling ever become professionally competent.

That may make you wonder why I'm convinced most people could succeed in selling beyond their wildest dreams. Well, every bit of my research on selling has been based on comparisons. When I set out to find out who could succeed in selling and what would cause them to succeed, at the same time I had to determine why most people who try selling fail and what caused them to fail.

Here are three things we know about salespeople who fail:

1. **Most salespeople who fail will fail within the first year.** In some fields of selling this figure can run 99 percent and even higher. Others will fail in the second year and also leave selling. Most of those who stay will reach their peak selling productivity in a short period, often 60 days or less. From then on, their sales and income will go down gradually. They (like the clerk in the convenience store) will develop a strong antipathy toward their customers, and

will get to where they like their jobs even less. Not a pretty picture, is it?

2. It may seem hard to believe, but the longer the incompetents stay in selling, the harder it becomes for them to make a sale. Don't take my word for that, just study the productivity record of long-term average salespeople, the ones referred to as "old hacks" or "lounge lizards." Think about that.

Perhaps as few as *one out of 1,000 of those who stay in selling become professionally competent,* but when they do, something altogether different happens. These salespeople discover that the longer they stay in selling, the easier the work gets, the less time it takes to make a sale. Their incomes continue to *climb* for the rest of their selling careers. Most important, they like their customers more and more. What an exciting career that would be, don't you agree?

Why then do most of those who try selling fail? *Anything* you do repetitively gets easier to do if it has been done for 21 days or longer. Psychologists tell us it will have become so easy it will require little or no conscious effort. Once it has gotten that easy, it will have become a habit to which the person is addicted. The longer the habit continues, the stronger that addiction will become, and the harder it will be to overcome.

In fact, all skills are developed through repetition—we've all heard "practice makes perfect." As any skill is practiced, it gets easier and easier and the person becomes more and more skillful. When it has gotten so easy it requires little or no conscious effort (about 21 days) it will then be a skill that has been perfected into a habit.

Effective productive skills are the most valuable assets anyone can have, because they make it easier for us to do what we have to do. They allow us to take less time to do something and permit us to do what we do far more effectively. Most important, no one can take effective productive skills away from us.

If that is true, how then is it possible for some people to "practice" selling for years and still get worse every year?

The problem is that while a few salespeople make a habit of practicing *effective productive* skills, others effectively practice *counterproductive* skills. The longer these *effective counterproductive* skills are practiced, the more habitual they become and the stronger is the person's addiction to them. In other words, these people get better at getting worse.

The worst liability anyone can have is an *effective* counterproductive skill. If you have effective counterproductive selling skills, they can doom you to a job that gets harder as your pay goes down as long as you follow a sales career.

3. The third element everyone agrees with when it comes to selling is that to succeed, salespeople must have desire. The greater their desire for success, the greater their chance of achieving it. That's all well and good, but it is the same as saying you have to have empathy and enthusiasm. How is anyone supposed to get desire? What causes it?

How did that young man in the convenience store gain the knowledge that caused him to react with such enthusiasm and complete empathy? Need. He had the same problem I did and was forced to find a better way to get to work or he would lose his job. That created a burning desire in him to find the best way to travel in the least time. Anyone with a genuine *need* to succeed will have an equally strong *desire* to succeed. (You will find this fully explained in the chapter entitled "The Secret of Self Motivation.")

Of the thousands of salespeople I have encountered in my interviews, the three I am about to tell you about will demonstrate best why I am convinced almost everyone can succeed in selling beyond their wildest dreams.

I was visiting a small city in the heart of Appalachia to interview a furniture salesman I had been told about. The economy in that town had been decimated by mine and steel mill closings. This salesman had been with the company for seventeen years, and if ever I met a man without one ounce of get-up-and-go it was he. He dropped out of school at sixteen because of failing grades and got a job as a helper in the carpet workroom, which was the lowest rung on the ladder and the lowest-paying job in this sixteen-store chain. I say he had no get-up-and-go because seven years later he was still the helper in the carpet workroom and still the lowest-paid worker in the company. It would be hard to imagine anyone with less get-up-and-go than that.

During that seven years, however, the helper had married and had two children. Now, he had reached the point where he could not afford to feed and clothe his family, let alone pay rent. He sent away for a mail order course on selling real estate he read about on the back of a comic book. The ad said he could earn up to $150 an hour in his spare time.

When the store owner heard about that, he called the man into his office. The owner told him that if he felt he could sell, why didn't he try selling for them? If he failed, at least he would still have his job. Could you imagine anyone who would seem less likely to succeed?

On the other hand, I doubt that there has ever been anyone starting out to sell carpets and furniture who knew more about which carpets were likely to best meet the prospective customer's needs, what customers who bought seemed the most satisfied with, or who knew as much about what customers who bought didn't like about carpets and why they had become dissatisfied or disliked them. That experience let the helper put himself in the shoes of anyone who had any need at all for carpet.

Within three months, he had become top salesperson in that company. He had been selling for ten years when I interviewed him and was one of the highest-volume, highest-paid furniture and carpet salespeople in the U.S. Despite the deflated economy in his area, his sales were better than five times the volume of most of the salespeople in the company where he worked.

He was still just a good old boy who didn't have any more get-up-and-go than he ever had. But his need had created the desire to earn enough money to support his family. His vast accumulation of specialized knowledge made it easy for him to develop effective productive selling skills, the same productive skills all professionally competent salespeople have. His need and desire to earn the money he needed had been satisfied long ago, but by then the productive skills he needed to succeed beyond his wildest dreams had already become habits to which he was addicted, whether he liked them or not. Selling, for him, would continue to get easier and his income would continue to go up. He still had his beer belly, drove his fancy pickup and would just as soon be hunting or fishing. But with his new prosperity he belonged to the country club and played a lot of golf. He had the time and money to do that because he still worked only 40 hours a week.

I would like to point out that sixteen percent of the sales in the company where he worked were carpet and 84 percent were furniture.

Forty-two percent of *his* sales were carpet and 58 percent furniture. I thought that was interesting.

The next day, I was in a company very similar to the one where the good old boy worked. It was in a small town 20 miles from Youngstown, Ohio, which at that time had the highest unemployment rate in America. The steel mills had shut down, never to start up again, and things could only get worse. In this store was another of those rare top professionals who will sell almost every prospective customer they come in contact with. His sales were in the top one-tenth of one percent of all the salespeople in his industry. His income topped $100,000 a year.

As I was leaving, he said, "Mr. Lawhon, I wonder if you would have time to answer a question for me?" He asked if I could give him any tips that might help him sell carpet, adding that he sold 100 percent of his prospective furniture customers, but he just could not sell carpet.

I said, "Let me ask you a question. How long have you been with this company?"

"One year," he said, but then said he had been selling where he had worked for seventeen years and had been the highest-volume salesperson in this part of the country for most of that time. I asked why he had left the other company. He told me that after the founders died, their kids got to fighting over the company and caused it to go bankrupt. When I asked him if they sold carpet, he said no. I asked him if he thought he knew much about furniture.

"Mr. Lawhon, I know more about furniture than anyone I know. I may even know more about furniture than you do, and I have a degree in interior design."

I said, "Then, I don't know why you asked me the first question." He wanted to know what I meant and I looked him right in the eye, paused a moment, and asked, "How much do you know about carpet?" He looked absolutely stunned as he mumbled, "I guess I really don't know anything about it."

I said, "I can't believe it. You have learned more about furniture than anyone you know and even gotten a degree in interior design. That incredible amount of specialized knowledge and information has permitted you to develop the productive skills to become one of the highest-volume, highest-paid furniture salespeople in the world. Don't you think that if you knew as much about carpet as you do about furniture that those same skills would make you one of the best carpet salesmen in the world and your sales would go up in this company over nineteen percent?" (In this company, carpet made up nineteen percent of the sales, furniture 81 percent.)

He just stood there saying over and over, "I can't believe it." Then he asked me how he could gain the carpet knowledge and information he needed.

I told him to take time off and volunteer to work with the carpet layers for one week and pick their brains to find out from them everything he could about what seems to satisfy customers most and what it is that caused them the most dissatisfaction.

With all the other knowledge he already had, during that week the salesman learned most of what he needed to know about carpet. Equally important, he learned what it was that he still needed to know and where to get that information. In less than a month, he was selling almost every prospective carpet customer he came in contact with, which caused his sales to go up *over* nineteen percent, because some of those customers bought furniture in addition to carpet. Not only had he made back what it cost him to take that week off, within thirty days his pay would be running better than 20 percent higher and that would continue for the rest of his career. I would call that a pretty good investment, wouldn't you?

If anyone ever tells you "selling is selling"— that if someone can sell one thing, they can sell anything, just remember that story. But wait, let's go back to that first good old boy salesman. He had done pretty much the same thing. Only sixteen percent of the prospective customers going to his company were shopping for carpet. With his incredible knowledge, he was selling almost 100 percent of the ones he waited on. But 84 percent of the prospective customers he came in contact with were shopping for furniture. Only 58 percent of his sales were furniture, so it is obvious he did not sell nearly as many furniture customers as carpet customers. When I said he had no get-up-and-go, nothing could offer greater proof of that than the fact that in all those years he had not taken the time to learn as much about furniture as he knew about carpet. If he had, with the incredible productive skills he had already perfected, his income could easily have doubled and possibly tripled.

Here we have two salesmen: one had no formal education, no skills and no get-up-and-go, but an incredible amount of specialized knowledge and information. So much that the productive skills he needed came almost naturally, just like when someone who knows is asked if they know the best route to the hospital would just naturally ask, "Which one?"

The second salesman had all the get-up-and-go in the world—he even had a university education—and had perfected the productive skills to make him one of the highest-volume, highest-paid salespeople in his field. But when he lacked the information his customer needed to make the best buying decision, he could sell diddlynothing.

I can't tell the story of this next salesperson without getting a few tears in my eyes, but anyone who hears about her will come to believe as I do that almost anyone can succeed in selling beyond their wildest dreams.

The owner of a chain of furniture stores had brought all his salespeople (over 150) to one store so I could speak to them for two hours. They had been using my first book, *Selling Retail,* as the basis of their sales training for over two years.

While I was speaking, I noticed way in the shadows, almost hidden at the back of the room, someone who seemed to be more intent on hearing what I had to say than anyone else there. Whoever it was seemed transfixed and I don't think moved a muscle for the whole two hours.

When I finished and they turned the lights on, I saw that person was a black cleaning lady. As soon as I finished answering questions and signing books, I worked my way back to where she was cleaning mirrors on a bedroom furniture setting. She was overweight, at least 50 years old, dressed like a charwoman, and her figure showed all the signs of a life of hard labor. She was not especially pretty, until she smiled, then her face lit up and somehow you forgot about how she looked and how plainly she was dressed. When she looked up and saw me, that incredible smile seemed to completely fill the space where her face had been, but almost faster than the smile had appeared it disappeared and fear took its place.

She said, "Oh, Mr. Lawhon, I hope you aren't upset because I listened to what you were saying. I read your book all the time. I must have read it a half a dozen times or more. When they said you were going to be here today, I came early just hoping I would get to see you." I spent a few minutes visiting with her.

Before I left, I told the sales manager and the owner of the company about this woman. "If you are not going to let her enroll in your sales education system and go on your sales floor, let me know because I know of other companies in this city who would give her a chance if I asked them to." I would like to tell you that today she is one of the world's highest-volume, highest-paid salespeople.

But she's not, although she is one of the top salespeople in that company and is making about four times what she had been, while doing a job she loves. It's also easier on her worn-out bones and yes, she has succeeded beyond her wildest dreams in selling. She doesn't have that look of fear in her eyes anymore, either. I guess that may be because she sure doesn't have to worry about her job security. There are plenty of companies in that big city that would give their eyeteeth to have her selling for them. The harder times get, the more they would like to have her. That's why she seems to have that incredible smile on her face so much of the time. I guess having the easiest job and more money than she has ever had in her life doesn't hurt either.

Yes, I did select three examples out of the thousands I could have used, but I felt these three made my point as well as it could be made. Not a single person who read early, unedited versions of this book has failed to agree that they too came to believe almost everyone could succeed in selling, even before they'd read the first ten chapters—despite the fact that at present very few of those who try selling stay in selling. And, very few of those who do stay in selling ever become professionally competent.

Read on and you will find out *why*.

3 / *Your Road to Selling Success I*

SUCCESS IS AN EFFECT. PEOPLE SUCCEED ONLY BECAUSE WHAT THEY DO CAUSES THEM TO SUCCEED. PEOPLE FAIL ONLY BECAUSE WHAT THEY DO CAUSES THEM TO FAIL. NOT AN OPINION, IT'S THE LAW OF CAUSE AND EFFECT.

THE GUIDED TOUR

EVERYONE WHO STUDIES SELLING AGREES that within moments, and possibly within a split second of when a salesperson first comes in contact with a prospective customer, something happens that gives the salesperson a better than 80 percent chance to make that sale or a better than 80 percent chance of not making the sale, with nothing in between.

Most experts have always assumed that this situation was something over which the salesperson had no control. We have known for years that most salespeople (probably over 99 percent) will sell fewer than 20 percent of the prospective customers they come in contact with, which means they must do something during that initial contact that gives them a better than 80 percent chance of *not* making a sale. Meanwhile, a very few salespeople in all industries will sell over 80 percent of their initial customer contacts.

In industries such as life insurance, over 80 percent of all insurance sales are made by fewer than fifteen percent of the salespeople, while over 85 percent of the salespeople account for fewer than 20 percent of all sales. Obviously, most of those unsuccessful salespeople do something every time that gives them a better than 80 percent chance *not* to make a sale and causes over 80 percent of their prospective customer contacts *not* to buy. (Please note: I said what they "do" causes most of their prospective customers not to buy, because those few salespeople who sell over 80 percent of their prospective customer contacts must "do" something that causes theirs *to* buy.)

There can be no effect without a cause: the natural Law of Cause and Effect. When a customer buys something that is "effect." Whatever the salesperson did "caused" that effect.

Until now, no one has ever written that when a customer has *not* bought, that is an *effect,* too. That salesperson did something that caused the customer not to buy.

When competent salespeople are selling over 80 percent of the prospective customers they come into contact with in a company where the average salespeople don't sell 20 percent, it is not the product that causes the customers to buy nor is it the terms, prices, service, advertising, or competitors. If it were, every salesperson in the company would be selling over 80 percent of their prospective customers.

No, the answer to this riddle can only be something productive the salesperson does that causes most of his or her prospective customers to buy. That means the other salespeople in the company are doing something counterproductive that causes most of their prospective customers not to buy.

Having observed this frustrating phenomenon for over 35 years at all levels of selling, it *caused* me to investigate why it happened. When I began my research, I owned about two hundred books on selling, all of which I had read, many of them more than once. Today, my library has almost four hundred books on selling. For some reason, I just didn't believe most of what those books were trying to teach about selling.

During the first nine months of my research, I interviewed salespeople, but I added a factor to my interviews that others had not considered. The answers I received let me define clearly for the first time exactly what it was that most salespeople "did" that *caused* most of their prospective customers *not* to buy. Because of this I was able to discover what it was that professionally competent salespeople "did" that *caused* most of their prospective customers *to* buy. I traveled across the U.S. and Canada for nine months. Whenever I found both types working in the same company, I interviewed them.

I began my research with interviews in companies located in major cities where I could find more easily those rare professionally competent salespeople who sold almost everyone they came in contact with, even prospective customers other salespeople in their company had tried to sell and dropped. These professionally competent salespeople did up to ten times the volume of the average long-term salespeople in the same company, and—this may seem hard to believe—they often worked fewer hours.

My interviews with each salesperson lasted over an hour; here are a few of my questions:

• Do you feel your company has any merchandise weaknesses or do you lose sales because competitors have better products, prices and brand names than you have?

• Is there anyone in this city who you feel has better advertising than your company?

• Do your competitors offer better terms or delivery than your company?

The salespeople who were selling almost every prospective customer contact answered every question of this type with a flat "no." They had nothing to add to their answers and did not hesitate before answering.

Those long-term average salespeople in the same companies who sold very few of their prospective customer contacts answered "yes" to these questions. If I let them, they would go on and on, telling me how bad the selection, services, advertising, delivery, and credit terms were in their company and how much better all of these things were, including the prices, at a number of their competitors' stores.

When I asked the average salespeople if they lost sales because of each one of these things, they said of course they did. When I asked if that was a lot of sales, they said, "A lot of sales."

During the interviews, I also asked each one, "If I went out into your showroom right now and lowered every price on every item, including sale prices, by five percent, would you make more sales?"

I would wait for them to answer, then pause a moment and ask, "What if I lowered all prices ten percent?" Again, I would wait for their answer, pause, and ask, "What if I lowered every price 25 percent—I mean every price, even your sale prices—would you make any more sales?"

Those long-term average salespeople who were selling very few of their prospective customer contacts replied, "Of course, we would make more sales if you lowered our prices five percent." They acted like the second question was stupid. "If we make more sales when you lower our prices five percent, we are certainly going to make a lot more sales if you lower them ten percent." At 25 percent, they said, "Mr. Lawhon, if you lower the prices in this company 25 percent, the customers would tear the doors down to get in. You would have to call the police to keep order."

Professionally competent salespeople, who were selling almost every prospective customer contact in that same company, said:

"No," at five percent.

"No," at ten percent.

"No," at 25 percent.

They did not even pause to think. They didn't have to explain. They simply and firmly said, "No, I would not make any more sales."

One of the highest-volume, highest-paid, top professionals in his field, who does ten times the volume of many of the salespeople in his company and who only works four days a week, made a statement about this that every salesperson in every field of selling should think about long and hard.

"Mr. Lawhon, if you lowered the prices in this company 25 percent, I would probably quit. I work all the hours I want to work. I have all the prospective customers I can sell. If you lower our prices 25 percent, you would cut my pay 25 percent, but that is not the reason I would probably quit. If you lowered the prices in this company 25 percent, I think most of the people who come to us would think we were carrying cheaper products and quit coming. That's why I would probably quit."

In many cities where I conducted these interviews, I was able to go across town and interview salespeople in one or more of the competing companies, where the salespeople who had said everything was wrong in their company had said everything was right at their competitors. It was hard for me not to react when the long-term average salespeople told me how everything was wrong in their company but everything was right in the company I had just come from.

Early on, I realized that *all* salespeople did one of two things every time they came in contact with a prospective customer. (And it did not matter what they sold or whether the customer came to them or they called on the customer.) What most of them did seldom resulted in a sale, what the others did resulted in a sale almost every time.

To demonstrate the "something" most salespeople do when they come in contact with a prospective customer, which doesn't result in a sale very often, I am going to use a real-life experience and a simple product. We'll be looking on from the time a prospective customer first enters the showroom until he or she leaves without buying. Then I will show you what a professionally competent salesperson would have done with this same prospective customer, in this same store, that would result in a sale almost every time. Before we're through, I will have clearly shown what one did that caused the prospective customer *not* to buy and what the other did that *caused* him or her to buy.

I had scheduled a meeting in Atlanta with the president of a large chain of furniture stores. I like to shop a company's places of business before I meet with their executives, so I sat in my car on the parking lot of one store, watching for just the right prospective customers. As a young couple got out of their car, so did I. I went in the door with them so the other salespeople would think we were together and I could follow along and eavesdrop.

As the couple entered with me, a salesman approached, "Good afternoon," he said. "What can I do for you folks?" When they said they wanted to see dinettes, he said, "Right this way, just follow me." He started off down the aisle at a fast pace and was waiting at the first dinette when they caught up with him. He said, "This is one of our best dinettes. It has a solid oak frame around the glass top. The base is brass and our price is $599 with all six chairs."

The young lady started looking it over, feeling the finish and saying things like "Well, it is pretty. . . " while the man sat in a chair, tilted back, banged on the side of the table and lifted it up to see how sturdy and heavy it was; each asked a few questions.

When the salesman had told them everything he could think of, he turned to the next set. "This is our starting price set. It is round, with a glass top, and four chairs. Our price is $299."

They didn't show much interest in that, so he turned to the next set and the next, then the next, next, next, until he had shown them all 27 of his dinettes.

At that point, he was rewarded with these warm and comforting words: "Well, we were just getting ideas today. We will probably be back."

He countered. "Here's my card. Be sure and ask for me." They left.

Almost one hour had gone by. One hour for which that salesman will not be paid one dime. To make it an even bigger waste, he had probably waited at least an hour for his turn to wait on this prospective customer. That is what happens most of the time when prospective customers come in contact with a company's sales representatives. I call it a "guided tour."

The salesperson starts right in showing and telling about his or her product, hoping against hope the prospective customer will like it well enough to buy. Very few do.

Actually, this was a good guided tour. The salesperson was polite and informative. It could well have been an "unguided tour." He could have said, "Just make yourselves at home. Look to your heart's content. I will stop by from time to time to see if you have any questions."

It could have been a "short guided tour." They could have asked to see the dinette that was advertised. In that case, he would have led them right to it. He would have said, "That's it. That's the one that was advertised on sale."

They would have looked at it for a moment and the lady would have said, "I don't think I can use it."

He would have said, "Let me show you something else."

She would have said, "No, I saw that one advertised and I thought that if I could use it at that price, I would buy it, but I can't," and they would have left.

In my 35 years in the business of selling, I have had many a guided tour while sitting behind the desk in my office by wholesale representatives who get out the pictures of their products and proceed to show them to me one at a time, hoping against hope I would find something I liked well enough to buy. I rarely did.

Automobile salespeople may be the very best at this. When prospective customers come in, they lead them around or let them look, hoping these prospective customers will see a car they like well enough to make an offer, any kind of an offer, so the salesperson can get them in what they call a closing room, where the sales manager or "closer" will try to negotiate, sweet talk, high pressure, or even trick customers into buying.

Real estate salespeople sometimes give guided tours that go on for months. They will call the prospective customer repeatedly, saying, "I have some homes I want you to see. I think they may be just what you are looking for." They set Saturdays and Sundays aside for guided tours of open houses. Same thing.

Whether it's jet airplanes, heavy-duty machinery, clothing, building sites, literally anything—when salespeoples' only objective is to get prospective customers to look at what they sell while they try to tell them about it, or to demonstrate it hoping the prospective customers will like it well enough to buy, it is a guided tour and it seldom results in a sale.

Some form of a guided tour is what most commissioned salespeople do. Once they get in that rut it becomes a counterproductive habit and they will go on doing it as long as they stay in selling. The most amazing thing about what they do is that it actually gets harder for them to make a sale. As the years go by, they become less and less productive, while their income slips ever so slightly, year after year.

It is a rare beginning salesperson who has even a small part of the specialized knowledge and information needed to develop effective productive selling skills into productive habits. Those who have any sales training at all before they start selling are shown how to point out the features of what they sell and to demonstrate the benefits. With that basic training, they are told to get out there and start selling. From the start, their only efforts are to try to get the prospective customers to let them show and tell about what they had to sell, hoping against hope that the prospective customer would like it well enough to buy. Very few do.

Within 21 days, these effective counterproductive skills become perfected into counterproductive habits that cause most prospective customers not to buy. The longer these skills are practiced, the more effective and counterproductive they become. The salespeople do almost everything they do with little or no conscious thought or effort. They are not even consciously aware of what they have done most of the time. Because all skills, whether productive or counterproductive, improve with practice, these people get better at becoming even more counterproductive.

Don't take my word for that. Study the sales productivity records of long-term average salespersons and you will see that they peaked within a short time after they started selling. Often within a month. From then on, year after year, allowing for inflation, they slipped ever so gradually, almost imperceptibly, as they got better and better at getting worse. The older they get, the harder it is to hold a selling job and when they lose their jobs, the harder it is to get another.

This process accelerates greatly when selling intangibles like life insurance where the percentage is the highest for those who try selling, fail, and change careers. They can't give guided tours so they rarely get past asking prospective customers if they can tell them about what they have to sell. In other fields of selling, guided tour directors will have enough prospective customers buy to hang onto their jobs. Since most salespeople are guided tour directors, the company has no choice but let them continue their counterproductive habits at the terrible cost of lost sales.

When they discuss this problem among themselves, I have heard many a sales executive say, "I would fire them all, but the ones I would have to hire to replace them probably wouldn't be any better and might even be worse."

While speaking to salespeople I often do my impersonation of the losers in the lounge. This gets the loudest and longest laughter of anything I do. Salespeople with tears of laughter running down their cheeks will stand up and yell across the auditorium at fellow salespeople, "He sure has your number down perfect," and yet, the ones doing this are the very ones I am mimicking. Because most of what they do is done unconsciously they are not aware they are doing it. They can see the other salespeople doing these things without realizing they are the very things they are doing, too.

Repeatedly, I have said what they do is counterproductive and causes most of their prospective customers not to buy. What they do and why it causes prospective customers not to buy cannot be understood until you can see what it is the professionally competent salespeople do that cause most of their prospective customers to buy. Before we look into that, it is important to understand the difference in liking something and needing it.

LIKES VS. NEEDS

Here is an example we can all relate to: Suppose a young man needs a necktie. He stops into a men's store and as he is looking through neckties displayed on top of a showcase, he finds the most beautiful tie he has ever seen in his life. He had never seen anything that he "liked" as well. He looks at the price tag and it is $100. He chokes, but even then, he "likes" it so well he is thinking of ways that he might buy it when the clerk approaches him.

"Sir, we have put all of those ties out for our sale. They are your choice, ten dollars apiece."

"You mean this tie is only ten dollars?"

"Yes," the clerk says.

Needless to say, the customer buys the tie and what a buy he made. Imagine: a $100 necktie he likes better than any necktie he has ever seen and he gets it for only $10. That's 90 percent off!

So he takes it home, holds it up to his suits and sport coats. It doesn't seem to go with anything in his closet. I can tell you what he will do. Because he likes the tie so well, he will wear it one day even though he knows it doesn't really go with what he has on. He will be uncomfortable all day long, and never wear it again. There is not a man reading this who doesn't have ties in his closet that he bought because he liked them, but never wears because they don't meet his needs. Any woman reading this has things in her closet she bought because she liked them (usually on sale) at a price too good to pass up. When she put them on, they didn't make her look the way she wanted, so she never wore them again.

Guided tour directors always start right out letting prospective customers look, telling about or showing them their products and demonstrating them, hoping against hope the customers will like what they see well enough to buy. Most of these prospective customers don't buy, but when one does, more often than not the decision was based more on how well they liked what was offered and its price, with very little consideration given to how well it would meet their needs. When they start using what they bought, the product (like the necktie) often doesn't meet their needs. When any purchase fails to meet the customer's needs, the customer becomes more and more dissatisfied with that buying decision.

It does not matter what is being sold and it does not matter how much prospective customers like it, even feeling they couldn't live without it. It doesn't even matter how low the price was. When the product fails to meet their needs, they are going to become dissatisfied and they will stop liking it.

Dissatisfied customers are the biggest liability any business can have. They won't return to that company and they will tell others not to. Unfortunately, dissatisfied customers will tell many times more people of their dissatisfaction than satisfied customers will tell others about their satisfaction. To make this even more destructive to a company, dissatisfied customers have often bought the least profitable products, as with the necktie, products that were sold at a huge loss. Too many dissatisfied customers will break any company.

Before I return to my prospective dinette customers, let's see what happens when the product purchased really does meet a customer's needs.

Suppose I need a necktie, but don't have the taste to coordinate my wardrobe, so I rely on a real expert. He has put together everything in my wardrobe and keeps a file on what I buy and knows each garment well. I stop in his store. He says, "Mr. Lawhon, how good to see you. What brings you in today?"

"I ruined my necktie and I am on my way to a meeting and need one right away." He says that must be ESP because only that morning he had been unpacking some new ties when he came across one and laid it aside for me, intending to give me a ring. He ran into the back room and brought it out. What do I know about neckties? I don't dislike it, but I don't particularly like it. He insists it's what I need. It's $25 and I buy it.

At the meeting, I get several comments on how good I look. Later, I found that tie went with everything in my wardrobe. I wore it every chance I got and every time I wore it I got compliments and felt well dressed. After wearing it about fifty times, it was soiled and even had gravy stains on it. I had it cleaned and wore it another fifty times before it was completely worn out.

Now I ask you, who made the best buy? The young man who paid ten dollars for a $100 tie he liked better than any tie he had ever seen, then got one lousy wearing out of it that cost him $10. Or me? I bought my tie for $25 after the salesman told me it would best meet my needs, even though I didn't particularly like it. I got 100 of the best wears anyone ever got out of a necktie. Each one made me feel well dressed. I got more compliments on how I looked than with any tie I had ever worn and each one of those incredible wears cost me only 25 cents. I wound up liking that tie better than any tie I ever owned.

But this was not a question of like or need, only a question of which came first. It is on that one point that a salesperson is either on a guided tour that does not lead to a sale very often (and when it does, those who do buy usually wind up dissatisfied to some degree) or on a road to selling success that will lead to a sale almost every time, and as you will see, to a satisfied customer.

The professionally competent salesperson has only one goal when he or she comes in contact with a prospective customer and it matters not what is being sold. That goal is to turn every prospective customer into a satisfied customer. One so satisfied with what he or she bought that when needs arise this satisfied customer will return to that salesperson in that company to do business again. Equally important is that the satisfied customer will recommend to friends, family and business associates that they, too, go to that salesperson in that company to do business.

Professionally competent salespeople have ten objectives that they must achieve in the same sequence every time they come in contact with a prospective customer. Once these objectives have been achieved, they have reached their goal and have a satisfied customer. Eventually, they will achieve this goal well over 80 percent of the time.

O B J E C T I V E # 1 : A GREETING THAT ESTABLISHES POSITIVE COMMUNICATIONS AT THE MOMENT OF CONTACT

This first objective requires a greeting that immediately establishes positive communication with the prospective customer and gets down to business.

In the case of the dinette salesperson the greeting used would not have been much different than the one used by the guided tour director. The difference is that the professional's greeting skills have been perfected to the point that they work literally 100 percent of the time.

When the woman said that she wanted to see dinettes, the professional salesman would have asked a simple question: "Do you mind if I ask whether you will be needing to seat more than four people at your dinette?" Regardless how she answered, he would have eliminated about half of his 27 dinettes. That question asked while the prospective customers are standing where they first met him would cut the salesperson's guided tour in half and, you must admit, make his job a lot easier. He asks another simple question, "Was there a particular style you need or have you already seen something you think you would like in a dinette?"

That question probably eliminated all but three or four of the 27 dinettes, and with no more than two or three more questions (asked before he even starts toward the dinette display), he will have achieved his second objective. What was it? To learn enough about this prospective customer and her needs to determine which of his 27 dinettes was going to best meet those needs.

Now let me ask *you* three questions: If you were that prospective customer and you had bought one of those 27 dinettes, which one would you hope you had bought? I guarantee that if you stop and think about it, you are going to say, "The one that best meets my needs, of course." Why? Because the more the dinette meets your needs, the more and more satisfied you will become and the better you will like it. That will always be true of anything anyone buys.

If you owned that company and the couple bought one of your 27 dinettes, which one would you hope they had bought? Before you say, "The one I will make the most money on," which is the answer I get most often, reconsider the question. If you do, you will say the one that is going to best meet their needs, of course. Why? Because as it better and better meets the customers' needs, they are going to become more and more satisfied. The more satisfied the customers become, the more people they will tell about that satisfaction and the more apt they are to continue doing business with you and your company. If they bought the one they liked the best or that you made the most money on, and it failed to do an acceptable job of meeting their needs, they will become more and more dissatisfied as they start to dislike the set more and more. And they will tell more and more people of their dissatisfaction, and they won't ever return to your company to do business.

If you were that salesperson and you had any chance at all of selling that prospective customer one of your 27 dinettes, which one do you think will be the easiest to sell? The one that will best meet their needs, of course. Why? Simply because as you point out and demonstrate how the benefits of each feature makes the dinette meet their needs better and better, your chances of making that sale increase.

The only goal all prospective customers ever have or ever will have when they start out to buy anything, is to buy what is going to best meet their needs, which means the product they will be the most satisfied with. Simply, that means these prospective customers' only goal when they came in contact with a salesperson was to wind up as satisfied customer. Isn't that incredible? The professionally competent salesperson and the prospective customer both have the same goal when they first come in contact.

Remember, I said that once the professionally competent salesperson had learned enough about the prospective dinette customer and her needs to determine which product was going to best meet those needs, he had achieved an important objective. No professionally competent salesperson will ever go forward with a sale until this objective has been achieved to the very best of his or her ability.

OBJECTIVE #2: DETERMINE THE NEEDS OF YOUR PROSPECTIVE CUSTOMER

Far more sales are lost because the salesperson has not learned enough about the prospective customer and that customer's needs than all other reasons combined. Another way to look at it is to say that no sale ever has or ever will be lost because a salesperson knew too much about a prospective customer and his or her needs. Every need for the benefits of a feature found on what the salesperson sells that he or she has gotten the prospective customer to tell them about also becomes a powerful reason for that prospective customer to buy when the salesperson demonstrates how the benefits of that feature meet that need. As one powerful benefit (reason to buy) that makes it better meet the prospective customers' aforestated needs is piled on top of another, they soon become overwhelming, and all the salesperson needs do to get the order is write it up.

But wait. It would not do the salesperson one bit of good to have all that information about the prospective customer's needs if he didn't know an awful lot about all 27 of those dinettes including the prices and how each one compared to the rest. If he had twelve dinettes, it would be which one compared to the other eleven. If he had 200, it would be which dinette compared to the other 199. To the salesperson, it is only a question of which of his dinettes, whether 12, 27, or 200, will best meet this particular customer's needs.

Suppose a new dinette salesperson who has never sold anything were to ask his first prospective customer these questions: "Do you mind if I ask what you are using for a dinette now and how long you have had it? There must be some things you have liked about it, would you mind telling me what they are? What are those things you don't like about it?" Each time these questions are asked, the salesperson will hear a different reason or two for liking what they have, and usually *more* reasons for *not* liking it.

The salesperson who has become an expert on what causes customers to become dissatisfied with dinettes can elevate a prospective customer's level of dissatisfaction even more with questions like these: "I have had a number of customers who had that type of dinette tell me that they had problems with [this or that feature]. Did you have any of those problems?" This is called a "leading question," but it reminds the customers of even more things they are dissatisfied with about their present dinette, but are not consciously aware of.

By the time the salesperson has asked ten prospective customers these questions, he or she will probably know more about what seems to satisfy dinette customers and what seems to dissatisfy them than 99 percent of the people selling dinettes today.

When the salesperson has asked these questions of 100 prospective customers, I can guarantee you he or she will know more about what satisfies and best meets customers' dinette needs and what makes them the most dissatisfied than most of the people who design and manufacture dinettes.

When these salespeople look at a dinette what do they see? Instantly, they see every feature of that dinette that seems to satisfy customers the most, as well as anything that might cause customers to become *dissatisfied*. When the factory representative or the company buyer comes in, the salesperson is going to ask why they have a feature that causes customer dissatisfaction on a dinette. If the representative or buyer can show how it has been improved or how the company has overcome the problem, the salesperson is now in a better position to help his or her prospective customers.

Remember, it is the salesperson's job to learn enough about each prospective customer's needs to help that customer buy what will best meet those needs. With that knowledge and information, the competent salesperson is far better able to help prospective customers find the dinette that will best meet their needs than if the customers were left on their own.

Where did the salesperson get that basic information? From the manufacturer or his company's buyer? No! No! No! *From the prospective customer.* It is the precise information the prospective customer needs to make the best buying decision, and the salesperson got the information direct from his or her customers. The more prospective customers who get asked those questions, the more of this precise or specialized information the salesperson gains and the more of an expert the salesperson becomes. This makes the salesperson better qualified to help each customer. This learning process continues for the rest of the salesperson's selling career, making the job easier and easier as his or her income goes up.

> **THE TECHNICAL BASIS OF ALL SELLING IS SUPPLYING THE PRECISE INFORMATION EVERY PROSPECTIVE CUSTOMER NEEDS TO MAKE THE BEST BUYING DECISION. IF SALESPEOPLE DO NOT HAVE THAT KNOWLEDGE AND INFORMATION, THEY CAN'T DO THE ONLY JOB THEY WERE HIRED TO DO.**

The more a salesperson can learn about a prospective customer's needs, the more that customer will become consciously aware of those needs. The more thoroughly you as a salesperson understand that fact, the better you will understand why more sales are lost because a salesperson did not know enough about a prospective customer's needs than all other reasons combined.

Just as crucial, the number-two reason sales are lost is because the salesperson did not know enough about the features and benefits of what is being sold. Almost every lost sale can be traced to one or both of these failures.

To achieve the second goal (to learn enough about the prospective customer's needs to determine what will best meet those needs), the salesperson continues to ask questions in order to reach a third objective:

O B J E C T I V E   # 3 :   ELEVATE THE PROSPECTIVE CUSTOMERS' LEVEL OF DISSATISFACTION WITH WHAT THEY ARE USING NOW

Remember, I said that for the furniture salesperson to know enough about his dinettes, he would have to ask every customer what they were using and what they liked or didn't like about it. The world's highest-volume, highest-paid salespeople regardless of what they sell, ask these same questions of every one of their prospective customers.

Almost every salesperson is taught that the only reason anyone ever has or ever will buy their products will be to get the benefits. In the case of a sleep set, for instance, no one will ever buy one because they want one. If they do buy a new sleep set, it will be because they want a better night's sleep. That is the *primary* benefit and they have to buy the sleep set to get it. But remember, there is nothing perfect on the face of the earth. So the question becomes, "Better than what?" Better than the night's sleep they are getting now. It is that *dissatisfaction* with their old sleep set that has caused these people to become prospective customers for a new sleep set. Wrong! Wrong! Wrong! It is the dissatisfaction with the night's sleep or *benefits* they are getting from the old sleep set that has caused them to need and want the benefits of a new sleep set. The greater their dissatisfaction with those benefits, the greater their need for the new sleep set. No! No! No! The greater their perceived need for the *benefits* of the new sleep set the more determined they will be to buy one.

And therein lies the catch. Most things don't quit working all at once. They wear out gradually. The longer a sleep set is used, the more it sags. The springs get squeakier and noisier, the padding lumpier and bumpier. The prospective customers find it harder and harder to get a good night's sleep. They become more and more dissatisfied, but that dissatisfaction is accumulating a little at a time in their *subconscious.*

For example, research has shown almost five years will elapse from the time a couple first starts complaining about their old sleep set until they begin looking for a new one. Wrong! Wrong! Wrong! They complain about the benefits they are getting from their old sleep set. One will say to the other, "Honey, I tossed and turned all night last night. I didn't get a minute's sleep. One of these days we are going to have to get a new sleep set." Until they buy, almost five years will pass. Incredibly, it is often after they have been on vacation and the sleep they got on the sleep set in the hotel made them aware just how dissatisfied they were with the sleep they got at home and *that* experience caused them to start shopping.

All that dissatisfaction accumulated in their subconscious a little at a time. These are needs they are not consciously aware of. In other words, they don't know they have those needs until someone makes them consciously aware of them, which is what sleeping on the sleep set in the hotel did. Competent professional salespeople know that very few of their prospective customers are consciously aware of very many of the needs they have for the benefits of the features of the salesperson's product. The salesperson's probing questions into what they have now and what they don't like about it make the prospective customers consciously aware of more and more needs, which increases more and more their dissatisfaction with the benefits of what they have now.

It will be the comparison of that dissatisfaction with the benefits they will enjoy when they own what the salesperson sells that will better meet their needs, that will cause them to buy. Professionally competent salespeople know that the more consciously aware they can make their customers of their dissatisfaction with the benefits of what they are using now, the easier the sale becomes and the less time it will take. That is the third objective, and like each previous objective it is achieved to some degree at least before the professional moves on to the next objective.

OBJECTIVE #4 : SET UP A COMPARISON SELECTION

The fourth objective of all professionals who follow their own road to selling success is called "the comparison selection." I have never met a top professional who did not set out to achieve this objective with every prospective customer. When prospective customers raise objections, it is usually because they want to shop more to make sure that they don't find something they "like" better, or they want to be sure they are getting the "best" deal. The comparison skill eliminates those two problems.

As the professional works with our prospective dinette customers, for example, the first three objectives determine what he is going to sell the prospective customers before he ever shows it to them. He knows which dinette that will be, but he does not take them to that one. He takes them first to a similar dinette that sells for about the same price, say $999. It is a good dinette and compared to what they have now would far better meet their needs, which makes them even more dissatisfied with their old dinette. But this dinette will not meet their needs as well as the one he intends to sell them. He will have them look it over, try it out, and then he will move to another dinette that is much better looking and one that will meet their needs much better than the first one, but it costs over $1,500.

Of course, the lady likes that one better, but as good as this set is, it will not meet her needs any better than the one he intends to sell her. But it does make her far more dissatisfied with what she has now. After seeing and trying it out, she certainly doesn't want to go back to using her old dinette, anymore than the people who got the better night's sleep in the hotel wanted to go back to their old sleep set. Then the competent professional takes them to *the* dinette that is going to best meet their needs. Can you close your eyes and see the woman as she says, "Oh, honey! I like this set so much better than the first one that we looked at. I even like it better than the second one and honey, it's over $500 less!"

It is not unusual for top professionals to have the prospective customer at this point say, "I love it. I want it. I will take it." It doesn't happen often, but you can see how it *can* happen, can't you?

Can you see why top professionals when asked what their closing techniques are, simply say, "I just write it up, why?" And the better they are, the more indignant they get when someone implies they would need tricky, sneaky, slick, and even high-pressure tactics to get an order.

Remember, these comparisons are between the set that best meets the customer's needs, the other two sets, and what the customer is using now. It doesn't really matter what they have seen on guided tours elsewhere, because they were not consciously aware of a fraction of the needs they are now aware of, so they had seen nothing at any price that could even start to come close to meeting their needs as well as this set.

This explains why a professionally competent salesperson with only twelve dinette models to offer will make the sale literally every time to the prospective customer who has just had a guided tour in a store that had over 200. The odds are that prospective customer will wind up with a dinette that will better meet her needs than anything she might have bought in the store with 200 sets. In that store, with a guided tour director, her decision to buy will be based almost entirely on how well she liked what she saw as well as the price she had to pay.

Odds are the bargain dinette she "likes" won't meet her needs any better than the $100 necktie met the young man's needs, even though he liked it better than any necktie he had ever seen and bought it on sale for ten dollars. It's exactly the same principle. If she had had a professionally competent salesperson when she shopped in the store with 200 dinettes, that prospective customer would not still be shopping. Can you see that?

Now the salesperson is ready for his fifth objective.

OBJECTIVE #5 WRITE THE ORDER

I'm sure you can see how the prospective dinette customer who is shown the dinette that will best meet her needs after the salesperson has achieved his first four objectives could take one look at that dinette and say to her husband, "Oh, honey! I like this set so much better than the first one we saw. I even like it better than the second one and it costs over $500 less! Let's buy it."

What these competent professionals told me about their presentations is vitally important to anyone who wants to master the business of selling.

Every one of the professionals has told me he or she can tell how effectively he or she has achieved the first four objectives by how long it takes to demonstrate the product and to get the order. We have already seen that once these masters have executed well enough their first four objectives, they have made the prospective customer so consciously aware of so many of their needs for so many of the benefits of the features of the product or service, that the customer takes one look at the dinette or product that is going to best meet their needs and says, "I will take it." The professionals "just write it up." Anything they have to do more than that to get the order they say, is how they measure their effectiveness in achieving the first four objectives.

When asked why they do these things, top professional salespeople all agree that it makes getting the order easier and takes a lot less time. None would consider starting a presentation or demonstration until all four previous objectives were achieved to the best of their ability. When long-term average salespeople who are selling in the same company are asked why they don't do these things, they always reply, "If you think I am going to waste my time doing those things you are crazy!" And that is why they often are not doing ten percent of the volume of the professionals!

Who should you believe? These two types work the same hours in the same company. It is obvious that the average salespeople waste most of their working time because they don't accomplish these first four objectives.

You could compare what the professionally competent salespeople do in preparing themselves and their prospective customers for the fifth objective to what a surgeon does in preparing a patient for surgery. First and always, the surgeon learns enough about the patient and his or her needs to be able to determine what is going to best meet those needs.

He makes the patient consciously aware of those needs. He even gives them comparisons with their options. There is a complete pre-op routine the patient and surgeon go through. And last, but not least, the patient is put under anesthetic.

No surgeon would ever consider cutting on anyone before those objectives had been carefully achieved to the best of his ability—and all of that was done just to get ready. The surgery does not actually begin until the first cut is made. This preparation can take weeks and even longer, although the surgery itself may take only two or three hours.

Now, imagine yourself being met at the door to the doctor's waiting room. He greets you with a big smile. "Boy, are you in luck! We are having the sale of a lifetime. Come on back here. Just step right in there and get your clothes off, then come on out here and hop up on the operating table."

"Why?" you ask.

"We're having a special on appendectomies!"

"Doctor! I don't need an appendectomy, I only have an ingrown toenail."

"Fella, we don't have time for ingrown toenails."

"But, doctor, I've already had my appendix out!"

"Buddy, at the price we have on appendectomies, you ought to buy two for your grandchildren."

Do you suppose you might object to this offer? What would you think of this doctor if he tried a bunch of sneaky, tricky ways to overcome your objections and even tried to cut his price, pressure or coerce you into letting him remove your appendix? To a greater or lesser degree, that is exactly what happens most of the time when a prospective customer comes in contact with the average salesperson.

Prospective customers are not consciously aware of most of their needs for the benefits of the features of what is being sold. To complicate this even more, most of the features and almost none of the benefits can be *seen*.

The only thing prospective customers will see when they take their first look is the price and they won't like it. Automobile salespeople call this "sticker shock." When customers get over the shock enough to have regained their speech, and say, "If you think I am going to give you my great big pile of money for that little bitty pile of benefits, you are crazy."

Remember, when the prospective customer is not consciously aware of a need, as far as that customer is concerned no need exists. That's why most of what the guided tour director will do are things that cause the customer not to buy—just like the make-believe doctor. The more he tried to convince you his appendectomy was a good buy without knowing anything about you or your needs the stronger your objections got. Everything he did would make you more and more determined *not* to buy and cause you to trust him less and less.

It is the same with the guided tour director who knows little or nothing about prospective customers and their needs. Almost everything the tour director does gives prospective customers more reasons not to buy and causes them to have less and less confidence in the salesperson.

People do not buy from salespeople they don't trust. When salespeople do things that cause the prospective customer to lose confidence in them and cease to trust them they are doing things that causes their prospective customers not to buy.

When professionals in the business of selling give prospective customers the first look at what they intend to sell them, the price has been neutralized by the selection comparison as in the dinette example. The prospective customer has been made consciously aware of so many needs that he or she immediately sees how what is being shown is going to meet enough needs to make it *almost* worth the price. On occasion, prospective customers will see that the product meets their needs so well at that price they will say they'll take it and you can write the order right then!

More often, however, the professional salesperson needs to make a presentation and demonstration to achieve objective five and write the order. In the case of the dinette salesman, he might start his demonstration like this: "You said most of the time you will only need to seat four, but you wanted a dinette that would seat six when the need arises. This dinette table comes with six chairs and has one leaf which is 24 inches wide. With the leaf inserted, you can see it will comfortably seat six. You might even add a couple of folding chairs without really crowding anyone and seat eight. I want you both to sit in one of the chairs. Close your eyes a moment. Lean back in the chair. I want you to feel how comfortable they are. They are even more comfortable than a lot of the occasional chairs on the market today, wouldn't you agree? They're certainly more comfortable than the chairs you are using now, aren't they? Many of my customers who have bought this set use two of the chairs in another room as occasional chairs or desk chairs. With their big casters they can easily be rolled into the dining area when needed."

He reminded them of their need to seat six some of the time. He showed them how this set would meet that need and, in a pinch, could even seat eight making it better meet their needs. At the same time he showed how the two extra chairs could meet other needs when not being used as dining chairs.

Can you see how this would give these prospective customers some very good reasons to buy and, in some cases, would be all the reasons they would need? Did you notice how he had them sit on the chairs and experience how comfortable they were while asking them to compare that comfort with what they were using now? He might even say, "I find these chairs even more comfortable than the chairs that come with the dinette I showed you that costs twice as much. You can feel how much more sturdy they are than those chairs, can't you?

"I remember your telling me it was impossible for you to get your old table pulled open by yourself to put the leaves in. You said at times you and your husband together had a hard time getting it open. You said it was an ordeal you hated to go through every time you had company. Mrs. Jones, the slides this table opens with are made of steel with large cog wheels mounted in them. As you pull out on one end of the table the cog wheels open the other end. I have already released the latch that locks the table closed when the leaf is out. Would you just take one finger and pull out on your end of the table? Isn't that incredible! I believe your five-year-old daughter could do that, don't you? Because it is steel, it will never warp or expand."

Again, the salesperson has reminded the customers of a need they said they had. He also reminded them how poorly that need was being met by what they currently were using. He had them actually experience the incredible benefits they would enjoy as this table met that need.

Even though the salesperson had only pointed out two features, he had them experience many benefits. Other than possibly having sat in one of the chairs, none of those benefits would have been seen or experienced on a guided tour. And yet, I think it is safe to say that most prospective customers would be ready to sign the order with only this many benefits having been demonstrated. Can you see how that happens? That point is so very, very important. If you don't feel that happening, then go back and read the last few pages again.

The average medium-priced dinette has at least twenty equally important features and each one offers a number of benefits that would make it better and better meet the customer's needs.

Remember that this salesperson had his customers actually experience the ownership of the benefits of these two features, the chair and the leaf extensions. You can bet that is all the demonstration most customers would need to say, "Oh, honey, we need a chair for your desk and I could use the other chair by the table in the family room. If this set didn't have anything but those metal slides and cogs, I would take it. Let's buy it!"

But, if he had to, this salesperson *would remind her of every need and every dissatisfaction that the benefits of the features found in this dinette would meet,* and long before he was halfway through his presentation and demonstration she would have experienced the ownership of so many of the benefits of the features that made the dinette so well meet her aforestated needs that he could have written the order and she would have signed it. Once that happens he has achieved his fifth objective.

There could be features on this dinette that offered benefits for which she had no use. If they did not create a problem that caused the set to not meet her needs, there was no reason to bring them up. If they would in any way keep the dinette from meeting her needs, this salesperson would not be trying to sell it to her. Period.

The most important point for you to understand about what this salesperson has done is this: He reminded the prospective customers of needs that they said they had and then demonstrated how the benefits of a feature met those needs. No prospective customers could find any reason to object to buying what the salesperson was selling as long as his demonstration was showing how it was going to better and better meet needs that they were consciously aware of—needs that they had told the salesperson they had.

If you have read many books that purport to teach a person to sell, you must wonder where the chapters are in this book that deal with overcoming the customer's objections to buying and closing the sale. After all, there has been more written on these two subjects than everything else combined. Many books on selling deal only with overcoming the customer's objections and closing the sale. Some go so far as to say that closing the sale is not the most important thing in selling, it's the *only* thing in selling. That statement is false. That one teaching has done more to damage the image of selling as a profession than all other things combined.

Let me establish a few facts. Overcoming the prospective customer's objections to buying and closing the sale are one and the same thing.

An objection to buying is a reaction or you could say an "effect." Something had to *cause* that reaction or effect. That's the Law of Cause and Effect again.

I started this chapter pointing out that most salespeople do something that *causes* most of their prospective customers not to buy. That means they do something that causes their prospective customers to object to buying what they are trying to sell them.

When a prospective customer objects to buying, that objection was the *effect* caused by something the salesperson did. No prospective customer can object to buying anything until a salesperson has let them look at it, tried to tell them about it, or asked them to buy it.

The most-asked question in selling gets the number one objection to buying: "Can I help you?" "No thank you. We are just looking."

"Can I help you?" was an effort to get to sell customers something and they objected to the salesperson even trying to do that. There are a thousand ways salespeople reword this question. The version of salespeople who call on their customers goes like this: "I would like to talk to you about what I sell," and most of the time prospective customers object to the salesperson even talking about it.

Something these salespeople did caused these objections. Whatever that was caused most of the prospective customers *not* to buy from them.

All the so-called sneaky, tricky, and even high-pressure techniques for overcoming objections and closing the sale won't overcome one factor that is at the base of every objection that every prospective customer has ever raised.

Every objection prospective customers have to buying anything can be traced to the fact that the salespeople did not know enough about the customers and their needs for what they sell before showing or telling them about it.

You could carry that a step further and say because the salesperson had not learned enough about the prospective customer's needs, he or she had not made the prospective customer consciously aware of those needs. Most of what the salesperson does from this point on will be counterproductive.

Books that claim to deal with overcoming customers' objections deal with two kinds of objections. *Legitimate* objections occur when prospective customers have no need for what is being sold. In that case, they are not prospective customers, and no effort should be made to sell to them. None. If an effort is made, it is because a salesperson did not know enough about their prospective customers and their needs. All the sneaky, tricky, high-pressure closing techniques in the world won't *legitimately* overcome that *legitimate* objection.

The books that concentrate only on teaching techniques for closing the sale, regardless of how well meaning they are, have given the profession of selling the image it has today. These books provide the most damaging and counterproductive of all advice on selling skills. All other objections are termed "requests for more information." Every single one of these objections or requests for more information can be traced to the fact that the salesperson did not know enough about the prospective customer's needs. Boil down all of the teachings on how you are supposed to overcome a prospective customer's objections and you will find you are told to ask more questions. About what? The prospective customers and their needs.

Now hear me and hear me well. These objections are not caused by what the salesperson has *not* done. They are caused by what the salesperson *has* done and it is this counterproductive effort that causes customers to object and that causes most of them *not to buy*. The salesperson simply let the customers look or tried to show them a product without knowing enough about them and their needs. That failure has caused more prospective customers not to buy than all other things combined. Every skill the salesperson used that got him or her into that mess was counterproductive. Of course, none of these objectives can be achieved if the salesperson has not become a real expert on what he or she is selling. And the truly accomplished salesperson will move from one objective to the next so smoothly that the prospective customer will not be aware of all the steps along the way to the sale.

Examine closely the first five objectives of the professionally competent salesperson:

Objective # 1:   A Greeting that Establishes Positive Communications at the Moment of Contact

Objective # 2:   Determine the Needs of Your Prospective Customer

Objective # 3:   Elevate the Prospective Customers' Level of Dissatisfaction With What They are Using Now

Objective # 4:   Set up a Comparison Selection

Objective # 5:   Write the Order

Once more: When the highest-volume, highest-paid, top professional salespeople are asked what their closing techniques are, they all answer indignantly: "I just write it up. Why?" The more competent they are the more insulting that question is to them and the more indignant their response.

4 / *Your Road to Selling Success II*

WHEN YOU ARE IN THE BUSINESS OF SELLING,
DO ONLY THOSE THINGS WHICH ARE IN YOUR
BEST INTEREST. YOU WILL DISCOVER THAT IF
WHAT YOU DO IS IN YOUR OWN BEST INTEREST,
IT IS ALSO IN THE BEST INTEREST OF YOUR
CUSTOMERS AND YOUR COMPANY.

OBJECTIVE #6 : ELEVATE THE SATISFIED CUSTOMERS' LEVEL OF SATISFACTION

IN MOST BOOKS ON SELLING this is called reinforcing the customer's buying decision. As you have already seen, there is a lot of fear in making a buying decision. After the customer has bought, this fear often returns, causing what is termed "buyer remorse." It is the cause of almost all cancelled orders.

This is a problem for the guided tour director whose customers have bought based almost entirely on how well they *liked* what they bought and how good the *price* was. Afterward, they can think of many reasons why they shouldn't have bought. *That* is buyer remorse.

It is even more of a problem when the customer has been coerced into buying, or in some cases, tricked or pressured. Needless to say, the percentage of those who cancel their orders goes way up when this is the case.

Today, we have laws that give customers a cooling-off period after they have made a major purchase. They have the right during that period to cancel their contract or purchase agreement for no reason at all.

Imagine needing a law that protects buyers from the illegal tactics and incompetence of salespeople and their counterproductive selling habits. This law is never a problem for the professionally competent salesperson.

When the professional has achieved the first five objectives, he or she has the order, but until this customer has returned to do business with this same salesperson and sends others to do business, the ultimate goal has not been achieved: to turn all customers into satisfied customers. How satisfied? The most satisfied he or she could possibly make them. You have already seen that in the case of the dinette customer, the young couple were satisfied that this dinette at the price asked was going to meet their needs so well after the demonstration of the benefits of only two features that they bought it and became very satisfied customers.

There were at least 20 important features on this dinette and each offered many, many more benefits. Each of these benefits would make the dinette better and better meet their needs, but as of the time the customers signed the order, these features had not been pointed out to them and the additional benefits had not been demonstrated.

This salesperson gave very little of his or her presentation and demonstration to get this order. Most of the time even top professionals will have given more of their presentation to get the order and all salespeople, even the very best, will at times have to give all of their presentation and demonstration. Sometimes on rare occasions they will have to go so far as to repeat the entire presentation and demonstration twice before they can write the order.

That means they must perfect the productive skills they need to make the most complete and effective presentation and demonstration of what they sell that could possibly be made, and be prepared to make this complete presentation and demonstration with *every* customer.

This constant repetition—doing the same thing the same way every time—makes it easier and easier. It takes less and less time and requires less and less conscious effort to perfect any skill into an effective productive selling habit. The catch is that all skills make us more effective, but the skills we perfect can make what we do counterproductive or they can be productive skills that make us *more* productive. That means the salesperson who wants to perfect productive presentation and demonstration skills will have to follow the same sequence from start to finish every single time he or she makes a presentation and demonstration.

By now, you remember that professionally competent salespeople measure how effectively they have achieved their first four objectives by how much of the presentation and demonstration was made before the order was written and signed.

The professional salesperson does not consider that perfection of the productive skills needed to achieve the first four objectives was a way to shorten the presentation and demonstration. The professional fully intends to make the most complete and effective presentation and demonstration *every time.* He or she will interrupt it to achieve the fifth objective, which is to write the order and get it signed at the earliest possible moment, but as soon as the order is written and signed, the professional returns to the completion of his presentation and demonstration.

Imagine if you can having bought something new such as this dinette, and how satisfied you would have been with the few benefits you had experienced at the price you had paid compared with the benefits of what you are using now and the other sets you had seen. Then try to imagine how much more excited you would be if you were shown feature after feature and experienced how each feature offered additional benefits that made this dinette better and better meet your own stated needs. If the benefits of only two of the features and what you had seen when you first looked at the dinette made it worth more to you than the price, all those added benefits would easily make that dinette worth several times the price you have paid.

Do you think that would make you an even more satisfied customer? Of course it would, and that's why the professional will always carry out objective six which is elevating the satisfied customer's level of satisfaction to the best of his ability every time. The more satisfied you are, the more likely you are to continue doing business with the professional salesperson, and the more people you will recommend to him or her. These people are in the business of selling.

One last question on this subject. If the dinette customer needed her buying decision reinforced, do you suppose this got that job done, too?

When the presentation and demonstration has been completed, the salesperson has achieved the sixth objective.

Many automobile makers now have a variety of programs where customers who have bought a new car are then shown all of the features of the car and how to get the most benefit from those features after the order is written. This certainly adds to the benefit value of the car and makes customers even more satisfied with their purchases.

What I find interesting about these programs is that for the most part, they are performed by someone other than the salespeople, who often haven't sold ten percent of the prospective customers they have come in contact with.

How many of that 90 percent of the unsold and unsatisfied prospective customers would have bought had they experienced all the exciting benefits that made the car meet their needs so much better than what they were driving and other cars they had seen? But alas, these features and benefits must be kept secret. Reserved only for those few who have bought and certainly not used to help anyone buy.

Residential real estate people say no two homes are alike so no two presentations can be alike. But the professionally competent salesperson presenting and demonstrating a home will start at the same point and follow the same sequence every time. That's how they perfect effective presentation and demonstration skills into productive habits.

Guided tour directors never start their presentation or demonstration at the same point nor do they follow the same sequence. They start wherever the prospective customer shows an interest and then launch into an effective counterproductive presentation and demonstration that causes prospective customers to object to buying and *not* to buy.

The sixth objective, elevating the satisfied customer's level of satisfaction and reinforcing the customer's buying decision, is one that many salespeople have a hard time relating to. I know of no professionally competent salespeople who do not achieve the first five objectives in selling almost every time they come in contact with a prospective customer. Nevertheless, there are more professionally competent salespeople who don't know about the sixth objective and have no plan to achieve it than there are those who do. But achieving the sixth objective is what brings satisfied customers back to the professionally competent salesperson again and again and gets them far more referrals.

Let's take the case of the dinette customer, where the salespeople are also dealing with other products for every room in the home. Furniture customers spend about $1,300 a year and make a significant purchase about once a year. They have many needs for other home furnishing products at all times. The only barrier that keeps them from buying everything they need or desire for their home is budget.

Budget is the key factor in the purchase of almost all big-ticket products. Although it may be two or three years before new car buyers will be buying again and we can't determine what they will be buying, we know one thing for sure and that is that most *will* buy again. How car salespeople can guarantee that their customers will buy from them the next time is different from the techniques of furniture salespeople, but those who are professionally competent all have the same goal and the same ten objectives that must be achieved.

In the case of home buyers, an average of seven years pass before they will sell the home they are living in and buy a new one. That's a long time between sales, but the professional knows the customer will be selling the old home and will be buying another. The objective of professionals selling in this field, as in all selling, is to have their customers so satisfied with the homes they bought that they will return to the same salesperson next time they want to sell their old home and buy a new one. Because these customers are so satisfied during that long seven-year spell, they are also going to send along many, many new prospective customers. Yes, all salespeople will have the same objectives, even those who sell something a customer will only buy once in a millennium, because the best source of prospective customers for these competent salespeople is their satisfied customers.

OBJECTIVE #7 : MAKING THE NEXT SALE

After the dinette sale has been reinforced and the sixth objective achieved, the customer is ready to leave. In this case, the salesperson says, "Mrs. Jones, because I do like to help my customers anyway I can, do you mind telling me what you think you will be buying next for your home? Then I can keep my eye out for you. If it goes on special or we get something in I think you will like better, I'll give you a ring or drop you a line. You may want to stop in and take a look at it." The customer will tell that salesperson what it will be every time and won't even have to think about it.

In hundreds of companies, salespeople who have been taught to memorize those exact words and ask them of every customer who has bought before they leave the showroom, have found they work every time. At least I have yet to have one who uses those exact words tell me of a case where it hasn't worked.

Suppose the customer says, "A reclining chair." The professional would then say, "Mrs. Jones, as long as you are here, would you mind walking through the reclining chair department on your way out and show me those reclining chairs you think would best meet your needs and then I will have an even better idea what to be looking for." It is a rare customer who doesn't.

This salesperson already knows a lot about this customer and her budget, but even so, between the time it takes to get from where he is and where the reclining chairs are, he will have achieved his second and third objective for this sale. He will take her to a good chair that will far better meet Mrs. Jones' needs than what she is using now, which is priced about the same as the one that is going to best meet her needs. After she sits in it and he has her experience some of the benefits, he will move to a much more expensive chair that she will like even better, but won't meet her needs any better than the one he intends to sell her. When he arrives at that chair, the buyers will react just as they did when they arrived at the best dinette for them: "Oh, honey! I like this chair so much better than that first one. I even like it better than the other one and it costs a whole lot less."

With little more demonstration than that in his effort to achieve his fifth objective, the professional will say, "Mrs. Jones, I don't know if you have thought about it, but if you really do want that chair I could go ahead and put it on your account right now. It would only affect your payments about 20 dollars a month and we could deliver it with your new dinette." Every time this is done just this way, about half the customers go ahead and make the second purchase because the sale has already been made.

That's easy to understand when you realize the professional has achieved all five objectives, so all he needs do is just write it up. Wait a minute. If he has achieved all five objectives, why is it that the other half of those customers didn't go ahead and buy? Budget won't permit. He has achieved his fifth objective and has made the sale and will write it up as soon as budget does permit. He isn't greedy. He is in the business of selling and he expects to be right where he is right now when their budget does permit. Do not forget for one moment that until they do come back and he does write the sale, his original goal, a satisfied customer, has not been achieved.

With furniture customers when budget does permit, as it does in cases like this about half the time, the professional writes the second order, reinforces their buying decision and is ready to start on that seventh objective again. When he reaches the point where he asks, now what they think they will be buying next, they will tell him and they won't hesitate one bit to think about it. The wife has been dreaming about all the things she needs and wants for her home and they are stacked up in the order of their need and priority in her subconscious. When one item has been bought and a need is satisfied, the next item has already jumped up to take its place. Once in a while, salespeople who do this every time will make a third sale and I have heard of one case where a fourth sale was made before the budget was used up. Even in that case, the salesperson made a fifth sale and set the date when the budget would permit him to write it up.

Back to the dinette salesman and his customers in the reclining chair. He has had them experience all of the incredible benefits of owning this chair, so he could write it up right then if their budget permitted. When they get home, they will have to go back to the old chair. If they were dissatisfied before and that dissatisfaction had been growing for several years, how much more dissatisfied do you think they become every time they use it and compare it with the benefits of that new chair they have experienced owning? How much faster do you think that dissatisfaction is going to grow? When this has been done the seventh objective has been achieved.

OBJECTIVE #8: PUT YOUR SATISFIED CUSTOMER TO WORK FOR YOU

The professional now sets out to achieve the eighth objective when saying "good-bye." Professional salespeople never act rushed and their entire attention is focused on the customer in front of them. Nothing is allowed to take precedence. They always walk the customer to the door and often all the way to their car.

When the professional is ready to say good-bye, he or she will have two business cards held between two fingers as shown in the illustration below, and will say something like this: "Mrs. Jones, it was such a pleasure to wait on you folks today. I want you to have my card because if at any time you should have any reason to call our company, I want you to call me first so I can see you are personally taken care of." With that, the salesperson hands her the two cards, but just as her fingers start to close on them, his fingers twitch as shown in this illustration.

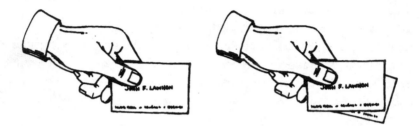

With a little practice, the salesperson finds the customer will react by taking one card and start to hand the other back saying, "You gave me two cards." The salesperson then says, "I know Mrs. Jones, but you and your husband were so nice I bet your friends and relatives are just like you and should any of them have any need for anything for their home, I hope you will give them one of my cards. I would be glad to set an appointment at their convenience and help them any way I can."

This is his first step towards getting this satisfied customer to send him more prospective customers. This might sound corny to some salespeople because most of them never form this kind of relationship with their satisfied customers and they couldn't do this with sincerity and be able to laugh when the customers laugh as they realize what had been accomplished.

All professionally competent salespeople develop methods that work for them to get their satisfied customers to send in prospective customers or to give them the names of prospective customers along with a recommendation for these salespeople, what they sell and the company they work for.

When the salesperson gives them his card, he says, "If you have any reason to call our company, I want you to call me first." Most salespeople don't want to have anything to do with their customers if they have a problem. They will tell them to call delivery, service, or the credit department. The professional knows customers do have problems and when those problems are promptly taken care of to their satisfaction they become even more satisfied than customers who have no problems. The professional wants to ensure that his customer's problems are promptly taken care of and he wants full credit for seeing to it himself. Do not forget he has not achieved his final goal until that customer is a satisfied customer.

OBJECTIVE #9: PUT YOUR SATISFIED CUSTOMER'S BUYING GOAL IN WRITING

At this point, the competent professional sets out to achieve his ninth objective. The satisfied dinette customer is gone and the salesperson turns in the order. At that time, he will handwrite a short note and hand-address an envelope. The showroom can be packed with prospective customers but he will still take the minute or so that it requires. Why does he do it then, not later? The emotional relationship with this customer is still a strong presence. If he writes the note right then, it will have the degree of sincerity that bonds that customer even closer to him.

Because he does this every time, he soon gets to the point where writing the note and addressing the envelope is done as unconsciously as turning in the order. It only takes a few moments, but those few moments have a powerful effect on his satisfied customer.

The note will say something like this:

Mr. and Mrs. Jones,
It was such a pleasure to be able to help you. I was so glad to see you take the solid oak dinette because I know it's going to take all the wear and tear that those three growing boys of yours and their friends are going to give it.
Again, my most sincere thanks.
John F. Salesperson
P.S. You can bet that if that reclining chair goes on special or one comes in that I think you will like better, you are going to be the first people I call.

This note goes in the hand-addressed envelope along with two more of his business cards. Yes, the man and his wife will probably get a chuckle out of the two cards, but that note forms a stronger bond between the salesperson and customers and it guarantees they will become even more satisfied. And this note has done something else for the customers that they are not aware of. It has actually put their buying goal in writing. They will be constantly reminded of their dissatisfaction with the old chair, which makes that dissatisfaction increase every time they and their guests see or use the chair, and you can bet that they will achieve that goal two or three months ahead of when they expected to.

This salesperson will fill out a 5 x 7 file card, similar to the one shown in the illustration below, for every prospective customer he comes in contact with—whether or not the sale was made. When a sale has been made the information on the card will include what and when they will be buying next. A color tab will be placed on the month that is two or three months before the customer said their budget would permit them to write the order for the reclining chair.

Basic Customer Accounting Card

FRONT SIDE. *This is how a basic customer accounting card might look. Of course you may modify your cards to meet your particular needs.*

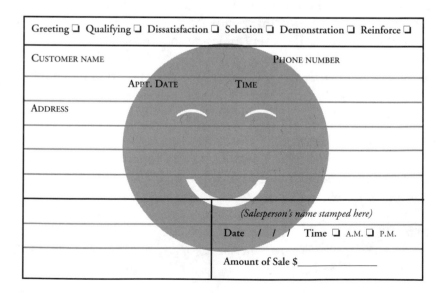

Greeting ❑ Qualifying ❑ Dissatisfaction ❑ Selection ❑ Demonstration ❑ Reinforce ❑

CUSTOMER NAME | PHONE NUMBER

APPT. DATE | TIME

ADDRESS

(Salesperson's name stamped here)

Date / / / Time ❑ A.M. ❑ P.M.

Amount of Sale $_____

BACK SIDE OF THE BASIC CUSTOMER ACCOUNTING CARD. *A green tab goes on the month when the next order will be written. Tabs attached for any other reason go on the blank to the right of the month.*

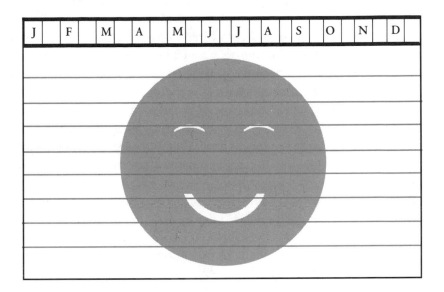

Professional salespeople often phone their satisfied customers after delivery is made to see that everything is to their satisfaction. This added concern makes them even more satisfied.

O B J E C T I V E   # 1 0 :   RESELL THAT SATISFIED CUSTOMER— AGAIN AND AGAIN

This card goes in the professional's customer filecase. Unless those people die or move far, far away, at that salesperson's convenience he is going to call this satisfied customer with the good news he or she has waited many months to hear. It is time to set the appointment and write the order. Salespeople who do this sell over 80 percent of these customers. They can separate the cards with color tabs for any given month and tell almost exactly how much they will sell that month, even if they don't get a single new prospective customer to wait on. Within a few years, these salespeople who are in the business of selling are working by appointment only. Their satisfied customers and the prospective customers they send them take up all of the hours they choose to work. Most of them elect to work shorter hours than the average salespeople in their company and they usually earn three to ten times the average salesperson's income. Those professionals who truly do perfect their skills and who put in longer hours, become the highest-paid people in any profession as they build their customer file.

When the reclining chair customers come back in and the order has been written, the salesperson's tenth objective has been achieved, his goal has been reached and he sets out to make them satisfied customers again.

Salespeople who sell things like homes, automobiles, boats, life insurance or whatever, where three to seven years may pass before the next purchase is made, will still write the thank-you notes and fill out the 5 x 7 cards, or something similar. They will maintain personal contact with their customers with two objectives in mind: (1) to ensure that when satisfied customers are ready to buy again they will buy from them and (2), to keep a steady flow of prospective customers coming in.

The chapter called "Your Road to Selling Success I," in simple form, shows what it is that most salespeople do regardless of what is being sold that *seldom* results in the sale being made. I call them guided tour directors. Then, it shows what it is the world's highest-volume, highest-paid, top professionals *do* that results in a sale almost every time, regardless of what is being sold.

There really are only two routes to take when salespeople come in contact with prospective customers: The first route will be a form of guided tour with little chance to make a sale. As guided tour directors do this repetitively, they will become more and more effective in doing so and they will quickly develop counterproductive habits to which they become addicted. This guarantees that the longer they stay in selling, the better they will get at becoming more and more counterproductive. They will find themselves having to work harder and longer as their income ever so gradually goes down and down. All anyone needs to do is look around at the long-term salespeople who are in fact nothing but guided tour directors.

Professionally competent salespeople on the other route have a clearly defined goal whenever they come in contact with a prospective customer. They have ten clearly defined objectives to achieve, in a set sequence every time. As these objectives are achieved, they reach their ultimate goal: a truly satisfied customer. Because they are trying to achieve the same objectives every time, this repetition causes them to become more and more effective, which means selling becomes easier and easier, while taking less and less time. The longer the competent professionals stay in selling, the easier it gets for them to make a sale, the less time it takes, and the higher their income will grow.

This book includes a complete set of instructions that shows every salesperson how to achieve each of these ten objectives in their proper sequence, while gaining the specialized knowledge and information needed to succeed. Follow these instructions and your selling success is guaranteed. This is a mathematical fact. You can read why this is a mathematical fact in the next chapter, which I call the most important thing you will ever read about selling.

It is true that there never has and never will be any two selling situations exactly alike. No two customers and their needs will ever be exactly alike. No two salespeople will ever be identical, but all those in the business of selling have only one goal and it matters not what is being sold. *That goal is to turn every prospective customer they come in contact with into the most satisfied cusomer they possibly can.* They will all have the same ten objectives and strive to achieve them to the best of their ability in the proper sequence with every prospective customer with whom they come in contact. That's what puts them in the business of selling—their own business.

To summarize the ten objectives — the ten mileposts — on "Your Road to Selling Success:"

Objective # 1:	A Greeting that Establishes Positive Communications at the Moment of Contact
Objective # 2:	Determine the Needs of Your Prospective Customer
Objective # 3:	Elevate the Prospective Customers' Level of Dissatisfaction With What They are Using Now
Objective # 4:	Set up a Comparison Selection

Objective # 5:	Write the Order
Objective # 6:	Elevate the Satisfied Customers' Level of Satisfaction
Objective # 7:	Making the Next Sale
Objective # 8:	Put Your Satisfied Customer to Work for You
Objective # 9:	Put Your Satisfied Customer's Buying Goal in Writing
Objective #10:	Resell that Satisfied Customer—Again and Again.

5 / *The Yardstick*

- WHAT CANNOT BE MEASURED, CANNOT BE IMPROVED.
- WHAT DOES NOT GET MEASURED, WILL NOT IMPROVE.
- WHAT CAN BE MEASURED, CAN BE IMPROVED.
  - . . . *WHAT GETS MEASURED, IMPROVES.*

*"THE MAN WHO QUESTIONS OPINIONS IS WISE;
THE MAN WHO QUARRELS WITH FACTS IS A FOOL."*
Frank A. Garbutt

THE MOST IMPORTANT THING EVER WRITTEN ON SELLING

NOTHING IN BUSINESS EVER HAPPENS UNTIL SOMEONE SELLS SOMETHING. Whether it's an idea, a product, or a service, nothing happens until someone sells it to someone else.

Once that sale is made, one of two things can happen: (1) That idea, product, or service will meet the needs of the buyers as well or better than they were led to expect and they will be satisfied with their purchase. The better it meets their needs, the more satisfied they will become, or (2) the idea, product, or service will *fail* to meet the buyers' needs as well as what they were led to expect so they will become *dissatisfied* with their buying decision. The more dissatisfied they will become as it fails to meet more and more of their needs. This principle is true of anything and everything that anyone wants to sell.

Government officials, educators, scientists, all professionals, religious leaders, tradespeople, and business successes or failures will be determined by these factors:

- Someone had to buy the idea, service, or product, which means someone had to sell it. If that hasn't happened, nothing else will.

• Once buyers have bought, they will become satisfied only to the extent that their purchase lives up to what they had been led to expect.

• After they have bought, they will become *dissatisfied* to the extent that their purchase *fails* to live up to what they had been led to expect.

The only legal goal of any sale is a *satisfied customer*. It is the only legal goal when a political idea is presented, a doctor's treatment is recommended, a religious belief is taught, a product is offered for sale, or anything else is exchanged by people.

Anyone selling anything with any goal other than a satisfied customer or buyer, is what we call a "shyster, quack, con artist, racketeer, swindler, or fraud."

When buyers of an idea, product, or service receive as many or more benefits than they had been led to expect at the time of their decision, they are satisfied and *will never begrudge the price they paid*.

When they feel they did not receive the benefits they had been led to believe they would enjoy at the time of their decision, *they feel they paid too much and have been cheated, because they were cheated*.

This is true for a student who is the buyer of an education, the citizen whose taxes pay for government, for patients, clients, and customers who buy and pay for ideas, products, or services.

The cold hard facts are that nothing happens, absolutely nothing, until somebody sells something. Without this honest exchange or trading in ideas, products, and services within the bounds of the moral laws, statutory laws, and the laws of nature, no civilization, business, government, profession, trade, craft, educational system, or social order can survive.

Incredibly, selling is most often seen as evil, criminal, even traitorous. In fact, look at the definition of the word "sell" in the Britannica World Language edition of *Funk & Wagnall's Standard Dictionary*:

> sell: (sel) *v.* sold, selling, *v.t.* 1. to transfer (property) to another for a consideration: dispose of by sale. 2. to deal in; offer for sale. 3. to deliver; surrender; or betray for a price or reward: to sell one's honor; 4. *colloq.* to cause to accept or approve

something; *they sold him on a scheme.* 5. *colloq.* to cause the acceptance or approval of. 6. *Slang* to deceive, cheat. - *v.i.* 7. to transfer ownership for a consideration: engage in selling. 8. to be on sale: be sold; *see synonyms under convey -n* 1. *slang;* a trick; joke; swindle. 2. on the stock exchange a stock that ought to be sold.

Not one time do you find the word "honorable" in any of these definitions. Note especially definitions 3, 4, and 6. This is how selling is perceived most of the time.

No one can read those definitions of the word "sell" and feel selling could possibly be an honorable profession and yet, the basis of all governments, religions, businesses, professions, sciences, trades, educators, is selling ideas, products, and services. That definition in the dictionary does not clearly define selling as an honorable and most needed of all professions compared with the deceitful, traitorous, scheming, betraying, cheating swindlers, and frauds who have nothing to do with selling and so they treat it as a joke. These types of people aren't salespeople but they create an image of selling as the most dishonorable and despicable of all man's acts. No human could stoop lower than to betray, cheat, or sell out his fellow man. The name "Judas" is synonomous with selling. Isn't that a tragedy?

In my opinion, Ralph Waldo Emerson's essay "Compensation" is the greatest of all man's writings. It says there are two sides to everything in life, one compensating for the other. There can be no honor without dishonor, no sweet without bitter, no kindness without cruelty, no joy without sorrow, and Emerson goes on to include all things. So it is with selling, there can be no honorable practitioners without dishonorable practitioners, but herein lies a factor that is never considered.

In all other professions we have standards that must be met before one is considered competent to practice. Selling is the most important of all professions, yet no skill standards have ever been established that are required before the profession can be practiced.

There are accredited textbooks for every profession and trade known to man and there are accredited educational programs or apprenticeships that must be completed and standards met before the trade or profession can be practiced.

Yet in the academic world, there is no fully accredited textbook on selling that fully defines both the knowledge and skills needed. There are no actual degrees in selling nor are measurements of competence based on skills set for the licensing of a person in the selling profession. (Certain tests must be passed in some fields of selling as in the sale of investment securities or real estate. These have nothing to do with selling competence.)

Because of this, we find the most important profession of man perceived as vile and evil. Is that because most salespeople are dishonest? Without scruples? I spent over thirty-five years in the business of selling, and I have been researching it for over twelve years; I guarantee you most salespeople are honest. Then why do most people perceive salespeople to be of questionable honor?

I am convinced that most salespeople are honest. But I am just as convinced that most of them could not by any stretch of the imagination be termed "professionally competent." The rarest creature in selling is a professionally competent salesperson.

When products bought from honest but incompetent salespeople fail to meet the customers' needs as well as they were led to expect, those customers feel cheated. That causes them to feel the salesperson was not honorable. Those customers feel they would be better off if they never had to put up with such a salesperson. When you take the percentage of salespeople who are of questionable integrity, the ones my daughters call "sneaky, tricky" people who try to pressure you into doing something you don't want to do, then include the frauds, swindlers, quacks, etc., and add them to the great majority of salespeople who are not professionally competent, the result is that people on the whole look down on selling and lump all salespeople together in a garbage heap. Yet, this world has never before needed more professionally competent salespeople in every field, nor had fewer of them.

When I say most salespeople are not professionally competent it is not an opinion, it is a well-known fact supported by the numbers. When I say the problem is not only bad, but getting worse—a lot worse—that is not an opinion, it is also a fact supported by the numbers.

Example. The life insurance industry has long had a reputation for having the best sales training of any industry. Because of this, life insurance companies are reputed to have the best-trained salespeople. In 1965, over 80 percent of all life insurance was sold by fewer than 20 percent of the salespeople. That meant that over 80 percent of the salespeople were making fewer than 20 percent of the sales. It is easy to see that at least 80 percent of the salespeople in what is reputed to be the best-trained industry were not professionally competent in 1965.

Since 1965, untold millions, perhaps billions of dollars, have been spent to improve sales training and the ongoing training of life insurance salespeople. Despite all that money, time, and effort spent, by the 1990s over 80 percent of all life insurance was then being sold by fewer than fifteen percent of the salespeople, which validates my statement that not only have they not improved or even stayed at the same level of incompetence—they have gotten *worse*. The biggest and the fastest growing single cost for the industry (especially the major life insurance companies) is turnover in sales personnel created by the failure of hiring and training programs.

To give you some idea how much money we are talking about, major life insurance companies send recruiters to universities and colleges. Those selected are given guaranteed subsidized salaries of around $3,000 a month for up to three years. They do not have to pay this back. They are furnished offices with all expenses paid. In addition to all of these costs, the companies spend up to $150,000 training each salesperson during that initial three-year period. They can have invested over a quarter of a million dollars in each salesperson who stays for the three-year period. That sounds expensive doesn't it? (It is—as a matter of fact that amount would have paid for the complete thirteen years needed for a medical education.)

But wait, of every hundred hired, subsidized, and trained by the insurance industry, only *four* remain at the end of one year. At the end of the second year, only *two* are left! Those pitiful few still there after three years are often lost because they set up their own agencies, etc. These are the industry leaders. The others don't do even that well.

This hiring and training effort has been stepped up every year, with more money being spent in an effort to improve its effectiveness. But things haven't gotten better. They've gotten worse, a lot worse.

Industry leaders can give you thousands of reasons why this has happened including the economy, changes in types of policies, the complexity of the industry, and so on. Not one of these excuses points the finger at the failure of hiring and training programs, so insurance companies go on spending more to do more of what they are already doing that doesn't work. They just get better at getting worse and they spend more money doing it. As incredible as this may seem, they trace almost 100 percent of this failure to the salesperson's inability to prospect. Which means the salespeople have failed to gain the knowledge and information they need and to develop the productive skills needed to learn enough about prospective customers' needs to help them buy the products that will best meet those needs. Which verifies my claim that more sales are lost because the salespeople have not learned enough about their prospective customers and their needs than all other reasons combined.

I have not singled out life insurance companies just to pick on them. I use them because they have the most accurate information and are considered the best in training and developing salespeople. It is true that the product they sell is an "intangible," not a "tangible" product like a home, automobile, or computer.

My research shows that this same hiring, training, failure ratio is as bad or worse in all industries and it gets progressively worse every year. Part of this problem can be better seen in sales where prospective customers come to the salesperson to buy (as in retailing) and have announced themselves to some degree as prospective customers. Salespeople usually take turns, so that at the end of any given month the salespeople in any one company will have had about the same number of prospective customers to wait on.

From those fields of selling, I often single out home furnishings because that is where I am most knowledgeable and have the most accurate numbers.

In 1964, the U.S. Department of Commerce figures showed that the average American who bought furniture that year had shopped at an average of four different companies. That means the salespeople were selling one out of four or 25 percent of the prospective customers they waited on. Over the next 25 years, the need for furniture out-paced other competing industries. The selection available to the public was hundreds, even thousands of times greater than in 1964. State-of-the-art showrooms and displays made it easier than ever before to select and buy furniture.

So there was every reason for salespeople to be selling even more of their prospective customers.

But current research shows that average furniture salespeople are now selling fewer than fifteen percent of the prospective customers they wait on. They not only haven't improved over the past 30 years, they have gotten worse, much worse.

This is true in all fields of selling. The automobile industry has all but given up on sales training to the extent that none of the big three have any in-house sales training programs.

From time, to time, we see sales training that seems to be effective, as was the case with IBM and Xerox in the sixties and seventies. Books were written about the incredible competence of their salespeople. Xerox was so sure its sales training was the solution that Xerox put its program on the market and sold it to other companies.

The Xerox sales training program had no more overall effect on the competence level of salespeople than any other. And in the case of IBM, computer companies no one had ever heard of have sales staffs selling circles around it today.

In those two cases, as in similar situations, both companies had almost a monopoly on the computer or duplicating markets. They had the best products with the best service capabilities while all their competitors had lesser products and almost no service capabilities. But their salespeople were not *salespeople.* They were the best-trained order takers and service representatives ever developed. When competitive products and service capabilities came on the market that met needs IBM and Xerox didn't meet as well, or in many cases at all, their order takers weren't any better than anyone else's.

I could write hundreds of books on examples that are documented by these numbers. The facts are that to date, no books, training programs, or any other efforts have shown any overall measured improvement of salespeople's competence. Let me make one thing very clear about sales training. Every bit of it, whether in books, audio and video tapes, or sales training programs, has the same objective: to improve the competence of salespeople.

The key word is "improve." It is a fact that a problem that has not been fully defined cannot be fully resolved. Obviously, until now, this problem has never been fully defined.

What you are about to read will explain why no book and no sales training program has had any overall measurable effect on improving the competence of salespeople.

I will now state a mathematical fact, one that is well known by all comptrollers and all mathematicians. This is not my opinion, it is strictly a mathematical fact: "What gets measured improves." I want you to think about that.

WHAT GETS MEASURED IMPROVES

There are no strings attached. No ifs, no ands, no buts. Here we are spending untold fortunes to improve the competence of salespeople without any improvement we can put our finger on and all the time it has been a mathematical fact that if you wanted to improve anything and had some way to measure that improvement, all you would have to do was use that yardstick or standard of measurement and what you were trying to improve would improve. That is a *fact*.

It is just as true that what cannot be measured *cannot be improved*. Any student of mathematics will assure you that is a fact, not an opinion. Even though you had a yardstick to measure what you wished to improve, if it is not used, it will not improve.

WHAT CAN BE MEASURED
CAN BE IMPROVED

That is a fact. If you can measure it, you can improve it.
Do not forget for one minute that what we are talking about is improving the competence of salespeople. If we have no yardstick by which to measure that competence or improvement, despite all the money, all the research, all the books, all the training programs, absolutely no improvement will happen.

No fact has been better documented in the history of man than this one. The competence of salespeople worldwide has not improved overall but, in fact, worsened. There are only four possible reasons why this could happen:

1. No one has wanted to or tried to improve selling competence.

2. There is no yardstick by which to measure the competence of a salesperson.

3. There is a yardstick, but no one it using it.

4. An inaccurate yardstick is being used.

Anyone looking for a solution to this problem can find it within those four factors, because *what gets measured improves.*

We can rule out number one because we know about the incredible efforts that have been made to improve selling competence.

Is there, then, a yardstick that measures the competence of salespeople? If so, what is it?

There is a yardstick, and it is the accepted standard of measurement in all fields of selling. That yardstick is volume. Ask any sales manager or company owner to name the best salesperson in the company and odds are almost 100 percent will say it is the top-volume salesperson.

That brings us to number three: "There is a yardstick, but nobody is using it." Oh yes, they are. It is used as the basis for selling competence world-wide. Companies may include many other considerations, but in the final analysis, volume is the basis by which salespeople are compared and the measurements are nothing more nor less than comparisons.

That brings us to number four: "An inaccurate yardstick is being used." If it was accurate the competence of salespeople would have been improving even if improvement was almost imperceptible. If the yardstick was accurate there would not only have been improvement, but *ongoing* improvement. Instead, we find competence continuing to decline.

This may come as a shock to the world of selling, but *volume has nothing to do with selling competence.* Suppose two salespeople work in the same company and take turns. Each sells 20 out of every 100 prospective customers they wait on and the average amount of each sale is about the same, so we could say they were equally competent. If one wanted to work harder, to hustle more prospective customers, and to work longer hours, at the end of the month he or she could have waited on twice as many prospective customers as the other salesperson and have double the volume, while still selling only 20 percent of them and having the same average volume per sale. (This would not make them one bit more competent.)

Many books and sales trainers will tell you that if you want to make more sales, you have to make more calls. *Working harder has nothing to do with selling competence.* A common phrase is: "Hustle is the name of the game." *Hustle has nothing to do with selling competence.*

The top-volume salesperson in most companies today is rarely any more *competent* than the other salespeople. I call them "hustling order takers masquerading as salespeople." They represent one of the most destructive elements in selling.

If one of the two salespeople who sold 20 out of a 100 prospective customers were to become more competent, you would see two things happen. The one who was more competent would start selling more than 20 percent of his or her prospective customers and the average volume of each sale would increase.

Before I go forward, I want to tell you about three experiences that I have had. The first of these occurred in my youth when I worked for a large company that had a floor covering workroom where materials were cut and made ready for the installers. Back then, workmen had to buy their own handtools, and one indispensable tool was a six-foot, wooden folding ruler. There was an older gentleman who worked full time in the shop. His ruler was always lying around and someone often took it. I don't say someone stole it, but they didn't bring it back, either. He came up with an idea that put a stop to people taking his ruler. He bought a new one, pried open the metal joints, and removed a six-inch section from the center. He now had a five and one half foot ruler and it worked just fine for him.

A day or so later, someone took it. It was the foreman of the shop. He went to the main location and cut the inlaid linoleum for three kitchen countertops. The next morning, two installers started out to do those three jobs. When they rolled the first piece out on the counter top, it was eighteen inches too short. They called the foreman and he said that they must have given him the wrong measurements. After measuring the top again, they assured him that he had cut the job short.

"Okay," he said, "you guys go on to the next job. I will go cut another piece and catch up with you." To make a long story short, he cut four jobs wrong before he discovered what caused his mistake.

Two points. Could you see where he would be far better off with no ruler than with one that was inaccurate? What if he had refused to accept the fact that the ruler was inaccurate? Can you see where this inaccurate ruler would cause things to get worse, and if he continued using it to cut everything, he could actually bankrupt his company?

The second of these experiences was when I received a call at my home from the owners of what was considered at the time the most successful company in their industry, having gone from one store to 39 in ten years, doing over half a billion dollars a year. They told me they were thinking of changing their commission schedule and wondered if I had time to let them run it by me first.

I said, "Sure, but let me ask you a question. Why are you thinking of changing your commission schedule?" They told me they wanted to put more incentive in it and were going to a graduated commission. Instead of paying a straight six percent, they were to pay four percent on the first $20,000 in sales each month and five percent up to $30,000, six percent to $40,000, seven percent to $50,000, and eight percent at $60,000, but these percentages were all to be retroactive. Whatever day of the month a salesperson hit each plateau, that extra one percent would be added to all sales up to that point. Which meant those selling $20,000 started getting five percent up to $30,000 but picked up one percent on the first $20,000 or $200 in added commission.

When the salesperson hit $60,000.01 in one month, that one penny paid him or her an additional $600 commission on the previous $60,000 in sales. Imagine the pressure on the salesperson and thus the pressure he or she would put on the customer as one of those sales plateaus was approaching.

I said, "It appears to me you feel that your salespeople could be selling more of the customers they are waiting on than they are selling now." They agreed. I said, "Then you must feel they could or should be more competent."

"Oh, no," they said, "we have the most competent salespeople in the world."

"That may be so," I said, "but if you feel they could or should be selling more of the prospective customers than they are selling now, you must feel they could improve."

They finally agreed to that. Then I asked, "What will this added incentive have to do with improving their selling competence?"

They asked what I meant.

I said, "There are only two things that will improve selling competence: increased specialized knowledge and information and more productive selling skills. What will your added incentive have to do with that?"

They said, "Nothing."

I said, "Incentive will not buy competence. Incentive only buys hustle. If you have an incompetent sales organization and you give added reward for hustling, it will be the biggest business mistake you will ever make."

They did not take my advice and put in the new commission program. Two years went by. They asked me for another meeting. They were having problems so they had brought in a major research firm at a cost of more than a quarter of a million dollars. The results of the research survey showed that for the most part, customers who had shopped the company and did not buy said they would not go back again because of the way they had been treated by the salespeople. For the most part, those customers surveyed who had shopped the company and had bought said that even though they had bought they would not go back to that company because of the way they had been treated by the salespeople.

How long will it take this company to put itself out of business? The company prided itself on its sales training program and was recognized for having what was considered the best in their industry. So this next finding came as a real shock: Most of the customers who were surveyed, both those who had bought and those who hadn't, said that of all the places they had shopped, the salespeople in this company were the least knowledgeable and least competent of any they had encountered.

The company had previously done customer surveys periodically that had shown during their growth years that they were selling around 20 percent of the prospective customers who shopped their stores.

When they told me about their problems, I said, "The first thing you should do is have an outside firm get you an accurate door count of customers." They did and discovered that at the time their salespeople were not selling ten percent of them.

They had put in the added incentives to get their incompetent salespeople to sell more of the prospective customers they were getting. This incentive only caused the incompetent salespeople to do even more of what they were doing that was counterproductive. The more they hustled and the harder they pushed the customer to buy, the fewer they sold.

Incentives won't buy competence. Incentives only buy hustle. That has long been the only argument against using commissioned salespeople. About the same time this problem came to a head, the third experience occurred: I was in Boston visiting another company, only this one was growing by leaps and bounds. They were all excited because they had just eliminated commissions and put all their salespeople on salary at $10 an hour, at a time when the local McDonald's was paying $8.50.

I asked, "Didn't you lose all of your best salespeople?"

They said, "Yes, but they weren't doing what we wanted them to do and besides, some of them were going to make over $100,000 that year and we could have several salespeople for what we would be paying one of them."

About three years later, they called me to set a meeting. Since they had gone to hourly wages not only had they lost their few competent salespeople, but they had added large numbers of even less competent salespeople who had no incentive to improve or make a sale, and they were faced with a very serious problem.

In both cases the problem was incompetent salespeople. Increasing the incentive didn't solve the problem and eliminating incentive didn't either. In both cases, sooner or later, incompetent salespeople are going to put these two companies out of business. Added incentives may speed up the process.

Multitudes of sales training programs and pay plans with all kinds of contests and awards have been devised to accomplish one thing and one thing only: to improve the competence and thus the productivity of salespeople. And *none* of them has ever caused *overall* sustained improvement because there has been no accurate measurement of what was to be improved.

What, then, is the basic measurement of selling competence?

1. How many prospective customers did the salesperson come in contact with and how many did he or she sell?
2. What was the average volume of each sale?

That is the basic yardstick for measuring competence of a salesperson: "Return on [Prospective] Customer Contact"© or ROCC©. I pronounce it "Rock." The more a salesperson's competence improves, the higher his or her return on prospective customer contacts will be.

A great many of the salespeople in the world today have negotiable prices on what they sell. It may come as a shock to most management and salespeople alike, but there are no negotiable prices in the business of selling. (Note: fixed prices with quantity discounts are not considered negotiable.)

Reread "Your Road to Selling Success I and II." You saw why the highest-volume top professionals in the world do not believe in lowering the price or negotiating prices while the great masses who sell a fraction of what those in the business of selling do, feeling that if they could lower their prices they could make more sales. Millions of cases prove that this is not actually true.

When companies lower prices for sales events they attract more prospective customers, but the percentage of prospective customers sold goes down for 99.9 percent of the salespeople even though their volume might be up.

Those salespeople who are selling fifteen to 20 percent of the prospective customers that they come in contact with will usually be selling fewer than ten percent during big sales events and peak traffic periods when accurate records are kept.

Long before you have finished this book you will have come to realize why the highest-paid, highest-volume salespeople in the world sell almost every prospective customer they come in contact with in good times, or bad, during peak traffic periods, and slow traffic periods.

Those people selling things like real estate, automobiles, airplanes, and so on, where negotiated prices seem to be the only way to do business because everyone seems to do business that way, will find it hardest to believe that there are no negotiated prices in the business of selling.

Some members of the automobile industry, after years of negotiating prices as a way of doing business, finally conceded that there was no integrity in their prices and it was counterproductive. The solution was not one price and it wasn't a negotiated price, either. The problem was and is incompetent salespeople—and negotiable prices or fixed prices won't change that.

If the salesperson's goal is a satisfied customer when contact is made and he or she is able to achieve the first five objectives to any reasonable degree, that salesperson will have the order and it matters not what is being sold.

The basic yardstick that measures how effective that salesperson was will always be his or her "Return on Customer Contact©."

In order to use this basic yardstick, the salesperson or management must know something that not one in a thousand salespeople or managers know. *Exactly how many prospective customer contacts did each and every salesperson have?* Guesses don't count when it comes to accurate measurements, not even educated guesses.

Many companies today have fairly accurate counts of how many customers shop their showrooms or sales lots by the hour, day, week, and month. They can total the number of sales made at the end of the month and easily figure what percentage of these prospective customers were sold. They know how many customers each of their salespeople had on average and what percentage each sold of that average. That information is totally useless as a measurement for improving selling competence, because it is based on *averages,* not on accurate counts of exactly how many prospective customers each salesperson had.

You cannot improve the competence of salespeople collectively. Their competence can only be improved individually. But as each salesperson improves, the sales force as a whole improves. This is the result of *individual improvement.* The basic yardstick needed to measure individual improvement requires an accurate count of every single prospective customer each salesperson comes in contact with. Without that information, there can be no accurate measure of how effective the salesperson had been, so no improvement is possible.

When I first began my research, I had the owners of all types of companies swear to me that their salespeople were selling over half the prospective customers they came in contact with. They were willing to bet any amount it was over 40 percent. In the first hundred companies where we installed an accurate customer accounting system, the salespeople in only two of those companies were selling more than 20 percent of the prospective customers they came in contact with. Most weren't selling fifteen percent, the salespeople in one company weren't even selling seven percent.

Three years into my research, I discovered a problem that would absolutely guarantee that as long as the problem existed no yardstick would ever be developed by which to measure accurately how effective an individual salesperson was. What I discovered was that *not one in a thousand salespeople (or managers) knew what a customer was.*

WHAT IS A CUSTOMER?

Do not think this a stupid question. Unless you know what a customer is you could not know what a prospective customer contact was and there would be no basis for measuring the effectiveness of a salesperson. My research convinces me that very, very few salespeople know what a customer is and that is just as true of management.

I made this discovery after interviewing salespeople for more than three years. On a tape of one of those interviews, I was asking the same questions I asked in every interview of long-term, average salespeople, and getting the same answers *every time.* In this case, I was talking to a salesman who didn't sell fifteen percent of his prospective customer contacts in a company where one salesman was selling over 80 percent of his prospective customer contacts and doing over five times the volume of this man.

I said, "You have been selling a long time, tell me what kind of a salesperson you think you are."

He leaned back in his chair, looked away, thought a moment and said, "Mr. Lawhon, I think I am a very good salesperson. As a matter of fact, I think I may be the best salesperson in this company." Every long-term average salesperson I interviewed gave me that same answer in almost those same words and I am sure my mouth fell open every time. How in the world could they possibly think they were good salespeople (let alone the "best" in their company) when other salespeople outperformed them so dramatically? It was what this salesperson said next which I had heard said so many times before, that finally made me realize why these salespeople feel that way.

"Because, Mr. Lawhon, every time I get a *good* customer, I make the sale. Mr. Lawhon, if this company really does want more sales, what they should do is get busy and get us more good customers."

That struck me like a bolt of lightning. These salespeople did not know what a customer was. No sir, they absolutely did not know what a customer was. To them, a "customer" was someone who *bought* something. If they bought a lot, then they were "good customers." If they bought a little, they were "bad customers." If they bought a little and took a long time doing it, they were "terrible customers." Yes, they had good customers, terrible customers, and everything in between, but in order to be a customer at all, they had to have bought, because if they had not bought, you can bet the farm that they were *not customers.* They were "lookers, browsers, tire kickers, mooches, fronts, time killers, idea getters," and a hundred other names the average salespeople have for anyone who does not buy. Of course they think they are the best salespeople in the company, because when they have a "good customer," they never one time in their lives have failed to make the sale. Not once. Of course in order to qualify as a *good* customer, the customer had to have bought and it had to be a big order. If it was anything less than a big purchase, they were still customers, but they weren't *good* customers.

That brings me back to my question, "What is a customer?" There are actually four kinds of customers:

1. *Prospective customers*
2. *Satisfied customers*
3. *Dissatisfied customers*
4. *Unsatisfied customers.*

What is a prospective customer? Anyone who has any need for the benefits of the features of a product or service. Of course we can all spot red-hot prospects who come in with money in hand, ready to buy, but they are the rarest of prospective customers. Most prospective customers are at best only lukewarm, with many being downright frigid. But to the professionally competent salesperson, anyone with the slightest inclination to own, even one so vague it is an unconscious desire, is a prospective customer. The professionally competent salesperson's only goal when he or she comes in contact with any prospective customer is to turn that person into a satisfied customer. That, my friend, includes what the other salespeople are calling lookers, browsers, tire kickers, mooches, and so on.

What is a *satisfied* customer? For prospective customers to become satisfied customers, they must have bought. At the instant the purchase has been finalized, they become satisfied customers, but in order for them to *remain* satisfied customers and for the professional salespeople to reach their goals, whatever was purchased must live up to the customer's expectations, which means the product must meet their needs as well as they were led to expect it would and they get what they were led to believe they would get in services. The better and better the product meets their needs, the more satisfied they will become. They will return to that salesperson in that company to buy again and they will send friends, relatives, and business acquaintances to that salesperson in that company to do business.

What is a *dissatisfied* customer? It is also true that customers must have bought and become, at the time, satisfied customers before they can become dissatisfied customers. When the services promised or the product bought fails to meet their needs as well as they had been led or left to believe, they will become *dissatisfied* customers every time. The less and less the purchase meets their needs, the more and more dissatisfied they will become and they will not return to that salesperson to buy again. They will tell others not to buy from that salesperson in that company. The more dissatisfied they become, the more people they are going to tell about it.

What is an *unsatisfied* customer? Prospective customers who have come in contact with a salesperson, but who did not buy. The salesperson left them with their needs unmet and thus, unsatisfied. They must continue their search for something to satisfy those needs. Do you know what the dictionary's one-word definition of unsatisfied is? "Disappointed." Can you remember when you set out all excited to buy something and failed to find it or were unable to buy it? Remember how disappointed you felt?

Most salespeople sell fewer than 20 percent of the prospective customers with whom they come in contact. That means they send over 80 percent of those prospective customers away, or leave them with their needs unmet, unsatisfied, and disappointed. Isn't that a shame? Many is the time I have heard a salesperson say after sending prospective customers out with their needs unmet, unsatisfied, and disappointed, "What is the matter with those people? They had no more intention of buying than the man in the moon. They wasted over two hours of my time. Don't they realize we work on commission?" Isn't that a shame? Shame! Shame! Shame!

The one thing I loved doing most in my business was standing at the entrance of the showroom greeting prospective customers as they entered and seeing to what extent I could "qualify" them before I turned them over to a salesperson. ("Qualifying" in selling means the same thing that diagnosing does in the field of medicine. It means learning enough about prospective customers and their needs so as to be able to show them how what is being sold will best meet those needs.) I also liked to talk to customers as they were leaving. You can learn a lot more from prospective customers who are leaving than you can when they arrive. Right up to the time I sold the company, whenever we kicked off a major event, I was flown to one of my operations to be at the entrance to the showroom on opening day of the event. I would get so excited I often spent the entire day at the entrance to the showroom having forgotten even to eat. There were three things that I saw happen hundreds, even thousands, of times that always mystified me.

There could be hundreds of prospective customers unattended in the showroom all day long and it never failed that there was a cluster of salespeople gathered around me at the entrance. As it came each one's turn to take the next prospective customer, they would say, "Get me a good one Mr. Lawhon, I haven't had a good one all day long."

In total frustration I would say, "That showroom floor is crawling with prospective customers. Get back there and start helping them." One and all, the salespeople would say, "Mr. Lawhon, there's not a buyer in that bunch. Everybody in there has been bumped. Some of them have been bumped by every salesperson at least once. They are just lookers."

I have watched salespeople go down a showroom aisle crowded with prospective customers, saying, "Anything I can help you folks with?" to everyone they passed, only to be told, "No thank you, we are just looking."

As I began my research, the one thing that intrigued me most was what those few professionally competent salespeople were doing. They never seemed rushed. They worked with prospective customers as though they were the only people in the showroom. They took enough time with every prospective customer to achieve each of their ten objectives and to send them on their way a satisfied customer. When they had walked them to the entrance to say good-bye, they turned as though they had radar, walking past dozens of people to one specific prospective customer, and in what seemed like no time at all, they had made another big sale. This was repeated all day long. Some days they would do up to 20 times the volume of many of the long-term salespeople. I asked myself how they knew which customer to go to next.

I soon discovered how those prospective customers were selected. They were the ones who had been in the store longest, who had been "bumped" or approached by the most salespeople. It was obvious to these professionals that any prospective customer who had been there that long and put up with that much harassment had to be very determined to do business with that company and had to need a whole lot of things. They always turned out to be the biggest sales that would be made that day and the sale usually took the least amount of time.

I have asked owners and presidents of all kinds of companies, "If a customer has bought one of your products, which one would you hope that they had bought?" I have yet to have one say, "The product that is going to best meet their needs." Without exception, their answers have been, "The one that we are going to make the most money on."

Ever since the book *In Search of Excellence* by Thomas J. Peters and Robert H. Waterman, Jr. was published, the buzzword in business has become "customer driven" and yet, I dare say, not one in a thousand people in business actually knows what the only goal of any business should be. Because they don't, they don't even know what a customer is.

If management and owners would work in their service departments, they would hear the same things coming out of their customers' mouths, and most of the time it would have nothing to do with defective products. This is what they would hear: "I don't care what you say, the salesperson told me." And then they go on to say they had been told or left to believe that what they had bought would do something it won't or can't do, or, they will say they were told that someone in the company was going to do something they were not supposed to do or can't do.

The only objective of most salespeople when they come in contact with a prospective customer, is a sale. The only objective of the professionally competent salesperson is a *satisfied* customer. There is all the difference in the world between these two goals.

When most salespeople make sales, what do their customers mean to them? Trouble with a capital "T." I have yet to interview a long-term, average salesperson who did not complain about having to take service calls, write credit applications, or the like. Thousand of times I have heard these words, "Mr. Lawhon, if we didn't have to do all these other things, we would have a lot more time to sell, and that's what they hired us to do."

I have yet to interview a professionally competent salesperson who, when giving his or her customer a business card, didn't say something similar to these words: "If you have any reason to call our company, I want you to call me first." Their only objective is a satisfied customer and it must be kept in mind that *satisfied* customers are those whose purchase meets their needs so well that they will return to that salesperson in that company to buy again and will send other prospective customers to do the same. It might come as a surprise to most people in business, but customers who have a complaint that is quickly taken care of to their satisfaction will become even more satisfied than customers who never have a complaint. Professionally competent salespeople want the credit for getting those complaints taken care of promptly.

It is just as important to remember that no sale ever has or ever will be lost because a salesperson has known too much about prospective customers and their needs. Every time professionally competent salespeople get an opportunity to learn something about a prospective customer, they take it. God forbid that they have an opportunity to take a credit application and learn everything there was about a customer's budget—where it was allocated and when current payment and lease accounts would be paid off—and did not take that opportunity. How else could they learn what best meets their prospective customer's needs?

Why do the professionally competent salespeople and the losers in the lounge see customers who have bought from such two utterly opposing viewpoints? I said that to average salespeople a customer is only someone who has bought and once having bought, the only thing that customer could possibly mean to that salesperson is trouble. Why? When their only objective is to get a sale, and they make that sale, the only things that could happen after that are all bad.

Their only reason for wanting the sale was the commission. When they have the sale, they have the commission, so their goals have been achieved, but, but, but—the credit could be turned down, the product might be out of stock or defective, delivery could foul up, the customer could change his mind, and this list goes on and on, spelling "trouble."

The salesperson loses the sale, loses the commission, and gets blamed for it.

No! No! No! Not on your life. That salesperson did not have anything to do with that sale after it was made. If the credit was turned down, it was the customer's fault and the fault of the credit department. The average salesperson thinks his or her only job was to sell. The credit department's job was to get it financed. Never did the salesperson give a thought to helping the customer find the product that was going to best meet his or her needs, which certainly meant something within that customer's budget. If they refused it on delivery, that was not the *salesperson's* fault, it was the delivery department's fault.

Yesiree, once they have a sale, the less they have to do with a customer the better! I have yet to ask one of these average salespeople why they don't do some of the things after they have made the sale that a professionally competent salesperson does and not have them say, "If you think I am going to waste my time doing those things, you're crazy."

So I ask again, "What is a customer?"

The average American is going to buy three homes and sell two. About seven years after buying a first home it will be sold and the second home will be bought. That home will be sold and the third home bought about seven years after that. When prospective customers are shopping for a first home in a modest neighborhood, are they just browsers who are looking only at modestly priced homes? Or are they prospective customers who will probably spend at least double that amount on another home in about seven years, and who knows how much on the next one? Will they be so satisfied with their first home that they will return to the same salesperson to buy their second and third homes, having that salesperson sell two homes for them in the process?

Are they customers who have become so satisfied over the years that they will have sent to that salesperson a steady stream of friends, relatives, and business acquaintances who are in the market for a home or looking to sell one? That is the way professionally competent real estate salespeople see all prospective customers with whom they come in contact. What makes their careers and their lives so exciting is that most of the time they achieve their goals with each prospective customer.

Americans buy cars every two or three years. They are also buying recreational and utility vehicles. From the time they buy that first car to the last vehicle they buy, they will have spent two hundred thousand dollars or more. Listen to me, that includes all the tire kickers, time wasters, up takers, browsers, lookers, fronts, and mooches, because that is what most of them were to the salespeople with whom they had come in contact and did not buy from. Hard to believe that is how any automobile salesperson could see a potential million-dollars in sales, isn't it? How did I arrive at that million-dollar figure?

To an automobile salesperson in the business of selling, anyone with a driver's license is a prospective customer for a least a million dollars in sales. The professional fully expects and usually succeeds in turning most prospective customers into *satisfied* customers—so satisfied they are going to come back to buy from that salesperson again and again and send along many more prospective customers who buy, which easily makes each of those customers potential million-dollar customers. Pretty exciting just to think about dealing with customers like that, isn't it? I guarantee you that it's a thousand times (no, a *million* times) more exciting than dealing with tire kickers, mooches, and fronts as the losers in the lounge see them.

The average American will buy $50,000 worth of furniture over a 35-year period, making a significant purchase about once a year. With so little effort you would not believe it, the professionally competent furniture salesperson will have every one of his or her satisfied customers buying their furniture from that salesperson and sending more prospective customers, who are easily turned into *satisfied* customers who send them more prospective customers, who are easily turned into *satisfied* customers, and so on.

So, *what is a customer?* A "browser" or "looker" as most average salespeople think? Maybe they are *bad* customers, who only bought a loss leader and wasted a lot of the salesperson's time doing it. Or are they customers who are literally an annuity who will pay big dividends like clockwork for the rest of that salesperson's career?

It matters not what is being sold, whether it is something the customer will buy more of often or only once in a lifetime. The goal of all professionally competent salespeople who are in the business of selling is the same when they come in contact with any prospective customer. *They want to turn him or her into a satisfied customer.* It is easy to see why a salesperson selling something the customer will buy frequently, such as furniture, would do this, but why would the salesperson whose customers will only buy once and never again have the same goal? Very simple. Satisfied customers tell others about their satisfaction. Often, these products don't even get advertised. Almost 100 percent of these salespeople's prospective customers come from their satisfied customers. It is not only the professional salesperson's *only* goal to turn every prospective customer contact into a *satisfied* customer, but it should be the only goal the company has if it intends to stay around.

Before I go on, I want to make a point about so-called customer driven companies. When their salespeople sell fewer than 20 percent of the prospective customers with whom they come in contact, that means over 80 percent of their potential customers left unsatisfied.

When the company has no record of who their prospective customers were or why the company failed to help them buy, then over 80 percent of that company's prospective customers can have nothing to do with making the company customer driven. That means the best most companies can hope for is to be 20 percent customer driven.

In the home furnishings industry, most salespeople sell fewer than fifteen percent of the prospective customers with whom they come in contact, which is as good or better than in many industries. Extensive research shows that over 54 percent of the people who bought furniture over the past few years in the U.S. have become so dissatisfied with their purchases that they will not return to that company or that salesperson to buy again. Over 75 percent of those people who will not return again to a company say that decision was caused by the salesperson. It's not the product, services, prices, terms, or anything else. I feel certain that is true in most fields of selling because the degree of salespeople's competence is about the same everywhere.

Fewer than fifteen percent bought. Of those, only 46 percent remained satisfied enough to return to the company to buy again. (The percentage of those buying a second time who actually asked for the salesperson from whom they had bought before was not even *one percent*.) So 54 percent of the fifteen percent who bought didn't return. That means that fewer than seven percent of the prospective customers who shopped in furniture showrooms wound up satisfied enough to return and do business there again. Virtually none are satisfied enough to want the same salesperson. That means they will tell very few people of their satisfaction. Over eight percent were so dissatisfied they will not return at all and especially not to that salesperson. These customers are very dissatisfied, which means they will take every opportunity to tell others about their dissatisfaction. While over 85 percent of those prospective customers left unsatisfied and disappointed, they may not broadcast it like those dissatisfied customers, but if asked, they will tell others of their disappointment. Is it any wonder the home furnishings industry has lost share of consumer disposable income every year for over 25 years?

Note: These are not percentages I just grabbed out of the sky. They are the result of an industry survey conducted over a four-year period and similar to numbers found in all fields of selling. Government figures show that over the last 25 years sales have fallen from 1.4 percent of consumer spendable income to less than .8 percent.

I hope you will forgive me for taking your time with all those statistics, but we cannot have customer driven sales forces until we have customer driven companies. We cannot have customer driven companies until everyone in the company, starting at the top, *knows what a customer is.*

I think it would be safe to say that almost everyone today agrees the future of any company and thus, the future of their salespeople, depends entirely on how customer driven they become. As more and more companies strive to become more customer driven, we will see more and more of those who didn't start soon enough go out of business. We can look around in every industry and see that happening right now.

Do you know the most incredible element of this whole problem? Prospective customers have only one goal. It may be only an inclination or a vague, even unconscious dream, but their only goal is to become *satisfied* customers, so satisfied that their greatest joy will come from telling others how they too, can enjoy the same satisfaction. It is the salespersons' job to help all prospective customers achieve their goals so the salespeople can achieve their own personal goals.

The only goal prospective customers ever have or ever will have, regardless of what the product is—whether an eight-penny nail or a jet airplane—is to buy the products that will best meet their needs so they can wind up as *satisfied* customers, so satisfied they will return to buy again and have a place they can recommend to others.

That statement may be the most important statement you ever read about selling. When every person in a company and all prospective customers have the same goal, then and only then will a company become truly customer driven, with the goal of turning every prospective customer contact into a *satisfied* customer.

How can you do that?

- **WHAT GETS MEASURED ACCURATELY IMPROVES.**

- **WHAT DOESN'T GET MEASURED WON'T IMPROVE.**

- **WHAT GETS MEASURED INACCURATELY WILL GET WORSE.**

Of all of the things I've written in this book, that last point is the hardest to comprehend and to accept as fact.

Remember: the only reason any book on selling was ever written or read was to improve selling competence. The only reason any sales training program was ever developed or applied was to improve the competence of salespeople. The only reason anyone ever has or ever will hold a sales meeting is in hopes that it will improve the effectiveness and productivity of what the salespeople do.

The key word is *"improve."* All improvement results from someone doing something repetitively that causes him or her to become more productive. Whatever it is anyone does repetitively will get easier. It will take less time to do and the person will become more effective at it. In fact, the task will get so easy that it will require little or no conscious effort. When something gets that easy, it will have become a skill that has been perfected into a habit. And the longer a skill is practiced, the more addicted the person becomes to the habit.

The most critical point that you must accept is that you can also get better at doing something *wrong* if you do it repetitively.

You can develop those effective *counterproductive* skills into habits that cause prospective customers not to buy just as you can develop productive skills into habits that cause prospective customers to buy. Repetition causes improvement.

Your yardstick alone, used accurately, will improve your effective productivity. Use it inaccurately and you will improve effective *counterproductive* skills, thus making your efforts even more counterproductive.

Used consistently, the yardstick will always tell you if the skill you are perfecting is *effective and productive* or *effective and counterproductive*.

WHAT GETS MEASURED WILL IMPROVE

FACTS

• The only goal of any business should be a *satisfied* customer.

• The only goal of a prospective customer is to become a *satisfied* customer.

• The only goal of all salespeople when they come in contact with prospective customers is to help those customers achieve their goals by turning them into *satisfied* customers. It is the job of everyone else in the company to support the salespeople in their efforts to achieve their goal.

• The technical basis of selling is having all the specialized knowledge and information the salesperson needs to help prospective customers make the best buying decision.

• *What gets measured improves.*

6 / *Putting the Yardstick to Work for You and Your Company*

> "HE WHO LEARNS TO DO THE LITTLE THINGS
> WELL CAN DO BIG THINGS EASILY."
>
> *Schiller*

THE FIRST REQUIREMENT FOR USING THE YARDSTICK is a plan that accurately records every single contact each individual salesperson has with a prospective customer. If a sale is made, the amount of the sale, and the time of day when the sale was begun and finished is recorded. When this information is tallied, it will reveal how many prospective customers the salesperson came in contact with each day and month-to-date; what percentage were sold; and, what the average amount of each sale was.

This basic yardstick, when used accurately, has shown measured improvement in each salesperson's return-on-customer-contacts (ROCC©). When all praise and recognition in a company is based on improvement instead of just volume, the rate of improvement is accelerated.

To use this basic yardstick, the salesperson would have to know what a prospective customer contact is:

• Anyone calling on the phone for sales information is a prospective customer contact for the salesperson who takes the phone call.

• Any phone call made by a salesperson in an effort to make a sale or to get an appointment.

• Anyone greeted when they arrive at the salesperson's place of busness is a prospective customer contact no matter what is said or what the prospective customer asks for, with only two exceptions: (1) The person is going directly to the office; or (2) The person asks for a specific salesperson. If that salesperson is there and waits on them, it becomes a prospective customer contact for him. If not, and the greeter-salesperson waits on them, it is his or her prospective customer contact.

• Any unattended browser approached in a sales area is a prospective customer contact. It does not matter if these people have been approached by other salespeople and dropped, it was still a prospective customer contact for them and any other salesperson who approached them. It was a prospective customer contact even though the people had gone to the office and were browsing on their way out.

• Any effort made to call on a prospective customer with or without an appointment must be accounted for—even when the salesperson didn't get to see the prospective customer.

Unless every single effort is accounted for, there will be no accurate yardstick. The purpose of the yardstick is to improve the productivity of those efforts.

Now that we all agree on what a prospective customer contact is, how do we get a record of exactly how many of these contacts each individual salesperson has had? I devised a basic way to accurately get this information that has been used, tested, and perfected in hundreds of companies by thousands of salespeople. Here's how it works:

Each salesperson has a supply of 5-inch by 7-inch customer accounting cards (see the illustrations on pages 76 and 77) and a self-inking rubber stamp that has his or her name on it. Each card used will be stamped with the name of that salesperson in the bottom, right-hand corner.

The first and most important purpose of this card is to make the salespeople consciously aware of the fact that they are about to come in contact with a prospective customer before contact takes place. A contact for which they must account.

Every time each salesperson comes in contact with a prospective customer, an accounting card with his or her name stamped on it must be deposited into a locked control box before he or she is allowed to approach, greet, phone or call on another prospective customer—whether the sale was made or not. The salesperson must record the time of day the contact was made and the amount of the sale if made.

These cards, when tallied daily, give each salesperson and management an accurate record of how many prospective customer contacts each salesperson had and each salesperson's average volume-per-sale. These records are tallied daily, month-to-date, and the cards are returned to the salespeople before they start the next day's work. With this information, management knows accurately how productive each salesperson has been. The ongoing accurate use of this basic measurement guarantees the improvement of each salesperson's selling competence.

How can this plan be used in all selling situations?

Companies who wish to improve the productivity of their salespeople when taking phone calls or calling prospective customers on the phone for appointments, should require the salespeople to have a customer accounting card out and in front of them with a pen handy before the call is taken or placed. When the call has been completed, regardless of the results, the card must be deposited immediately in a locked accounting control box. If any information was gained and an appointment made, it is to be recorded on the card along with the time of day.

After the cards have been tallied they are returned immediately to the salesperson with the day and month-to-date results before he or she begins the next day of business. Most companies have the locked control box for phone calls a short distance from the phones which forces the salesperson to get up and walk to the box and return before another call is handled.

In companies where the customers come to the salespeople, the accounting control box with a slot large enough to easily insert a 5 x 7 file card is placed in the most conspicuous and convenient location. Every time a salesperson comes in contact with a prospective customer—before he or she may approach or greet another prospective customer—he or she must walk to the box and deposit an accounting card.

I can tell you from thousands of experiences that this, like anything else people are asked to do for the first time, will meet with resistance. As simple as it seems, it will be hard to do at first. The salespeople will forget. A few may even forget intentionally, but because the control box is in plain sight, monitoring this vitally important plan is easily accomplished. When anyone is observed failing to deposit a card immediately after having approached or greeting a prospective customer, discipline must be immediate.

When the plan is administered with integrity and consistent discipline, it will soon have become so easy to deposit the card that it will be done as unconsciously as turning in the order and money after each sale is written. In fact, it will have become a habit that makes it get easier and easier for the salespeople to deposit the accounting card. It is not long before management is saying, "How did we ever run our company without this plan?"

The only consistent objection I have found among salespeople when first put into use is, "Why do we have to deposit the card after each prospective customer contact? When we are overrun with customers it wastes a lot of our time!"

It is true that salespeople are least productive during peak traffic periods. They bounce from prospective customer to prospective customer with their counterproductive harassment of "Can I help you?" It doesn't work, so they say these contacts were not customers. Remember, the first and most important purpose of the accounting card is to make the salesperson consciously aware of the fact that they are about to come in contact with a prospective customer—a contact for which they must account.

I can only guarantee you that no accurate measurement can be taken if salespeople are not required to drop the card immediately after they have finished with each prospective customer.

Companies using this accounting system have found dramatic improvements in the productivity of the salespeople when they are required and have agreed to file an accounting card after every single prospective customer contact.

Home, automobile, boat and trade shows, too, are the same thing— just attending one of these shows stokes the fires of prospective customer's desires, making them all even hotter prospective customers. Depositing the card immediately does two things: 1) It makes each salesperson consciously aware of the fact that they are about to come in contact with a prospective customer before that contact is made, and 2) reminds the salesperson that there will be a record and accounting of that contact, causing him or her to derive more out of each contact. Managements who want to see improved results from these product shows must measure what they want to improve and when they do, improvement is guaranteed.

How can you use the card accurately when salespeople call on their prospective customers?

The salespeople must have their customer accounting card out before the call is made—whether by appointment or not. If it is the same card created to get the appointment there should be important information already on the card and it should have been reviewed. If the salesperson keeps a file folder for his or her customers, the card should be clipped to the folder. He or she must have a separate case in which to deposit the card after completing each contact—even if he or she didn't get to see anyone but the receptionist. The card must have the time that the call was made and the time it was completed. If a sale was made, that amount should be shown on the card.

The cards should be tallied at the end of each working day and turned in or faxed to the home office if the salesperson is on the road. The times shown on the cards will help both salesperson and management to measure the time spent on each call and the time between calls.

Once the basic yardstick is in place it can be used to measure any specific thing that needs improvement. You could easily see, for example, how an accurate record or measurement of the time spent *between* prospective customer contacts would be a productive aid in accounting for your time and also the time spent on each contact, resulting in improvement.

Companies requiring salespeople to have the prospective customers' names, addresses and phone numbers before they left, whether a sale was made or not, found the salespeople developing the skills to do this 100 percent of the time—almost at once. Just showing this interest in every prospective customer contact caused improvement. When these companies required that salespeople write on the card what the prospective customers are using now; how long they have had it; and what they liked or disliked about what they are using now, they were able to achieve even more dramatic improvement. The reason is simple. Before using the yardstick salespeople asked the prospective customers if they could help them and when customers said they were only looking, the reaction of the salespeople was that they weren't prospective customers, but tire-kickers, time-wasters, and so on. But once the salespeople *knew* something about their needs and what they were using now, they saw them as customers. Amazing how that one measurement accurately taken, improved their ROCC©!

There are ten clearly defined objectives to be achieved in proper sequence if the salesperson is to reach his goal to turn a prospective customer into a satisfied customer. As salespeople improve and perfect the productive skills needed to achieve each of these ten objectives in their proper sequence, they will find themselves turning more and more of their prospective customers into satisfied customers.

Even though the basic yardstick will cause improvement and the improvement is guaranteed, management will soon realize that measuring how effective each salesperson has been with each productive skill needed to achieve each of the ten objectives greatly accelerated improvement.

To reach any goal, you must know where you want to go. Then, you must determine where you are. You must have a plan to follow that will get you from where you are to where you want to get—and you must follow that plan. It is that simple.

Professionally competent salespeople know that their goal is a satisfied customer and their yardstick tells them where they are when they come in contact with a prospective customer. The ten objectives establish the plan. They simply follow their plan and thus, reach their goal more and more often until they are reaching it almost every time.

Incredibly, results have shown that each time an effort is made to achieve one of the ten objectives and the results recorded, further learning objectives and goals are established. These cause salespeople to gain more of the specialized knowledge and information they need to improve their selling skills and make them more productive.

Once the basic yardstick is in place, how can it be used to measure how effective each salesperson has been in achieving each one of the ten objectives?

There has never been a fatality on take-off. The passengers are killed when the plane comes down. The pilot, not only wants to be sure he can get his plane in the air, but far more important, he wants to be sure that he can get it safely back on the ground. During his career, he will have taken off and landed thousands of times but every single time—right up to his last flight—before take-off, he physically goes down a written check list. He could probably recite that list forward and backward, but should he rely on his memory and miss only one check point, it could be his last flight, so he relies on that written check list every single time he flies. He does not pass a single check until he has seen that it was done.

Examine the illustrations below which show the front and back of a professional salesperson's basic checklist.

• First, you see a smiley face.
• You see the ten objectives listed across the top on the front side.

ADVANCED CUSTOMER ACCOUNTING CARD

FRONT SIDE. *This is only a suggested card. A few of the boxes are basic check-offs. As you are ready to perfect another productive skill, put a check box on your card for that skill.*

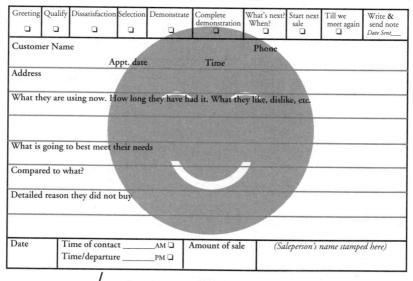

Greeting	Qualify	Dissatisfaction	Selection	Demonstrate	Complete demonstration	What's next? When?	Start next sale	Till we meet again	Write & send note
❏	❏	❏	❏	❏	❏	❏	❏	❏	*Date Sent___*

Customer Name | Phone

Appt. date | Time

Address

What they are using now. How long they have had it. What they like, dislike, etc.

What is going to best meet their needs

Compared to what?

Detailed reason they did not buy

| Date | Time of contact _____AM ❏
 Time/departure _____PM ❏ | Amount of sale | *(Saleperson's name stamped here)* |

This measurement will greatly improve time efficiency.

That is your checklist. You should be able to check all ten of those when you have finished with any prospective customer contact. It will be obvious when your efforts to achieve any one of those objectives worked, and this will cause you to repeat that productive act. Repetition will cause improvement. When you see that it had not worked very well, or at all, it tells you to go back to your instructions (the book) so that you don't repeat those things that didn't work. It guarantees your improvement.

The professionals not only use a form of this customer accounting card to measure any improvement in their ROCC©, they use it to measure and accelerate the improvement of their ability to more easily achieve the

ADVANCED CUSTOMER ACCOUNTING CARD

BACK SIDE. *The month squares are for green tabs. They denote the month the next sale is projected. Use the blank squares to schedule follow-up communications.*

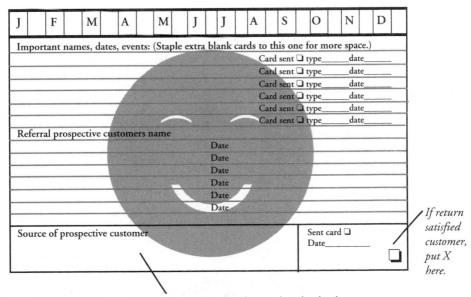

J	F	M	A	M	J	J	A	S	O	N	D

Important names, dates, events: (Staple extra blank cards to this one for more space.)

Card sent ❑ type_____ date_____
Card sent ❑ type_____ date_____
Card sent ❑ type_____ date_____
Card sent ❑ type_____ date_____
Card sent ❑ type_____ date_____
Card sent ❑ type_____ date_____

Referral prospective customers name
Date
Date
Date
Date
Date
Date

Source of prospective customer

Sent card ❑
Date_____

If return satisfied customer, put X here.

If the source was a satsified customer, write the name here and send a thank-you note. Put this name on the file card of the customer who was referred.

objectives in their proper sequence. They would no more think of not doing this than the pilot. Your checklist should be no different or less crucial, than the pilot's—whether he's flying a Piper Cub with a short list or a 747 jet with a long list. The objectives are the same!

I don't know a single one of the world's top professional salespeople who do not have extensive customer files. How do you think they got them? By what, for them, had amounted to their customer accounting card. It is the information they have gained from each individual customer contact over the years. It measured how productive they were in what they did. That measurement caused them to improve their amount of specialized knowledge and information they had on an ongoing basis. It also caused their productive skills to improve and make them even more productive until the last day of their career. (I have yet to find a long-term average salesperson who has an ongoing customer file.)

Not one top professional started out to build a customer file. It was the information gained (in their efforts to improve) that wound up in a customer file. When satisfied customers are your satisfied customers they are your biggest assets. You can either deposit those assets in a safe place and draw interest on them from then on—or you can trash them.

> • You will note that there is a line for the source of the prospective customer. This tells you where your prospective customers are coming from—TV, radio, mail, word-of-mouth, Yellow Pages, magazines, newspapers, etc. This information must be noted on the card if advertising is to improve.

> • There is a place to list what the prospective customer is using now and what they like and don't like about it, to remind you that you must have this information every time.

> • There is a place for you to write what you recommended to best meet that prospective customer's needs. (If you sold them, you need that information. If not, you can analyze what you did that didn't work.)

Discuss with other salespeople what questions you might have asked or product(s) you might have offered to learn more about what would have better met the prospective customer's needs. The odds are the sale was lost because you had not learned enough about the prospective customer and their needs and therefore did not make them consciously aware of enough of those needs. They are still a prospective customer and you still have the same goal. Keep the information on file and keep getting more until you have learned enough about them and their needs to get the order. It beats counterproductive bitching in the losers' lounge and it's productive.

• There is one line on the card for special occasions. Obviously, there isn't enough space for dates of all the birthdays, anniversaries, events, and so on that you will need to list to permit you to maintain ongoing communications with the prospective customer. That line is to remind you to staple a lined 5 x 7 card to the back of the master card for that purpose.

• Across the top of the back side of the card are small boxes with the twelve months of the year printed with a blank square in the middle. If you are to send a birthday or special event card, call to set an appointment to write up the next order, or anything else, you should put a color tab on that month's square as a reminder flag. You should review the tabs for each month no later than the third week of the preceding month. The blank square or box next to each month is for a different color tab to remind you that you are currently working on something for this customer. (A word of advice: Use metal tabs. The plastic ones don't stay on the card as well.)

• Optional: Many companies have a space to check when an effort to make an add-on sale was made. Companies which sell fabric protection, credit life insurance, undercoating, or extended warranties, to name a few, always have check boxes for their add-on items. Remember this checklist is supposed to be a measurement of anything that you wish to become more productive at doing. It will include a record of the times you tried and it measures those results. That measurement will cause improvement if accurately kept.

Let's re-cap: As a salesperson, what you would like to do is sell more of the prospective customers you come in contact with than you are selling now. You would like for this to become easier to do. You would like for it to take less time and you would certainly like for the average volume of each sale to increase.

When you religiously use the basic 5 x 7 customer accounting card and accurately tally the results daily, month-to-date, and year-to-date, that alone will cause every one of these things that you want to happen to happen. It's guaranteed. If you opt not to do this whether you use this form of measurement or some other method, you will not improve—and that also is guaranteed.

When you first start out and measure how effective your selling efforts have been, you should use only the basic card. No one, not even Einstein could learn everything at once. Keep it simple. Forget everything else until your greeting works. Each time it works, focus entirely on your qualifying skills. Ask more and more questions improving the questions and the sequence in which they are asked. Ask more and more questions about what the customer is using now, what they like, what they don't.

As your greeting works more often and better, you will get a chance to practice your qualifying skills more and more often. As these skills improve, you will get a chance to practice your selection technique more and more often, and so on. Keep it just that simple. You will not be ready to fly a 747 for some time.

Focus on the development of the productive skills needed to achieve each objective one at a time in its proper sequence and as the one you're focused on becomes more and more effective, you start to focus on the next one. Remember, a study of each objective in and of itself shows you that the productive skills needed to achieve that objective can be easily developed. The yardstick will focus you on each objective and this focused repetition guarantees you that your productive skills will be perfected into productive selling habits.

No truer words have ever been written than Schilling's: "He who learns to do the little things well, can do big things easily."

It may be several years before you realize what powerful and productive skills you have mastered and how they have skyrocketed your sales. But make the use of the yardstick a habit from day one and it will reward you as long as you are in the business of selling. Reselling the satisfied customer again and again using the 5 x 7 customer file card becomes a productive habit. You did not start out to build a customer file, you set out to master productive skills and to gain the knowledge you needed to turn prospective customers into *satisfied* customers. As you succeeded in achieving that goal, you wound up with a file full of satisfied customer cards with the information you need to continue selling them as well as their friends, relatives, and business associates. *It has put you in the business of selling.*

The salespeople who do these things habitually wind up earning many, many times what the average salespeople in their industry earn and they often work fewer hours to do it. While it may take tremendous effort in the beginning to develop these productive skills into productive habits, once you do, they make selling easier the longer you practice them and they guarantee your success beyond your wildest dreams.

When you have a customer file card for every prospective customer contact, that means you will wind up with a yardstick for measuring your improvement. To the degree that you have become successful in achieving your goal of a satisfied customer, the information you need to follow up on that *satisfied* customer is available on your card. Other family members' names, birthdays, anniversaries, and so on, may be notes on the card, too. What they will be needing next and when, where they work and how long they have been there may be on the card; whatever you think is important.

Automobile salespeople who have recorded the ages of the customer's children know when it will be time for the children's first car. They can make the most memorable sale in that young person's life. No satisfied customer has more prospective customers for friends than the young man or woman buying a first car. To professional automobile salespeople, this is the kind of knowledge that causes them to put extra effort into this sale, knowing it could turn into the biggest return on a single customer contact they will ever have. This search for and use of information about every customer's needs in any field of selling is the basis for your success in selling. Using your 5 x 7 customer file card (or a form of one) will cause you to wind up with the most valuable information any salesperson can possess.

Caution: Here is where it can all go down the tubes. The first thing most managements want to do today is to put the information from your customer file into the computer and eliminate the card.

One day, I was walking through a huge upholstered furniture warehouse with the company owner. There were racks to stack furniture four levels high. Every item and its location was recorded in the computer. I stopped at one of the rows, turned, and walked to the end of it, climbed through the racks, and came out on the next row. I asked the owner if he allowed his salespeople to let prospective customers take cushions home to make sure the fabric and color would be all right.

He said, "You know better than that, John. Of course we don't."

I said, "I didn't think you had a plan for them to do that, but I counted 32 missing pillows and cushions on just the two aisles I walked down. The only way that could happen is if salespeople were letting prospective customers take the cushions from your floor samples. When they weren't returned, they had to take one from the warehouse stock to replace it. That information isn't in your computer. The only way you can ever be sure of what you have in your warehouse is to walk through it yourself. Look at the merchandise for yourself. Put your hand on it to be sure it's there. Lift the end of cartons or you could have a warehouse full of empty boxes. It is the same principle with your other assets, including money and satisfied customers."

That 5 x 7 card represents a live, walking, talking prospective customer, a *satisfied* customer. As long as it is out there in front of you, you can see it and visualize that customer. If it is only in a computer it is out of sight and not available to you when you need it most.

Two further points: If management required a salesperson to punch a computer station after every prospective customer contact before they were allowed to approach another, the odds of having an accurate count would be absolutely zero. Any psychologist can tell you why. The most honest people in the world who have never lied to another person in their entire lifetime, lie to themselves. The reason most people have a weight problem is well known. They exaggerate their exercise by almost 50 percent and they underaccount for about 50 percent of what they eat (their calorie and fat intake). They may be honest to the nth degree with all other people, but not with themselves.

Nothing will replace the card or a form of the card unless it is *visible* to the salesperson before the prospective customer contact is made, then deposited and another one in place before the next contact is attempted. Only the knowledge *before contact* that the salespersons' actions will be monitored assures their compliance.

I know more and more salespeople are using their own computers. And of course the information they put on this card can be put in the computer. But don't ever eliminate the card just because its information is in your computer. That 5 x 7 card represents a tangible live, walking, talking prospective customer or a satisfied customer with whom you have had a personal experience. When that card is pulled out and held in your hands, the emotional involvement of that experience is recalled. You may put all that information in the computer just like you would your inventory, but when you want to know what the inventory is, you'd better be able to look at it and feel it.

When you want to call your customers on the phone or greet them when they come in for an appointment, nothing will replace having reviewed the card for that person and having it right there in front of you. That may change as computers become even more advanced, but I doubt it.

I recently received a catalogue from a company stamped with large, red letters on the front it said, *NOTICE: IF WE DON'T RECEIVE AN ORDER FROM YOU WITHIN 30 DAYS, THIS IS THE LAST CATALOGUE YOU WILL RECEIVE FROM US.* Their computer had just told them I was no longer a customer. But no human being bothered to ask why. That reminded me of something I heard a minister say once. Two men were fashioning a cross on which a third must die and no one stopped to ask, "Why?" And why? And why?

Some salespeople I know have metal file cabinets and use manila file folders for each customer. But stapled to the front of the folder is the file card. Others I know fill up one card and staple another one to it. They may have a half dozen or more stapled together for one customer, but they never discard any. Each card has emotional impact because it represents wonderful experiences with a satisfied customer.

Every referral customer the salesperson has gotten will be noted on the card of the satisfied customer who made the referrals, along with a checkmark indicating that a personal note had been sent to thank the customer for that referral, along with a follow-up thank you phone call. This will be cross-referenced to the referred customer's card.

To professionals, selling is a business, their own personal business, and they are successful only to the extent they run it like a business. Their only assets are prospective customers and satisfied customers. Professionals take great satisfaction in seeing their assets out in the open. The salesman who sells me my shirts in New York City has all of his customer file cases stacked on the counter for everyone to see. He loves to be asked about them. His greatest joy is telling new customers about long-standing satisfied customers whom he has satisfied for 50 years or longer, even though they live all over the world and he may rarely see them.

When he pulls out a card, you can see him run his fingers over it as he pictures the satisfied customer in his mind. You know that by the way he tells about his experiences with that person. Yes, he sells nothing but ready-made medium-priced men's shirts in a tiny store off Park Avenue in New York City, but he probably has more people he can call friends than most people in that great city. By the way, he has become a very wealthy salesman.

You may say his record keeping takes too much time. Well, it took him just as much when he started out. He could have all that data in a computer, but then he couldn't see his friends any time he wanted to. Or what's more, show them off to his prospective customers. As I say, "The card is a walking, talking, living satisfied customer and should be kept that way."

Please! Before you argue this point: When you make a sale the information the company needs to run their business is on the order form and other documents. That is not our problem. When you are not using the card and over 80 percent of the prospective customers leave without buying, neither the salesperson nor anyone in the company has that information. You can bet that salespeople will go on losing sales for the same reasons forever in spite of all the well meaning sales training in the world.

On the other hand, the 5 x 7 card also records your effort to turn a prospective customer into a satisfied customer. We know that when you fail to do that the number one reason is that you haven't yet learned enough about the prospective customer and his or her needs. In many types of selling, the salespeople can take what they have learned and see how much more there is to learn. If they are persistent enough, the odds are that in time they will learn enough to make that sale and achieve their goal.

But what if salespeople and their managements don't make this effort, which is what happens well over 80 percent of the time in all fields of selling? If there is no customer card accounting for that prospective customer with that salesperson, the company has no record of what happened. As far as the company is concerned, there was no customer. The company that is not as vitally concerned about why a prospective customer has *not* bought as it is about why one *has* bought, cannot claim to be customer driven. At best, they would only be 20 percent customer driven. You can trace every one of the problems of industry giants like General Motors, IBM, and Xerox to this single issue.

The 5 x 7 customer accounting card can be used to monitor how effective and productive everyone in the company has been. When salespeople cannot come up with something that will best meet their customer's needs and they go to management before they walk the customer, if management can't come up with a solution, that can become valuable customer driven information that should be in the computer. It can tell management that their selection needs attention or their product needs improvement, and so on. When a company correlates traffic count to advertising costs and sales along with average volume per sale and the salespeople's batting averages, that will measure how productive advertising has been.

When referral customers who buy are logged in the computer by management, the company can easily see who is making maximum use of their satisfied customers and that measurement tells management how they are doing that. Plans can be developed to focus the other salespeople on developing the productive skills of the top salespeople. When satisfied customers return to buy again, it is important to know whether they returned to the same salesperson. Logging service calls, credit turn downs, delivery problems, and complaints for all salespeople helps them improve because that is customer driven *measured* information.

For salespeople who sell something that is to be sold again, such as wholesale, what they know about their customers is vital. But when wholesale salespeople know *more* about their customers' customers needs than their customers do, then and only then can they help their customers buy what will best meet *their* customer's needs. (If that didn't make sense to you, read it again, because it *is* correct.)

In many fields of selling, the toughest information for companies to compile accurately is why they didn't get an order. If there was a legitimate reason for a prospective customer to buy a competitor's product, a company needs to know that, but it must be accurate information. If there *wasn't* a legitimate reason for a prospective customer to buy a competitor's product, the company needs to know that, too. Can you see that this information influences an entire company because it puts a yardstick on everything the company does? Using the yardstick accurately guarantees improved competency and productivity throughout a company. And where did the information come from? Customers, those who *bought* and those who *didn't*. This is pure customer driven information. If managers think this information can be gathered accurately other than through the company salespeople, let me point out that fewer than four percent of those who become dissatisfied with any purchase ever complain to the seller. And, of course, those who didn't buy—as far as the salespeople without the yardstick are concerned—were not prospective customers.

Management may question the wisdom of letting salespeople in on what management is trying to do or should be doing. If a company is truly customer driven, its only goal is a *satisfied* customer. That becomes the only goal of all salespeople in that company. Supporting the salespeople in achieving that goal becomes the job of everyone in the company. That, however, will never happen until everyone in the company realizes the only goal of any prospective customer is to become a *satisfied* customer. Incredibly, all prospective customers have the same goal! The better you understand the needs and goals of your prospective customers, the better you can help them achieve those goals. *There are no secrets in a truly customer driven company* and the more everybody understands what everybody else is trying to do, the better they support and assist those efforts.

Working with many of the world's largest fine department stores, I have been convinced that without a systematic way to account for every prospective customer contact the salespeople (and the clerks) have, most of these companies selling higher quality products will be out of business within a few years. I have noted that as the competence of the people who wait on a company's prospective customers has gone down, so has the quality of their products. Cheaper and cheaper products with more and more sales events claiming wilder and wilder savings are the order of the day. That obvious direction gets them closer and closer to doing what the discounters do, yet department stores with their overhead, cannot compete with the discounters. A quick review of Sears' history reveals this happening.

So when there is a yardstick to measure how successful a salesperson has been, his or her productivity will improve. Right? Wrong! Wrong!

Only when there is a yardstick that accurately measures how successful *every* prospective customer has been who came in contact with that salesperson will there be a yardstick that improves not only selling competence, but *everything else* in that company.

Why should salespeople agree to use the card? Because what gets measured improves. Selling becomes easier and takes less time. They will make more sales and more money.

What does not get measured won't improve. It will get worse. Selling will become harder and harder. They will make fewer sales and take longer to make them. They will make less money. These are mathematical facts.

Surprisingly, the only salespeople who resist using the card are the losers in the lounge. It is a tough call, but we are not dealing with opinion—nor options. A salesperson who chooses not to accurately measure his or her productivity has opted to fail—or they are only selling as a stop-gap measure until a better career opportunity comes along. I have found through experience that those who have been offered the opportunity to use the accounting card and refused were long-term average salespeople.

Newly-hired sales trainees who have been made to understand that the use of the accounting card (yardstick) is the only thing that will guarantee their success have been willing to use it and reject any efforts made by losers in the lounge to ridicule them for its use.

The same situation happens when a person has been hired to drive a truck. When things slow down, if the boss asks him to help in the warehouse, sweep floors, or even tidy the rest rooms, even though his pay remains the same, he will far more often than not refuse saying, "That's not my job." It wasn't in the terms of his employment. Had this same man been told when he was hired that most of his time would be spent driving a truck, but when times were slow, he would work in the warehouse doing any job that needed doing as the terms of his employment, then management would have eliminated the problem.

Many current salespeople will agree to *try* to use the yardstick. Forget it. They might as well *try* to be a brain surgeon. It isn't a question of whether the yardstick will work or not. It is only a question of whether or not we wish to improve. Many a manager has related to me that when they discuss it with a salesperson, he or she is told that they "will try to improve." They don't, because they can't.

    Managements who choose not to accurately measure the productivity of each individual salesperson have opted to fail, jeopardizing their companies. Everything on the face of this earth that can be done in efforts to improve selling competence may be done by salespeople and management, but if they have no accurate way to measure competence, or if they opt not to accurately measure it, there will be no improvement.

    The decision to use the yardstick or not is a management decision. It is one that guarantees the future of the company and the future of the jobs of the people in the company, including theirs. To get the yardstick used accurately, the salespeople must agree that they want to improve and they must agree to accurately use the yardstick while supporting all others use of it. It is managements' job to get that agreement and to monitor the use of the yardstick so that stray dissenters won't undermine its use.

    When managements have had their salespeople *read the book* and shown them how using the yardstick is *in their own best interest,* most of the salespeople opt to use it. At first, its use must be closely monitored until the salespeople are habitually depositing the card. There should be added public praise and recognition for any and all improvement made by the salespeople. And because *it works,* salespeople will fight anyone who tries to take it away from them.

    A plaque awarded each month to the salesperson showing the most improvement in any company will be worth its cost to the company. A master plaque, hung on the main office wall where everyone can see it, with the salesperson's name on it is just as important. Plaques and monthly awards for salespeople showing the highest return on (prospective) customer contact (ROCC©), the highest percentage of sales made to prospective customers, the highest percentage of repeat sales made to satisfied customers, and so on.

    Anything you wish to improve can be measured with this basic yardstick. Added praise and recognition given for improvement of anything will accelerate improvement.

7 / I Can See How That Would Work for Other Salespeople, but What I Sell Is Different

THE EASIEST THING FOR ALL MANKIND TO SEE IS THE FAULT IN OTHERS. THE HARDEST THING FOR ALL MANKIND TO SEE IS THE FAULT IN THEMSELVES. PERHAPS THE WISEST ADVICE EVER GIVEN WERE THESE WORDS WRITTEN BY SHAKESPEARE: "UNTO THINE OWNSELF BE TRUE AND IT FOLLOWS AS THE DAY FOLLOWS THE NIGHT THAT THOU CAN BE FALSE TO NO MAN."

I CAN SEE HOW THAT WOULD WORK FOR OTHER PEOPLE, but what I sell is different. I have heard those exact words from people selling everything from brushes door-to-door to jet airplanes. I rank my next-door neighbor as one of the top life insurance people in the nation. His huge mansion with the grand ballroom on the fourth floor attests to his success as a life insurance salesman and a builder of life insurance companies. When I had questions about problems selling life insurance, he was the person I turned to.

I asked him if he would read the first four unedited chapters of this book and give me his opinion. I had been in a writer's slump for about a month when I received a call from him. Summing up his report, he said, "I have never read anything like it. It read like a novel. One thing led to another. I couldn't put it down. I could see where it is just what automobile, real estate, and retail salespeople really need. John, if you put an ending on those four chapters you will have the biggest selling book ever published on selling."

Needless to say, that snapped me out of my slump. I said, "Wayne, you didn't say anything about life insurance salespeople."

"John," he said, "selling life insurance is different. Life insurance customers rarely come to the salespeople and when they do, it is only those shopping price or those who are uninsurable and know it. When a life insurance salesperson calls prospective customers on the phone or approaches them in person to ask if he can talk to them about their life insurance, the customer says, 'I don't need any. Period.' So I can't see where your 5 x 7 card would be of any use at all."

I reminded him that in a previous conversation he had told me that the reason for the failure of people who are hired and trained to sell life insurance is because they never learned to prospect. "You just said when a salesperson calls prospective customers on the phone or in person and asks if he can talk to them about life insurance, they say, 'I don't need any. Period.' Would you agree that very few of these salespeople have developed an effective greeting that will get them past this point?"

"Yes."

"Let me ask you a question. Have you ever one single time asked anyone if you could talk to them about their life insurance?"

He thought back over his career and said, "Not that I can recall."

"When you and I were talking the other day, you were telling me how you expected life insurance sales to boom when the new inheritance taxes go into effect. It will mean the heirs will have to come up with a lot more cash to pay those taxes; the only place most people will be able to get this needed cash is life insurance. This made me aware of a need for life insurance that I did not know I had. It caused me to think about my own life insurance and to ask myself if I had enough."

I went on. "Another problem you mentioned was how diversified life insurance had become over the past few years. Today, there are hundreds of different kinds of policies available for every conceivable need. I can assure you that prospective customers for life insurance are no more consciously aware of their needs than are prospective customers for any other products or services. As a matter of fact, most of them are even less aware of those needs—needs that change often in today's world. More life insurance sales are lost because the salesperson has not learned enough about the customer and his or her needs than all other reasons combined."

My friend tried to argue, but I charged ahead.

"When a life insurance salesperson starts right out telling the prospective customer he would like to talk to him about life insurance, he has tried to give that customer a guided tour. Life insurance is intangible. You can't give guided tours. Over 85 percent of all life insurance salespeople account for less than 20 percent of total sales, but none of that 85 percent last. Once they have sold their relatives and friends, they are through. It's not like furniture or cars, where about one out of seven prospective customers *will* buy, so guided tour directors can at least hang in there. In the life insurance industry you are either competent or you aren't. Is that true?"

"Yes."

"Then I will guarantee you that if you personally stop and think about it before you even try to talk to customers about the insurance you intend to sell them, you have achieved the same four objectives as all other professionally competent salespeople. You have made your customers consciously aware of every need they could conceivably have for the benefits of what you are about to sell them. You have made them consciously aware of what will be lost if they don't have those benefits. This increases the level of their dissatisfaction. You have told them about a good policy that would cost about the same, but not meet their particular needs near as well as the one you intend to sell them. You tell them about a second policy that will meet their needs much better than the first one, but cost up to twice as much. And that's before you even begin the presentation on the policy that's going to *best* meet their needs, yet only cost about the same as the first one."

He pondered what I had said for a moment, kind of looked away and to himself said, "Then I just write it up."

I laughed. "Of course you do. Now, let me ask you a question. Where do you get your prospective customers?"

"What do you mean, John?"

"Just what I asked. Where do you get your prospective customers?"

He pondered that for some time before he said, "I guess mostly from those people with whom I do business."

"Would you call those people your *satisfied* customers?"

He managed to produce a smile as he said, "Yes."

"Have you ever talked to anyone about life insurance from the time you first started selling without having some record of that encounter? You know what I mean, name, address, phone number, and all other pertinent information?"

"No, I keep it all in 8½ x 11 file folders."

"There's your equivalent of my 5 x 7 file card and you have created one for every prospective customer you have come in contact with from the day you started. That yardstick measured how effective and productive you were. It showed you what you did that worked and what was counterproductive. It told you what you needed to know and why."

As we discussed the topic further, I was able to show him that right from the start, his objective when he came in contact with any prospective customer had been to turn him or her into a satisfied customer who would continue doing business with him from then on. One who would send friends, relatives, and business acquaintances to do business with him. "I bet you have some customers right now, today, whom you sold in your first months of selling."

He nodded.

"Then there is no telling how many millions of dollars worth of insurance you have sold to each one of them, their friends, relatives, and business acquaintances. Is there?"

He thought a moment, reliving some of those early experiences. "No, and there have been a lot of them."

All professionally competent life insurance salespeople and their prospective customers have only one goal when they come in contact with each other and that's for the customer to wind up a *satisfied* customer. Life insurance salespeople set out to achieve the same ten objectives in the same sequence as all other salespeople.

I admit it is almost impossible for a life insurance salesperson to see how his or her product is the same as selling an automobile. What makes this humorous is that automobile salespeople feel the same way.

Remember, all salespeople say, "That may work for someone else, but what I sell is different, so it won't work for me."

An automobile salesperson will say, "Other salespeople don't have to deal with trade-ins." Trade-ins have nothing to do with selling a new car. Professionally competent salespeople who have learned enough about their prospective customers' needs and made them consciously aware of those needs have learned enough about their budgets as well. The trade-in is only a part of how the prospective customer will pay for a new car.

When the guided tour directors start out showing their new cars, all they want their prospective customers to do is find a car they like well enough to make an offer on—any kind of an offer.

There are two things we know about such customers:

• The price of every new car they look at is too high—way too high.

• Prospective customers think their trade-in cars are worth a whole lot more than they are.

When professionally competent automobile salespeople achieve their first four objectives, they have already made the new car worth a whole lot more to their prospective customers. More important, they have made their prospective customers far more dissatisfied with what they have now. So price is no more of a problem to them than it is to any other professionally competent salesperson.

During the demonstration, the competent professionals have their customers experience owning more and more of the benefits of the features of the new car. That elevates the value of the new car even more and makes the customers even more dissatisfied with what they have. See how the value of the new car has gone up, up while the equity in the old car has gone down, down? It's all the same. The customer doesn't want to lose those incredible benefits he or she has experienced and go back to the same old car and its benefits, which he or she is now so dissatisfied with. The competent professionals just "write it up."

A prospective life insurance customer or automobile customer who is shopping price is no different from any other prospective customer shopping price. These people are no more consciously aware of their needs than any other prospective customers. Like all other sales, more automobile and life insurance sales are lost because the salespeople did not know enough about their customers' needs than all other reasons combined.

Bankers see themselves as being above all of this. To imply they are "salespeople" would be a sacrilege. In the boom years created by the OPEC bloc and the inflation it caused, many bankers forgot that their only objective should be a *satisfied* customer. Many went bankrupt. Some went to prison.

The only objective of any business should be a legitimately *satisfied* customer, and that includes banking. The success of all business depends entirely upon the competence to get and keep *satisfied* customers.

So don't ever say, "It may work for others, but what I sell is different." If you and your prospective customers both have the same goal when you come in contact and that goal is for them to wind up satisfied customers, in order for you to succeed, you will need to gain the specialized knowledge and to develop the productive skills to achieve the same ten objectives in the same sequence. It does not matter what you sell. And all of your good intentions and efforts will fail if you don't have a yardstick by which to measure your improvement or if that yardstick is not used accurately.

If you do have a yardstick and use it accurately to measure how effectively you achieve those ten objectives, success is guaranteed beyond your wildest dreams. Just close your eyes and visualize my next-door neighbor's huge Tudor mansion with its fabulous collection of priceless antique furnishings and art. Picture yourself in the pool, playing tennis, or strolling through the rose garden. Could you ever in your wildest dreams imagine yourself owning and living in that mansion? Want to know something? Even in his wildest dreams, when he started selling, neither could my neighbor.

Fortunately for him, he started right out using his own form of a customer file card and that measurement caused him to gain the knowledge and develop the skills that led to his success. I don't want you to doubt for one minute that he didn't work harder than most life insurance salespeople. Had he only worked half as hard, he would still be successful far beyond his wildest dreams. He would still be wealthy, but he would have had a lot more time to smell his roses. Of course, he probably wouldn't have that grand ballroom on the fourth floor of his mansion.

8 / *How To Get The Most Out of This Book*

SALESPEOPLE WHO HAVE NEVER SOLD BEFORE OR WHO ARE LEFT ON THEIR OWN TO LEARN HOW TO SELL WILL FIND THIS CHAPTER INVALUABLE IN THEIR BUSINESS OF SELLING.

IN THE CHAPTER ON HABITS you are reminded of the times you have bought things that required some assembly. You read the page of instructions, then tried putting the thing together and when something did not fit, you went back to the instructions. Then you said, "Oh. Now I see what they mean." Even on the simplest of products with only one page of instructions—which you have read completely and are sure that you understand—you will still have to go back to those instructions a half a dozen or more times before you have gained enough comprehensive understanding of what you are supposed to do to complete the assembly. It will seem to have taken forever and your result didn't make you proud of your job. By the time you had completed the third product, it had become much easier, taken less time and it was a job that you could be proud of.

The key thing for you to remember is the fact that you had gone back to those instructions a half a dozen times or more before the first product was assembled and you had referred to the instructions several more times before you were doing a reasonably good job in a reasonable amount of time.

Each page of this book may be viewed as though it was a one-page set of instructions. If you have never sold before and even if you have been selling for years, as you read each page for the first time, you will gain very little comprehensive understanding of what you have read. Even those who have been selling for years (unless they are way above average) will have gained very little comprehensive understanding the first time they read the book even though they may feel that they did fully comprehend it.

If you have never sold before you should have read this book carefully from cover-to-cover before you start your first selling job or approach your first prospective customer. Long before you have completed reading the book you will realize why you should read it before you start selling.

If you are selling now or are a new trainee who has already read the book prior to starting your first job you will need yellow, blue, and red highlighters.

Set aside a time of day to read a part of the book at home every day. Those who are really serious prefer rising earlier every morning to read when their minds are fresh. You will need enough time each day to complete the book from cover-to-cover in two weeks. Highlight in yellow all of those things that seem important to you as you read. It is best, to take the full two weeks to read the book, giving yourself time to ponder and to even re-read portions as you go along. Start reading an hour a day. This time allotment can be increased or reduced as you see what is needed to complete the book in two weeks.

Over the following four weeks, at the same time each day, you should read the book again from cover to cover. This time highlight anything that now seems important in blue—over those things highlighted in yellow that now seem even more important—this will turn the yellow green (money green, we like to say). Think about some things as you go along and re-read anything that seems cloudy or unclear.

Because you are working a regular selling schedule as you read the book it is like reading the instructions, trying to assemble a product, and when something doesn't work you go back to the instructions again.

During this 42 day or six week period, you should keep your book near at hand for reference. Every minute you are not with a prospective customer should be spent gaining more of the specialized knowledge that you need. Make a list of every feature and every one of its benefits of what you sell. List them in the order that your presentation will be made and qualifying questions will be asked. Come in on your day off and stay late to gain additional knowledge and to practice involvement presentations. This should be the rule during these six weeks or more—if needed.

From then on, as you refer back to the instructions (the book) anything that now seems important should be highlighted in red.

You should start initiating a customer accounting card for every single prospective customer contact without ever forgetting or failing to do it from the very first. These cards should be tallied every morning before your morning reading session. That puts all those things that worked and those things that didn't uppermost in your mind. (I am assuming that you are doing this on your own because your company is not using the book. If you can get other salespeople in your company to use the book also, working together with the others will enable you to increase your comprehension and accelerate the improvement of your productive selling skills. The more salespeople (both in and out of your company) using the book whom you can discuss what is working and what isn't increases your comprehension. The improvement of your skills will be greatly accelerated.

Psychiatrists tell us that people who do anything repetitively for 21 days will have become so skillful at doing it and it will have gotten so easy to do that it has become a habit to which they are addicted. If you follow this simple plan for six weeks that is twice as long as it takes to perfect a skill into a habit. You will discover that you have perfected the most productive of all learning skills into a productive reading/skill habit, one that very few people in selling have. Continue this productive reading skill/habit at the same time every day and it will continue to improve every day as long as you do so.

By this time, you will have proven to yourself something that very few people in the world of selling really comprehend. Each time you have referred back to the instructions (the book) it has increased your comprehension. Those things highlighted in blue, green, and red are absolute proof of this. This is your measurement of how much your comprehension of the profession of selling has improved.

Your yardstick (the customer accounting card) will show you how many more prospective customers you are selling than before. That leaves no doubt that your efforts are starting to pay off and you will not need anyone to tell you that it is getting easier and easier to make a sale while taking less and less time. You are making the sale more and more often and your income is going up, up, up! Just keep this vision uppermost in your mind as you go through those first six weeks of selling, putting in lots of overtime learning hours. Use your yardstick accurately—it guarantees that your effort will turn that vision into reality. You will find yourself in the business of selling.

The plan that you have just read has worked and continues to work for thousands of salespeople who have had to do it all on their own. Their letters to me tell of their successes, how it has changed their lives, and the lives of all those they love—truly the greatest personal satisfaction I receive from doing what I do.

I dare say that many, if not most, of the thousands of companies that now use this plan as a basis for the sales education and training in their companies got started because a salesperson on his or her own, followed the plan and had shown phenomenal improvement.

HERE'S HOW THOUSANDS OF COMPANIES HAVE USED THIS SIMPLE PLAN AS A BASIS FOR THEIR SALES EDUCATION AND TRAINING.

I believe that it is probably the most widely used plan that there is. The reason for this is simple: It works, whether the company does anything to help it work or not. Of course, the more support management gives the basic plan the better it works.

No one can get a medical education without a textbook. The same thing could be said about an education in any other field of learning and that certainly includes selling. What makes a book an accredited textbook? The professor (or one responsible for what is to be learned) selects the textbook. What was the basis upon which the decision was made? He or she read the textbook and said, "This is what and how I want my students to learn."

Who is qualified to accredit a textbook for the education and training of salespeople in a company? Only when the head of the company has read the book and says to management, "This is what I want the salespeople in this company to know and do," does that book becomes the accredited textbook for sales education in that company.

This plan, which is now used as a basis of sales education and training in thousands of companies, started to develop when the heads of companies —large and small—read my earlier book, *Selling Retail,* and decided it was what they wanted their salespeople to know and do. It evolved into the plan as it is today as I worked with hundreds of companies passing along those things that worked and didn't work as they were told to me.

One of the first discoveries we made was that the plan worked better when the salespeople bought and paid for their own books.

The next discovery was a way to get all of the salespeople in a company to buy and pay for their own book. This proved to be quite simple and has now worked successfully in several thousand companies.

The company orders enough books for every salesperson and its management staff. In a meeting with management present, the salespeople are told about the book and how salespeople who have read the book and done some of the things discussed in it found themselves making sales easier, more often, and in less time. This resulted in their jobs getting easier and them making more money. I have never heard of a salesperson not liking *that* idea.

Then the salespeople are told that management wants to make the book available to every single salesperson who wants one. All they need to do is to sign their name to a form that authorizes the company to take the cost of the book out of their next two pay periods and they can take the book with them. (I am sure that there have been cases where a salesperson has not taken a book when it was presented just this way, but to date I have not heard of one.)

Now the salespeople have the book but do not have a plan to follow. Without the company's support very few of them will ever finish reading the book because most people—even many well educated people—don't have good reading skills.

Most companies follow a simple plan based on what has proven most successful for new and current salespeople who bought the book and used it on their own. This becomes the basis of the sales education and training program.

Here is how the basic plan is used: In the meeting when the salespeople get the book, they are told that they will find a simple plan at the end of Section I of the book that tells how salespeople who use the book have been most successful. It is recommended that they read that first, along with the chapters entitled, "Habits" and "The Four Advanced

Educational Sciences: How We Learn" (Section II).

The plan is initiated at the next sales meeting. The use of the highlighters is demonstrated and they are passed out. Then the daily reading assignments are made for the coming week. The salespeople are told that they are to bring their books with them to sales meetings and that everyone's name will be put in a hat for a drawing. The person whose name is drawn will get to lead a fifteen to twenty minute discussion of what the salespeople had highlighted that week. The manager should thumb the pages of two or three salespeople's books at the meeting, holding them up so that all the salespeople can see how much was highlighted.

This is continued—following the same six-week schedule outlined in the salespeople's individual plan, with a different name drawn to lead a short discussion period. Keep these short—say, fifteen minutes or so. After the first six weeks, the reading assignments are reduced to no more that two or three chapters that will deal with any area where the salespeople need the most help. This will usually be one or two chapters that deal with a specific skill and one or two chapters that deal with the revelations or why's of that skill. These are to be read on Monday, again on Wednesday and on Friday mornings. That way, salespeople read what they are supposed to do and why, then try to do it for two days, read it again, try to do it for two days, then read it again.

When individual salespeople have problems in a given area, they can be given special reading assignments.

There are some companies using the plan that don't do more than this, and don't even do it very well, who are more than pleased with the results only because the salespeople are so much better than they were.

The more support a company gives this program

• the more attention is paid to the use of the yardstick, and

• the more praise and recognition is based on how much an individual has improved his or her batting average or return-on-prospective-customer-contact, the greater the results.

One of the biggest benefits of this plan is that it permits the company to start a new sales trainee on any Monday. The trainee will work with salespeople who are all trying to achieve the same objectives and goals. Instead of complaining about why things don't work—like the losers in the lounge—these salespeople start right in discussing what *does* work and how to make it *work better.*

If you want more help in developing a sales education and sales training plan for your company, call 1-800-234-9384.

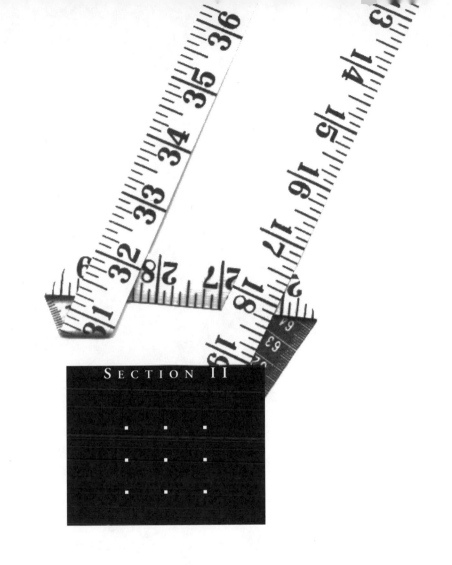

SECTION II

INTRODUCTION TO
THE BOOK OF REVELATIONS

AFTER 35 YEARS IN THE BUSINESS OF SELLING, having had thousands of salespeople work for me, I've built up quite a list of whys.

Why salespeople did what they did that didn't work, and even after they knew it didn't work, would go on doing it to the end of their careers.

Why prospective customers did what they did that didn't make sense and even seemed stupid, when I knew they weren't.

Most of my *whys* were the result of things taught as gospel about selling.

The objective of what I call "The Book of Revelations" is to give any salesperson who reads it easy-to-understand answers to the *whys* of selling.

I call the answers "revelations" because I have not found them anywhere else. They all come from my research. You will find very little in this book of what is generally taught about selling—in fact most of what is generally taught about selling you will find refuted or negated.

As you read each of these revelations, you will come to understand why it is in your best interest to do only those things that will cause you to become more productive. When you pursue your career in selling and see the prospective customer, the boss, or the people in your company doing something that doesn't seem to be in your best interest, you will ask *"why?"* As the whys arise throughout your career, the odds are good you can find them explained in the chapters of "The Book of Revelations."

These revelations will help you understand what really is in your own best interest and *why.* As you understand better and better these *whys* of selling, you will see that you should only *do those things that are in your best interest.* You will discover that when you understand what is in your best interest you will be able to do what you want to do, not what someone ordered you to do. When you reach this level of self-motivation, you become your own boss and you will own your own business. A business within a business—a "business of selling" franchise.

9 / The Secret of Self Motivation Revealed for the First Time

"GIVE ME A STOCK CLERK WITH A GOAL AND I
WILL GIVE YOU A MAN WHO CAN CHANGE THE WORLD.
GIVE ME A MAN WITHOUT A GOAL AND I WILL
GIVE YOU A STOCK CLERK."

J.C. Penney

YOU WILL NEVER FIND a successful person who is not goal oriented. You will never find a successful person who is not self motivated.

If that's true, then those two things must be the key to success. Wise men have known that for thousands of years.

The great retailer J.C. Penney once said, "Give me a stock clerk with a goal and I will give you a man who can change the world. Give me a man without a goal and I will give you a stock clerk."

Millions of living examples prove conclusively that the more clearly defined a person's goals are, the more self motivated they are, and the more successful they become.

We *all* want to succeed—regardless of what the losers in the lounge might try to tell themselves to keep from seeing themselves as they really are. The praise, approval, and recognition that go with success are the fertilizers that feed our spirits and make us grow. They build our self image and make us more confident. No one *chooses* to lack confidence and be fearful. No one. If that is so and those who set goals succeed, become more confident, and self motivated, why doesn't everyone set goals?

Let's ask that question of salespeople, because not one in a thousand has any goals. These are people who on the whole have above normal IQs. In no other profession are goals a bigger issue. Almost all salespeople are given sales quotas (which are goals) and yet, not one in a thousand achieves any real degree of success.

Why? Because sales quotas or goals were *given* to them. They were *company* goals, not *their* goals. The only goals anyone will work hard for are their *personal* goals. Nobody, not a spouse, mother, father, children, or boss can set someone else's goals. So why don't salespeople set their own?

It may sound dumb, but our fear of failure *guarantees* our failure. Every goal is a commitment. When we fail to achieve a goal, we have proven to ourselves we are failures. It is that fear that keeps everyone from setting goals.

And what is the biggest cause of fear? *Incompetence.* When we feel we are not competent to do something we lack the confidence we need to try it. The more we lack confidence, the greater our fear.

I do not believe you will find a book on selling or anyone who teaches selling who won't assure you that if you want to succeed, you must set goals. They will even go much further than that. They will tell you how to set your goals and yet, most salespeople have none at all.

Why? Most people have no goals because having set goals in the past and having failed to achieve them, they abandoned goal setting entirely. Obviously, there is more to goal setting than most have been led to believe.

Most goals set are the equivalent of "hoping to win a lottery." That's not a goal—it's blind luck and has nothing to do with goals as they are talked about by men like J. C. Penney or Napoleon Hill (in his book *Think and Grow Rich*).

If there is no plan for you to follow in your efforts to achieve your goal, it is no goal, only a wish. While many a book will tell you that if you can see yourself achieving any goal you can achieve it, they don't tell you *how* to see yourself achieving a goal. What you need is what I call a **Personal Action Plan.**

A city slicker slid to a stop at a county crossroads in south Georgia. He asked an old timer which road to take to Dalton. The old timer said, "Can't say as I rightly know."

"What do you mean you don't know? How long have you been living around here?"

"All my life."

"You've been living around here all your life and you don't know which one of those roads goes to Dalton? What's the matter with you, are you stupid?"

"I may be stupid, but I ain't lost."

In order for anyone to establish goals and achieve them, there are several things they have to know about goal setting. This story is the best example of people who have goals, but fail to achieve them.

• The city slicker has a goal: to get to Dalton. He can't reach it because he doesn't know where he is.

• The farmer knows where he is, but he has never wanted to go to Dalton.

• Neither of them is stupid, but they are both incompetent when it comes to getting to Dalton.

Most people have only been told they must have goals. They might even have been told how to set goals, but there are four things you must know if you are to set and achieve a goal.

1. You must clearly define your goal. The better defined that goal is, the quicker you are going to achieve it. The more you want to get to Dalton, the sooner you will get there. It's the same principle.

2. You must know where you are. If your goal required you to have more money, you would need to know when you would need it and how much more and you would need to know how much you have now.

3. You have to have a plan. The city slicker knew where he wanted to go. The farmer could tell him where he was, but if the driver had no map or plan to follow, he was not going to get to Dalton, not even by accident.

4. You must follow the plan.

That's it. Your **Personal Action Plan.** You do those four things and you will achieve any goal you set. You might say, "Okay, now that I know where I am, know where I want to get, and have a plan to get there, what do I have to do to follow my plan?"

Once you actually have a well-defined goal and a plan to achieve that goal, the only things you need to do are those things you choose to do because you *want* to do them, not because somebody made you or because you *had* to.

Your goal alone will motivate you. You could say your goal made you self motivated. How motivated? The more clearly defined your goal, the stronger your desire to achieve it, the more motivated you are, the sooner your goal is reached.

In 1989, I saw clearly for the first time what causes a goal to be achieved and a person to be self motivated.

When my daughter C.C. was sixteen, she was given national recognition for her studies of French and was invited to spend six weeks in France with students from all over the world. The first four weeks they would travel by bus across France, winding up the last two weeks in Paris. There would be 60 people in each bus, made up of fifteen students from four different countries, all speaking French. Each week they would be in a bus with three different groups from three other countries. What an incredible experience! The award was given in October and the trip was to start on June first.

This young lady can get very, very excited at times, but I have never seen her more animated than she was in March when she said, "Daddy, you know how you are always talking about 'Your Personal Action Plan'? When I won that trip to France, I decided I would like to have $600 of my own money to spend on clothes when I got to France. So I started a personal action plan in October and today I have my $600 in the bank."

Wait a minute. Where did this sixteen-year-old girl, whose only visible means of support is "moi" get $600 in less than five months? I said, "Honey, that's incredible. Let's sit down over here and see if we can figure out what caused that to happen."

She was a very popular girl, so parties and dates were important to her. She was also much in demand as a babysitter and she was on Sak's Fifth Avenue's fashion council, so she was often asked to model and help in other ways for which she was paid.

But now she had a goal that put a *priority* on her *time* and *money*. When she was asked to babysit or work at Sak's and had a date, she now had to decide which she wanted to do more: work to get the money or take the time for a date. She still led a very active social life but, given the choice, she often chose to earn money. She had an allowance she was free to spend as she liked. She could buy that new CD, cosmetics, pizza, and so on, or she could save the money. She didn't go without the things she needed, but other things her money might have been spent on just didn't get bought.

Her goal had set a priority on her time and money. It caused her to achieve her goal two full months ahead of time. By June first, she had over $750 in the bank and I was so proud of her I rounded it out to $1000.

We had spent a week in Paris the previous year, and C.C. had seen the incredible selection of clothes available there. She visualized herself in Paris again with $600 just to spend on clothes. At sixteen, nothing seemed more important to her. It would be hard to find anyone with a more clearly defined goal.

Note: C.C. did not have to do one single thing to reach her goal that someone ordered her or told her to do. She did what *she* chose to do, because she wanted to do it. Not only *wanted* to, but was excited about doing so. You can't get much more self motivated than that.

She knew exactly what she wanted and when she wanted it. Based on her current earnings and allowance, she could see herself having the $600 by June first. The goal caused her earnings to go up and her spending to be less than she had planned. She not only achieved that short-term goal, but she achieved it in less time than she dreamed possible. That is why she was so excited.

There is no cause without an effect. C.C.'s goal caused that to happen. How did it do that? By creating a yardstick that measured what she did with her time and money. It gave her a choice. She had to decide for herself which she wanted most every time she had a chance to work. It was easy for her to see herself with more money in Paris so "blah type" dates got left out. She still did all the social and school things that were important to her. She just stopped wasting time on things that weren't important or rewarding both mentally and financially.

She studied those cosmetics, CDs, trinkets, and all the other things on which money could be frittered away and decided which she wanted more: them or the clothes in Paris. At no time did she feel she was sacrificing or giving up anything. At no time did she have to be told she *couldn't* buy something. As a matter of fact, she was motivated and excited *not* to buy. Why? What gets measured, improves.

A well-thought-out personal goal puts a yardstick on everything you do with your time and your money. Can you see that the more clearly that goal was defined and visualized, the more you would be seeing in your mind's eye the object of that goal each time you had a choice to make as to what to do with your time and/or money? The more you desired the object of your goal, the more motivated you were to choose in favor of the goal and the sooner the goal is achieved.

Here's the catch. In order to achieve any personal goal, you are going to need more time and more money. Where is that going to come from? The only place that will come from is your source of income: your job or your career.

The boss is going to have to give you more time off and/or more money or you're not going to achieve your personal goals. When you tell the boss about your personal goals and ask for the time off and extra money, I believe you will be turned down and probably fired. He couldn't care less about your personal goals any more than you do about his.

So, where *is* the extra time and money going to come from? Those with goals not only achieve them, but become more successful in the process. What causes that? Salespeople who have personal goals must look at the hours they work and the income this brings in. These salespeople must now make more money in less time if they are to achieve their personal goals, which is to have more time and money. How can they do that? They must sell more of the prospective customers they come in contact with than they are selling now. They must do it in less time and their average sale needs to be larger. How can they do that? The same way they achieve their personal goals. They now have career goals set up to achieve their personal goals. This puts a yardstick on how effective and productive they have been with every customer they come in contact with and by now, we should all know that what gets measured, improves. No yardstick, no improvement, no goals.

Give me a person, any person, who has personal goals and I will give you a salesperson who can succeed beyond his or her wildest dreams. Give me a salesperson who has *no* personal goals and I will give you a loser in the lounge.

Isn't it amazing that when salespeople can see how to achieve their personal goals by selling in the company where they work, they buy into that company's goals? When they can't see how their personal goals can be achieved in the company where they work, they won't buy into their boss's or their company's goals. The masters of selling in company after company are loyal to that company and its customers to a fault because each one has personal goals that can be achieved in the company where they work.

In those same companies, the losers in the the lounge are just as quick to blame the company and its customers for their failure. They can see no career path in the company because they have no goals that measure what they do with their time and money against what they want out of their lives.

If you look at what those professionals of selling do, you discover they have long-term goals they wish to achieve. They want to work more hours, or even full-time, in their churches, Boy Scouts, or other rewarding activities. They want a chance to enjoy the nicer things of this life. Better homes, cars, schools for their children, and more time to enjoy those things. They want to smell the roses while they are young enough to enjoy them.

Most people dream about what they would do if they won a lottery. Those ones out of millions who win rarely do any of those dreamed-of things because they have made no plans. Just read the case histories of those who have won multi-million-dollar lotteries and you read horror stories, because they had no plan and no goals.

Those who do have goals always set intermediate goals or lesser goals for those things they want that can be achieved in less time. These goals are more easily achieved and make the goal setter more confident. This confidence makes them even more confident that they will achieve their long-term goals.

They also have immediate goals. These goals are also easily achieved, which builds their confidence even more. The more confident they become that they will achieve their goals, the more self motivated they become.

In order to achieve their long-term, intermediate, and immediate personal goals, they have only one career goal and that is to turn every prospective customer they come in contact with into a satisfied customer, and to continue to get better and better at achieving this career goal, which means it takes them less and less time as they become more productive, earning more and more money.

How can you do that?

You can't if you do not have an accurate record of the percentage of prospective customers that you are coming in contact with. That is your yardstick.

There are only two things that you can to do improve your batting average or ROCC©(return on customer contact):

- Increase the level of your specialized knowledge and information.
- Improve the effective level of your productive selling skills.

The goal of improving your ROCC puts a yardstick on what you do with your working hours that measures how productive they are. Every minute spent on unproductive activities while on the job is not just unproductive, but counterproductive and will not only keep you from achieving your personal goals but can guarantee you a failed career. When this option is compared to doing those things that are going to help you achieve your personal goals, you will find yourself doing those things that are the most productive. This repetition will cause them to become even more productive and that Personal Action Plan, when followed, causes you to achieve your personal goals *and* your career goals.

Once you have determined how much more time and money that you will need to achieve your personal goals, your yardstick shows you where you are. It tells you how many hours you are working and what percentage of your prospective customers are being sold and the average volume of each sale. You can easily figure how many more prospective customers you will have to sell out of every 100 contacts in order to achieve your goal. You know that it is a guaranteed fact that when you accurately use that yardstick your batting average will improve.

Now you know what your goal is, where you are, and you have a Personal Action Plan that will get you from where you are to where you want to get. Follow that plan and you cannot help but reach your goal.

Do you want to know the most exciting things about career goals? When you have them, you go to work because you want to. You call on customers because you are eager and excited to get the opportunity to call on customers. You like your customers because they like you. It is truly amazing how much you like the people who help you achieve your goals. That's why they like you. Yes sir, you are the best person they have ever met when it comes to someone who's excited and enthusiastic about helping them achieve their goals.

You like the boss because he or she is also helping you achieve *your* goal. And your boss likes you because you are helping achieve *his or her* goal.

Isn't it a tragedy when you realize that most people will never know this satisfaction and sense of success, or feel this confident and unafraid, all because they have no goals? Goals are the yardstick that measures how effective your life has been. What gets measured, improves. What doesn't won't, because it can't.

Back in 1965, six billion dollars' worth of home furnishings were sold in the United Sates; women spent well over 30 billion dollars' on cosmetics. About 90 percent of those cosmetics were never used and were thrown away. Surveys then and surveys now show that most teenagers, when asked how they would describe the furniture in their home, said, "Early Nothing." Their mothers and fathers had no goals that put a priority on their spendable dollars, so billions of dollars were frittered away with nothing to show for it, with no improvement in their lives. In 1965, one hundred billion dollars was spent on non-tangible recreation.

America became the greatest nation in the world because the pride of America was in the home. We have recently put that pride in those things that give us instant gratification. What a terrible price we have to pay because we lost sight of those long-term personal goals that had improved our lives so much.

The money spent in 1965 on cosmetics that were thrown away would have permitted parents to spend almost six times as much as they had on furniture. Every year since 1965 the percentage of dollars spent on cosmetics has risen and the percentage of cosmetics thrown away has too, while every year a smaller percentage is spent on home furnishings.

The salespeople of the world today who believe their customers are better off because they own what the salespeople sell and who are professionally competent to help their customers find a way to own it, drive our economy. They can set meaningful buying goals for our industries as well as for our citizens.

It does no good to have career goals without personal goals. The only reason you are motivated to achieve your career goal is so you can achieve your personal goals.

What Are Your Goals?

What do you want and what do you need right now? Maybe to pay off your debts and have some money in the bank? Could it be a new wardrobe or self image? The goal I gave myself as soon as my book *Selling Retail* was completed was to lose 30 pounds and get back in shape. At the time, I was 58. I went to a fat farm in Tecate, Mexico, for one week. That seven days helped me develop a whole new set of eating and exercise habits. Within 90 days, I was jogging three miles a day and the 30 pounds were gone. My reward? A complete new wardrobe.

One of the best books ever written is *Think and Grow Rich* by Napoleon Hill. He says you can achieve anything you can imagine yourself achieving. That is true. If you can imagine something, you have imagined owning the benefits you will enjoy.

The more clearly you have imagined what you wish to have or to do, the more clearly you have defined your goal, and the stronger your desire will be to achieve that goal.

If you are afraid of setting a big goal or a long-term goal, set smaller short-term goals. Visualize one goal, find out how much more time and money you will need, allow enough extra money and time to permit you to enjoy the goal once you have achieved it.

Suppose it is a trip somewhere that you have dreamed of taking but never believed would happen. Visit a travel agency. Let the people there help you plan the trip and give you the costs. Allow 25 percent more than the cost of the trip for spending money. Decide when you want to leave, then book the trip. Now set your career goals because that's the plan you follow to achieve your personal goals. Get every piece of available information you can about where you will be going and where you will be staying. Put the pictures around your mirror at home, hang a picture on the sun visor in your car, so you are reminded of your goal. Talk to people who have been there. Check out a book or two from the library on where you will be going and you, just like my daughter, C.C., will not only be taking that trip, but you will have even more spending money than you had planned on. The trip will be anticlimactic because you are going to enjoy getting up and going to work more every day the closer you come to achieving your goal, and you will already be setting new goals by the time you leave. By the way, the greatest part of your trip will be the increased confidence you have and the excitement of getting back to tackle that next goal.

Give me a salesperson, any salesperson, who has personal and career goals and I will give you a salesperson who will succeed beyond his or her wildest dreams. (Yes, and one who will change the world!) Give me a salesperson without these goals and I will give you a loser in the lounge.

Give me a manager who has personal goals with career goals and I will give you a manager who will drive a company to new heights. Give me a manager without these goals and the company is in serious trouble.

A manager's success depends on his or her salespeople's success, and their success depends on their customers' success.

A manager's personal goals are achieved as the company's sales and profits increases. When managers have personal goals that gives them career goals which measure what they do with their time and money. And that puts a yardstick on what they do with the people who work with them. The manager's job is to help his or her people succeed; the managers' personal goals motivates them to do that. But none of this will work with these motivated managers if their people have no Personal Action Plan. It is the manager's job to help the salespeople and/or encourage them to set their own personal goals and show them how those goals can be achieved with their career goals. The salespeople can then set their own realistic sales quotas, and you can bet those quotas will be raised as their competence and productivity improves and their confidence grows. I believe this may be the most important part of management's job and not one in ten thousand can find it today in his or her job description.

Managers, if your salespeople use this book and you are one of those one of a thousand who has set and are following your own Personal Action Plan and you are able to encourage and assist your people in setting their own realistic Personal Action Plans, think how their confidence in you is going to go up.

We all have to have goals. They measure how effective we are in our lives, which guarantees that we will be more successful and that causes us to be self motivated. Then, we do what we do because we want to, not because someone has ordered us to. We gain confidence and become less fearful: That's *The Secret of Self Motivation*.

10 / Habits: "That Won't Work for Me"

THERE IS NO SUCH THING AS AN *INEFFECTIVE* SKILL.
EVERY SKILL—NO MATTER HOW POORLY DEVELOPED—
TO SOME DEGREE MAKES IT EASIER FOR SOMEONE TO DO
SOMETHING BETTER THAN THEY COULD IF THEY HAD NO
SKILL AT ALL.

IN MY INTERVIEWS with many of the world's highest-volume, highest-paid professionally competent salespeople, I've noticed that the productive skills they use seem so simple and easy it would appear a child could acquire them. In the companies where they work, I have asked hundreds, even thousands of long-term average salespeople, who often didn't make a fraction of the sales, why they didn't do some of the simple things done by these masters of selling. I get the same answer every time: "I tried that and it won't work for me."

I was absolutely mystified. I would tell my daughters who were eight and ten at the time of some of these simple things and ask them if they could do them and they said, "Sure Dad, why?" (Note: Ask a child a question and they always ask one back.) This is a skill used by all professionally competent salespeople.

I am sure everyone reading this has at some time purchased something that required some assembly. It probably said on the carton: "Some Assembly Required." "Easy Instructions Enclosed." It might have even gone so far as to say: "So Easy to Assemble a Child Can Do It!" You got out all of the parts, read the instructions, and start putting the contraption together. Immediately, something didn't fit. What did you do? Throw a tantrum shouting, "I read those instructions. I tried doing what they said to do and that won't work for me." No, you didn't. You went back to that part of the instructions dealing with the problem, read it, looked at the problem, and the instructions, and probably said out loud, "Oh, now I see what they mean." When you read the instructions the first time, you had no comprehensive understanding of what they were teaching you to do. It was only after you had tried to do it and it didn't work, then went back and read the instructions again, that comprehension was gained. So you got that part together and what happened? Something else didn't fit, so it was back to the instructions again. On even the simplest of easy-to-assemble products with only a page or two of instructions, you will still have gone back to them six or more times before the product is assembled. It took you forever to do it. If you could get your hands on that guy who said it was so easy to assemble a child could do it, you would probably throttle him.

If you have ever purchased three of the same easy-to-assemble products, you probably had problems with the first one. But the second one was far easier. It took a lot less time. You hardly had to refer to the instructions at all and it was put together better. Often you discover something you did wrong on the first one and had to re-do it. By the time you assemble the third product, it takes a fraction of the time of the first. It is put together a lot better and you probably say, "By golly that was so easy a child *could* have done it."

It matters not what you do for the first time, you will find it hard to do, even those things so easy that a child can do them. No better example of this principle exists than chopsticks. If you have tried using them, the first time you probably said, "If I had to eat with these things, I would starve to death." Most people will try using them once and never try again. If you will hand an oriental person a fork who has never used one, you will see that it is even more difficult for that person to use than it was for you to use the chopsticks—so difficult that those Orientals moving to countries that use knives, forks, and spoons continue using chopsticks for the rest of their lives. Yet, using a knife, fork, and spoon is so easy little children at the age of five can use them as expertly as adults. But wait, go to an Oriental restaurant where Oriental families eat and you will see little children using chopsticks with such dexterity you find it hard to believe.

Whatever anyone does repetitively gets easier and easier. As a matter of fact, as you do anything over and over, you become more skillful. Psychologists tell us that anything done repetitively for about 21 days will have gotten so easy that it requires little or no conscious effort. Once we have become so skillful that we use little or no conscious effort, then that skill has become a habit to which we become addicted. The longer we continue doing it, the more skillful we become and the stronger our addiction to the habit.

We can demonstrate this with people who follow the same route to and from work every day. They don't realize it but the longer they have been using the same route, the easier it has become to go that way because the repetition has made them so skillful that in fact, sometimes when they aren't going to work and come to one of the corners where they normally turn, they have turned before they realized it. They did that unconsciously. Had they been consciously aware of it, they would not have turned.

If this has happened to you, you know you did not set out to develop that skill. The skill was developed through repetition. It was perfected into a habit without your even knowing whether you wanted that skill/habit or not.

All skills are developed when we do the same things the same way every time. We saw ourselves growing more skillful when we assembled each of the second and third easy-to-assemble products. Because our skill improved, the assembly got a lot easier, it took less time, and the quality of what we did improved.

Think about that. Any skill will make it easier for you to do something—so easy, in fact, that it requires little or no conscious effort. It will take less and less time to do as you become more skillful at it. The quality of what you are doing will greatly improve.

It is absolutely essential to the success of any career that you understand these things about your skills/habits:

- All skills/habits will be effective the longer you practice them; the more skillful you become, the stronger your addiction to the habit will be.

- There are only two classes of skills: Productive skills and counterproductive skills.

...ger you practice a productive skill, the more effective you ... and that will make you more productive. The longer you ... counterproductive skill the more effective you will become and ... counterproductive you will be.

... selling, as in all other professions, most of what salespeople do is done repetitively. When people first start selling, they are going to develop effective selling skills whether they like it or not. They don't even have a choice. The only choice they have will be whether they choose to develop *effective* productive selling skills into productive selling habits. If they don't take this option, they will develop effective *counterproductive* skills into habits.

••• Here's why: It requires no knowledge and information, yardstick, or ••• conscious effort to develop effective counterproductive selling skills. It is ••• so easy that they are developed and perfected into habits without the salesperson ever being consciously aware of it. Once developed, they are habits to which the salesperson has become addicted—an addiction that becomes stronger the longer that person is permitted to stay in selling.

Because these effective skills are counterproductive the more effective they become, the harder and harder it gets to make a sale and the less productive the salesperson becomes.

Developing even the simplest of effective productive skills demands that you have at least the basic specialized knowledge and information that you need. Once you do, it will require conscious effort when you start. Those early efforts, like your first attempts to eat with chopsticks, will fail. You will not be very effective and what you do will often be embarrassing when it is done in front of your peers and management. But like all productive skills, every conscious effort results in your becoming a little more effective. That means you are getting a little more productive. The work becomes easier every time and will continue to get easier the longer your productive skills are practiced. Imagine if you can a career that gets easier and easier, with each new sale taking less and less time. The size and quality of the sales never stops improving and your income never stops going up.

••• Considering the alternative, you probably can't imagine anyone ••• choosing to develop effective counterproductive habits, can you? To my ••• knowledge, no one ever *knowingly* has. No, they developed those effective counterproductive selling skills into habits not because they chose to, but because they had no yardstick, they failed to *choose* to make the effort to learn what they had to learn to develop *effective* productive selling skills into productive habits.

Old adages become so because there is an element of truth in them.

"We are creatures of habit."

"Old habits are hard to break."

"It's hard to teach an old dog new tricks."

These are three old adages most of us have heard quoted all our lives. What do they really mean?

We are all creatures of habit simply because there is at least some degree of routine to everyone's life. Everything done routinely develops into a skill that becomes a habit. We have all perfected the skills to do everything done routinely, yet most people are never consciously aware that they have these incredible skills.

Take a woman who wears lipstick. She can whip out that tube of lipstick and hardly glancing in a mirror, apply it with three almost invisible strokes with the skill of a fine artist. All this is done and the lipstick put away without her ever being consciously aware of what she was doing. Ask that woman to get in front of a mirror and put her lipstick on in reverse order. She will find that it takes all of the concentrated, conscious effort that she can muster. It is going to take her a lot more time and when she gets through, it will look like a five-year-old child did it. She would be too embarrassed to be seen in public.

But suppose for some reason she *had* to start putting her lipstick on in reverse order? Developing the new skill wouldn't be all that hard. The problem would be the old skill practiced unconsciously, just like the person unconsciously turning at a corner who didn't mean to. Old habits don't go away and they *can't* be unlearned. They will get weaker and lose their strength the longer they remain unused. Every person who has ever tried to quit smoking has learned that. They really have two habits. One is an addiction to getting a cigarette out and lighting it 20, 40, 60, even 100 times a day. They are so skillful at doing this that they sometimes have two cigarettes going at the same time. The second habit isn't actually a habit, it's an *addiction* to a narcotic. A habit or skill for using an addictive narcotic may be harder and more painful to break, but all habits are hard and painful to break.

The first day any smoker tries to quit is so hard it is mentally and physically painful. The second day is even more so, and the third day is the worst. This is true of all habits, we call it "burn out" day. If you get past day three, things become easier and less painful, but it is so gradual it is almost imperceptible. In about 21 days, you will have reached the point where it is about as easy not to smoke as to smoke, but it only takes one cigarette to bring the old habit back in full force. Each day from then on the old habit unpracticed will get weaker and weaker as new habits gain more strength. No matter how long the old habit lies dormant it never goes away. That's why they say an alcoholic will be an alcoholic the rest of his life even though he never takes another drink.

Smokers can leave their cigarettes at home so even though they reach for a cigarette and lighter unconsciously out of habit, they won't find them and can't fall back easily or unconsciously on the old habit. But salespeople cannot leave their effective counterproductive selling habits at home. Those counterproductive words that cause customers not to buy are spoken unconsciously before they know it and then it is too late. To overcome counterproductive selling habits not only requires constant concentrated effort on the part of the salesperson, but everything he or she does will take more time. It will all be much harder. At first, most of what that salesperson tries to do won't work and can even be embarrassing. He or she can truthfully say, "I tried that and it didn't work for me."

Professor Edmund C. Lausier at the University of Southern California in Los Angeles had major grants for studying selling. He called my book *Selling Retail* the most right-on book he had found among the hundreds he had studied. He said to me, "You have run into the same stone wall we have: 'Habits.'" This was about a year after the publication of *Selling Retail*. By then, I had been experimenting with focused repetition (see the next chapter entitled "Four Advanced Educational Sciences: How We Learn") for some time and was satisfied that I could not only fully define this problem for the first time, but come up with a way to resolve it completely.

No one can read *The Selling Bible* without seeing the effective counterproductive selling skill/habits used by most salespeople today defined clearly. At the same time, they will see side-by-side the *effective* productive selling skill/habits of the top professionals in all fields of selling. With this book all salespeople, young, old, just starting their careers, or who have been selling for years, will be able to choose for the first time whether they want to acquire effective productive selling skills that once perfected will be productive selling habits that will make selling easier. The longer they practice these skills, the less time it will take to get the sale. The size and quality of their sales will improve and they can expect their incomes to continue to rise the longer these productive skills are practiced, because that practice will cause the skills to become even more productive.

If you should choose to develop these effective productive selling skills into selling habits, there is a simple plan for you to follow—so easy a child could do it—in this book. When you do and when you use the standard that measures your improvement, your success in selling is guaranteed. Depending on your goals you may even find yourself counted among the highest-volume, highest-paid salespeople of the world.

11 / *The Four Advanced Educational Sciences: How We Learn*

MANY TEACHERS TEACH, BUT THE STUDENTS DON'T LEARN.

OBVIOUSLY, MUCH OF WHAT IS BEING DONE IN EDUCATION
TODAY IS COUNTERPRODUCTIVE.
YET, EVERY YEAR WE SPEND MORE MONEY SO TEACHERS
CAN DO MORE OF WHAT THEY DO THAT IS COUNTERPRODUCTIVE.

MORE AND MORE EDUCATORS are realizing that very little useful knowledge is gained in classrooms. You saw a simple example of that in the previous chapter on "Habits," when I showed you how one reading a page of simple instructions gave the person no applicable understanding. Only when that person tried to assemble the simple product and hit a snag, then went back to the instructions, was comprehension fully gained. From then on, it was try to do it, and when it didn't work, back to the instructions.

Today, we call these learning processes "spaced repetition"—reading the instructions at spaced intervals between trying to do what is taught. When we try to do what was taught, we call that "interactive learning."

Canada has an experimental program in some universities that uses these two advanced educational sciences. It is a cooperative program offered as an option to students.

The traditional course of study for a student who wants a career in a certain field is to go to the university for two four-month semesters a year for four years to get a degree in his chosen field.

Suppose the career was mining engineer. At the end of four years, mining students will have gained an enormous amount of information. But they have little or no comprehensive understanding of it.

Of course, they will have read thousands of pages of instructions over that four years, telling them *how* to be mining engineers. They were required to memorize enough of it to pass the tests. Each page could be likened to the instructions for the assembly of a simple product. Except four years go by after they read the instructions for the first simple product, before they ever get their first chance to assemble one.

Therefore, their degrees are mostly useless. In fact, the degree is only a license to begin *learning* how to be a mining engineer. If a student can get a job after college, (many can't) it will be as an apprentice at apprentice wages. If the graduate then develops the productive skills needed to be a mining engineer, he or she will one day become a mining engineer. Many don't.

On the other hand, the mining engineering student who opts for the cooperative program in one of Canada's universities goes to the university for two four-month semesters, then works four months for a mining company at the most menial starting jobs at the lowest rate of pay. Then the student returns to the university for two four-month semesters and then it's back to the mines for another four months. From then on, four months at the university and four months at the mining company for a total of five years, by which time the student has a mining engineer's degree and a job as a functioning mining engineer at a mining engineer's rate of income with all the productive skills needed to succeed. This program has been so successful in those fields where it has been offered that I predict it won't be long before it's the only way a person will get a degree in anything.

As you read this book you will see that when you follow the instructions both of these advanced educational sciences are working for you to the maximum extent. Instead of reading the instructions for four months, then trying to do what was taught, you are reading and trying things out on a continuous—almost on a day-to-day basis.

Spaced repetitive reading of this book interspersed with repeated efforts to apply what is taught, results in a salesperson who develops effective and productive reading skills as well as the productive selling skills. Productive reading skills are the foundation on which all other productive learning skills are based.

My first objective in this book is to get you to develop productive reading skills. Very few people, including many university graduates, have productive reading skills.

If you read the newspaper, you probably read it daily at the same time, sitting in the same place—usually first thing in the morning. The longer you have been doing this, the more skillful you have become and the stronger the habit. Just to discover how addicted you are to this habit, think back to those times when you went out to get your newspaper and it wasn't there. You reacted like a smoker who reaches for a cigarette and finds there are none.

Rising earlier and reading this book each and every morning will be one of the most painful things you will ever do, because you have no skills for getting up earlier let alone reading important things. However, every day that you do it, it will be getting easier to do. You will become not only more skillful at reading (which is the most productive of all learning skills) but you will become more skillful at rising earlier. Soon, you will have developed the two productive skills into productive habits. Taking advantage of your brain's peak hours is what prompted the old, but true, adage, "Early to bed, early to rise makes a man healthy, wealthy, and wise."

You must set aside a certain amount of time at the same hour every day to read and reread this book, highlighting those parts that seem important to you. After six weeks of repetitive reading at the same time every day (that's twice as long as psychologists tell us it takes to develop a habit), you will have perfected your reading skill into a productive habit. The longer you practice your new habit, the stronger its addiction, the more effective and productive the skill becomes. This skill will bless your life and reward you more than all other productive learning skills you may acquire.

RECAP OF SPACED REPETITION AND INTERACTIVE LEARNING

You will have to read this book all the way through at least twice before you can develop a comprehensive overview of its teachings. Always do your reading at the same time every day (preferably first thing in the morning). Space out your reading equally over a two-week period the first time through and highlight in yellow whatever seems important. Your second reading should span a four-week period, only this time highlight what seems important in blue. Whatever you highlighted the first time in yellow that now seems important should be highlighted again with the blue highlighter. This turns the yellow into green.

Follow this process and you will have an overview of the book and at the same time acquire a productive reading skill that is a habit. When you highlighted something in blue you proved conclusively that this reading skill interspaced with trying to do what is taught has caused you to gain even greater comprehension, which means you learned even more during the second reading.

Some of these chapters were written and rewritten by me as many as a hundred times, a couple, even more. I spent over four months rewriting just the chapters on the greeting after it was completed and edited. Why? After writing anything, when you wait a couple of days and reread it, you gain even more comprehension and say to yourself, "I could do an even better job of explaining that if I rewrote it."

It is a well-known fact that the secret of success in writing is rewrite, rewrite, rewrite, and to keep on rewriting. This is just as true when it comes to reading something that teaches you how to learn.

I have spent over eleven years on this book, after 35 years of experience. I feel safe in saying that no book on selling was ever rewritten as many times as this one.

I know that each time you reread any part of this book, your comprehension will increase if you are a practicing professional salesperson. If you follow the reading instructions and develop your reading skill into a productive habit, the habit will cause you to continue practicing the productive learning skill. Once you've read this book—twice—you may intersperse your continued reading and reference to this book with other good books.

Look at it this way. Would you visit a doctor who had been practicing medicine for 50 years, but who had not read a book or made any effort to keep up-to-date on the advances in the healing profession? Of course not.

Why should you want to continue learning? So you can continue to improve. Why? Because the little bit of time you spend learning saves you a lot more time in selling, while making what you do easier and easier. Along the way, *learning* becomes a habit, too, so it gets easier.

LEARNING BY OBJECTIVE

This is another of those advanced educational sciences that for the most part is used only in experimental or progressive educational programs. I have integrated it into the learning processes taught in this book.

I used the example of the thousands of sales trainees I had seen who were sent out onto showroom floors to learn all they could about what they would be selling. There might be as many as 25,000 different things, yet the trainees felt they had seen everything there was to see and learned everything there was to learn in an hour or less. How could they possibly think that?

What if you had never sold anything in your life and you got a job selling dinettes? After you had looked at every dinette you had to sell, you would think you knew all there was to know, but if you were to ask everyone you came in contact with what they were using for a dinette now, what they like most about it, and what they were the most dissatisfied with, it would not be long before you knew far more about what seemed to best meet a dinette customer's needs. You'd know more about what caused any prospective customer to become most satisfied and what caused them to become dissatisfied. You would probably know more than most of the dinette salespeople in the world today.

Any time you looked at any dinette you would instantly see anything and everything that customers had told you about what made them more satisfied or caused them to become dissatisfied.

Those questions you asked of customers established your learning objectives. They told your eyes what to see when you looked at what you sell. They told your nose what to smell, ears what to hear, your palate what to taste, and your fingers what to feel.

It matters not what you sell. What satisfies customers most and what causes them to be *dissatisfied* is what you must know (and you must know more than they do) if you are to help them find what best meets their needs.

As you try to achieve your second and third sales objectives, the answers you get to the questions you ask will establish these learning objectives. That puts this advanced educational science to work for you. It will cause you to learn more and more about what you sell and that will enable you to better and better meet more and more of your customer's needs. What was the source of these learning goals? Your prospective customer. This is customer driven information. It's the information the prospective customer needs that you must supply.

FOCUSED REPETITION

Through focused repetition you perfect all your productive skills into productive *habits*. That simply means you must do the same thing the same way every time. As you do, it gets easier to do because you are becoming more skillful.

In every profession, art, or trade where productive skills are needed, learning and training programs are followed that result in people developing the skills they need. Until now, that has been true in every profession *except* selling.

For example, when children take their first piano lesson, they are told a little bit about the piano and what the notes and keys are, then asked to put one finger on middle C and punch C, D, E, over and over and over, focusing that finger on those three keys in that sequence. They are sent home to practice C, D, and E, one hour a day for one week, by which time they have become so skillful at doing that exercise they can do it blindfolded, and it has driven their folks nuts. That effort progresses with students focusing on more and more complex arrangements. This constant, focused repetition of hitting specific keys with specific fingers in a specific sequence perfects their skills. You'll never learn to play the piano skillfully by randomly pounding on the keys one hour every day. Focused repetition is how all productive skills are developed.

In every field where productive skills are required, the same thing (whatever it is) must be done the same way every time.

In selling, there never has been and never will be two products that are exactly alike. No two salespeople have ever been identical either and no two selling situations ever have been or ever will be exactly the same.

It has always been assumed that no salesperson could or would ever do or say exactly the same thing. Therefore, we have never had one way to focus salespeople on doing and saying the same thing the same way every time from the time they come in contact with a prospective customer until they part. Yet, if you watch individual salespeople who have been selling for any period of time at all, you will discover each of them doing and saying whatever it is that they do and say the same way every time they come in contact with a prospective customer. It does not matter what they sell, whether their customers comes to them or they go to the customer. Believe it or not, this is true whether they are the worst salespeople in the world, the best in the world, or somewhere in between.

If you watch skillful people you will discover ever-so-slight differences in everything they do. While those who have become the greatest artists in the world never do things the same as anyone else, each mastered the productive skills that enabled them to achieve incredible success. The more skillful they became, the less time it took them to create a work of art and the more masterfully it was done.

For the first time, in this book you will find a simple set of instructions that will make it easy for you to develop the productive skills you need to achieve each of the ten objectives mentioned earlier in their proper sequence. You will also discover a yardstick that tells you how effectively each of these objectives was achieved with each prospective customer you came in contact with. This will permit you to read the instructions, then to practice the skill. When what you do doesn't work the yardstick tells you it didn't. Go back to the instructions each time this happens and you will become more skillful and more productive. It is this focused repetition that perfects productive selling skills into habits.

When you follow the instructions in this book you will have all four of these advanced educational sciences working for you.

The 9-Dot Puzzle

NOBODY—NOT EVEN THOSE WHO ARE SLOW-WITTED— EVER
INTENTIONALLY DOES STUPID THINGS.

THERE ARE THREE STAGES IN EVERYONE'S LIFE. The first is infancy, when we are all completely helpless and can do nothing for ourselves. We cry: "feed me, change me, hold me." Fortunately, everybody loves a baby, and we grow out of that stage.

The second stage is juvenile, when we're sure we know more than our parents, teachers, and elders: "Please, Mother, let me do this by myself. If I can't do it, nobody can." When things go wrong, they're not our fault. Some people never outgrow this stage, and it has nothing at all to do with their intelligence.

The third stage of life is maturity: "Let me help you get that job done."

Throughout our lives, we all go through every one of these stages every time we undertake anything new. We start out like a baby the first day of our careers as salespeople. We are completely helpless and don't even know where the restrooms are. We must ask someone else to help us.

In no time it seems, we pass into the juvenile stage of our selling career. We can do this job all by ourselves. If we can't sell them, nobody can. But if we don't make the sale, it isn't our fault. Most people who stay in selling seldom advance beyond this stage. Why?

Many psychologists think the answer to that question may be the most important lesson we all have to learn and the hardest lesson there is to learn—so hard a lesson most people never learn it.

Today, many educators are using a puzzle to teach this lesson, because it is the best tool they have found.

PLACE YOUR PEN OR PENCIL ON ANY DOT. MAKE
FOUR STRAIGHT LINES IN ANY DIRECTION: UP,
DOWN, ACROSS, OR DIAGONALLY, AND
CONNECT ALL NINE DOTS WITHOUT LIFTING
YOUR PEN OR PENCIL FROM THE PAPER.

THE 9-DOT PUZZLE *

*If you have not seen this puzzle and don't know how to solve it, do
yourself a favor and try to solve it before you look on page 183 for the
solution.

Almost everyone starts to look for the solution inside the framework formed by the nine dots. But within those nine dots there is no solution. Educators use the 9-dot framework to represent the human brain. Everyone is limited in their ability to solve a problem by the amount of knowledge and information they have inside their brains. It is human nature to try to solve a problem within the framework of the problem itself. The knowledge and information inside our brains puts the framework around that problem.

The first lesson to be learned by the 9-Dot Puzzle is that no solution can be found when we don't have inside our brain the knowledge and information we need to solve the problem.

The second lesson is that when you do have the necessary knowledge and information, the problem doesn't exist. What is a problem or puzzle to the person who lacks knowledge or doesn't know the solution is no puzzle and no problem to someone who knows the solution and has the knowledge. Please go over that again. Remember, like all puzzles or problems, the 9-Dot Puzzle ceases to be a puzzle or problem to you once you know how to work it.

The third lesson is that you could have enough knowledge and information to solve a problem, but not enough to find the best solution.

There is an unanswered question raised by the 9-Dot Puzzle that educators believe is the most important: What causes people to become arrested in their careers or educations at the juvenile stage if it is not caused by lack of intelligence?

> Ignorant - One who doesn't know.
> Ignoramus - One who doesn't know, but pretends to know.
> Stupid - Very slow of apprehension or understanding. Dull witted.
> *Funk & Wagnall's Dictionary*

A major stumbling block we all have, which keeps us from answering this most important of questions, is that we can't separate the meaning of the words "stupid" and "ignorant." How many times have you said to yourself, "I can't believe I could have done anything so stupid. If I had known then what I know now, I would never have done it." Everyone has 20/20 hindsight. What you did may have been stupid, but you didn't do it because *you* were stupid. You did it because you were *ignorant* just as you yourself said, "If I had known then what I know now, I would not have done it." It was your lack of knowledge that caused you to do something that turned out to be stupid.

Most people are not stupid, not even those with below-normal IQs. People do not intentionally *do* stupid things. That is the hardest lesson that salespeople can ever learn about themselves and everyone else, including their prospective customers. Any salesperson who fails to learn that lesson will find his or her career arrested in the juvenile stage.

All people (especially prospective customers) have logical reasons for doing everything they do. That logic is based on the amount of knowledge and information inside our brains when we make the decision to do something.

When a customer says, "I can't believe I was ever stupid enough to have bought that. If I had known then what I know now, you can bet I would not have bought it." That explains why they needed a salesperson. No! No! No! Why they needed a *professionally competent salesperson*. For the lack of one, this person is now a dissatisfied customer, and that wasn't their fault, the product's fault, or the company's fault. It was the *salesperson's* fault.

It is easy for any of us to see someone do something we think was stupid, but our opinion is based on the knowledge and information we had inside our own brain. It never occurs to the "juvenile" to say, "Those certainly aren't stupid people or prospective customers. I wonder what logical reason they could have had for doing what they did?" Nor do they think the person might have known something they didn't. It may be that what the prospective customer did was the best thing for that individual. The "juvenile" looked at what the person did *inside* the 9-dot framework of knowledge and information in his or her brain to find the reason for the prospective customer's behavior, without knowing enough about the individual or his or her reasons, so the behavior seemed stupid to the juvenile salesperson.

I have never met a *stupid* salesperson. I have known a few who were slow-witted, but they weren't stupid, either. I can truthfully say the same thing about prospective customers, although I have met many a slow-witted prospective customer who would try the patience of God himself.

It should be apparent that ignorance arrests a person at the juvenile stage of life and it is ignorance that arrests people at a juvenile stage in their careers. Juveniles drop out of school not because they are stupid, but because they are convinced they know all they need to and certainly more than their teachers. That lack of knowledge arrests them at a juvenile stage for the rest of their lives if they do not learn the lesson we try to teach with the 9-Dot Puzzle.

In every profession except selling people must gain the specialized knowledge and information they need before they are allowed to practice. There are prescribed educational programs they must enroll in and tests they must pass to prove they have the knowledge and information they need to succeed in their chosen professions. Not in selling. Yet, the technical definition of "selling" is supplying the information the prospective customer needs to make the best buying decision. If prospective customers need no information to buy what is being sold, they do not need a salesperson. An ordertaker can get the job done. On the other hand, if they do need information and the salespeople don't have it, they can't do the only job they were hired to do. They are nothing more than ordertakers masquerading as salespeople.

When I say a problem is the biggest problem facing the business world today, it is because everyone is searching for the solution within the framework of the problem. When no solution is found, it is because no solution can be found *inside* those nine dots. Once we look outside those nine dots, though, even the biggest problems in the world cease to exist. Just as solving the 9-Dot Puzzle ceased to be a problem as soon as we looked outside the nine dots.

What a simple statement that is. Within it is the answer to every problem facing mankind today. Tragically, it is the hardest lesson for everyone to learn, so most never learn it. We are all locked inside our own nine-dot prisons. I don't pretend to know the answer to the world's problems, but I would like to propose a solution to the biggest problem facing business and industry today: getting products sold, and winding up with *satisfied* customers.

Here are a few observations my research has turned up.

Anyone can get a group of average salespeople talking about their prospective customers and they will all agree that the prospective customers in their market are the most knowledgeable to be found anywhere. Isn't that interesting?

Only one group of these salespeople in only one of those locations could possibly be right and all the others would be wrong. What logical reason could they have for feeling that way? I have asked thousands of average salespeople about their prospective customers and been told in these exact words, "My customers are *very* knowledgeable. They know what they want. I am only here to help my customers." Now "very" is a comparative meaning "very" compared to what? But in this case, it is compared to the salesperson who made that claim. What this salesperson actually said is, "Compared to *me,* my customers are very knowledgeable. They know more about what they need and more about my products than I do, and I'm only here to help them solve their problem within my nine dots." That's interesting, isn't it? Inside the prospective customer's nine dots the best solution does not exist, so that's why they need a salesperson. Inside the salesperson's nine dots, the best solution does not exist, either. That becomes a case of the blind leading the blind.

What I find even more interesting is that you can't read a trade publication in any industry or listen to speakers at industry conferences without reading or hearing that prospective customers are more knowledgeable today than ever before in history. They are more discriminating and harder to please. The people who write and say these things are recognized as experts.

Just join groups of industry leaders, as I have at conventions, and listen to their conversations. They often wind up talking about how much more knowledgeable prospective customers are toward what they sell— more knowledgeable they agree than ever in history. The only thing they all agree to be an even bigger problem is their inability to find good salespeople. Note: I said "find." I think "find" is pretty funny. Here they are all agreeing that none of them have a fraction of the competent salespeople they need and they are looking for a solution within the companies in their industry.

If none of them can find competent salespeople within their own companies, how can they hope to find them elsewhere? Sounds stupid to me, and these are not stupid people. No, they are just locked inside the nine dots.

Let's do a quick recap: Selling is simply supplying the information a prospective customer needs to make the best buying decision. But salespeople, industry experts, and leaders all agree the prospective customer has become more knowledgeable than ever before. In other words, they say prospective customers in all industries need less help to make the best buying decision than ever before, so it would follow that salespeople are needed less today than ever. And yet, these same people agree the biggest and fastest growing problem the business world faces is finding enough competent salespeople. Are you as confused as I am?

What logical reason could these leaders possibly have for feeling that way? It demonstrates a global lack of understanding of the difference between general and specialized knowledge.

Example: When in my teens, I had a little general knowledge about headaches. If I got one, I knew enough to go to the drugstore. I could choose from aspirin, Alka-Seltzer, Bromo-Seltzer, B.C. Headache Powder, and maybe one or two other products. They only came in one size and I could read everything written on the container on all of them in less than five minutes. I bought one and took the recommended dosage. If my headache didn't go away and got worse, what did I do? I went to a doctor. Why? Because he had *specialized* knowledge. He knew far more about what caused headaches and about the best remedies.

Today, in just Tylenol there are almost 50 different formulas on the market in who knows how many sizes. That's just one brand of headache remedy. If you go to a super-size drugstore and read everything on the packages, printed inserts and materials available for just one of each brand of headache remedy, it would take you 37 days, reading 24 hours a day. That is 53,280 minutes. That would be more than 10,000 times as long as it took me to read everything on those things available for headaches only 50 years ago.

With that incredible volume of useless general knowledge, if you buy one of those remedies, take the recommended dosage, and your headache doesn't go away but gets worse, what do you do? You go to a doctor, of course. Why? For his or her *specialized* knowledge. That massive amount of general knowledge hasn't caused you to need the specialized knowledge of a doctor any less—anymore than it has caused anyone to need the help of a professionally competent salesperson less—instead, it has caused us to need that help even more, thousands of times more! To prove that point, I will bet everyone who reads this who has kids is giving them a pain reliever a doctor told them to use.

Now, that's only one of the thousands of everyday products we all purchase. But consider the complexities and improvements, along with the selection, available in products we only buy once every few years, such as a computer, and you can see the problem from the manufacturer's viewpoint as well as the prospective customer's. Both are at the mercy of the nine-dot framework in the minds of salespeople. It's not simply that salespeople need to know enough about their product, they must also know enough about the individual prospective customer's needs, or there is no solution to be found within those nine dots.

Because of mass media influences and the incredible proliferation of products and knowledge, the average five-year-old child will have absorbed thousands of times more bits and pieces of useless general knowledge than a 100-year-old adult only 50 years ago.

We have truly become a world where almost everyone knows a little bit about a lot of things, but very few know *a lot* about anything. This is why our need for those who have specialized knowledge in all fields is the fastest growing need in the world.

Only when a salesperson accepts that prospective customers *lack* enough comprehensive understanding of their own needs, then and only then will a salesperson be able to see beyond the nine dots of the prospective customer. This knowledge precedes everything else. More sales are lost because the salesperson did not know enough about the prospective customer and his or her needs than all other reasons combined. We saw in the chapter "Your Road to Selling Success I," that as the salesperson asked the questions in an effort to learn enough about the prospective customer and his or her needs, the salesperson was actually making the customer consciously aware of those needs. That process took both the prospective customer *and* the salesperson outside the 9-Dot Puzzle they were locked inside of when they first came in contact with each other.

Like everyone else in this world, you have a logical reason for doing everything you do and your customers have logical reasons for doing everything they do. You may have to think about that point, but when you do anything, no matter how big a mistake or how stupid it may prove to be in the future, it seems logical to you at the time you do it.

In other words, people don't intentionally do illogical things. They don't do things contrary to their own understanding or reasoning. While it is easy to understand that about ourselves, it is the hardest thing to understand about other people. You can only understand it when you have complete empathy for another person's problems or needs. You must be able (like the young man giving me directions in the convenience store) to say, "I know! I know! I take that route every day. You are right!" If you remember, I was only looking for a solution to my problem within the square framework or nine dots formed by Telegraph Road, 14-Mile Road, Warren, and 8-Mile Road. The young man's best solution was 7-Mile Road, a full mile outside my nine dots. What was a problem to me was no problem at all to him.

PROSPECTIVE CUSTOMERS CAN ASK FOR THE STUPIDEST THINGS

So you think prospective customers sometimes ask for stupid things. Of course they do. But what they ask for is based on how well they understand their own needs and how much they know about what is available to meet them. Usually, that is not much, even with simple products. Lack of information keeps the prospective customers locked within *their* nine-dot puzzles, where there can be no adequate solution. And that is where an *informed* salesperson is crucial to the prospective customer. The competent professional recognizes this. But the guided tour director says, "We don't carry that. Let me show you something else," and the prospective customer leaves without buying. The tour director blames his or her failure on the prospective customer, yet the tour director's ignorance of the customer's needs was even greater than the customer's.

The competent professional takes a different approach: "I am sure you have a good reason for asking for that particular product. Do you mind if I ask what that reason is?" Inside that prospective customer's nine dots there is no solution and certainly no *best* solution. It is the competent salesperson's task to pull the prospective customer outside those nine dots where far, far better solutions can be found. As you read this book, you'll see that in all situations where a prospective customer asks to see a specific item, even when the salesperson has that exact product in stock and even if it was an item advertised on sale, the professional will always start right in with: "Do you mind if I ask why you're interested in that particular product?" or, "Do you mind if I ask what you are using now?" The professional will continue asking questions in order to get prospective customers outside their nine dots where far better solutions can almost always be found.

I rarely tell jokes to make my points, but this one does the job better than any other example I can give. Remember, we are talking about learning what many believe to be the hardest and most important lesson there is to learn in selling. Often, we remember a story long after we have forgotten the lesson. When we recall the story, that reminds us of the lesson it was teaching.

A man goes to a doctor and asks to be castrated. The doctor says, "I can't do that." The man tells the doctor that if he won't do it, he has the money and is sure he can find a doctor who will. Reluctantly, the doctor agrees and performs the operation. The man comes out from under the anesthetic in a semi-private hospital room with a patient lying in the next bed. He asks the other patient what he was in for. The man says, "to be circumcised." The first man snaps his fingers and says, "That's the word I meant."

He had told the salesman (doctor) what he thought he wanted and the salesman (doctor) let him buy it. I think it would be safe to say that was one very, very *dissatisfied* customer.

Think about this story any time you start to make the fatal mistake of thinking prospective customers know what will best meet their needs. Even on the rare, and I do mean *very* rare, occasion when a prospective customer does know, it is still your job to make sure. A dissatisfied customer is the worst thing that can happen to a salesperson, and enough of them will put that salesperson and his or her company out of business.

I think that doctor would have been well advised to have asked this question: "Sir, I am sure that you have a good reason for wanting to be castrated. Do you mind if I ask what that reason is?"

The minds of men, women, and children everywhere are being crammed with so much general knowledge through mass media that they are like the memory banks of computers that have reached their capacity. This general knowledge and the constant technical advances in every product known to man are making it harder and harder for prospective customers to make even half-way intelligent buying decisions on small products, let alone big-ticket products and expensive services. It is hard enough to try to understand this lesson when we are only dealing with the nine dot framework that limits the prospective customer and the salesperson. Now we have to add in the other people who may be involved in completing your sale.

How many times have you heard another salespeople blame the delivery or credit department for costing them a sale?

If salespeople will work in their service departments for awhile and take complaints from dissatisfied customers, they will find that more often than not a complaint occurs because a salesperson has led the prospective customer to believe (or left them believing) that what had been bought was going to do something it couldn't do; or, that someone in the company (usually the credit department, delivery, or installers) would do something they couldn't or weren't supposed to do.

Here are some of the words of dissatisfied customers when they have complaints: "I don't care what you say, that salesperson told me...." In this case, the information could have been intentional on the part of the salesperson, just so he or she could get the sale. Tragically, that is true too often in selling, but most salespeople would rather not do something wrong, especially when it could cost them a sale or even their jobs. Usually, what they told the prospective customer the product would do (or left the prospective customer thinking it would do) was based on the amount of knowledge the salesperson had at the time. That is also true of what salespeople tell prospective customers about what services other people in the company will provide to complete the sale.

When I developed my Sales Education System© for Selling Retail International, one of the toughest problems I had to overcome was to convince management they needed a special learning work schedule for newly hired salespeople for at least their first week on the job. Six ten-hour days at minimum wage: One day would be working (and I do mean working) on a delivery truck, one in the warehouse, and another in every other operational area of the company including the credit department. I wanted those new salespeople to experience how things got done in their company, who did them, and who got them to do it. In companies where customer's service calls are logged in a computer with the name of the salesperson, they found the newly trained salespeople were logging 50-percent fewer service calls than the current sales force.

Stop for a moment and think about this: Selling is supplying the information a prospective customer needs to make the best buying decision. And in every sale, one of the vital bits of that information will be delivery. You can tell a person all you want about delivery and you might as well be telling them how to swim. They won't know what you are talking about until they have been in the water. And you won't know what you're talking about either, until you have been on a delivery truck doing the job yourself. Most salespeople will tell the customer what they believe is going to happen based on the nine dots of understanding they have about what actually does happen.

So when the salesperson says, "Those stupid delivery people," and the delivery man says in turn, "You won't believe what that stupid salesperson told that customer," neither of them is stupid and neither one is right. Can you see how this third-person factor makes it even harder to understand the simple lesson the 9-Dot Puzzle is trying to teach us?

Please pay close attention to this: You saw how much sense it would have made for that doctor to have asked, "I am sure you have a good reason for wanting to be castrated. Do you mind telling me what that reason is?" So whenever you see somebody doing anything that seems stupid to you, in all likelihood it is *not* stupid to that person.

If the people in your credit department turn down your prospective customer's credit, they had a good reason. If you visit them and say, "I am sure you had a good reason for turning down that customer. Do you mind telling me what it was? Then I will be able to do a better job in the future." When you do this every time a problem of any kind arises with a customer's credit, it won't be long before you have learned far more about what causes credit to get approved without problems. Even more important, you'll know what holds up credit approvals or causes credit to be turned down. In no time you will discover that the people in your company's credit department aren't stupid, nor are they looking for reasons to turn down credit. Not at all. Their job is to get every prospective customer approved if there is any way possible. The better you understand what they are trying to do the better you can help them and *presto,* credit turndowns and credit problems will cease.

Most salespeople spend their entire careers never having gained this vital knowledge, never once visiting the credit department. If they ever did, it wasn't to learn why credit had been turned down, but jump on the staff and tell them why they should have approved it. This approach results in the salesperson thinking the credit staff is stupid and their thinking the salesperson is stupid. In fact, they are all quite sane and reasonably intelligent—intelligent enough to have resolved this problem without anger or confusion.

Now stay with me, because this is a two-way street. Although the credit department person who turned down the sale couldn't understand why the salesperson had even turned it in, did he or she say to that salesperson, "I am sure you had a good reason for thinking this prospective customer could qualify for this amount of credit. Do you mind telling me what it was?"

No. Instead, they go on turning down what they are supposed to turn down, blaming the salesperson, and the salesperson continues to turn in sales when the prospective customer can't possibly qualify for the credit. Each one is locked within their own nine dot puzzle, ignorant of what the other is trying to do.

Yet, when either one takes the initiative, they both learn more about what the other is trying to do, and what they would need to know to do it. Why? That little word is the key that opens the door to get everyone outside of those nine dots where the solution to both of their problems exists. Once they get outside those nine dots, their problem disappears.

This principle applies to every situation that causes one person to think another is stupid. We have all done things in our life that we look back upon, asking ourselves how we could have been so stupid as to have done it when it wasn't stupidity at all, it was a lack of information, which means we didn't know what we needed to know. We weren't stupid, and the other person wasn't stupid, either, but we sure were ignorant. Ignorance costs salespeople more sales than all other reasons combined. How do you overcome ignorance? The greatest teacher we are ever given is the mistake.

I have asked thousands of average salespeople why they didn't do some of the simple things top professionals do. I've heard the same answer every time: "I tried that and it won't work for me." They are saying it was a mistake because the method didn't work. Instead of asking *why* something didn't work, the long-term average salespeople go on making the same mistakes over and over until they develop ineffective counterproductive habits that doom their careers. They continue doing truly stupid things only because they remain ignorant and *pretend* to know when they don't. That makes them ignoramuses.

Look back on those most embarrassing moments in your life and ask yourself if you would have done what you did when you did it, if you had only known what you know now. The bigger the mistake, the greater the failure, the more embarrassing the experience, the greater your lesson—on one condition: that we admitted it was *our* failure, not the customer's, not the company's, not the merchandise's, but *our* failure to make the sale. Instead of blaming others you must learn to go to whomever it was that you would blame for having lost the sale and say, "I am sure you have a good reason for feeling the way that you do about this or doing what you did. Do you mind telling me what that reason is?"

Suppose it's your merchandise. You can blame the buyer or you can blame the manufacturer. In either case, nothing will change and every time it costs you a sale, you can get rid of your frustrations by calling the manufacturer stupid, or you can go to the buyer or factory representative and say, "I am sure you had a good reason for buying this or making it this way. Do you mind telling that reason? Once I know, I am sure I will be able to sell a lot more of them." Each time you do this, you will have learned more than you knew and thus become more of an expert.

I have heard many, many salespeople talk about the stupid questions prospective customers have asked them. When prospective customers ask stupid questions and salespeople don't know the answers to them, they can simply say "I don't know"—and go on not knowing for the rest of their careers, wasting both their time and their prospective customers' time. Or they can say, "I am sure you have a good reason for asking that question. Do you mind if I ask what your reason was?" You will be amazed what you will learn every time you ask that question.

Let me give you a classic example. One of the most frequent questions asked by customers in the furniture business is what size something is. So often do they ask that even the worst of ordertakers carries a tape measure. I do an awful lot of eavesdropping as I go around the country. I have yet to hear a salesperson who measured something ask the prospective customer, "I am sure you have a good reason for needing to know the height of that table. Do you mind telling me what the reason is?"

Now, please, please, please. One more time: Whenever a prospective customer asks you a question and you know the answer to that question, but not *why* the prospective customer asked it, you can go ahead and answer it and *still* not know one thing more about that prospective customer and his or her need than you did before. In every case, you should ask *why* the customer asked. Note: Many times it is wisest to say, "I will be glad to answer that question for you, but before I do, so that I might better understand it, do you mind if I ask *why* you felt you needed to know more about that particular feature?

Teachers can teach, but students will never learn until they ask, "why?" It is said that we have all asked, "why?" by the time we are five years old more times than most of us will ask during the rest of our lifetimes even if we live to be 100. But when we quit asking, "why?" we quit learning. This is the hardest lesson to learn and yet it is the most important lesson because it takes us outside our own nine dot puzzle. When you don't ask you remain ignorant, arrested at the juvenile stage, which leaves you an ignoramus.

- No sale ever has or ever will be lost because a salesperson knew too much about the prospective customer and his or her needs.

- No sale ever has or ever will be lost because a salesperson knew too much about what he or she was selling.

- No sale ever has or ever will be lost because the salesperson knew too much about his or her services.

Almost every sale that has ever been lost can be traced to the fact that salespeople did not know enough, and the reason they didn't was because they didn't *ask*. That lack of specialized knowledge locked them inside a nine dot puzzle where the best solution to the prospective customer's need could *never* be found.

Every question you ask increases the size of your nine dot framework. As your nine dot framework gets bigger and bigger than that of your prospective customers', you become more and more competent to help them make the best buying decision. Just ask, "why?" But be polite, always ask for permission to ask. The words "Do you mind if I ask?" show common courtesy. Courtesy costs you nothing, but it sure pays big dividends in selling.

The principle of the 9-Dot Puzzle can be applied to every problem in a company and it will cause those problems to disappear. I certainly don't want to take on the world's problems, but the principle of the 9-Dot Puzzle could do the same for those problems.

13/ *The Principle of Reflection*

"THEY HAVE EYES THAT SEE NOT AND EARS THAT HEAR NOT...."

The Bible, King James Version

WHILE IN TORONTO, CANADA, for a speaking engagement, I watched the morning news on television while I was getting dressed. A magician who was appearing that night for a charity event was introduced. Just as I started to tie my necktie, he said, "The eye sees what the mind tells it to see and that is why magic works. I would like to use this white cup and red ball to demonstrate." He continued, "I am going to put the ball under the cup and when I lift the cup, the ball will have disappeared. If you want to see how this trick works, you must keep your eye on the cup. I am a magician. It is my job to get your eye off the cup, and I am pretty good! So, let's see if you can keep your eye on the cup."

With that, the camera zoomed in for a closeup of the cup and the ball. I watched intently as he put the ball under the cup and when he picked up the cup, the ball was gone. He asked, "Did you see it?"

I muttered a "no" to myself as he said, "I told you that I was pretty good! I am so good that I can fool most people with this trick in slow motion. We are going to play the trick back in slow motion. If you want to catch me, you are not only going to have to tell your eye to stay on the cup, but you are going to have to tell it not to look at anything else."

He wasn't going to fool me in slow motion. I quit tying my tie and stared hard at that cup. Slowly, the camera zoomed in. Slowly, he put the ball under the cup. Slowly, he raised the cup. The ball was gone! The camera cut to him and he asked, "Did you see it?" I said, right out loud, "No!"

He said, "You see, you haven't paid a bit of attention to a word I said! I started right out telling you that magic works because the eye only sees what the mind tells it to see. I then told you the ball was going to disappear and for you to watch the cup and you did, didn't you? The cup didn't disappear, did it? Now, I want to play this trick back on video tape while you tell your eye to watch the ball." I did, and he was good. I only saw a whiff of red as he flicked it into the palm of his hand, but then something happened (and to this day, I find it hard to believe). As he lifted the cup, not six inches away on that small television screen, he had turned his other hand over with the red ball right there in plain sight and I hadn't seen it! Then, to add insult to injury, he played it back in slow motion.

Truly, this was the best demonstration of the Principle of Reflection. It is one of the most important things that a salesperson can know about selling and yet I have never heard it taught or read about it in any book.

The eye will see what the mind tells it to see. The eye will not see what the mind tells it not to see. In this case, I had told my eye to see that cup and under no circumstances to get tricked into seeing anything else.

What made that experience even more intriguing was that I could have seen that trick performed many, many times, trying my hardest to see how it worked, without once seeing that ball go into the magician's hand. But once I had seen the least little glimpse of that red ball as it went into his hand, I could never again watch the trick being performed and not see the glimpse of red. Think about that.

Many years ago, a wealthy customer of mine was giving an afternoon tea party. Her sofa was upholstered in a very fine fabric with a rose floral print pattern that she just loved. One of her guests without thinking said, "That is such a beautiful sofa. Isn't it a shame that the roses go across the top of the back on the left side and across the bottom on the right side?" This sophisticated woman had owned that fine sofa for more than two years and neither she, the members of her family nor anyone else had ever noticed that glaring defect until the guest told their eyes to see it. Once my customer had seen it, she could never look at that sofa again without seeing it. In fact, from that moment on when she looked at the sofa, the defect was the only thing she would see.

With both the red ball and the sofa with the mismatched pattern, until the mind told the eye what to see, it had not seen. In "The 9-Dot Puzzle", we are taught why this happened. The mind cannot tell the eye to see something unless it knows what it is it wants the eye to see.

The eye will see what the mind tells it to see. Once the eye has been told what to see and sees it, it will never be able to look at what it saw again and not see it.

You can get a small spot on a necktie or dress that won't come out. Chances are not one in a hundred people would ever notice the spot, but once you've seen it, you can never again look at the tie or dress and not see the spot. As a matter of fact, from then on you will never see the dress or tie again. You will only see the spot, and because of the spot, odds are you will quit wearing the garment.

When prospective customers are asked if they can be helped, most will respond with, "No, thank you. I am just looking." If they haven't told their eyes what to see, they will be looking at everything, while seeing nothing. If the salesperson knows nothing about the customer and his or her needs, there is no way that the salesperson can tell them what to see. It truly becomes a case of the blind leading the blind.

People never have nor ever will be able to describe what they want someone else to see if they haven't seen it themselves. Simply, it is impossible for you to react with empathy for a prospective customers' needs if you have not experienced with your senses what you want them to experience.

I frequently visit new furniture showrooms when I travel. The managers always ask how I think their showroom looks and I say, "Beautiful," because they are. Then I ask if they would like for me to critique the showroom for them and they eagerly agree.

Standing in one place I may look across the showroom, point to a piece of upholstered furniture with only the top of the back showing and say, "That sofa has the wrong legs on it." I will then point out at least a dozen crooked pictures in one corner alone, the crooked lamp shades, along with three light bulbs which have burned out. I might point out the missing drawer pulls on the bedroom group in the far corner, or count the pieces of furniture without price tags.

How could I (a perfect stranger) walk in the door, take one look, and see all of these things that made a showroom harder to sell in when the manager, salespeople, tag, and display people can't see them?

Thirty-five years of experience for one thing. There is hardly anything that could be wrong in a showroom that I haven't seen—and know what caused it to be that way. When I walked in the door and the manager asked me how I thought his showroom looked, I looked at the showroom and what I saw was beautiful. But, when I asked my eyes to see crooked lamp shades, I saw every one in the showroom instantly, the same way I saw the flash of red as the ball went into the magician's hand. (Try doing this yourself when you enter a showroom.)

The same was true of burned out light bulbs. You might wonder how I knew the sofa had the wrong legs or the drawer pulls were missing. I know that most upholstered furniture is shipped with the legs in plastic bags tucked under the cushions to be installed by the retailer. It's not uncommon for factory workers to put a bag of legs that are one inch too long or one inch too short with a piece of furniture. I told my eye to see if there were any pieces of furniture in matched groups that were a little higher or lower than the others. It's a rare showroom floor where I don't spot this problem at least once. I know most drawer pulls are in bags inside the drawers when they are shipped. It's not uncommon for a bag to be short a drawer pull. When a customer discovers this and comes in when the service department isn't open, the salesperson will often take the pulls off a floor sample to satisfy them.

Because they aren't supposed to do that, the salesperson doesn't tell anyone. It's a rare showroom that doesn't have some hardware missing.

I must tell my eyes specifically what I want them to look for or see, but if I don't know what I want to tell them to see, I can't tell them to see it. (No pun intended, but) you can see that, can't you?

Sometimes you must be able to describe what you want someone to see. How many times have you had someone say to you in a crowd of people: "Hey, look. There's (so and so)!" and you say, "Where?"

"Right over there."

"I don't see where you are looking."

"See that clock on the wall?"

"Yes,"

"Look down below it about ten feet to its left. He has a blue suit on."

"Oh, now I see him!"

Most big-ticket products have many features and each of those features may offer many benefits. Some things like a home could have hundreds of features that offered a multitude of benefits that would make it better meet a prospective customer's needs. Many of these features cannot be seen and almost none of the benefits are visible.

Few prospective customers have a comprehensive understanding of their needs. The product that they should buy will be the one that has the most features that offer the most benefits that meets the most of their needs within the price range that they can afford. But no matter how many features, even those that are the most visible, and no matter what the benefits of those features, unless the prospective customer's eyes are told to see them, for the most part they will not be seen.

So the professional salespeople have three obstacles to overcome that few prospective customers are aware of:

• They must make the prospective customer as consciously aware of his or her needs for the benefits of as many of the features of what they sell as possible. Remember, if prospective customers don't know they have a need for the benefits of a feature, as far as they are concerned, the need doesn't exist and thus they will have no interest when the salesperson tries to show or demonstrate it.

• They must be able to get the prospective customer to see what they want them to see.

• They must get their prospective customers to experience emotionally how the benefits of what they see meets some of those needs they are now consciously aware of.

As far as the prospective customer is concerned, every need for every benefit of every feature found on what was being sold did not exist if he or she was not made consciously aware of that need. Every feature the prospective customer had not seen did not exist on what was being sold and thus, no benefit value existed.

Here is the best example I can give of a product with features that offers benefits everyone will need once they own it. The feature can't be seen and most prospective customers are not aware of the need they will have for the benefits of this feature once they own it.

Over the past 50 years, millions of sofas with fold-out beds have been sold and they have been greatly improved every year to the point where it is now possible to get a very good bed along with the sofa. Over the years as these improvements have taken place, there remained two things that combined to cause customers to become dissatisfied: (1) They are too heavy and (2) you can't move them to clean under them. I find that incredible because no sofa is easier to clean under than a sleeper sofa. You simply open it half way as shown below:

Then take one finger and the entire sofa will tilt forward, as shown below. You can vacuum under it and with one finger tilt it back in place. Few owners of sleeper sofas know about this incredible feature. Because of that, not one in a thousand owners of sleeper sofas enjoys the benefits of that feature. Because they don't, this continues to be the number one complaint of sleeper sofa owners.

Why don't the salespeople make their prospective customers aware of this feature and its benefits? Prospective customers are not consciously aware of their need to clean under it when they buy the sofa. The first time they fold the bed out at home is usually for guests. Only then do they discover they can see the floor under the sofa with the bed folded out and notice the dust balls and grunge that has collected. The sofa is too heavy to move and it is nearly impossible to get in and around the mechanism to do a good cleaning job. So from then on, the longer they have that sofa, the more they have to clean under it, the more dissatisfied they become.

They own the feature, but they don't know it's there and they don't know how to enjoy the incredible benefits that would make it far better meet their needs and, thus, make them a more *satisfied* customer.

That's only one feature. But it is always a combination of how well all of the benefits of all of the features of what you sell combined that makes it best meet the prospective customer's needs and gets the order.

It is entirely possible for a professionally competent salesperson to make a sale to a prospective customer who has just shopped where another salesperson offered a product with more features providing more benefits that would have made it better meet their needs, and at a lower price! Not only could the professionally competent salesperson make that sale, he or she would wind up with a more *satisfied* customer than had she bought the product that would better meet her needs at a *lower* price.

The other company's salesperson had failed to make the prospective customer aware of most of his or her needs for most of the benefits of the features of what he sells. As far as the prospective customer is concerned, those features and benefits (like the tilting mechanism on the sleeper sofa) never existed and even if that customer owned what was being sold, he or she would never enjoy most of those benefits, benefits unexperienced that *could* have made that customer even *more* satisfied left him or her *dissatisfied.* Professionals make their prospective customers consciously aware of every conceivable need that they could have for every conceivable benefit of every feature on what the salesperson is selling. The involvement demonstration has them experience emotionally the maximum benefits of each feature.

What's even more amazing is that when *incompetent* salespeople with a better product with more features and benefits at a lower price hear that the customer bought from competitors, they say the customer was stupid and the salespeople crooks.

When what the customers have purchased lives up to what they were led to expect and meets their needs, they are satisfied and never begrudge whatever price they paid.

When what customers bought fails to live up to what they were led to expect, as in the case of sleeper sofa buyers, left to expect, they become dissatisfied and feel they were cheated because they *were* cheated. In selling, the sin of omission is often greater than the sin of commission.

You read how one salesperson with a lesser product at a higher price than the competitor could wind up getting the sale and producing a more satisfied customer. The same results can be achieved with the benefits of any one feature on a product. Two products may have the same features that offer the same benefits, but the salesperson who can have his or her prospective customer experience more of each benefit will get the sale.

One of the most amazing things about the eyes is summed up with a statement we often hear, but few understand: Beauty is in the eye of the beholder.

Not only does the eye have to be told what to see, but when we are dealing with benefits that cannot be seen, salespeople must be able to paint pictures that can be seen in the prospective customer's mind's eye: "This room is so bright and cheerful it is the perfect place for you and your family to have breakfast, don't you think?"

Can you see the difference in what prospective customers treated like this will see versus what they would have seen had their eyes not been told to see it? We *can't* see cheerful, soothing, warm, comfortable, sturdy, solid, and so on, with our eyes, but sales professionals know all they have to do is remind prospective customers of a need so that they become consciously aware of it. Then, what the professional says will paint a word picture in their imagination—a picture so strong that it can never be erased. That family will be having breakfast in a "bright, cheerful" breakfast room as long as they live there. The guided tour director's customer, if he gets the sale, will just be having breakfast every day in the breakfast room. Who is going to be more satisfied?

"Imagine your friends seeing you driving this new car." These words have painted in the prospective customer's mind's eye the most powerful of all benefits. One I call the ultimate benefit: "Pride of ownership." If you want to be sure your prospective customers can visualize their friends or competitors in business watching them enjoying the benefits of what you are selling, you are going to have to ask them to see that image in their own mind's eye.

For example, the salesperson might say, "This is sure going to take the wind out of your competitor's sails when they discover you have fully automated your factory." Yes, the eye will see what the mind tells it to, but the mind must know what it wants the eye to see. In this case, the prospective customer sees his state-of-the-art factory and a defeated competitor.

Prospective customers will rarely see more than what the salesperson makes them aware of their need to *see,* then tells them how to see it. Salespeople will never be able to describe what they want their customers to see if they have not seen it themselves. The more features and benefits the salespeople have actually seen, the more they can help their prospective customers to see.

What is true for the eyes is also true of the other four senses.

There are only five ways we can get anything inside our own brain and there are only five ways we can get something inside the prospective customers' brains and that is through the senses.

If an image or idea is in the brain, it got there through the eyes, ears, nose, taste buds, or the sense of touch. No one can transmit anything to another person's brain that is not in the first person's brain to begin with.

"They have ears, but they hear not."

"It just goes in one ear and out the other."

"You weren't listening to a word I said."

My wife and daughters felt I was losing my hearing so they made an appointment for me with a specialist at a hearing clinic. After thorough testing, the doctor said, "Mr. Lawhon, you have perfect hearing and that's quite unusual for a man of your age. Your problem is that you don't listen. If your wife and daughters want you to hear what they say, they must be sure they have your attention and that you are listening."

When prospective customers have no interest in what the salesperson is saying, it is because they are unaware of their need. If salespeople want prospective customers to hear what they are saying, they must be certain they have *their* attention.

Most people who study selling believe salespeople fail because they don't listen to their prospective customers. Listening is a skill, perhaps the most productive of all selling skills. Think hard while you consider that fact. *More sales are lost because the salespeople did not know enough about their prospective customers and their needs than all other reasons combined.* The main reason they haven't learned enough about them and their needs is not just because they haven't asked questions, it is often because they have not listened closely to what their prospective customers say.

Prospective customers don't listen to salespeople because they have no interest. They have no interest because they have no need or think they have no need. Far more often than not, salespeople do not listen to what their prospective customers say because *the salesperson* has no interest. Here is the problem: The mind must tell the eye what to see and it must also tell the ear what to listen for. Salespeople must learn enough about their prospective customers and their needs in order to be able to help their customers find those things that will best meet those needs. In the process of doing this, the professional salesperson makes the prospective customer consciously aware of those needs. This means the salesperson must show an interest in the prospective customer and his or her needs. The salesperson shows this interest not only by asking questions, but by *listening* to the answers.

Barbara Walters is considered one of the best interviewers ever. The object of all interviews is to get the subjects to open up and tell everything of interest about themselves. Watch Walters closely when she asks a question. She is all ears. She is listening to what they say and how they say it. If they wander away from a point, she brings them back with another question, otherwise she hears them out.

She was replaced on NBC's Today Show by a man and woman who did not listen. They had the questions they wanted to ask written down for them just like Barbara Walters had. However, you could tell when they read a question that they did not listen to the answer. They let the person answer, but they were already looking at the next question so they could read it the instant the subject paused. Often, follow-up questions seem stupid because the interviewer had not listened to what the subject said. Clearly, they were not aware of that or they would not have done it. They had good reading skills, but absolutely no listening skills.

Some salespeople compound that flaw. They must listen to the prospective customer, which means they must tell their ears to listen. Then, they must be sure they have the customer's attention. The only way you get that is to show genuine interest in them. Then you can listen and you will actually hear what the prospective customer says.

The opening words used most by top professionals when they greet a prospective customer are: "So that I might save you a lot of your valuable time, do you mind if I ask you a few questions?" Sometimes, of course, you have to do more to get the prospective customer's attention. The owner of a company whose prospective customers, for the most part, were blue collar dock workers, told me that when his salespeople approached their prospective customers with this question, the prospective customers were not consciously thinking about saving time, so just ignored them until one young woman said to herself, "If I am going to make a sale, I am going to have to get my prospective customers not only to talk to me, but I have to get them to *listen* to me."

The next time she said to a big, burly dockhand, "Sir, so that I might save you some of your valuable time, would you mind if I ask you a few questions?" He ignored her and she pulled on his sleeve to get his attention. Then she said, "Excuse me sir, let me ask you another question, do you really have a lot of time to waste today?" Well, he heard *that* loud and clear, because her question made him aware of his need to save time. When he said, "No," she said, "In that case, so that I might save you a lot of your valuable time, let me ask you a few questions," and she did. Once she showed a *serious* interest in him, he took a serious interest in what she said and *heard* what she said.

Most salespeople are so busy thinking about what they are going to say or ask next that they don't hear the prospective customer's answers. And if the saleperson ever quits listening to what they say, that prospective customer will instantly lose interest in the salesperson.

Suppose the benefit of a feature is the sound it makes? Once a salesperson has learned to listen to his or her prospective customers, he or she must then realize that if the benefits of one or more of the features of the product is the sound it makes, the salesperson must learn how to get the prospective customer to hear as much of that sound/benefit as possible. That's where "The Principle of Reflection" comes in.

Did you know you can hear better if you close your eyes? The reason is simple. You focus all your mental effort on listening. When your eyes are open, what you *see* distracts you, so you don't listen as well.

If a competitor had asked a prospective customer to listen to his audio system and you later had asked them to close their eyes and *hear* the same audio system, yours will sound better than his—and that makes it *worth* more.

How many times have you heard someone ask, "What was that noise?"

"What noise?

"You didn't hear that?"

"No, what did it sound like?" The person would describe what it sounded like. "It sounded like a car horn." At that point, you say, "Oh, *that* noise. I think it *was* a car horn." In that case, you had actually heard the horn, but had not even been consciously aware of it.

If salespeople want prospective customers to hear something, they must tell the prospective customer's ears what to hear because the customer doesn't know what to listen for and when they don't know what to listen for, they don't hear.

Did you know that almost all major big ticket products have features that eliminate or reduce noise? The value of that benefit lies in the fact that, by comparison, you don't hear much of anything. Two of the biggest advances over the last ten years in automobiles has been the reduction of noise levels inside cars and absolutely incredible audio systems. This is old hat to most car salespeople today so they either don't mention it or, at best, say something like, "We have the quietest riding car you can buy." Or, "The audio system is fantastic!" This "fact/feature" goes in one ear of the customer and out the other.

Professional automobile salespeople will discuss audio systems with their prospective customers, learn what they like to listen to, and put a tape or CD of that kind of music in the audio system before beginning the demonstration drive. This will start with the salesperson driving the demonstrator, then having the prospective customer drive it.

The salesperson gets the car up to 65 on a crowded, noisy interstate, then runs the window down and asks the prospective customer to close his or her eyes and listen to the roar of the wind and the traffic. Next the salesperson asks him or her to listen to the absolute silence as the window closes. The comparison prospective customers hear with their own ears makes this the quietest-running car they have ever been in. Compared to that roar, the silence is deafening. Then the salesperson says, "Because it is so quiet, you will enjoy the music on the audio system far more than you ever have before." The salesperson switches the music on and asks the customer to close his or her eyes and listen, describing the sounds the salesperson wants the customer to hear.

No salesperson can do this well who has not gone down the freeway at 65, opened the window, told his or her mind to hear all of the roaring noises, listened for trucks, horns, wind, sirens, and the like, then closed the window and listened to the absolute silence. Absolute, compared to the noise he or she had just heard. No salesperson is ready to tell the prospective customer's ears to hear the incredible audio system unless he or she has listened intently to its sounds—each instrument, each high note, and so on.

In offices or factories where machines make noise and distract others, the quieter a machine is, the better it meets the user's needs. It is always the comparison demonstration that convinces prospective customers best and gives them more reasons to buy. The professional tells the prospective customer's ears to listen to that silence while the guided tour director only tells the customer the machine doesn't make as "much noise." What the *tour director* says goes in one ear of the customer and out the other.

Now, how do you *feel* about that? Whether the prospective customer buys or doesn't, the answer will depend on how they *feel* about it.

When prospective customers have seen how the benefits of a feature make the product meet their needs better, they will *feel* that way because of how well they have been convinced it will better meet their needs. The more they experience—and become consciously aware of—how benefit after benefit of feature after feature make the product meet their needs better, the stronger and stronger their positive *feelings* will be about buying.

The value of the benefits of the features of many big-ticket products determines how that product *feels* to the prospective customer. Our sense of feel or touch is the strongest of our senses. No one ever has or ever will *see or hear* "feel." When the benefits of the features of a product are "How it feels," often the only way that customers can experience that benefit is to have them *feel* that benefit, because it can't be seen. Salespeople must describe what it is that they want their prospective customers to feel. They may deny their sense of seeing or hearing, but they don't deny what they have felt. We have all heard people say, "I can't believe my eyes," or "I can't believe my ears," but never their sense of touch. No one can describe to another person what they want them to feel who has not felt it themselves.

Our minds can convince our tastebuds that what we are about to taste is going to be delicious or that it's going to taste terrible. No salesperson will ever master the profession of selling until he or she fully comprehends what that means, because it is true for all five senses.

If you haven't smelled Limburger cheese, take a sniff. A small one! If you have, you know what I mean when I say, "How in the world could anyone's mind ever convince their taste buds that what they had smelled was going to taste good?" I don't know, but I do know that an awful lot of people have convinced themselves Limburger is delicious.

It costs plenty in a fine restaurant for six escargots. Now, those are snails, but we eat them as *appetizers.*

We eat raw oysters and tell those who have never tried them they are delicious. They try one and gag trying to get it down. Then we explain you must *develop* a taste for them. In other words, your mind must keep telling your tastebuds how delicious they are until your mouth waters every time someone mentions good, fresh, raw oysters on the half shell. I will bet you that the first time you ate one, it was only after someone talked you into it, telling you, "Try it! You'll like it!"

My point: all our senses can be convinced that something is good or bad and nowhere is this more apparent than in the food we eat.

How often have you been dining with others when someone asks a question like this: "What's that spice in this soup?" You taste the soup again and roll it around your palate asking your mind to tell you what the spice is. The soup may have many ingredients that make up its flavor. You don't taste any of them as your mind asks your tastebuds to taste only the spice.

You may say, "I don't know, what does it taste like to you?" and they reply, "I think it's clove." You taste it again and say, "You are right, I believe it is clove." You see, someone had to describe what it was of all the flavors in that soup that they wanted you to taste before you could separate it mentally and taste that benefit.

There is no question that good pots and pans make it easier to prepare good food, but they, like the spice, are only one element of that food. Every person who has ever sold pots and pans can tell you that if you can get several couples together and fix them a good dinner with your pots and pans you can sell a set to almost everyone who attends. Yet, the pots and pans were only one of the factors that made the dinner taste good. What *really* did the job? Was each person telling their palate to taste how good the pots and pans made the carrots, potatoes, pot roast, gravy, and hot rolls taste? Then, each person described how good each thing tasted to the others. Can you see that? Was it those pots and pans that made a memorable dinner? No, no, no. The salesperson had made it a memorable meal! He or she was the one who described what to taste and what to enjoy.

Benefits can *only* be experienced through our *senses*. It is only as our mind tells our senses what to experience that these benefits are experienced. The more benefits we can be drawn to experience through our senses, the more benefits we *can* experience. The customer only buys for benefits. When the pile of benefits gets high enough they become overpowering and the sale is made.

Even the simplest of products has a multitude of benefits that can be experienced. There is no reason for the competent professional salesperson to ever, ever, ever have to lie about a product or its benefits to make a sale.

"Close your eyes. Take a deep breath. This mountain air is so invigorating. Smell the pine needles—the wildflowers. That's about as close to heaven as you get in this life!" In springtime, there are flowers all around us, but few actually stop and close their eyes, take a deep breath, and tell their noses to experience one of life's greatest joys. We really don't stop and smell the roses.

The aroma afforded us by what we sell can sometimes be its most valuable benefit. It is said that the person who perfects a spray that keeps the "new car" smell inside it will make a fortune. Yet, if the average car salesperson even mentions the "new" smell, it's rarely more than to say, "it still smells new." The professional has the prospective customer close his or her eyes and take a deep breath to get the full effect of the new car smell.

To the degree that salespeople have their prospective customers experience the full benefit of a feature with their senses—to that degree only—the customers have experienced the value of that benefit.

Even when we fully understand this principle, there is still one factor that has led to the downfall of many a salesperson.

When I was about twenty, I was taken to see the Chicago stockyards on an August day when the temperature hit 106 degrees. To this day, I have never experienced such a gut-wrenching stench. That was over 45 years ago and I still can't eat canned ham because I catch a slight scent of what I smelled on that day. I said to those who I was with, "How could anyone work here, let alone live here?" They said, "Oh, you stay around here awhile and you get used to the odor. You soon get to where you don't even notice it." Salespeople soon get "used to" the features and benefits of what they sell, too. Eventually, they don't even notice them at all. That, my friends, is the beginning of the end. They think everyone knows about the features and every product has them.

If you want to see how excited a person can get about the benefits of the features of a product that everyone in the world thinks everyone knows about. . . sell a young man his first car. It may be a ten-year-old clunker, but every benefit puts stars in his eyes. Listen to him telling his buddies about every feature. It may have been old and worn out to the last four or five people who owned it, but it is all brand new to him. So it is to everyone we sell, regardless *what* we sell.

It does not matter how long a product has been on the market. It doesn't matter how many people have owned it or used it. It doesn't matter if every person on the face of the earth knows about it. They are not aware of the benefits. They may have even gotten so used to them they don't even notice them. When a salesperson has a customer experience how even the most minor of benefits makes that product better meet their needs, it is all brand new to the customer. (Don't you know that the people at that dinner had all had pot roast, potatoes, carrots, and gravy hundreds of times, but they never had a meal that tasted this good because their tastebuds were told to search out every hint of flavor and they were telling each other how good every bite tasted.)

I have owned several Rolls Royces, including classic cars that were

40 years old or older. When I get in a Rolls, the first thing I do is inhale the rich aroma of the Connelly leather they use on the seats. I tell you that benefit is one of the greatest pleasures to be found in owning a Rolls Royce. When they tell you it's taken from cattle that have never been exposed to barbed wire, then point out that there is not a blemish or a scar on the hide, your eyes enjoy a heady benefit that few people will ever own. It is as exciting to me right this minute as it was the first time I experienced these benefits.

But! Here's the catch! When a person has no need or is unaware of the fact that they have a need, they have *no* interest. Customers who have no need will not buy. They are not interested in your product or the benefits of your product; what you say goes in one ear and out the other; they can't see a thing about it they like.

It is the salesperson's first job to make customers aware of their needs. The professional does this by asking questions to make customers consciously aware of their needs. The salesperson is learning about those needs as well. When the salesperson has learned enough about the customer's needs to be able to determine which product will best meet those needs, the salesperson can then (and only then) demonstrate how the benefits of each feature make the product better and better meet the customers' needs.

The same factors operate with the benefits of everything sold in this world today. It may all be old hat to the losers in the lounge. Everybody may know about it. Features and benefits may have been around for years as far as a salesperson is concerned. But customers are all eyes and ears when they encounter features that offer benefits that make a product meet their needs better. That makes their mouths water. They want to smell it. They can't wait to taste it. The better it meets their needs, the more excited they get. The more excited they get, the more enthusiastic the salesperson gets. That makes good *sense* for the salesperson who is in the business of selling.

14 / The Fear of Loss Is Greater Than the Desire to Gain

A FEAR MORE POWERFUL THAN THE FEAR OF DEATH ITSELF WORKS FOR THE PROFESSIONALLY COMPETENT SALESPERSON AND GETS THE SALE ALMOST EVERY TIME. BUT IT WORKS AGAINST MOST AVERAGE SALESPEOPLE AND CAUSES MOST OF THEIR PROSPECTIVE CUSTOMERS NOT TO BUY.

THE FEAR OF LOSS IS GREATER THAN THE DESIRE TO GAIN. Concealed in that simple statement is one of the most powerful forces affecting the entire world economy. In fact, fear of loss can be even more powerful than the fear of death itself. In any sale, fear of loss is the most powerful force a salesperson deals with, a force that works against the guided tour directors as effectively as it works for professionally competent salespeople.

I would like to start with some examples that show how the fear of loss can be even more powerful a force than fear of death, then we'll see how this powerful force affects buyers and salespersons.

A young woman is told she has a rare disease. If she even conceives a child, she drops dead at once. You can bet that young woman will not risk her own life to bear a child. Now, suppose this same woman has a child and her child is in a life-threatening situation, such as being trapped in a burning building. This time, you can bet the woman would risk her life to save her child. She will not risk her life to get a child, but she will risk her life to keep from *losing* a child that is hers.

You might say, "That could be true with something as precious as a child, but it would not be true with something less valuable." Almost every news report tells us about people who have been killed by robbers, the victims risking and losing their lives merely to keep from losing the few dollars they own. When that happens to store clerks, it isn't even their own money they're defending. All salespeople must understand the frightful power of this force before they can begin to comprehend how powerfully it affects the buying and selling of everything.

A young man wants to buy a new car. He spends days pitting dealer against dealer, dickering for the best possible buy. Finally, he gets one $25 lower than the others and buys. He pays nothing down, won't have to make this first payment for six months, and gets a $500 cash rebate. The young man jumps in the car, races to his job and runs inside. "Hey, everybody! Come on outside and see my new car."

In the parking lot, a coworker asks if that car is really his. "It sure is. I just bought it today."

Wait a minute. He hasn't paid a dime down on this car, he isn't going to pay anything on it for six months, and he has $500 of the dealer's cash in his pants pocket. Whose car is it, anyway? It *is* his. The title is in *his* name. He owns every benefit that car has to offer. Six months go by and the first payment is due. At that point, the owner probably owes about three times what the car could possibly bring at a dealer's auction. He makes the payment and will continue to make payments until the car is paid for or he trades it in on another, if there is any possible way for him to do that.

Why would this young man, who spent days quibbling over price, be willing to pay three times what he could replace that car for? It's as if the price was of no concern at all. Simple. If he doesn't make the payments, he will *lose* his car. Wrong! Wrong! Wrong! He doesn't "own" the car and won't until it is fully paid for. If he doesn't make the payments, he will *lose* the benefits he now owns and enjoys.

I would like to point out that even if the car the young man bought did not do a good job of meeting his needs and he had lots of service problems, even if he became very dissatisfied with the car and the company he bought it from, he still makes those payments because he will lose what few benefits he owns if he doesn't. He will go on making those payments on a car he wouldn't consider buying again to a company he would not do business with again. That's how powerful the fear of loss is.

The only reason people ever have for buying anything is so they can enjoy the benefits. In our example, the young man's good credit permitted him to own the benefits of the car with no sacrifice or cash outlay on his part. But his fear of *losing* those benefits he now owns, which include his good credit, is so powerful that there is almost nothing he will not do to keep from losing them. No price is too high, no effort too great, because the fear of losing the benefits he now owns can actually be greater than the fear of his own death.

Most big-ticket products are bought with some kind of credit, which permits people and companies to own the benefits of something while they pay for it, even though they wind up paying a lot more. The result is that we have built a credit-driven world economy. The fear of loss drives all credit purchases. And without this powerful force, the world's economy would collapse.

To demonstrate better where the force fits into buying and selling, I would like to use two experiences from my very first selling job.

Back then, we had a federal law called "The Fair Trade Act." It permitted a manufacturer to put a retail price on his product and it was a federal crime for a retailer to sell it for less. The company where I worked couldn't cut the price on their premium sleep sets because they were "fair traded," so they made a special offer: Anyone buying a premium sleep set could sleep on it for thirty nights. If they were not satisfied that they were getting a better night's sleep, we would pick it up and buy it back. It would cost the customer nothing. I set new bedding sales records for this company, and all the time, I was afraid we would have to buy back a lot of the sleep sets. We never had a single customer ask us to buy back a set.

This sale had been so successful for me that I went on making the same guarantee after the special offer expired and over the next 35 years of my career, anyone who bought a sleep set from a company I managed or owned could sleep on it for 30 nights and if they were not satisfied with the night's sleep they were getting, I would buy it back and it would cost them nothing.

In the sixties, when Simmons was the world's largest bedding maker, I became Simmons' biggest dealer. In the seventies, when Ohio Sealy became the biggest maker of Sealy products in the world, I became *their* biggest dealer. After having sold tens of millions of dollars worth of bedding with that guarantee, I could count on the fingers of one hand the number of sets we were asked to buy back. The few times that happened, it was because we couldn't get the buyers to sleep on the new set for more than a night or two.

To understand why this was so effective, you have to realize how powerful the fear of loss is. The reason these people had bought a new sleep set was because they had become so dissatisfied with the night's sleep they were getting on their old sleep set. They could buy the new sleep set on credit so they could have the benefits right then for no money down. The first night they tried sleeping on the new sleep set, they found it hard to adjust to. The second night, it got a little easier to get comfortable. After 30 days, it had become so comfortable, they had gotten used to it, and it gave them the support they needed to get a better night's sleep than they had been getting on their old sleep set. If they didn't keep the new set, they would lose the benefits of the better night's sleep they now owned. The fear of losing those benefits was so great you couldn't buy back the sleep set even if you paid them a premium.

In the purest sense of the word what I had gotten the customer to do was enjoy the "ownership" of the benefits of the new sleep set when in fact they had not really bought it. Let me tell you just how big that risk to me really was. Since the thirties, we have had a national bedding stamp act. You've seen the tag on anything sold as bedding that says, "Do not remove this tag under penalty of the law." It says on the tag that only new materials have been used. It is forbidden for a retailer to sell used bedding. Had very many customers demanded that I buy back their sleep sets, I could not have resold them because they had been used, and that could break any company.

When you take a close look at what is happening when professionally competent salespeople make their presentation and demonstration, you will see that they are having prospective customers actually experience owning the benefits of the features of the product with as many of their senses as they can, in every way that they can. The professional's presentation of those benefits will continue until prospective customers have experienced owning so many benefits they simply have too much to lose if they don't buy. So all the salesperson has to do, as those masters of selling all say, is "just write it up." The more skilled these professionals become with their demonstration, the quicker customers reach the point where the fear of losing these benefits they have experienced is so great the salesperson just writes that order.

Many an executive jet airplane has been sold when a professionally competent salesperson has learned enough about the CEO of a company and its financial capabilities. These professionals let the CEO use the airplane, complete with the flight crew, for thirty days at no cost other than fuel. At the end of that thirty days, the salesperson has a lease all prepared and cleared. All the CEO needs do is sign the lease and he or she will not lose all of those absolutely incredible benefits. Believe me when I say that the greater the benefits, the greater the fear of loss. But as we see even in small robberies, the fear of losing even an insignificant amount can sometimes be greater than the fear of death.

I said I had two experiences on my first job that taught me about this powerful force. The second experience demonstrates a factor in selling I have never heard mentioned nor found explained in a book.

Shortly after the company had run its offer of a guaranteed better night's sleep, it ran a trade-in sale on bedding. (Back then, old sets were given to the Salvation Army.) A prominent local doctor and his wife selected my best sleep set and said they would buy it if I could deliver it that day.

That evening, one of my fellow workers and I delivered the new sleep set. As we were removing the old sleep set, I saw something that to this day I find hard to believe. The doctor's mattress had a hole in it. I don't mean a little hole. This was a hole sunk into the mattress on the doctor's side that was about six inches deep and big enough for him to curl up in. The sleep set was so worn out that we just dropped it at the city dump.

The next morning the doctor's wife called. She was highly distraught. The doctor had tossed and turned all night because he could not find his "nest." Those were her words. She asked if there was any way possible for me to return their old sleep set.

I told her it was in the city dump and I was sure that it would be unusable. I explained that once the doctor got used to the new sleep set, he would find himself getting a much better night's sleep. I was in that small city for another two years and every time I ran into the doctor or his wife, they did, in fact, confirm how much they enjoyed their new sleep set.

Now this is how the fear of loss can work against a salesperson. This doctor could not get a good night's sleep curled up in his nest, but it was like a child's security blanket. In order to have a sleep set that would give him the support he needed to get a good night's sleep, one that was far better than he had been getting, he would have to lose the benefits of his nest or security blanket.

Even though he couldn't get a decent night's sleep and awoke with every joint in his body aching, rather than lose the benefits of his nest, his fear was so strong this doctor couldn't stand that loss until he began enjoying the benefits of the new sleep set.

Psychologists say that a buying decision is such a fearsome thing that some people will even reach a point of temporary insanity when trying to make up their minds. We probably see this more clearly in the furniture industry than anywhere else because over 97 percent of all furniture purchases are initiated by a woman. Men would rather spend the money on cars, boats, guns, and so on. Out of the blue, I have seen men whose wives had decided on furniture that they wanted to buy, go into a rage, turn on their wives and say, "I don't know how you got me into this mess. We just came in here to look. I had no intention of buying anything." This ranting might last a minute or so, then all of a sudden the man sits down and is silent a moment. Then he says, "If she wants it, go ahead and write it up." He had just lost the power to buy the benefits of a new boat, car, gun, or whatever he wanted instead of furniture.

Guided tour directors know nothing of the power of the fear of loss and couldn't do anything about it if they did. When they get prospective customer objections, what the prospective customer is saying is that I wouldn't give up the benefits of what I have now to get the benefits of what you are trying to sell me, let alone pay you additional money for it. The professionals make their prospective customers so aware of their needs and so aware of their dissatisfaction with what they are using now that when they actually experience the ownership of the benefits they will enjoy compared to what they have now, their fear of losing the benefits of the new products is far greater than the fear of losing the benefits of the money that it will cost. When that has happened, the fear of buying disappears and all the professional has left to do is write the order.

This is one of those factors in selling that can be made to work more and more in salespeople's favor, the better they understand it. You should reread this chapter from time to time and take every opportunity to discuss it with other salespeople. You must admit that if you could have a

power assisting you when you are selling that is more powerful than the
fear of death, that would be a pretty good tool. And you certainly
wouldn't want such a powerful force working *against* you.

The Best-Kept Secret
in Selling

MOST PROSPECTIVE CUSTOMERS A SALESPERSON COMES IN CONTACT WITH
COULD AT BEST BE DESCRIBED AS ONLY LUKEWARM AND MANY ARE
DOWNRIGHT FRIGID.
WHEN SALESPEOPLE SELL MOST OF THEIR PROSPECTIVE CUSTOMERS THEY
MUST DO SOMETHING THAT TURNS LUKEWARM AND ICE-COLD PROSPECTS
INTO RED-HOT PROSPECTS WHO BUY.
WHAT THEY DO IS THE BEST KEPT SECRET IN SELLING....

THE RAREST CUSTOMER any salesperson ever encoun-
ters is the red-hot prospect with money in hand,
ready to buy. Instead, most prospective customers can at
best be described as "lukewarm." Many will even be
downright "frigid."

The Law of Cause and Effect says there can be no effect without a
cause. You cannot even look for a cause until you have experienced its
effect. You cannot determine what caused a noise until you hear it. If you
heard a noise and wanted to repeat it, you would have to find its cause
before attempting to duplicate its effect.

The 9-Dot Puzzle taught you that most people look at the effect and
never go outside the framework of that effect to figure out what caused
it. When your customer has bought, that is an effect. I dare say not one
salesperson in a thousand knows what causes a prospective customer to
buy.

When a salesperson sells almost every prospective customer he or
she comes in contact with, it is obvious that salesperson must be doing

something that *causes* customers to buy. Most of those prospective customers were at best lukewarm and many were downright frigid prospects. Whatever the salesperson did must have turned them into red-hot prospects who bought. *How he or she causes that to happen is the best kept secret in selling.*

When salespeople sell almost every prospective customer with whom they come in contact in a company where the rest of the salespeople are selling less than fifteen percent of their prospective customers, it was not what the successful salesperson was selling that caused prospective customers to buy. It wasn't the product, the price, the terms, the display, advertising, location, services, competitors, or anything else that caused them to buy. Had it been those things that caused the prospective customer to buy, every salesperson in the company would have been selling almost every prospective customer they came in contact with, and they were not.

When any prospective customer does not buy, that is an *effect* just as with prospective customers who buy. In each instance, there has to be a *cause.* No improvement in selling competence will ever take place until salespeople and management alike accept the fact that cause and effect is a law. When a prospective customer does not buy, the salesperson did something that *caused* the customer not to buy.

Why a prospective customer buys is the easiest lesson to learn about selling because there is only *one* reason people ever have for buying anything:

PROSPECTIVE CUSTOMERS BUY IN ORDER TO GET THE BENEFITS OF WHAT THEY PURCHASE.

No one ever has or ever will buy a one-inch drill bit because they want one. If they buy a one-inch drill bit it's because they *need* a one-inch hole. To get the hole, they have to buy the bit. The *hole* is the benefit. And that's the only reason prospective customers buy.

Why *would* a person NOT buy a one-inch drill bit? Is it because he or she does not need a one-inch hole and never expects to need one, thus has no need for a one-inch drill bit and will not buy? No! No! No! Because they have no need for the *benefits* of the drill bit. *That's* the only reason for them NOT to buy. In fact, if they had no need for the one-inch hole they were not a prospective customer for a one-inch drill bit.

Notice! If the prospective customer needed the hole, but did not know he or she needed it, as far as that person is concerned there is no need for the benefits of the drill bit and that person will not buy it, because he does not consider himself a prospective customer.

All salespeople must realize that when one of their prospective customers is unaware of the needs of any benefits of the features of the products they sell, that person is convinced he or she has no *need* and will *not* buy. This is a critical point, because as you will see, prospective customers for big-ticket products rarely have a comprehensive understanding of their needs. In other words, they are unaware of their need for most of the benefits of most of the features of whatever product the salesperson is selling.

Those are the basics of why customers buy and why they won't. If you understand what causes customers to buy, you have learned the best kept secret in selling. If you don't have a comprehensive understanding of these basics, you will never figure out how to turn lukewarm or ice-cold prospects into red-hot prospects who buy. Any more than you could learn algebra before knowing how to add or divide.

Okay, add this need of the benefit to the basics: The more prospective customers feel they need that one-inch hole, the hotter prospects they become, the more motivated they are to buy, and the more they are willing to pay.

Notice: How much more prospective customers feel they *need* the hole is determined by comparisons. They must feel they need that drill bit more than it will cost or they won't buy, right? No! No! No! They will have to feel they need the *hole* more than the cost of the drill bit or they won't buy. There is a vast difference between these two statements. The drill bit doesn't matter at all if the person has no need for the hole because they are not a prospective customer.

When a product has two or more features, each offering two or more benefits, the more customers feel they need each of those benefits, the stronger their reasons become for buying. Needing a one-inch hole is only one reason for buying that drill bit. Of course, the more the customer felt he or she needed the hole, the stronger that reason would be. However, if a product had two features and each feature offered two benefits, that would total *four* benefits. Thus, a customer for that product could have four times as many reasons for buying it, and the more he or she was made to feel the need for each of those benefits, the more compelling the reasons for buying would become.

What if the customer did not need the benefit of one of those features? That could become *two* reasons *not* to buy. The stronger the customer's feelings that he or she didn't need those benefits, the more compelled the customer would be *not* to buy. It is absolutely critical that you comprehend this, so I recommend you think about it carefully and discuss it at length with other salespeople.

The benefits of any feature can be a customer's reason for buying or for not buying. Example: Suppose a young couple with young children is buying a home. If its location is close to schools, that would be a feature that offered benefits that gave them a good reason for buying that home. If an older couple were looking for peace and quiet for their remaining years, that proximity to a school might be the only benefit that would keep them from buying.

But what if a buyer *needed* the benefits of that feature but was *unaware* of his or her need? Unless the buyer was made aware of those needs, he has *no* need, so those benefits will not be a reason to buy and can even be a reason for *not* buying.

Big-ticket items incorporate many, many features, each offering multiple benefits. A home could have hundreds of features offering a multitude of benefits. Most features of big-ticket products are not apparent or visible and almost none of their benefits can be seen. Look closely at the product you sell. How many of its features can you see? Now ask yourself how many of its *benefits* you can see. Then consider this: It is a rare customer for any big-ticket product who has a comprehensive understanding of his or her needs. Which is why that customer needs the help of a professionally competent salesperson, and that's the *only* reason you have your job.

Benefits are the *only* reason any customer will or won't buy and all benefits are based on need, and all needs depend on comparisons. We call those *perceived* needs. Most of the time, your customers perceive no need for the benefits of a feature on your product because they are unaware of this need. When they do *perceive* a need, it becomes a question of how strongly they want the benefits. The greater the perceived need, the hotter the prospective customer becomes.

Why do customers feel they need something? If you can answer that question you have learned what causes *every* customer to buy. Then and only then will you know the best kept secret in selling.

When I was about five years old, the first bicycle with coaster brakes on it arrived in Stillwater, Oklahoma. Until then, the pedals on a bicycle turned when the wheels did. You couldn't coast down a hill with your feet on the pedals because the pedals went around as fast as the wheels. The faster the bicycle went, the faster your feet had to go to stay on the pedals. I can tell you that every kid in Stillwater from five through their teens ran or rode their bikes many a mile alongside that first bike with coaster brakes, amazed at how the owner could be rolling along without the pedals having to go around. Every single kid would have given his eye teeth to own that bicycle. Even kids who had brand-new bicycles were made dissatisfied with what they had and that caused them to want a bicycle with coaster brakes. No! No! No! Their dissatisfaction with the *benefits* of what they had was caused by wanting a bicycle with coaster brakes. And kids who had no bike at all were made even more dissatisfied. We can all relate to that!

• • •
• • •
• • •
Note: This one feature offered three benefits that caused the kids who saw it to become dissatisfied with the benefits of what they had. For one moment, close your eyes and imagine yourself riding that bicycle, with every kid in town running beside you or riding their bikes trying to keep up with you. Would you ever want to go back to your old bike after you had experienced owning those benefits? How much more do you think riding that bike would make you want it instead of just seeing someone else ride it? How much more dissatisfied would you become with the benefits of your old bike after you had ridden the one with coaster brakes? No! No! No! It was not your old bike or that new bike that caused your dissatisfaction, it was the benefits of your old bike *compared* with the benefits of the new bike. This is so important for you to comprehend that you should give it plenty of thought and discuss it often with other salespeople to see how it applies to what you sell.

Perhaps the most important point is this: Your bike without coaster brakes could have been almost brand new, yet the benefits of the coaster brakes could have caused you to become so dissatisfied that if you had
• • •
• • •
• • •
the money, you would have bought the new bike. Can you see that? The reason it is so critical for all salespeople to understand this point is that most big-ticket products don't fail, quit working, or wear out overnight,

they wear out over long periods. As they do, the owner becomes more and more dissatisfied.

Example: Each little squeak or rattle in a car makes the owner a little more dissatisfied. As the squeak or rattle seems to get louder, that dissatisfaction increases. Each and every little thing, from a ding on the door to a dead battery increases owner dissatisfaction. Once your ears heard the squeak or rattle, or saw the ding in the door, you could never use the car again without seeing the dent, hearing the squeak. That's the principle of reflection. The more you saw and heard them, the bigger the dent became and the louder the noise seemed to be, causing your dissatisfaction to grow.

The neighbor next door, whom you don't like, gets a new car and causes you even more dissatisfaction with the benefits of your car. All of that dissatisfaction is happening a little at a time. But it collects in your subconscious. Imagine what happens when a new car model comes out with a whole bunch of new features and each one offers benefits your car doesn't. You are just like one of the kids who saw that bike with the coaster brakes. Your dissatisfaction takes a giant leap. Then, imagine what happens when you actually experience all those benefits for yourself, even the "new-car" smell. Your dissatisfaction soars to white-hot heat. Can you see that?

Bikes with coaster brakes had been on the market long before they appeared in Stillwater. But no bike riders were dissatisfied until they became aware of the coaster brakes and their benefits. As kids, we didn't know or perceive that we had any need for those benefits, and so as far as we were concerned we had no dissatisfaction. Had we seen the coaster-brake bicycle in a store window we might have liked it, but would have had no idea of its amazing benefits. If someone told us about them, that would not be enough for us to comprehend what the benefits would do for us nearly as much as actually seeing them demonstrated. Mr. Automobile Salesman, that one point can be worth the price of this book a thousand times over when it is comprehended and put into use. The power of *seeing* the benefits is nothing compared to the effect of customers experiencing the ownership of those benefits for themselves.

I'm not trying to identify all the things that cause buyer dissatisfaction, but it is dissatisfaction that *causes* customers to buy. As a rule, their dissatisfaction doesn't happen all at once, but builds over a long period and accumulates in their subconscious. More important, all of their dissatisfaction is created by *comparison,* not by need. It is comparisons that cause us to perceive needs and it is comparisons that cause us to buy.

Example: My wife is driving a car she loves, with only 4,000 miles on it, so it still smells new. It is a state-of-the-art vehicle that was quite expensive. Then she saw an ad for the new model of her car that listed eleven new features. The ad described the benefits of each one. As she read them to me, I could see how each one caused her to become a tiny bit more dissatisfied with her beloved car.

The result was she wished she had those features on her car now so she could enjoy the benefits. Thank goodness she wasn't made to feel she needed them badly enough to feel she *needed* the new model. I dodged that bullet for another year, but by then, there were lots of minor things causing small dissatisfactions to accumulate in her subconscious. The next new model may come in new colors and probably eleven more new features with new benefits, and by then, her ash trays full, she will feel she needs a new car so badly she absolutely has to have one. So we will trade in her old "wreck," with ten or twelve thousand miles on it, before it falls apart.

Can you see that all of this need was only *perceived?* She did not really *need* a new car and wouldn't for at least ten years. Very few salespeople understand this basic element of selling. They only understand the effect. Almost all research on selling is done through customer surveys or customer-oriented research. It deals with why customers think they bought and why they think they didn't. It has nothing to do with what causes them to buy, but whether they are satisfied or dissatisfied.

All salespeople can understand that every customer's only reason for buying is so he can own the benefits.

But that is where selling breaks down for most salespeople. They think they are selling homes, automobiles, sofas, airplanes, computers, and so on, and so they start right in *showing* their product to try to sell it. Then they wonder why most people who said they needed or were interested in buying their product don't buy and, in fact, don't seem too interested in what the salesperson has to say about it. Two things cause this to happen: (1) The prospective customers are not consciously aware of their need for the benefits of the features of what is being sold; (2) the salesperson knows little about the prospective customers and their needs. The salesperson is trying to put the cart before the horse or, in this case, the effect before the cause. *That* is the best kept secret in selling. We can all understand that no one ever bought a one-inch drill bit because he or she wanted one. It was the need for a one-inch hole that *caused* the purchase. You must understand fully the basics of this example if you want to use The Best Kept Secret in Selling, the one that permits professionally competent salespeople to turn lukewarm and even ice-cold prospects into red-hot prospects who buy.

In the case of the drill bit, I dealt with a product that had one basic feature and offered one basic benefit. In the case of the bicycle, I showed how one new feature could offer many benefits—your legs can rest when coasting, which makes riding much easier. Brakes lock the rear wheel just by pressing on the pedals. "Look Ma! No hands!" And the most powerful benefit of all: pride of ownership. Oh boy, how we all wanted to be that kid with the first coaster brakes!

"STOKE THE FIRES OF THEIR DESIRES AND YOU'LL NOT FAIL TO MAKE THE SALE."

The definition of "desire" in the Encyclopedia Britannica/Funk & Wagnall's standard dictionary is: "Desire - To wish or long for; covet; crave; yearning; requesting or asking for. Synonymous with appetite; longing, hankering, inclination."

Inclination is the mildest of these terms, a quiet, vague, or even unconscious tendency. However, desire begins with the slightest of inclinations, no matter how vague, quiet, or even unconscious they may be. Desire is often seen by many folks as a far-off dream that seems unattainable. Although desire ranges from the merest of inclinations to a raging, burning need, all desire is created by *dissatisfaction*.

Everyone has been caused to have many desires simply because any time people see something that offers more or better benefits than they are getting from what they have, has been caused to be dissatisfied... like a person walking when someone sails past on a bicycle. Today, those who live in advanced nations are caused to have thousands of desires jammed into their brains by mass media. Most of those desires lie buried in their subconscious. Besides, most of those desires are really just inclinations.

And therein lies the key to the best kept secret in selling.

Adages persist because they are true. So what does that old adage mean, "Stoke the fires of their desires and you'll *not fail* to make the sale."?

If you have ever used an old-fashioned coal-burning furnace or have camped out, you learned to rake the burning coals into a pile and cover them with ashes at night. Then in the morning, you sift through the ashes, find an ember still glowing, then put on a little tinder and blow on it. Even though that ember has all but burned out, it will produce a tiny flame in the tinder. When you add kindling to that flame, you get a little fire going, then in a few minutes you pile on the logs or coal on top of that small fire. You turn that all-but-burned-out ember into an inferno. That is what is meant by "stoke the fires."

You have already seen dissatisfaction fuel the flames of desire. That boy who was passed by the cyclist with a coaster brake was *caused* to be dissatisfied with the benefits he got from his old bike and a desire was created to own the benefits of the new bicycle. If he had no money, then that desire was only a dream. Even so, that dream was lodged in his subconscious—a burning ember that would never burn out completely. You saw how that desire could be made stronger if the boy actually rode the new bicycle and enjoyed its benefits for himself. That experience stoked the fires of his desires and made them burn even brighter.

Anyone who ever walked the docks of a marina looking at the sailboats and power boats feels a powerful desire to own one. No! No! No! A desire to own the *benefits*. No one can attend an automobile show without experiencing a desire to own the benefits of some of the new cars. The desire to own a new car was already there, buried in the ashes of the subconscious. It may only have been a vague or unconscious inclination, but when the person saw those new cars, all of a sudden it was right at hand. What had been an impossible dream became possible and that fueled the fires of their desires.

Couples living in homes that would be the envy of 99 percent of the world's population, spend a Sunday afternoon browsing through homes that are being shown by realtors or at a parade of new homes. The benefits they see that they would enjoy compared to the benefits of their current home stokes the fires of their desires. Haven't you experienced this?

The professionally competent salesperson knows that these

browsers, lookers, tire kickers, idea getters, time killers, and dreamers who, at best, only have an unconscious inclination that causes them to be looking, also know that budget permitting, each and every one of them can be turned into red-hot prospects with burning desires who buy. The professionally competent salesperson understands what *causes* the customer to buy. That's The Best Kept Secret in Selling.

The most important point for all salespeople to comprehend is that the *comparison* of the benefits that the customer enjoys with what he or she has now and the benefits that he would enjoy if he or she owned the product that the salesperson has to offer is the key. *That* comparison stokes the fires of the customers' desires, otherwise how could those professionals wind up selling most of the customers they come in contact with? *It is not just the comparison with a competitor's product.* The competitor's product may have stoked the fires of the customer's desires enough to cause customers to continue shopping, *but not enough to cause them to buy.* Why?

Big-ticket products always have many features, and each offers at least two or more benefits. Sometimes a feature can offer *dozens* of benefits. It is a rare customer for a big-ticket product who has a comprehensive understanding of his or her needs for even a few of the benefits of those features. Most features are invisible. Almost none of the benefits are visible. When the customer is unaware of a need for the benefits of any one of those features, as far as that customer is concerned, there is no need and no interest. When customers have been made consciously aware of each of their needs of the benefits of each of the features, the presentation and demonstration can stoke the fires of the customer's desire until the salesperson *never* fails to make the sale. All he or she need do to get the order is just write it up. Can you see that?

Let's go back once more to the bicycle with the coaster brakes. That bicycle had at least two dozen features and each one offered more than one benefit, but it was that one feature and its three or four benefits that stoked the fires of every kid's desires to the point that he or she would buy, budget permitting. To some degree, this principle applies to all big-ticket products. It is not unusual to find a single feature in a home, car, boat, airplane, or similar product that causes a customer to like it better and make the feature seem more important than any other. Many books call this the customer's "hot button" and suggest that the salesperson focus on that one feature and its benefits, to make the customer want those benefits more and more, thus turning the customer's desire into a raging inferno, forgetting all other features and benefits.

This is a fallacy. No better example of the dangers of this fallacy exists than in "Your Road to Selling Success." When that young man bought the $100 necktie on sale for $10, he thought he had made the buy of a lifetime because he liked it better than any tie he had ever owned. That was the one factor that caused him to buy with no consideration for any other feature or benefit. When the tie failed to meet his needs, because he had nothing to wear it with, he became more and more dissatisfied with it and liked it less and less.

There are two important lessons to learn: The first—how satisfied a customer will be depends ultimately on how well all of the benefits of all of the features cause that product to meet that customer's overall needs. Only rarely is that achieved by only those benefits of one or two features that seemed so important to the customer at the time of the sale.

Being the first person to own an Edsel was all it took to get a lot of people to buy one. When the fad wore off and it failed to be a car that was going to best meet the customer's needs, the Edsel turned out to be the worst mistake in automotive history.

The second lesson is that there is nothing perfect on the face of the earth and that certainly includes everything made by man. There will always be some features on big-ticket products that offer some benefits for which a customer has no need. Since the prospective customer may know about these features and benefits while knowing very little about the dozens or even hundreds of features and the multitude of other benefits, the familiar ones become reasons not to buy. They will show up as objections to buying, and as I have pointed out, sometimes the benefits of only one feature can be enough to keep a prospective customer from buying. In such a case, how would you stoke the fires of their desires and still not fail to make the sale?

First you must accept that you have already achieved your first and second objectives, which means you have already learned enough about your prospective customer and his or her needs to determine which of your products are going to meet those needs best. At this stage, it is unlikely that your product has a feature and benefit that will absolutely preclude your customer from buying. So the sale becomes a question of how many reasons you give the customer to buy versus the reasons not to. When the benefits of all of the features that are positive reasons to buy are stacked up against those few negatives, the positives become overwhelming. When those benefits are stacked up against the benefits of what they are using now, which caused their dissatisfaction in the first place, the sale is made.

If you have completed your presentation and demonstration and still do not have the sale, then you have yet to elevate the prospective customer's perceived need or their comprehension of the need as well as his or her comprehension of the value of the benefit of the features. You still haven't overcome objections to buying and those objections include price. As the presentation and demonstration of the benefits of each feature are repeated a second time, that spaced repetition increases the perceived need and thus value of each benefit, which causes the customer to want the product even more. In other words, "stokes the fires of their desires."

Masters of selling tell me they have repeated some presentations and demonstrations as many as three times if that was what it took to get a sale. They knew it was not a question of *"making"* the sale. It was only a question of stoking the fires of the prospective customer's desires until the sale was made, and that has nothing to do with sneaky, tricky, or high-pressure tactics.

The longer professionally competent salespeople follow their careers and the more effective they are, the fewer times they will complete a presentation the first time before they write an order. Doing a second presentation rarely happens, let alone a third, because more and more of their prospective customers are taking one look at the product that is going to best meet their needs and say, "I like it. I want it. I will take it."

As soon as I entered a large showroom in Salt Lake City, the top salesman in that company, a true professional who is one of the highest-volume, highest-paid salespeople in his industry, stopped me. He said, "Mr. Lawhon, I wonder if you would have a minute to answer a question for me?"

I said, "Sure, what is it?"

He told me that the evening before, the company had a special sale from 6:00 PM until midnight. He said the store was packed with customers the entire time, but it took him almost four hours to sell his first customer. Even though the sale was $3,200, he felt that in the same amount of time, had he dropped that customer, he could have made sales of $12,000 to $15,000. At that point he said, "Mr. Lawhon, my question is this: How long do you stay with a customer like that before you drop them and get another one?"

"You are the last person in this world I would have expected to ask me that question," I said. "Now, let me ask you one. When you had been with those people for five minutes, did you feel you would make a sale?"

He told me of course he did.

"At the end of 30 minutes, were you sure that you had a sale?"

He said, "Of course I was, or I would not have stayed with them."

"In other words, you felt you had the sale right up to the time that you wrote the order four hours later?"

"Of course."

I asked him how many times during his 20-year career it had taken him four hours to make a sale.

He thought a long time. "Come to think of it, I guess that was the first time it ever happened."

"Well then," I said, "here you are, one of the highest-paid highest-volume, top sales professionals in the entire world. You have gained so much specialized knowledge and so perfected your productive skills to the point that you rarely miss a sale, and it seldom takes you more than a few minutes to make even larger sales. Once in a while it takes you 30 minutes or longer, on rare occasions more than an hour, yet the first time in your entire career that it takes you four hours, you want to stop doing what has made you what you are today. So I will tell you when to quit. You don't quit after one hour, one day, or one month. Provided you think you have a sale, you never quit. When you start every sale intending to wind up with a satisfied customer, maybe one more time in your life it will take four hours to make a sale if you live long enough, but I doubt it."

He stood there with tears forming in his eyes. "Mr. Lawhon, I really needed that. I can't believe I asked that question. I will never be able to thank you enough."

By now, you realize that everything that happens to prospective customers from the time they enter a showroom or when a professional salesperson first calls on them has already started stoking the fires of their desires. Every question you ask in qualifying stokes those fires. Those questions you ask make the customer consciously aware of the dissatisfactions that had put them in the market for your products in the first place, and really, really stokes that fire of their desire. The comparison stokes it even more, making, as the professionals say, the sale easier to get and making it take less time.

The involvement presentation is just like having the boy ride the bike with the coaster brakes. The customer actually experiences owning the benefits of those coaster brakes, but with big-ticket items, every benefit of every feature when experienced, to a greater or lesser degree, has the same effect on a prospective customer. And every one of those benefits creates more and more desire until the customer is aching to own your product. That's when you add the one factor more powerful than the fear of death itself. Every time prospective customers have experienced the ownership of even one benefit of one feature, they have something to lose if they don't buy. Each benefit, once experienced, adds to that fear of loss.

Believe me when I say once you understand what causes the customer to buy—The Best Kept Secret in Selling—you will quickly see that most of the time when you become proficient in achieving each of your first five objectives, you will already be selling twice as many of your customer contacts as the average salespeople in your company. As you continue your efforts to become more and more productive, dealing with each objective in its proper sequence, you will see the most exciting things that can happen to anyone in any career, happening to you:

- Making a sale is going to get easier and easier the longer you follow your career.

- It is going to take less and less time to make bigger and bigger sales.

- Your income is going to rise ever so gradually year after year for the rest of your selling years.

- You will have a job selling as long as you live or you will be inundated with management opportunities.

Yes, it all becomes a reality when you actually realize that if you will stoke the fires of the desires of every prospective customer you come in contact with, even those who are just looking, browsing, getting ideas, kicking tires, and even those who seem to be ice-cold prospective customers, you will not fail to make the sale. But understanding what causes customers to buy won't be easy *at first*—that's why it remains The Best Kept Secret in Selling.

Service Is a Benefit

BUSINESS EXISTS BECAUSE SOMEONE HAS GAINED THE SPECIALIZED
KNOWLEDGE AND DEVELOPED THE PRODUCTIVE SKILLS REQUIRED TO DO
SOMETHING THAT PEOPLE NEED DONE BETTER THAN THEY COULD DO IT
THEMSELVES.
PRODUCTS ARE ONLY A BY-PRODUCT OF THOSE SERVICES. THE VALUE OF THE
BENEFITS OF WHAT YOU SELL IS DETERMINED ENTIRELY BY THE VALUE OF
THOSE SERVICES.

THE ONLY REASON anyone ever has or ever will have
for buying and paying for anything is to own the
benefits of what is being sold and only then when the
value of those benefits compared to what they are using
now exceeds the price they must pay.

Over and over I make this point when I say that no one ever has or
ever will buy a one-inch drill bit because they want one. If someone
bought and paid for a one-inch drill bit it was because that person needed a one-inch hole more than what the drill bit would cost. The hole was
the benefit. The prospective customer had to buy the drill bit to get that
benefit.

But wait a minute. The man who owned the hardware store had
bought the drill bit for about one half what he sold it for. There was not
one single benefit the retail buyer could have gotten out of that drill bit
that he or she couldn't have gotten if it had been bought directly from
the factory just like the owner of the hardware store had done.

Why would the customer feel that the benefits from the drill bit
made it worth twice what the retailer had paid for it? Without doubt this
is one of the hardest things for most salespeople to understand about the
prices they must charge for what they sell.

Most people in selling feel that any markup over and above what is
being sold has cost the company is profit. If we were to carry this to the
extreme we could say that the one-inch drill bit was nothing more than a
few cents worth of case-hardened steel. Why should the prospective cus-

tomer have to pay $20 for it?

It is obvious that many people have done something to that piece of steel that would permit it to do something that it would not do before. Whatever was done did not add to the value of the steel. It was the services performed that added features to the steel which permitted it to offer needed benefits. Those services had made the piece of raw steel worth many times what the drill bit maker had paid for it.

The value of the drill bit was not determined by the cost of the steel alone. It was determined by the services that were performed which turned it into the one-inch drill bit and then made it possible for those needing its benefits to find and buy it when that need arose. Those services added value to the steel many times over what it cost.

The valuable benefits of all things made by man are created by services that were performed on the raw materials, not by the raw materials themselves. Even a diamond in the rough has no value as a gemstone until services are performed on the raw material.

All trades and professions exist for one reason and one reason only, and that one reason is that people have gained the specialized knowledge and developed the skills to perform services for other people better then they would have done it themselves.

I am often asked how much something costs. I have a stock answer: "What's it worth? To whom, when, and where?"

Some of the wealthiest people in the world who were aboard the sinking Titanic offered everything they had for a life vest that had cost the shipline no more than a dollar or two.

Consider the Stone Age man when it was first discovered that tying a stone to the end of his war club made it an even more effective weapon. Then he discovered he could chip a sharp edge on the stone making it even more effective. It wasn't long before it became apparent that some members of the tribe had more talent and could produce better arrowheads than the others in less time. These guys weren't stupid. When their lives were at stake pride fell by the way. When the benefits of one tribe member's arrowheads made it easier to kill game and protect their own lives, they said, "You stay here and make arrowheads. We will trade you a part of our kill for your services." The arrowhead maker gained more and more specialized knowledge of stone and developed more productive skills. He became the wealthiest member of the tribe. Never had to risk his life and had the easiest job of all because of the skilled services he performed on what had been worthless stone. Yes, he was the first to gain the specialized knowledge and perfect the skills that permitted him to perform services that others needed *better* than they could perform them for themselves. How much value did those services add to the value of the rock? Without them the rock, like the raw diamond, was worthless.

Yes, the arrowhead maker enjoyed a far easier, safer way of life at a much higher rate of pay.

I can hear those Stone Age people with their primitive language grunting, "How much does it cost?" There must have been those who were in the business of selling way back then who had a stock answer, "What's it worth to whom and where?" Archeologists have found some of the finest arrowheads as many as 3,000 miles from where they were quarried and made. This happened at a time when most people never got more than a few miles from where they were born. Who knows how many times those arrowheads changed hands over that 3,000 miles? You can bet that every time they did they had cost the new owner a lot more than they had cost the previous owner.

Things were simpler back then and much of those basics that the business of selling are founded on have been forgotten. There is one that I think we are in serious need of reviving: In those days when an arrowhead maker foisted off an inferior product and created a dissatisfied customer, if the customer survived, he returned to the seller and beat his brains out with his war club, which is how it should be in the business of selling. Yes, down to this present day.

Inferior products are the result of inferior service. Period. Superior products are the result of superior service. Inferior service has become a luxury the world can no longer afford. The biggest waste of the world's natural resources is caused by inferior services performed on raw materials by man. Period.

Superior services can multiply the value of this earth's natural resources millions of times over. Continued waste created by inferior services used to make inferior products to be sold by guided tour directors at the lowest price possible, threaten these resources within a few generations.

The world can no longer afford anyone in the business of selling who performs inferior services or sells products of inferior quality.

Napoleon knew that Krupp, the German cannon maker's cannons were so superior to those made by French and English companies that, while the Germans themselves and other nations were buying French and English cannons because they cost far less money, Napoleon paid double the price for the Krupp cannon. The reason: The Krupp cannons would shoot almost one mile farther than any other cannon. Napoleon could blow the enemy to bits before they could get within a mile of them with their horse drawn cannons. Makes sense to me.

Most salespeople do not understand how value is added to a product through services, yet it is the one factor they need to understand best. The reason for this lack of understanding is simple: They are not in the "business of selling." They don't have the specialized knowledge and skills they need to competently perform the services their prospective customers need. They perform no services that add value to what they are selling and they are not entitled to be paid one penny more for what they sell than what it had cost their company. And they don't understand the value added by the services of others. They admit their ignorance when they claim that price is the number one reason for losing a sale.

Today, prospective customers are rarely greeted with a genuine welcome smile by someone who is competent to help them learn enough about their needs so as to be able to buy those things that are going to best meet those needs. The benefits to the prospective customer of that smile alone shines out like a radiant beacon. Small common courtesies that are all but forgotten add untold values to the benefits of your services and what you sell. Even such seemingly insignificant services as these when honestly and competently performed will put you way out in front of the pack. They will cause people to want to do business with you and I can guarantee you that this will result in your doing more business easier. You will find being in the business of selling life's most rewarding career. Oh yes! And the value of what you sell to your prospective customers will so far exceed the price asked that all you will need to do to get the order is—just write it up.

It is the multitude of services that went into the creation and making of what you sell coupled with the services that you and your company perform that create the benefits for your prospective customers of what you sell.

It is your job to know and understand everything you can about these services and how they combine to make what you sell best meet your prospective customer's needs.

Not one in a thousand salespeople believe what they sell is really worth more than what it cost their company. This attitude makes the job of those who are in "the business of selling" much easier. I hope this book causes the changes that put all salespeople in the business of selling. Until that happens, don't let up. Don't ever think you don't need to gain this knowledge and develop these productive skills. Get a head start now and the competitors will never catch you or your company.

The Losers in the Lounge

MOST SALESPEOPLE NEVER ASK THE PROSPECTIVE CUSTOMER FOR THE ORDER.
WHY?

As LONG AS I CAN REMEMBER companies have been conducting customer surveys. As customers are leaving the sales floor they are asked if they had found what they were looking for. When the customer says, "Yes," they are asked if they bought it. When the customer says, "No," the questioner asks, "Why?" and over 75 percent of those customers always give the same answer: "Nobody asked me to."

Let's be sure we get this straight. Prospective customers risk their lives on a freeway driving several miles at considerable cost in time and money to buy something they need. They find it, the price is fine, terms are great, and delivery was just right. They still need it and the only reason they give for not buying was, "Nobody asked me." Right. Most salespeople never ask a prospective customer to buy.

It amazes me that these same surveys go on year after year, always getting the same answers, yet no one who has this information asks, "Why?" Why did the prospective customers have to be asked to buy? Why didn't the salesperson simply ask them to?

Let's consider the prospective customer first. Psychologists say making a buying decision is a fearful thing—so fearful that there is often a moment of temporary insanity when the buyer weighs what they will lose versus what they will *gain*.

Most of us have a hard time making even the simplest buying decisions, like deciding whether we want soup or salad in a restaurant. We turn to the waiter to give us the confidence we need to make such a momentous buying decision. If we choose only one, we lose the benefits of the other and that fear of loss is always stronger than our desire for gain. The more confident we are as to which will best satisfy our palates, the easier it is to make the decision.

The bigger the buying decision, the less confidence we have, and the greater our fear. Sometimes, automobile salespeople lose sales just because they cannot get the prospective customer to decide on a color. That fear of choosing one and finding out out later they really liked another better is all it takes to keep some customers from buying.

You can see how hard it would be for a couple looking at home after home to decide which they like best. One has a master bath that they both like, another a kitchen the woman would die for, another a garage big enough for the man's workshop, and so on. When they choose one house over another they lose the benefits of all of the features of all of the homes they looked at and liked better, but the home they chose didn't have. Imagine how strong this fear of loss can be. The more homes the guided tour director has shown them, the greater this fear will be and the harder it gets to make a sale.

It should be easy to see why prospective customers who have found what they need and like best still cannot make a buying decision when you remember that the fear of loss is always stronger than the desire for gain. The prospective customer's lack of confidence caused that fear. That's easy enough to understand. But why doesn't a salesperson just ask them to buy? Same reason. Fear. These salespeople are even more afraid to ask the prospective customer to buy than the customer is to buy. So most salespeople never and I do mean *never* ask a prospective customer to buy. They have perfected a skill that guarantees they will not lose the sale.

I call it "the best-known secret in selling." It is used by all the losers in the lounge. Learning and practicing this secret will guarantee every salesperson that they will never lose another sale as long as they live. It is the most effective and most often used of all selling techniques to keep from losing a sale. It requires little or no practice to master. It requires no high pressure, no sneaky, tricky closing techniques, and it is guaranteed to be 100 percent effective. This technique is used by millions of sales-people, some of whom have been selling for fifty years or more without a single known instance of one of them ever losing a sale.

Every word you have just read is true. No gimmicks or tricks. Here is all those salespersons need do: *Don't ask for the order.* That's it. As long as you have not asked for the order you cannot lose the sale. You may

a tricky way to say something else. No. The fact is *most*
er ask for the order. They never ask their prospective cus-

aking on this subject in Coeur d'Alene, Idaho. A man came
terwards. He said, "My father-in-law taught me that lesson
the first day I went to work in his furniture store. As I arrived, a man and
his wife followed me in the door. My father-in-law said, 'There's your
first customer, turned, and went into the back room. He came out when
they left. It had been almost an hour and he asked how I had done. I told
him they had picked out over $900 worth of furniture. He asked if they
had bought. I said, 'No, but they assured me they would be back.' He
went in the back room and came out with a brand new $100 bill. 'Young
man, you have already put in a hard day. I want you to take this $100 bill
and go buy a new suit. You have earned it. There is only one catch: you
can shop anywhere you like, but you cannot buy the suit unless you can
get the salesperson to ask you to buy it."

This man reminded me that back then $100 would buy the best
readymade suit on the market. He said he went out the door walking on
air, but when he returned long after all the men's clothing stores had
closed, he still had that $100 bill. He had not been able to get a single
salesperson to ask him to buy a suit.

Let's look at what this man said to his father-in-law. "I made the
sale. I will write it up as soon as they get back and they will be back." If
he had asked them to buy and they said, "No," when his father-in-law
asked how he did, he would have had to say that he did not make the
sale. His fear of disapproval would not let him admit that he had not
made the sale. He had discovered how never to lose another sale as long
as he stays in selling, *"Don't ask for the order."*

THE NEED FOR APPROVAL AND THE FEAR OF DISAPPROVAL

Everything we do is an effort to gain approval or to avoid disapproval. No person can ever hope to succeed at anything who does not
understand these two forces in their own life and in the lives of all other
people.

Approval, praise, and recognition are what feed the spirit of man and make it grow. They make us strong and build our confidence. Disapproval kills the spirit of man. Destroys our confidence. Makes us fearful and weak.

Not one average salesperson has ever told me he or she lost a sale because of something that salesperson had done. If the prospective customers did not buy, these average salespeople all assured me that they had made the sale and would write it up as soon as the customer returned or the next time they called on the prospective customer. What makes them believe that?

Prospective customers are afraid to buy because they are not confident their buying decision will gain them the approval of all those whose approval is important to them. Salespeople are afraid to ask prospective customers to buy because they are not confident the customer will say, "Yes." This lack of confidence makes salespeople more fearful the customers will say, "No." That is seen as disapproval, and that is exactly what it is.

When salespeople let prospective customers look at what they sell, tell them about or demonstrate what they sell, and the prospective customers have not bought, these customers have disapproved of both the offer and the salesperson.

Many books on selling tell salespeople they should not take personally a customer's refusal to buy. It should only be seen as a rejection of the offer, not as a rejection of them. This confusion will never be cleared up until the salesperson admits it was what he or she did that caused the offer to be rejected or accepted!

The professionally competent salesperson has reduced the buying decision to an easy comparison of good, better, and best as soon as he or she has achieved the first four objectives.

The residential real estate salesperson has helped his or her prospective customers understand and become consciously aware of what their needs really are. The realtor knows far more about what homes are available that would best meet their needs. Because of this awareness when he or she shows the prospective customers the first home, it meets their needs better than what they have now and have seen up to this time. The realtor shows them a second home that will far better meet their needs, but may cost up to twice as much. Then he or she shows them the home that will meet their needs as well or even better than the second home, yet may cost about half as much. Sometimes, it so obvious that it best meets their needs that they have the confidence to say, "I will take it" the minute they see it. But if they don't, it is only a question of the salesperson's demonstrating how the benefits of feature after feature make it better and better meet their needs until all doubt and fear or questions have been eliminated. They aren't fearful of buying and the salesperson isn't fearful of asking them to.

Although those simple facts have never been expressed until now, *the number one cause of failure in selling is the fear of disapproval.* This fear is due to a lack of confidence and that lack of confidence is due to a lack of competence.

Even if average salespeople are selling only half of their prospective customers, they could not stand that rejection ratio because their fear of rejection is greater than their need for approval. But most average salespeople don't sell one out of seven of their prospective customers and no one could possibly stand that high a rejection or disapproval rate, so most average salespeople who are hired and trained to sell fail, turning to some other career. And what about those long-term salespeople who never become professionally competent? How do you think they handle the massive doses of disapproval and rejection they face every day?

THE LOSERS IN THE LOUNGE

Actions that are rewarded tend to be repeated. They become learned, then they become habits. Actions that result in frustration tend to be avoided. They are never learned.

Therefore:

> IF YOU ARE DOING SOMETHING WRONG AND
> YOU CAN FIND A WAY TO GAIN APPROVAL FOR
> DOING IT, YOU WILL TEND TO GO ON DOING IT.
> THAT ACTION WILL BECOME LEARNED AND IT
> WILL BECOME A HABIT.

Convicts give each other approval for what they have done. That approval causes them to repeat their criminal acts, acts that are learned and have become habits. Ever wonder why we call repeat offenders "habitual criminals?" Fourth- and fifth-time criminal offenders don't mind prison so much because they get more and more praise and approval from their peers for committing more and more crimes. They form a mutual admiration society. The longer they are permitted to repeat their criminal acts, the better they become at doing what they do.

In selling, I call these mutual admiration societies "The Losers in the Lounge." Others call them lounge lizards. To show how they work, let's consider five salesmen in a furniture company and see how each of them deals with a prospective customer for a reclining chair.

I

Prospective Customer:	"Do you carry Superaction reclining chairs?"
Salesperson:	"No. We carry XYZ and they are just as good. Let me show them to you."
Prospective Customer:	"No thanks, I have already picked out the Superaction reclining chair I want and I am looking for the best deal I can find."
Salesperson:	"Well, I can't help you ma'am. You come see us again, ya hear."

I I

Salesperson:	"Can I help you ma'am?"
Prospective Customer:	"No thanks, I am just looking."
Salesperson:	"I'll be glad to show you around."
Prospective Customer:	"I really only want to look."
Salesperson:	"Well, what is it that you are looking for?"
Prospective Customer:	"I am thinking about a reclining chair for my husband for Christmas and thought that I would look around to see what's available."

Salesperson:	"Come on back here and I will show you where they are. You just look to your heart's content. If you have any questions, I will try to answer them. See anything there you like ma'am?"
Prospective Customer:	"No, but thank you for letting me look."
Salesperson:	*(Handing prospective customer his card)* "Well, if you don't find anything you like better, you come on back and ask for me."

I I I

Salesperson:	"Good morning ma'am, can I show you something today?"
Prospective Customer:	"Do you have something in a dark-blue, velvet reclining chair that rocks?"
Salesperson:	"Lady, we don't have a dark-blue recliner in this whole place, let alone one that rocks. How about some other color? Can I show them to you?"
Prospective Customer:	"No thanks, I need blue and I am in a hurry."
Salesperson:	"Well, you come back and see us."

I V

Salesperson:	"Good afternoon. What can I help you folks with?"
Prospective Customer:	*(Older woman with her husband)* "We are looking for a reclining chair for him."
Salesperson:	"They're right back here folks. We have about

150 of them and the best prices in town. I bet you can find just what you are looking for."

Prospective Customer: *(After almost an hour looking and trying every chair)* "Well, you sure have some pretty chairs, but we have some more places we want to look."

Salesperson: "Thanks a lot..." *(under his breath)* "for wasting my time."

V

Prospective Customer: "I want to see that reclining chair you advertised in today's paper."

Salesperson: "Which one ma'am?"

Prospective Customer: "I don't know. It was advertised regular $399 for $299 on sale."

Salesperson: *(Calling to other salesperson)* "Hey Joe, did we have a reclining chair advertised today?"

Other Salesperson: "I don't know. Check with the office." *(The salesperson checks with the office and gets the information.)*

Salesperson: "Okay, ma'am. Now I know just which one it is. Follow me."

Prospective Customer: "I sure hope it is the one we looked at last week that my husband wanted so badly."

Salesperson: *(Arriving at the reclining chair department.)* "There it is. Is that the one you wanted?"

Prospective Customer: "Oh, yes! That's it. Is the sale price $299?"

Salesperson: *(He fumbles for the price tag)* "Let me look. Yes ma'am, it's reduced to $299."

Prospective Customer: "I'll take it. When can you deliver it?"

That was one approval and four disapprovals. There is not a person reading this book who could not have made that fifth sale. This sort of prospective customer rarely totals more than five percent of the prospective customers salespeople come in contact with.

The professionally competent salesperson with a reasonable selection of reclining chairs would stand an almost 100 percent chance of selling Prospective Customers I, II, III, and IV. Let's go back and examine the salesperson in each case and see how the salesperson managed to gain approval from each lost sale.

Prospective Customers I, II, III, and IV: The outcome with these prospective customers was the same—no sale. Surely the salespeople involved can't expect approval from that result, or can they? Remember, they crave approval and they die a little with every bit of disapproval. So if they can't find a quick way to get some offsetting approval to the prospective customer's disapproval and their lost sales, their careers will expire even faster.

Therein lies the secret that keeps alive the sales career of an ordertaker, while actually selling fewer than one prospective customer out of every seven.

The ordertaker always blames someone or something else for his or her failure to make a sale. Most often the ordertaker blames the prospective customer or the company, neither of whom is present to defend themselves, thus removing any blame from the ordertaker while gathering full support from colleagues in the lounge. Because the ordertaker is able to get their full approval, the ordertaker *believes* his or her own excuses and goes right ahead masquerading as a salesperson. Even as the prospective customer is leaving, the ordertaker has started his campaign to gain full approval as he or she joins the losers in the lounge.

About PROSPECTIVE CUSTOMER I, ordertaker says: "Well, there goes another Superaction recliner customer. I will bet you 75 percent of the reclining chair customers we get want Superaction. I don't know why we don't carry them instead of this stuff we have. Once a customer has seen a Superaction, you can't sell them anything else. We either have the dumbest buyers in the world or they are taking kickbacks."

The other losers in the lounge agree with these excuses and give supporting testimony of similar experiences. See how easily the ordertaker gets their full approval for not making a sale? Of course, the other losers will expect this person's approval of them when they fail to make a sale, too. That's how all mutual admiration societies work.

About PROSPECTIVE CUSTOMER II, "Damned people come in here taking up my time and wasting it. I waited over an hour for my turn and that woman didn't want a damned thing. She didn't even sit in one of those chairs. She probably doesn't even have a husband. I swear I haven't had a decent customer in a week. If this company doesn't get their prices down and start doing more advertising, we're all going to starve to death."

About PROSPECTIVE CUSTOMER III, "If we don't get a better selection of recliners, we might as well shut down this department. It's hard enough to get a decent customer in here and when we do, this company never has the colors they want. They work our fool heads off to make the sale and the credit department turns it down or that sorry delivery department messes it up. I have had three credit turndowns already this week. They don't care. It's not their sale or paycheck. They get paid anyway. We are the ones who suffer."

About PROSPECTIVE CUSTOMER IV, "What's the matter with these people anyway? They wasted over an hour of my time. They didn't any more intend to buy than the man in the moon. Don't they know we work on commission? He went one way and she went the other. I don't think either one of them had enough sense to know what they were looking for."

About PROSPECTIVE CUSTOMER V, "Yesiree!" (He says as he snaps his fingers.) "You give me a good customer, I sell 'em every time and it doesn't take me that long to do it." (He snaps fingers again.)

This loser is going to get maximum mileage out of this sale. You can hear the yell clear across the showroom, "Hey boss! I just sold another one of those $299 recliners. When I got through with that lady she was tickled to death." He or she claims every bit of the credit that can be claimed. Reread the story of this sale. This person wasn't even a qualified "ordertaker." He or she didn't even know the chair was advertised, what it was, or where it was, had to look on the tag for the price, but was quick to demand 100 percent of the credit. The salesperson who first showed the customer the chair last week, the company's advertising, and a 25-percent price cut had nothing to do with it as far as this goof is concerned.

These comments about prospective customers are called "bitching." I have asked hundreds of long-term average salespeople how they feel about it. They all shrug and agree "it's a way of letting off steam and that's a right all salespeople need." The longer these people had been selling, the more adamant they were about their right to bitch.

Let me set the record straight right now. Bitching is the ordertaker's chief method for gaining the approval that masks his or her selling incompetence. Of all the bad, effective counterproductive habits in selling, bitching is the most destructive and the most counterproductive.

Ask any top professionals in any field of selling how they feel about bitching and they will say in just these words: "It is counterproductive. I won't have anything to do with it."

There are two guaranteed ways to fail:

- "I don't have what I need to do my job."
- "Things aren't the way that they are supposed to be."

Now listen to what the losers in the lounge are saying: "I don't have the merchandise, prices, advertising, terms, inventory, delivery, or anything else I need to sell for this company." Any one of those attitude guarantees failure. "Nothing in this company is being done the way that it should be for me to do a good job of selling." That attitude guarantees failure.

It is generally believed the extrovert has a much better chance of succeeding in sales than the introvert because the outgoing personality has a greater need for approval. The greater anyone's need for approval, the greater the fear of disapproval. The two come in equal measure. I assure you the fears of an extrovert are just as powerful as the fears of an introvert. Whether the fear is great or small, if we lack the confidence to face it, that's only because we are not competent to handle that situation.

I make this point because some of the most successful salespeople in the world are some of the biggest introverts you will ever meet, yet others are the biggest extroverts, too. The same effect occurs in all professions. Some of the world's greatest doctors, lawyers, scientists, actors, educators, poets, have been extroverts and some have been introverts; so that trait has nothing at all to do with their competence.

It is fear that drives the rookie salesperson into the company of the losers in the lounge, and there is only one thing that will get him or her out of their clutches: competence. Don't think for a minute that I'm saying once a person has joined the losers in the lounge he or she can't get away. Not so. But I am saying the longer they stay in that poisonous company, the harder it will be for them to become competent.

"Old habits are hard to break" became an adage because it has stood the test of time. There will never be a customer-driven company that has two or more losers in the lounge. They will continue along their counterproductive destructive paths until they and management agree on one very, very important point: When a salesperson has let prospective customers look at what he or she sells, told them about it, or demonstrated it, and the prospective customers have not bought, the customers have *disapproved* of both the salesperson and the offer and that was the salesperson's fault.

This problem will never be resolved until all salespeople know full well and admit that it was what *they* did or did not do that caused their offer to be accepted *or* rejected.

When salespeople create customer file cards each and every time they come in contact with a prospective customer, they have taken their first giant step down the road to selling success. They have admitted to themselves and anyone else who is interested that they had a prospective customer and did something that either caused the customer to buy or not to buy. That is the first step forward, but the first time a salesperson fails to create that file card to account for that prospective customer contact, he or she has taken two giant steps back—just like the reformed smoker who succumbs to one cigarette. Each backward step makes the next step backward even easier. If you have two prospective customers in a row you did not create a file card for, you have taken *four* giant steps back. When you don't account for three prospective customers in a row, that is *sixteen giant* steps back. All bad, counterproductive habits are developed by taking what at the time is the easy way out, which is backstepping. Bad and counterproductive habits develop much faster than effective productive ones because no conscious effort and no specialized knowledge is required.

It is no harder for the long-term average salesperson to develop effective productive selling skills than for the new sales trainee. In fact, it can be easier because the long-term salesperson already has a lot of the knowledge and information he or she needs.

What makes it harder for the long-term counterproductive salespeople is their hard-earned bad habits. Those old counterproductive habits will keep them mired in the cozy security with the other losers in the lounge. That is their "comfort zone."

If these counterproductive, negative people are permitted to continue their destructive ways, that is a management decision and it becomes management's failure.

It is easy to blame salespeople for failing when in fact the failure of any employee to succeed must be considered a management failure. Until companies admit this fact, managements can go on blaming their salespeople and salespeople can go on blaming customers.

But the 5 x 7 customer accounting card shows salespeople in black and white when they have succeeded and when they have failed. That causes them to quit doing the things that caused failure and to do more of the things that cause successes. This card measures the success of management, too, because it measures the results with each prospective customer. The information on those cards is truly customer-driven, and only when *that* information drives the company, is it a real customer-driven company.

A sales manager's success or failure is determined 100 percent by how much the competence of the salespeople he or she supervises improves. That improvement will have nothing to do with what is being sold, prices, advertising, services, or the nation's economy. The improvement in sales productivity can only be determined by measuring how many prospective customers each salesperson came in contact with and how many they sold. As the sales manager improves his or her productive management skills, the salespeople improve right along with the manager. How much both management and salespeople have improved is measured by the 5 x 7 customer file cards.

When no one in a company actually knows how many prospective customers every salesperson has come in contact with, there is no way to measure how productive those salespeople were, and worse, there is no way to measure how productive anyone else in the company has been.

Example: A sales manager could have improved the batting average of his salespeople 50 percent by taking them from selling 20 percent of their prospective customers to 30 percent. If traffic fell off over 50 percent because of ineffective advertising, sales would have gone down despite the sales manager's incredible success. Not only would this manager not get the praise and recognition he or she deserved, in all probability the manager would get the blame along with the salespeople. But when a company knows accurately how many prospective customers their salespeople had coming to them and that number declines, then they can pinpoint the problem and solve it.

Once there is an accurate measurement of how successful salespeople are with prospective customers, then you have a yardstick by which to measure the competence and productivity of everyone else in that company. That measurement alone guarantees that the competence of everyone measured will improve, and not only the salespeople. Without this vital yardstick, only the losers in the lounge will prosper because they've caused everyone else in the company to form their own mutual admiration societies in self-defense.

There are two guaranteed ways to fail in anything you attempt:

• Claiming you don't have what you need to succeed (that includes claiming you don't have the competent people you need).

• Claiming things aren't the way they need to be for you to do your job.

The 5 x 7 customer file card eliminates these two excuses for everyone in a company and guarantees the company's success. Why? Because what gets measured accurately, improves. That's a mathematical fact. When used effectively, the yardstick leaves no place for the losers in the lounge to hide.

Incompetence causes fear and fear keeps everyone from exposing their incompetence to others and that keeps us from measuring our own competence. That fear will always drive the incompetent into the waiting arms of the losers in the lounge.

I once saw a company destroyed after putting in an incentive program that could have doubled the commission rate of a sales force that didn't sell 20 percent of its prospective customers. The added incentive only encouraged incompetent salespeople to push even harder and to hustle more prospective customers. Two years later, that company was in deep trouble. Their surveys showed:

• Prospective customers who shopped there and did not buy said they would never come back because of the "pushy" way they had been treated by salespeople.

• Prospective customers who had shopped and did buy said even though they had bought they would not buy there again because of the way they had been hustled and pushed into buying.

• Both customers who did and did not buy said of all the places they shopped the salespeople in that company were the least knowledgeable.

• These later surveys showed the salespeople to be selling fewer than ten percent of their prospective customers (only one-half of the 20 percent they had been selling) and advertising costs had more than doubled.

• Surveys also showed the company needed at least twice as many salespeople.

When management tried to install a customer accounting plan and hire more salespeople, the current salespeople issued an ultimatum: either release the newly hired sales trainees and drop the accounting plan or they would join the union. When management caved in to that threat, for all practical purposes those losers in the lounge were running that company.

Managements might wonder why I would put this story in a book written primarily for salespeople. I did so to make the point that salespeople cannot support management when they feel that what management wants to do is not in their best interest any more than management could support what salespeople are doing if they didn't think that it was in management's best interest.

But when the goal of everyone in a company is to turn every prospective customer the salespeople come in contact with into a satisfied customer, then we discover that the success of everyone in the company depends on success with prospective customers.

That means the customer becomes the head of the company and organizational charts showing who works for who would look like this:

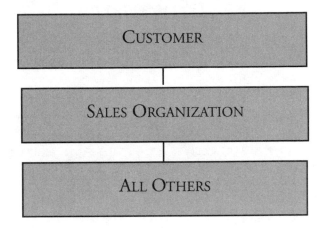

In a real sense, the competent salespeoples' job is to service the needs of their customers, which means they are working for the customers. The customer is their boss. Everyone else's job is to support the salespeople as they service the customer's needs.

The job of management is to work for the success of those under them, which means they are actually working for them instead of the other way around. The president of any company works to help everyone beneath him to succeed. His success depends entirely on the success of those he "works for." In a truly customer-driven company, success in achieving satisfied customers determines the president's and everyone else's success.

Only the 5 x 7 customer file card can tell everyone in a company, including the losers in the lounge, just what a prospective customer is.

We will see the greatest turnaround in business history when all companies become truly customer-driven. Until then, business will stay on a downhill slide, greased by the losers in the lounge.

18 / "I Can't Buy Without Approval"

THE LAST THING PROSPECTIVE CUSTOMERS *WANT* IS TO PUT OFF A BUYING DECISION UNTIL THEY HAVE SOMEONE ELSE'S APPROVAL— WHETHER THAT SOMEONE IS A PARENT, FRIEND, SPOUSE, CHILD, BOSS, OR COMMITTEE. YET, MOST BOOKS ON SELLING SAY THAT SALESPEOPLE SHOULD NEVER TRY TO MAKE A SALE UNTIL THEY ARE SURE THOSE WHO HAVE THE AUTHORITY TO APPROVE THE BUYING DECISION ARE PRESENT.

PERHAPS THE MOST COMMON EXCUSE for not buying is the need for other people's approval. That is when the prospective customer says, "I am sure that I will buy it, but I must have my spouse see it," or "my boss," or "the committee."

The reason you will hear this excuse more than all others is that it works. Prospective customers have found that when they give a salesperson other excuses or objections to buying, they get all kinds of hassle. Whereas there is no real argument against this excuse for not buying. It works for the prospective customer. They know it works; so they use it more often than less effective excuses for not buying.

It works so well that all the books I have read that deal with this problem say that salespeople should not try to make a sale unless they have the person or persons present who have the authority to approve the purchase.

Because this is about the *only* thing salespeople are taught, the excuse works. The prospective customer can get out of buying at the time and the salesperson can assure the boss and losers in the lounge that the customer will "be back."

This term is often heard in the retail industry. Professionally competent salespeople don't believe in tooth fairies and they don't believe in "be-backs." If they are working a sale that requires them to make a second call or for the prospective customer to come back, it will be done by appointment.

In retail, where most salespeople don't sell fifteen percent of the prospective customers, that means at least six of those who told the salesperson they would be back didn't come back and the one out of seven who bought was rarely a prospective customer who had come back. That's why I don't believe in "be-backs."

This chapter will give the salesperson some insight into this problem.

I would like to remind you that we are all driven to do what we do and say by our need to gain approval or to avoid disapproval. Prospective customers do not want the disapproval they know they will get from the salesperson when they don't buy. They love to get the salesperson's approval when they do. This "be-back" excuse lets them not buy and to avoid most of the disapproval and it does the same thing for the salesperson.

This is not a problem for the professionally competent salesperson. To understand why, let's look at three different customers buying a simple product that must meet the needs of someone else and who has to approve the purchase. Keep in mind the same issues would apply to a person buying for a company (things that would have to meet the needs of others in the company or things that will be resold by that company and would have to meet the needs of prospective customers of the company.) The issues would be the same when a committee has been asked to approve a buying decision.

A study of this situation in its simplest form can help all salespeople understand it in its most complex form.

Suppose a woman's husband says to her, "Would you run down to the hardware store and get the cheapest one-inch drill bit they have?" She hurries to the hardware store and asks for the cheapest one-inch drill bit. The clerk points it out to her and says that it is $4.95, but that there were some one-inch drill bits in a barrel of assorted items that are offered your choice for one dollar. She digs down into the barrel and near the bottom finds a one-inch drill bit. She buys it for one dollar. She can't wait to get home and tell her husband how she got what he needed for only one dollar when the going price was five. Needless to say, inconsiderate bum that the husband was, he praised her for her buying decision and bragged to his buddies about the great buy *he* made.

In this case the woman/buyer has become a very satisfied customer.

Here's the only point of this simple example: Do you think that woman would rather call her husband on the phone and say, "Honey, they have two, one-inch drill bits: One is five dollars, the other is just like it, but it's on sale for one dollar. Which one do you want me to buy?" First of all, he would probably say, "What's the matter with you? Can't you do anything yourself? Stupid, get the one dollar drill bit and get a move on it. You have wasted enough of my time already." No! No! No! She does not want to give up one bit of the credit for having found and bought the five-dollar drill bit for one dollar. Whether its a five-dollar item on sale for one dollar that meets her husband's needs as well as the five-dollar drill bit, or a five-million-dollar product that she buys for one million dollars that meets the needs of those who use it as well as the five-million-dollar one, she wants all the praise and approval. All of it. And the bigger the purchase, the more of it there is to be gained.

Those are exaggerated numbers and exaggerated savings, but there is no exaggeration in what the buyer wants. Now listen to me. Customers only buy to get the benefits of what is being sold. This buyer does not want nor need the benefit of the one-inch drill bit, so what benefit will she get out of buying it? The approval of the person who needs the benefits of what she bought.

Same scene, different house. Wife hurries to hardware store, finds the one-inch drill bit in a barrel, buys it, and rushes home. Her husband takes one look at it and says, "You dingbat, this drill bit only works in a half-inch chuck. Mine is a 3/8-inch. Take it back and get me a one-inch drill bit that will fit a 3/8-inch chuck."

"I can't. Those were sold as is and cannot be returned." I could carry this scene of disapproval to the point where the husband physically abuses his wife or the employee who made a similar mistake gets fired. It's the same thing. In this case, the buyer has become a very, very dissatisfied customer.

Same scene, different house. Wife hurries to hardware store, tells the clerk she wants his cheapest one-inch drill bit. He asks what she wants to drill, a hole in metal, wood, or mortar, and what size chuck her drill has. She doesn't know and there is no way on God's green earth she can or will buy. In that case, the clerk would be a fool to go ahead and sell her or try to sell her, and the books that say the salesperson should not try to make a sale unless the person with the authority to make the buying decision is present is still wrong! Wrong! Wrong!

There will be cases where that is true, but they are the exceptions. This customer, even more than the others, wants the approval of her husband for having bought the drill bit that was going to best meet his needs at the best possible price. Her problem is she doesn't know enough about his needs.

If there were any way possible for that clerk to help her learn enough about her husband's needs without the husband finding out, then help her buy the drill bit that was going to best meet those needs at a fair price, you can bet your boots he is going to make one very, very satisfied customer.

I don't care what you sell. I don't care who you sell it to, and I don't care how many times the buyer is removed from the end user, your only objective is a satisfied customer. You will have the same ten objectives, you will need the same specialized knowledge and information that the end user will need, plus the knowledge and information that those in between the buyer and the end user need, and you will need the productive skills to reach your goal.

If all of these things were not needed, no one would need you. If you don't have the knowledge and information or the productive skills to use it, prospective customers don't need or want you and it won't matter if the end user is involved in the buying decision—or if the losers in the lounge approve of your action.

I can assure you that this little chapter is a fooler. It takes a few minutes to read. Put a color tab on the first page of this chapter. Every time you have parted with a prospective customer without an order with only an assurance that he or she will be back to you after getting someone else's approval, read this chapter and apply what it teaches to that situation. Every time you do this, I promise you will gain a much more comprehensive understanding. When you do, remember: That is true of every chapter in this book.

You will discover that there are no excuses for the professional in the business of selling.

19 / *Service Beyond the Call of Duty*

THE FIRST BASIC PRODUCTIVE SKILL IN THE BUSINESS OF SELLING IS ONE THAT YOU HEAR OVER 99 PERCENT OF ALL SALESPEOPLE PROCLAIMING LOUDLY: "THAT'S NOT MY JOB!" YET IT IS ONE PRODUCTIVE SKILL USED TO START AND COMPLETE EVERY SALE BY THE HIGHEST-PAID, HIGHEST-VOLUME SALESPEOPLE IN THE WORLD.

COURTESY COSTS NOTHING, but it pays giant dividends in selling.

Time was when common courtesy was a basic skill in selling, but it is one that has been all but lost and with it goes one of the skills that made selling really enjoyable. What had been a cause of pride in selling, making it a gentle art, has turned into the most disgusting comment that we hear coming out of the mouths of losers in the lounge, "It's not my job."

I started as a commissioned salesman while still in my teens in Greenville, Michigan. I was very poor, very cold, and had a limited formal education. If I didn't sell anything, I didn't eat.

One of the first prospective customers I had was a woman about 50 years old. She was looking at what was called a Venetian mirror. When I approached her, she said, "$14.95 is too much for that mirror."

I said, "But ma'am, that mirror is plate glass."

She turned to me and with a scathing look that I will never forget said, "Sonny, don't you think that I know that," turned, and walked out the door.

I want to tell you that destroyed me. I was so upset I did not sleep at all that night. All I could do was ask myself, "How in the world are you, a gangly teen-aged kid, going to get a woman to let you tell her what she needs for her home?" By the time I went to work the next day, I had decided what I would have to do if I had any hopes at all of succeeding. I was going to have to become one of those young men that all the young girls don't want anything to do with if I was to succeed in selling. You know the kind I mean. They are so polite and so helpful—the kind of young men that every mother wishes her daughter would marry and the daughter can't stand.

I became what I called a "service-rendering salesperson." I was so polite and would do so much for my prospective customers that they had to buy from me. In those days, furniture was not displayed in room settings as it is today. All sofas were displayed in one area while chairs, tables, lamps, and so on, was each displayed in its own area. Salespeople had to walk their prospective customer all over the showroom going back and forth several times to sell a sofa, chair, table and lamps. That could use up the better part of a day.

From that day on, after the Venetian glass mirror episode, no prospective customer of mine was going to have to do anything that I could do for them. When one of my prospective customers had found a sofa she liked and wanted to know what chairs would go with it, I would say, "Mrs. Jones, you just sit right there. You can't really tell how a chair looks with a sofa until you have seen them together." With that, I was off like a shot.

I was young and strong and could whip any chair up on my shoulders and carry it at a dead run for a city block without being winded. I would find a chair that would go with the sofa she had decided on, toss it over my head, take off on a dead run until I reached the point that she would see me. Then I slowed down, walking as if I were carrying a heavy burden. I strained as I put it down beside the sofa and took several big breaths to get my wind back. "You see, Mrs. Jones, you really couldn't tell how well it goes with the sofa without seeing them together." I might have repeated this seemingly exhausting effort until I had three or four chairs beside the sofa. I worked so hard to satisfy that prospective customer and had been so polite that she owed me so much she could not bring herself not to buy.

I would repeat these actions if she needed tables, sometimes having to clear some things out of the way to show more if that's what it took to get the sale. My favorite and most fun part of this sale would be the lamps. Again, I would say, "Mrs. Jones, there is no way you can tell how a lamp will look with this furniture until it is displayed together," and off

I ran to get a lamp. If it had a bulb in it, I took out the bulb, rushed back (always a little out of breath), put the lamp on the table, plugged it in, looked and saw that it had no bulb and said, "One moment, Mrs. Jones, there is no way you can see how well this lamp goes with this furniture if it isn't lighted." With that I was off to get the light bulb. Running back with it, a little out of breath, I put the bulb in the lamp. When she said she would take it, I would say, "Just stay right where you are, Mrs. Jones," as I took off to get the order form and returned a little out of breath to write it up.

I killed them with kindness, courtesy, and service. In that company with over 3,000 stores, 25 years after I left, my personal sales records had not been broken. You could look at it any way you want to, but if you were as hungry as I was back then and the more services you could perform for your prospective customers, the more sales you could make, you would have gone out of your way as I did to create services you could perform.

I used to think how much more successful I would have been if I had only one leg. Can you imagine how much that prospective customer would owe me after I had hopped on one leg to the other end of that store to get two or three chairs and hopped all the way back?

In those days, almost all customers came to the store to make their payments and we had a space in the top right hand corner of their ledger cards where it said how much their credit limit was. The salespeople in that company all felt that collecting payments wasn't their job, and they avoided payment customers like the plague. But from the very first, I couldn't run far enough fast enough to take a payment. I would ask these customers what they would be needing next. After they had left, I would get the price of what they wanted next, go to the payment line on their ledger card to find when their balance would be low enough for them to add that product to their account and write what they wanted next in code on that line so only I knew what it was.

When they came in to make that payment, I would say, "Mrs. Jones, I was thinking about you this morning when I was going over my ledger cards. I remembered you telling me you needed a new bedroom group (or whatever). We have a special on bedroom furniture right now and I could put the one you seemed to like the best on your account without even raising your payments. Let me show it to you." I don't think I ever failed to make one of those sales.

I always walked my customers to their cars. When it was raining, I kept a golf umbrella handy so I could keep them dry. In no time I was making more money than the store manager. I don't know that I was the best salesperson in the company or even a really good salesperson. I do know that I was rendering more services for my satisfied customers and prospective customers than the next 50 salespeople combined and I was getting the order almost every time. Yes, every mother did wish that her daughters would marry someone just like me.

Going out of the way to render a service or to perform an act of common courtesy is a thing of the past because it is beneath the dignity of most salespeople today to have anyone think that they are subservient to the needs of a prospective customer, and yet, that is the only reason they have their jobs. It has been so long since anyone has done these things in many companies that most salespeople today have never heard of service and courtesy being the basis of their jobs.

I started realizing how important this was to selling when I made my first trip to the Chicago furniture market as a buyer while still in my teens. I was looking at a suit in the window of a men's store on Michigan Avenue.

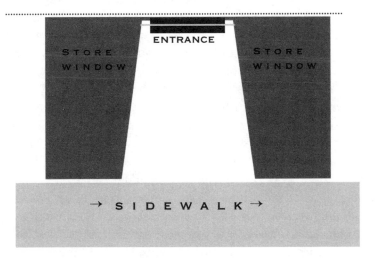

Later, I realized that this window had been designed to make customers think they were standing outside the store and just window shopping when, in fact, the store showrooms actually started the minute a person had crossed the line to look in the window. The door to the showroom was recessed over 30 feet from where the front of the store was. The owner came out the door, walked out on the sidewalk and then approached me from the street side as I was looking at the suit.

He said, "Young man, you must be a perfect 38 long." (Looking at me today you might find that hard to believe, but at that time I was.) He continued, "You look so good in that suit you have on that I would be proud if someone who looked that good was wearing one of my suits."

That was over 45 years ago and I can still remember how this man made me feel with that compliment. At that point, he reached out and knocked a deadly spider off of my shoulder and quickly squashed it under his foot as he said, "Goodness, you had a spider on your shoulder!" What do you owe a man who has just risked his own life to save yours from a deadly spider?

I remember how he brushed some lint off of my other shoulder as he bent to straighten the flap on my coat pocket. Yes, he sold me a suit and for many years I scheduled myself through Chicago just so I could buy my clothes from him. When I married, my wife wondered why I went so far out of my way. It was hard to explain how good I felt no matter where I was in the world knowing that there was a seller of mens' suits in Chicago who was proud of the way that I looked in his suits. Besides, he had saved my life on six different occasions from deadly spiders.

You can laugh about this and yes, I did come to realize that he was creating the deadly spiders, but by then I had come to know him so well that I knew that if there really was one he would risk his life to save mine, and I liked to see him stay in practice.

Back in those days, service beyond the call of duty had been perfected to a gentle art form by the true masters of the profession, but its' a lost art today. Did it work back then? Yes, it worked and it caused prospective customers like me standing outside window shopping with no intentions of even looking inside not only to go inside, but to buy those things that would best meet my needs and become satisfied customers. So satisfied that I continued to return to buy again and to send others to buy from that master salesman until the day he died.

Will it work today? In those days common courtesy was common and salespeople had to perform services beyond the call of duty to out-perform their competitors and reap the benefits of their efforts. Today, there is almost no courtesy shown by salespeople and a prospective customer would go into shock if someone performed a service that was beyond the call of duty. By comparison, those services and courtesies that worked 45 years ago, and made extra sales, will work far better today and make even more sales.

I frequently walk down into the audience when speaking and say to a woman, "How often have you been sitting in your car in front of a store when it's pouring down rain waiting for it to let up and had a salesperson come out with a big golf umbrella to usher you inside just as dry as can be? Has that happened to you a lot lately?"

When the laughter dies down, they always answer, "No, it has never happened to me and if it did, I would probably drop dead."

I then say, "But if it did happen, how would it make you feel?"

Common courtesy costs you nothing, but in selling, it pays giant dividends.

It is easy for the salesperson to learn almost anything he or she wants to know about customers buying a new car today. The salesperson should learn how many miles each year the customers drove their last car and about when they will be ready to replace the car he or she just sold them and/or be ready to buy another vehicle for another member of the family.

Most new cars need check-ups and minor service every so many miles and most of this work is done under warranty. The salesperson could have an appointment with a satisfied customer to pick up their car and take it in for service, leaving a demonstrator to be used until the customer's car is returned on the salesperson's way home. If I were an automobile salesperson, I can assure you that any time I saw anyone driving a brand that I sold with a competitor's name on it, I would get that prospective customer's name and see if I could make an appointment to pick it up, have it serviced in my shop and returned, leaving my new demonstrator for that customer to use.

By the time these prospective customers were ready to buy again, I would know a hundred times more about them and their needs than that joker who had sold them that car and I would have performed so many services they would have to buy from me. I would have caused these satisfied customers to become dissatisfied with their original salesperson while I made them my satisfied customers. It sure beats hanging around with the losers in the lounge trying to think up new names for a bunch of people who waste their time just looking and kicking tires, who certainly aren't customers to them.

Professional salespeople don't wait for the opportunity to arise to perform services beyond the call of duty.

In today's crime-infested world when customers—especially a woman or mothers with small children—are walked to their car, helped with the children, having the door opened for them, being asked to be sure and buckle up, and then seen safely on their way, it is bound to make that customer dissatisfied with where he or she has done business before and determined to return to that salesperson when needs arise.

"Let me hold that door for you. Let me look that number up for you. Let me carry that for you. Let me see if I can find out for you. Let me see if I can get that done for you." Yes, there are thousands of opportunities going to waste every day to be of service beyond the call of duty.

What I have discovered is that salespeople who won't take these opportunities when they arise are the same salespeople who don't take the opportunities to improve their own competence when those opportunities arise. As more and more managements are made aware of these two facts, salespeople who don't take these opportunities will find it harder and harder to hold a selling job and harder and harder to get a selling job.

Don't worry about this if you already have a job selling and the company doesn't expect improvement or require service beyond the call of duty, because that company won't be there very long anyway.

"No, I am not going to let you do that Mr. and Mrs. Customer, because that's *my* job," will be the secret of success in selling as we enter the 21st century.

We find all different kinds of ways to perform service beyond the call of duty in different fields of selling. When all of the salespeople and employees in a company have the same objective, which is a *satisfied* customer, new ways to perform services beyond the call of duty will turn up every day. Each time someone does anything that works, that person should tell the other salespeople in the company. When it is working for everybody, a way to make it work even better will pop up. Contrast the effect of this group of salespeople with common objectives to the losers in the lounge who say, "That's not my job."

To the extent these services beyond the call of duty are performed with competence, with genuine sincerity, and with no strings attached, they will bond a satisfied customer even more to the company and that salesperson. It will make selling them, their friends, relatives and business acquaintances much easier and take the salesperson a lot less time to do so.

One last reason for doing these things. Psychologists know that it really is more blessed and rewarding to give than to receive. Giving these services that are above and beyond the call of duty costs the salesperson nothing, but they sure make him or her feel a whole lot better, while making selling a lot more fun.

Tragically, the losers in the lounge aren't proud of what they do and they don't have much fun doing it. They aren't in the business of selling.

SECTION III

INTRODUCTION TO THE BOOK OF KNOWLEDGE

> IGNORANT: ONE WHO DOES NOT KNOW.
> IGNORAMUS: ONE WHO DOES NOT KNOW, BUT PRETENDS TO KNOW.
> *Funk & Wagnall Standard Dictionary*

THE TECHNICAL BASIS OF SELLING IS SUPPLYING THE INFORMATION THE PROSPECTIVE CUSTOMER NEEDS TO MAKE THE BEST BUYING DECISION.

THE PROBLEM UP UNTIL NOW is that the knowledge and information needed has never been fully defined. Consequently, you find almost nothing in any book on selling about what you need to know; why you need to know it; or how to learn it. I have almost four hundred books on selling in my library. If you took everything out of those books telling what knowledge and information a salesperson will need, why it is needed, and how to get it, and eliminated duplications—what was left wouldn't amount to more than two or three pages. For the most part all those pages would tell you is that you must love what you sell and know everything there is to know about it. That is equivalent to saying that if you want to be a surgeon, you must love cutting on people and know everything there is to know about it.

Specifically, the salesperson needs to know *what* it is that they need to know about what he or she sells and *why* he or she needs to know it. Then, the salesperson needs a plan for acquiring this information, which none of these books offer, thus salespeople are lead to believe that knowing their product is all the knowledge and information they need.

To compound this problem, much of the knowledge and information needed is constantly changing.

For example, in real estate, properties are coming on the market and being sold hourly. No real estate salesperson will ever start a new day with the same inventories or prices as the day before. Yet, his or her success depends on their ability to help prospective customers find and buy those properties that are going to best meet their needs. This changing inventory problem is obvious in real estate, but to some degree, this happens constantly in all fields of selling.

The technology in computers advances so rapidly that by the time a "new, advanced" model gets to the marketplace, newer advanced models have already been developed that make it obsolete. This example, too, is easy to understand when we talk of computers, but to some degree, all things that we sell are being improved and changing creating a need for up-to-date knowledge and information.

When you read the chapter entitled, "Who Can Succeed in Selling," you saw that the good old boy's knowledge was knowing what caused customers to become dissatisfied with carpet as much as his knowledge of carpet. You saw in "Your Road to Selling Success" and "The Best Kept Secret in Selling" that it was the prospective customers' dissatisfaction with what they were using compared to the benefits of what was being sold that caused them to buy. Without this broad base of previous and current knowledge and information, none of the skills needed to achieve the first six objectives can be achieved.

Why aren't more salespeople professionally competent? Because very few salespeople know what they need to know. They have no plan to routinely follow that would get them this knowledge and information, much less keep it up to date.

If you start trying to sell before you have the basic knowledge and information you need to develop the basic skills needed to achieve your first six objectives, it will be a mistake. If you are using your yardstick, you may succeed, but it will take you far longer to become professionally competent. Chances are, too, that you will never succeed to the level that you could, had you gained this basic knowledge and information first. The reason that you can't will be due to the fact that without it, counterproductive habits will soon be developed which will impede your progress.

When people choose any career other than a sales career they know they are going to have to gain some specialized knowledge and develop productive skills. They know that a lot of their time and a lot of their money will be required.

It currently costs $6,000 tuition and requires 600 hours of classroom training to learn how to be a welder. People pay $5,000 to $10,000 tuition and attend 40 hours a week for nine months to become a beautician. Three thousand dollars and 300 classroom hours are what it takes to learn how to become a bartender. Most people go into debt to get their education with no income while they are studying. If they do have income, it is usually because they are putting in twelve- to eighteen-hour days. Upon graduation, if they can get a job, not one of the above could hope to earn half of what any commissioned salesperson (who had the basic knowledge and information and the basic productive skills needed) would be earning almost from the day he or she started. Those salespeople who go on to become professionally competent can expect to be earning what the average doctor earns.

I am not talking about "selling" as most people have been led to believe, but about a career in the business of selling.

People with limited formal educations—often without high school educations—who have gained the specialized knowledge they needed and developed the productive skills they needed to become professionally competent have gone on the become some of the highest-paid people in the world.

The basic education needed in many fields of selling is no more than knowing how to add, subtract, divide, multiply, and read and write with some degree of competence.

Getting the basic knowledge and information needed to develop the basic skills in most fields of selling doesn't require the time it takes to learn most trades. Once a salesperson gains the basic knowledge and information, then he or she begins to practice. If the yardstick is accurately used from the very first day and the instructions in this book are followed, the salesperson can expect his or her income to double the national average while most are still in trade schoolrooms.

If a person has chosen selling as a career and he or she is not willing to make the effort on their own to gain the basic knowledge and information before they start trying to sell—even if it means working for nothing or borrowing money to do it—they are not likely to succeed. The reason is simple. A personal commitment must be made.

The more education you have had, the more fields of selling will be open to you. But having a doctorate will not make you a competent salesperson. You will still need five groups of specialized knowledge in your chosen field of selling and much of that can only be learned in the company where you will be selling. (Novices: Refer to the chapter, "Getting the Job That is Best for You.")

The odds are that the company you work for will have some sales training programs in place. Do not be surprised if these programs consist of little more than instructing how to write and process and order. Whatever the programs, you must support them wholeheartedly. Whether or not the company has a plan for you to learn what you must learn doesn't really matter. *You must learn it* and this book and its plan only make it easier for you to do that. When you're ready to make that commitment to yourself, you are ready to start on a career that will put you in the business of selling.

You will need five basic groups of knowledge. And the more of this knowledge and information you have, the more competent you will become and the easier it will be to make a sale.

- Know how things get done in your company—who does it and who gets them to do it.
- Know your product
- Know your inventories and availabilities
- Know your terms
- Know your advertising

You saw in the chapter entitled "The Principle of Reflection" that when you looked at a retail showroom you saw everything while *seeing* nothing. Learning is the same. You don't learn arithmetic and English in the same classroom at the same time. You may only learn a little about each subject in a separate class each day, but you must focus only on that subject while in that class.

So it is with the five groups of knowledge. You must focus on each of them one at a time. And, you must do so according to a plan. You cannot merely tell yourself, "I'm going to learn something today."

Only two things cause improvement in selling: 1. The salesperson's specialized knowledge and information increases; and 2. The salesperson's productive skills improve. Productive skills can *only* improve as the specialized knowledge and information increases.

20 / Learning How Things Get Done in Your Company

HOW IS IT POSSIBLE FOR PROFESSIONALLY COMPETENT SALESPEOPLE TO FEEL THEY HAVE THE FINEST DELIVERY AND SERVICE WHILE THE AVERAGE SALESPEOPLE IN THE SAME COMPANY FEEL THEY HAVE THE WORST?

MOST HIGHEST-PAID, HIGHEST-VOLUME salespeople in the world today started in the "back end" of the company where they work. Often, in the warehouse or delivery. They worked their way up through other company areas before they started to sell. They knew how things got done in their companies, who did what and who got them to do it. Consequently, they learned far more about what seemed to best meet customers' needs and what caused them to become satisfied customers. Equally important, they learned far more about what caused customers to become dissatisfied. They knew that most customer dissatisfaction was created by salespeople. If the company you sell for has a plan for you to gain this vital information before you start selling, it will make acquiring this knowledge much easier. If not, remember that it is essential to your success.

If you wanted to be a medical doctor, you would borrow the money, if necessary, to get the education you need, right? You would be better off volunteering to work with no pay in each area of your company until you understood how things got done, who did what and who got them to do it—even if you had to borrow the money to afford it. (And this would be just as vital to a salesperson who is switching companies.) A minimum of one day actually working in each area is required. Ideally, you should work in each area as long as it takes to thoroughly understand what is going on. If your business is with a manufacturing firm, working in the factory and customer service—even sweeping floors—gains you essential knowledge.

An expert furniture designer I knew in the 50s did all of his work in his company's factory at night using the factory's equipment to build samples. His success gained him an international reputation, while many a designer's designs weren't produced because the equipment needed wasn't available. Knowing what a factory can do was critical to his success and it is just as critical for the professionally competent salesperson.

You should never be permitted by management nor should you allow yourself even to try and make your first sale before you have a basic knowledge of how things get done in your company, who does it, and who gets them to do it. That includes the credit department, inventory, warehousing, delivery or shipping, and advertising. Without knowledge of all these areas you are not competent to help any prospective customer. Skip this learning process and it will virtually guarantee that you will have developed your few effective selling skills into effective counterproductive selling habits that will doom your career before you can get it started.

Whenever I interviewed long-term, average salespeople, I asked them if they had competitors with better delivery and credit terms. Every one said, "Yes." I asked if they lost sales because of this. They said, "Of course." I asked if it was a lot of sales and they said, "Yes sir, a lot of sales!"

In the same companies when I asked those same questions of top professionally competent salespeople they said "no" to every question. To make this even more interesting, on a number of occasions I was able to go to one of the competitors who the average salespeople told me had so much better terms and delivery that they lost sales to them—and I asked the other company's salespeople the same questions. I got the same answers out of both the long-term, average salespeople and from professionally competent salespeople.

How could some salespeople in a company think they had the best terms and the best delivery of anyone, while others felt they had terrible delivery and terms that caused them to lose lots of sales to competitors who supposedly had far better terms and delivery?

Surveys consistently show that about 75 percent of customers who have become so dissatisfied with a company that they refuse to do business with them again, say it was the salespeople of the company that had caused them to be so dissatisfied, *not* what they had purchased.

They were told or caused to believe someone in the company was going to do something he or she did not do or they hadn't done it when they said they would.

If that happens often to the customers of some salespeople in a company and rarely to the customers of other salespeople in that company, then it must be what some of those salespeople do that causes their customers to get bad service and what the others do that causes theirs to get good service.

No professionally competent salesperson is going to tell a prospective customer what they are buying will do something it won't and can't do.

No professionally competent salesperson is going to tell customers someone in their company is going to perform services that are not going to be performed the way the professionals said they would, when they said they would. Nor is he or she going to leave their customers with any doubts about what services will be performed, how they will be performed, and when. These customers remain *satisfied;* they *don't* complain, and these professionally competent salespeople feel they have the best delivery and service their customers can get anywhere.

When customers are not made correctly aware of what will be done and when it will be done when something does go wrong, they rightfully become dissatisfied. They complain to the salesperson, who blames the people who were supposed to perform the services. The salesperson feels his company gives the worst service and everyone else has better services.

There are many, many reasons why these long-term, average salespeople's customers become dissatisfied with a company's services, but most of these problems were the result of that salesperson's incompetence, which caused the customer to lose confidence. These incompetents tend not to tell their customers some things for fear of losing the sale. They will not tell customers other things they need to know about what they can expect in the way of service, because the incompetents often don't know. They will promise something will be done and when it will be done, that can't possibly be done. Sometimes this is promised even though they *know* it can't or won't be done. More often than not, a time factor is promised by the incompetent, that is unrealistic and can't be met.

Knowing everything you possibly can about the services your company offers customers is not only critical to your success, but no other knowledge can help you avoid so much grief or aggravation.

You must know everything about the people who perform services in your company, why they do what they do, and how. These people will be your best source for that information. Working with them long enough to get a good idea of what you need to know is a must. Learning from them what you can do to make it easier for them to do their jobs, as well as what causes them the most problems, is some of the most valuable information you as a salesperson can ever have.

When someone in service or delivery has a problem with one of your customers, you can blame it on them, blame it on the customer, blame it on what you sell, complain to the boss, bitch about it to the losers in the lounge, and none of that will solve the problem. It will only cause it to get worse, a whole lot worse. Or you can go to those in service and delivery, ask them if there was anything you did that caused the problem. Find out how you might have prevented it, and your services are only going to get better. And like all professionals, you will soon find you have the finest services your customers can find anywhere, the quality of service you must have if your are to achieve your goal and wind up with a *satisfied* customer.

Follow that plan and you are going to gain more of the knowledge and information you need to make your job easier, and you'll also eliminate a lot of grief. Even more important, you will form more and more of a bond with the people who have to do the things that make your customers even more satisfied.

It does not matter how competent your service people are or how hard they try to satisfy your customers. If the customers expect them to do something they can't do or are not supposed to do, those customers are going to be *dissatisfied.*

When those average salespeople said their company had lousy service and it cost them a lot of sales, they were telling the truth.

When the top salespeople in that same company said their company had the finest service of anyone, they were telling the truth, too.

What neither of them realized is that it was the salesperson who had made those service people succeed or fail, productive or counterproductive.

Remember, the prospective customer of a *salesperson* who effectively achieved the first four objectives would sometimes take one look at what was going to best meet his or her needs and say, "I'll take it," without the salesperson having promised that the product or the company would do anything at all.

But guided tour directors start right in promising that what the prospective customer was looking at would do things for them and the company would do things for them, too. Because these tour directors are not aware of the prospective customer's needs, they have promised that the product would do more and the company would do more than they actually can. If the tour director gets the sale, his or her customer winds up getting less than was promised and becomes dissatisfied because of that. Meanwhile, professionals have promised very little by the time they get the order, so their customers wind up getting far more than they had been led to expect.

The competent professional *never* promises, presents, or demonstrates any more of what he or she is selling than it takes to get the order. Once the professional gets the order, only then does he or she show the customer how much more can be expected from what was bought and how much better the services will be, as the salesperson reinforces the sale.

Weak salespeople whose delivery will take several days, weeks, or even months, will often promise much quicker delivery to get the order, figuring that somehow someone can stall the customer.

When I was selling, it usually took us two days to get something delivered locally and up to ten days out of town. I say "up to ten days" because we scheduled our out-of-town deliveries over a ten-day period. Truth was, the next delivery schedule for someone making a purchase for out-of-town delivery could even go out the next day or any time within those ten days. I knew those schedules. I knew what day every customer's out-of-town purchase would go out.

So whenever I got to the question of delivery, if it was local and I said they could have it in two days, they would want it sooner. So, I would say, "I could have your goods delivered one week from today," That was not a lie. I simply under promised. I don't recall ever having anyone who didn't object to that promise. When they did, I always said "let me check to see if perhaps I can squeeze you in sooner." When I came back and told them I could have it in their home by day after tomorrow, they were overjoyed and a much more *satisfied* customer. On out-of-town deliveries, whatever the date of the next delivery truck in their area, I would say I could have it delivered ten days after that. And I *could*. When the customers screamed bloody murder, I said, "Let me see if there is anyway possible for me to get it to you sooner." When I came back and told them it could be there ten days sooner, they were overjoyed, and I had made them much more satisfied customers. I gave my customers a choice. When I said one week and then delivered in two days, they were overjoyed. If I'd said two days and taken a week, they would never be as satisfied.

You can't do that if you do not have all the information you need on deliveries.

In many selling situations the buyer may need services your company does not perform. The professional will know far more about who performs those services, how competent they are, what their schedules are, and how competitive their fees are. Having this information readily at hand is an important service the salesperson performs for a prospective customer.

Most of the time, the prospective customer will not buy until he or she is sure of the availability of and costs for these services. No professional is going to take a chance on that. It may take the salespeople some time to get enough of this information to be able to give their prospective customers the options and permit them to select the service that best meets their needs. Left on their own, it would take customers as long or longer to get this information, and the odds are they would never have as much of this information as the professional salesperson who gets it once and has it ready for every customer from then on.

When competent professionals make their customers aware of the need for the service, and show them their options, they have made it far easier for these prospective customers to say "yes."

Service is a *benefit*. And that means it is a part of the *value* of what is being sold. Every service included in the salesperson's price must be treated as a feature. Prospective customers must be made aware of their need for the benefits of the services during the salesperson's efforts to achieve the second objective. Then prospective customers are shown how these services make the product best meet their needs. When you have this knowledge and develop these productive skills and use them effectively the same way every time, you will become more and more productive. Only then will you discover that those in your company who perform services for your customers truly are the best. After all, it's your service and delivery department because it's *your* business when you are in the business of selling.

21 / *Knowing Your Product*

IF SALESPEOPLE DON'T KNOW HOW TO MAKE A BASIC PRESENTATION OF THE
BENEFITS OF THE FEATURES OF WHAT THEY SELL IN A SET SEQUENCE, THEY
HAVE NO BUSINESS APPROACHING A PROSPECTIVE CUSTOMER BECAUSE MOST
OF WHAT THEY WILL DO WILL BE COUNTERPRODUCTIVE.

WHEN I SEE FURNITURE SALESPEOPLE carrying a tapemeasure with them, I always ask them, "Why?" They say so they can measure things for their prospective customers. I walk over to a dinette display and say, "In other words, if a prospective customer wishes to know how high the table is you get out your tapemeasure and measure it?"

They say, "yes."

I squat down so my eyes are level with the tops of the tables and look out across them. "These tables are all the same height. Do you suppose you could memorize that height once and then when your prospective customer asks you can be an expert instead of a flunky or an ignoramous?"

Then I ask them how many different widths and lengths of tables there are. Tables rarely come in more than three widths and three lengths. I ask how many different sizes their leaves come in (usually two and never more than three). I ask them how many different sizes their round tables come in (usually two, never more than three). Now, this is information these salespeople are going to need with almost every prospective dinette customer they come in contact with. It is *information* anyone can learn once, and because it is used all the time, that salesperson can look at any table or leaf and tell you every dimension. When salespeople can give the prospective customer this specialized information without having to look it up or measure it, that gives the prospective customer more confidence in them. When the salespeople do not have the information ready, of course the prospective customer loses confidence.

This knowledge and information is basic. Perhaps 80 percent of the knowledge and information you need to make any sale is *basic*. You need it every time!

I have heard salespeople say, "I couldn't possibly learn the size of every table I sell." Like most products, dinette tables for the most part come in only a few standard widths and lengths, generally in six-inch increments. Anyone can tell the difference between a 36-inch and a 42-inch round table top from some distance. That is true of most products where size is a consideration for the prospective customer.

I was visiting once with the salespeople in a retail furniture company in Ocean City, Maryland. Most of their prospective customers were buying all the furniture they would need for new condominiums. I asked the salespeople if their prospective customers usually needed measurements of what they were looking at so they could go back to their apartments to see if the furniture would fit. They said, yes, that was almost always the case.

When I asked, "Why?" they looked at me with blank expressions. Again, I asked, "Why?" When no one answered, I said, "I arrived in this city at four o'clock yesterday. I stopped at three real estate offices on my way to the hotel." I held up a sheaf of paper. "Here are the floor plans of almost every condominium with the measurements of every room in Ocean City."

Surely you can see the difference in making a sale when you have this information that you are going to need with almost every prospective customer, not to mention the selling time it will save you. It is the difference in your being an expert in the eyes of your customer and being ignorant. Don't take offense at the word "ignorant"—that doesn't mean stupid, it simply means "one who doesn't know."

What is the one fact all salespeople must know in order to complete the sale of anything? The price. It is a rare salesperson anywhere who can tell you the price of what he or she is selling without hunting for the price tag or looking up the product on a list. Nothing these people do causes prospective customers to lose more confidence more quickly.

I have bought millions of dollars worth of products at markets. When I walk into a showroom I am not acquainted with, I always ask to see the best-selling product. If the salesperson can't tell me, I leave. It could not be much of a product line if the salesperson doesn't at least know that. I will guarantee you that for every salesperson who can tell me the price of only the best sellers there will be many, and I do mean *many*, who can't. When they do tell me what their best-selling product is and I ask the price, if they can't tell me, I leave. It could not be much of a value if they don't know, and I don't have the time to waste while an ignorant salesperson hunts for his price list to look it up.

Ask yourself how you react when a salesperson doesn't have simple, basic information when you ask for it. Any salesperson selling anything, large or small. I'll bet you react the same way I do when I am a prospective customer. (You may not react as strongly—or you may react even more strongly—but you have the same negative reaction and no positive communication is going to take place.)

How many times I have heard salespeople say, "Mr. Lawhon, we have over 200 reclining chairs [or some other product] in our showrooms, how could I learn all those prices?" I ask how many different price points they have, and how many mechanisms. They rarely have more than six different prices and three different mechanisms. "How many different models do you have? 30, 40, maybe 50? You really only have 30 or 40 different chairs, in six price points, with three different mechanisms. The rest are duplications in other colors."

It wouldn't take anyone thirty minutes of one day on three different days to learn those prices. Thirty minutes of your time when you have no prospective customers to wait on, but I can guarantee you one thing: in your efforts to learn those prices you are going to have to learn something more about each chair. That's right. You will have to learn something more about the chair so you can remember the price, and when you have memorized the price and learned enough about each chair to be able to remember its price, you will know more about your reclining chairs than most of the reclining chair salespeople in the world today.

My point: There are exceptions to almost everything, but there are no exceptions when it comes to knowing the price of what you sell. You aren't going to complete any order without including the price. I defy you to find a professionally competent salesperson who can't quote you the price on most of what he or she sells without having to look it up.

While learning the prices of everything you also had to get quite a lot of the other basic information you will need.

Historical knowledge of what you sell is vital. The more you know about how your product has evolved and been improved over the years the better for you. Remember, many big-ticket purchases are only made once every-so-many years. Knowing the improvements made over the past years and why they were made can be critical to selling someone who is replacing an old product. Comparing the benefits of the features and how much better they make the new product meet prospective customers' needs than what they are now using is vital to getting you the sale.

RAW MATERIALS

If there is metal in your product, chances are it has been greatly improved over the years or it may even be one of the new strategic metals that offer truly *superior* benefits to the owner. *Knowing* how it has been improved, and why it makes what you sell better meet the customer's needs, is a must. Every historical improvement in the processing of metal was done to make it do something better for those who own it. That kind of information enables you to paint word pictures in the prospective customers' minds so they can experience the ownership of benefits.

If your product is wood, you can't know too much about a tree. All trees, but especially the trees your wood came from. You must know how and why it was processed the way it was to understand the benefits that are going to better meet the prospective customer's needs. Like fingerprints, no two trees or the patterns of their grains are ever the same. Each is a one-of-a-kind heirloom. Rolls-Royce uses some of the world's most beautiful and expensive woods for the interiors of its cars. A part of every tree that has been used in every Rolls-Royce has been saved, and the serial numbers of the car it was used on recorded. If the wood ever needs to be replaced, Rolls-Royce can supply it from the same tree that the rest of the wood in the car came from. This knowledge, and a whole lot more, makes it possible to sell a Rolls-Royce for $250,000.

Incredible value can be added to products with wood in their construction when you can tell the customers why that particular wood offers benefits that make it far better meet your customer's needs than other woods.

Plastic and Synthetics

The very word "plastic" conjures up "cheap" in most customers' minds. There are forms of plastic today that are stronger than the hardest steel, moldable synthetics that meet customer needs better than any natural materials. Knowing the history of plastic materials and their improvements over the years is not only interesting, but that information adds to your expertise.

One of the fastest-growing health problems in this decade are allergies. Most synthetics are non-allergenic. When they were first introduced in carpet, I sold many a carpet job when I said to my customer, "I have no sons and if my daughters were to present me with a grandson it would be one of the happiest days of my life. If there was one chance in a million that he was allergic to wool carpet and couldn't come to visit my home, that would be all the reason I would need to buy carpet woven of non-allergenic synthetic fibers."

Synthetics have become so much a part of our world that salespeople assume customers know everything there is to know about them. Not one salesperson in a thousand is consciously aware that synthetics are mostly non-allergenic. Professional salespeople who have products with any non-allergenic components always ask questions that make their customers consciously aware of the allergy problems almost everyone has today. Then they demonstrate how what they sell is non-allergenic. That one feature and its benefits often gets the sale.

When the first Corvettes were made, their fiberglass bodies would warp and split in the summer sun of Arizona. Getting them repaired was nearly impossible and was very costly. Today, the materials used are in many ways superior to steel. What is that material? What is it made of? How is it made? How has it been improved over the years?

Forty years ago, the number one problem with fabric was fading. Technical terms like "heat set dyed," "solution dyed," and so on, that we throw at our prospective customers describe two processes that put the color inside a nonporous fiber. In other words, when the nylon is in liquid form, color is added to the liquid before it is converted to fibers. The color is inside as if it were in colored glass. It *can't* fade. The technology used in plastic and synthetics, even those mixed with or used on natural materials to improve the benefits, is improving daily.

Every improvement means better benefits.

The salespeople who are on top of these improvements have products to sell that will far better meet their prospective customers' needs than the salesperson who is not up-to-date on this knowledge even though they are selling the same product. Only the salespeople with this knowledge can get the sale when earlier synthetics had caused customer dissatisfaction.

What is true of plastics and synthetics is true of all components. Electronics and computers are prime examples. Dolby, chips, watts, bytes, ROM—this is technical terminology everyone hears, but not one in a thousand prospective customers has any comprehensive understanding of how it makes some things better meet their needs. Professional salespeople never fail to make their prospective customers aware of the benefits, then put those technical terms into words the prospective customer can easily comprehend as the salesperson demonstrates how the benefits of modern-day electronic miracles make what they sell better meet the prospective customer's needs.

Antilock brakes, disc brakes, hydropneumatic suspension, four-wheel independent suspension, electronic ignition: "Everybody has them, everybody knows about them." Baloney! Translate those terms into language that the prospective customer can understand and you will make more sales easier, while having your prospective customer actually experience the ownership of those benefits.

Note: Historic as well as up-to-date state-of-the-art knowledge is most important to the real estate salesperson. Efficiency and security factors have changed almost every element of new structures, while the old, solid qualities of historic properties are increasingly desirable and valuable.

DESIGN

Music appreciation and art appreciation are two courses taught in colleges and universities. If we are going to help another person learn to appreciate music or art, we must be able to appreciate music and art ourselves. We cannot do this unless we have told our ears what to hear or our eyes what to see. The better we have described what we want our ears to hear, eyes to see, and inner self to feel, the more of the benefits we experienced of what was heard, seen, and felt. To the degree that salespeople describe these things to their own senses and experience those benefits, the better they will be able to describe them to their prospective customers.

• • •
• • •
• • •
All designs are works of art. Their objective is to make what is being sold esthetically more desirable while not interfering with its function. (That's very important.) If design improves function, that is the ultimate achievement.

We describe home styles as Mediterranean, Early American, Contemporary, Victorian, or Southwestern. The professional knows that the more Mediterranean, Early American, or Contemporary it is to the person attracted to the style, the more benefit value it has. Design features are pointed out and their historical significance described, causing the prospective customer to see more of what they like. Even the smallest and seemingly least important elements of design can often be made the most important to the owner. We call these "conversation pieces." They are unique, often concealed elements of design that the owners are able to tell their friends about. I know that a sliding panel concealing a secret drawer in the design of a piece of furniture was always very exciting to my prospective customers. This is important information for a salesperson to have and to use.

• • •
• • •
The historical background of various design styles is of vital importance to the expert. Understand the history of what you are selling. It adds romance to the value of the product. That's why salespeople love what they sell and, often are said to be "romancing it" with their presentations. My wife says that if I am able to put my arm around what I am selling, I can sell it.

DETAILS

The way a seam fits, the number of stitches per inch, the effect of damaging sun-ray reduction due to tinted glass, a dit here and a dot there, can all be seemingly insignificant details to most salespeople, yet any one of them could be the very reason a prospective customer buys.

FUNCTION

What a product does, how it does it, and why. Every function of what you sell is there to meet the needs of your prospective customer. The salesperson must not only know what the function is, how and why it does what it does, but that salesperson must have experienced the benefits of these functions with all of his or her senses to the fullest extent possible. Salespeople should be constantly on the lookout for any new needs that any function of what they sell might meet. This gives more people more reasons to buy and makes selling easier.

One day, I received an envelope with a nut in it and a letter that said, "This is the nut we are using on a chair that goes with a new dinette that we will be introducing at the market." It went on to tell how superior the quality of the nut was compared to what was used on most dinettes, and wound up saying that if I would keep the nut, I would receive another letter that would show me how they used it. A few days later, another letter arrived with a bolt. The letter described the superior quality of the bolt and said that if I would keep it I would be receiving a letter that showed me how the nut and bolt would be used on the new dinette chair. Over a period of about 90 days, parts kept arriving one at a time with letters telling what made each part superior to anything found in any dinette chair. The day the final part arrived, which completed the chair, the sales manager arrived to get my order ahead of the market introduction. I am glad he did, because that was the number-one selling dinette chair for years. I tell this story to make a point. When they got through, I had assembled that chair in my office and knew everything there was to know about it. I mean every nut, bolt, and part.

I showed my salespeople the letters and parts as they arrived. Before we were through, they knew more about that dinette chair than any salesperson had ever known about a dinette chair. It was the most expensive set we carried and it was the easiest set for them to sell.

When you know that much about what you sell, what every component does, and why it does it, you will find it easy to sell. When I say "know what you sell inside and out," that's what I mean. Will you ever need *all* of that information to make a sale? No, probably never, but, but, but, you will *never* and I mean *never* know in advance which part of it you *will* need to make the sale.

How can salespeople know that much about what they sell when they begin? Most of the time they can't, but they must have at least the basic information when they begin and they should *never* stop learning about what they sell if they are to remain in the business of selling and succeed at it.

Selling never gets old to the salesperson who keeps on learning. As long as you are learning, you are growing. When you stop learning, you stop growing, and you start to rot and tragically, all things get old to those in selling.

Always study what you sell from the standpoint of how you will make your presentation. The presentation, like all productive skills, should be done in the same sequence every time. Of course, the yardstick will help you determine what works, what works better, and what is counterproductive. It will keep you improving your presentation as long as you continue to use it. It is far better when several salespeople can get together with their checklists of features and benefits to discuss what is most productive for them as well as the sequence to follow when making a sale. Just like a golf swing: No two will ever be exactly alike, but the objective and goal of each golfer is the same. Even the tiniest of tips can have a dramatic effect on your selling career. The degree to which you are able to perfect your productive skills will be determined by the amount of specialized knowledge you have gained.

The technical basis of selling is supplying the knowledge and information needed to help your customers make the best buying decision. No salesperson ever has or ever will lose a sale because he or she knew too much about what they sold. No one will ever know how many sales were lost because the salesperson didn't know enough.

22 / *Knowing Your Inventories*

THOSE SALESPEOPLE WHO HAVE THE INFORMATION THEY NEED WHEN THEY NEED IT ARE SEEN AS EXPERTS BY THE PROSPECTIVE CUSTOMER. THIS CAUSES THEIR PROSPECTIVE CUSTOMERS TO HAVE CONFIDENCE IN THEM AND BUILDS THEIR TRUST.

THOSE SALESPEOPLE WHO DO NOT HAVE THE INFORMATION AND MUST GET IT (EVEN IF IT'S ONLY A PRICE, INVENTORY, OR MEASUREMENT) ARE SEEN AS FLUNKIES BY THE PROSPECTIVE CUSTOMER AND IT CAUSES THEM TO HAVE NO CONFIDENCE OR TRUST IN THE SALESPERSON.

PROSPECTIVE CUSTOMERS DO NOT BUY FROM THOSE THEY DON'T TRUST.

KNOWING WHAT YOU HAVE, WHAT YOU CAN GET AND WHEN YOU CAN GET IT

I SPEND A LOT OF MY TIME BETWEEN FLIGHTS in airports at airline clubs. I overhear salesmen on the phone trying to get prices, inventory and shipping information. It is easy for me to figure out that they have called on a prospective customer, possibly made a sale depending on their ability to supply something on time. They are in the airport on their way to their next destination without having made the sale. Once they get the information, they must try to get the sale on the phone or fly back for another meeting with the prospective customer.

I can't help but overhear these calls because the people are usually so frustrated in their efforts to get the information they need that their voices are raised. In selling situations, you would think salespeople would have learned everything they possibly could about their customers and their needs *before* starting on the trip, including knowing everything they possibly could about current inventories and availabilities, what shipping schedules were, and their alternatives.

If this salesperson on the telephone at the airport makes the sale, which is doubtful, it will be at much greater cost in time and money. Those salespeople reading this who go to prospective customers' work places will easily agree that it would be foolish to spend hundreds of dollars, even thousands, on airlines, hotel, and expenses to make a sales call when you didn't have the information you needed. Everything is a comparison. It is just as foolish for a salesperson to start any sale without the current, basic information he or she needs to complete the sale. With computers, fax machines, and our telephone system capabilities, current information is always available, except when you *need* it. That's right. When you are with the prospective customer and you need information, it always seems that is precisely when you *can't* find anyone who has that information.

The bigger the sale, the less time the prospective buyer has, and the more confidence the buyer must have in the salesperson. When the salesperson doesn't have the necessary information, the buyer's confidence drops with a big thud. That is what happens in every selling situation.

Inventory and availability information is needed to complete any sale. Therefore, it is needed *every* time. The confidence of the salesperson and the trust of the prospective customer goes up or down with the amount of this information the salesperson has. Because this information can change, most salespeople think it is a waste of time to try to keep up with it. Those who master selling review the basic status of their inventories by habit at the same time of day every day. Those with large selections will do so even more often than those with smaller selections and more stable stocks.

Truly professional car salespeople will know every demonstrator on hand. That can give them a reason for calling a prospective customer. They know what their prospective customers are currently driving and when they expect to sell them their next car. When they have prospective customers whose needs would be best met by an automobile that one of their satisfied customers is driving, having a ready buyer for that car makes selling the new one even easier. Reviewing their satisfied customer file cards during downtime can turn up information like this and often make a sale. It sure beats complaining to the losers in the lounge because business is so bad you have no prospective customers.

Master salespeople call this information their "aces in the hole." Knowing there was a canceled order that made needed inventory available could also give a salesperson information needed to call a prospective customer. Why? Because it was information the prospective customer needed. It is even more valuable information when it can be offered at a discount. Knowing the condition of demonstration products and when they will be sold, odd lots, new products coming on the market—these are door openers for the professional who has the information and knows how to use it.

Multilisting can be the greatest thing that ever happened to a real estate salesperson or it can be the worst. It can give the professional an unlimited selection from which to determine the home that will best meet any prospective home buyer's needs or it can take a guided tour director on never ending tours. Never ending, because they rarely result in a sale.

Keep one thing in mind regardless what you sell. No one ever has or ever will lose a sale because he or she knew too much about what was in inventory, what was available, and how soon it could be delivered.

"Ignorant" means only that you "don't know," but that is easily remedied. All you have to do is look it up. Knowing what you need to know by finding out is what distinguishes the experts from those who are ignorant.

Like all five of the groups of knowledge, the more you know about your inventory, the more sales you are going to make and the easier it will be for you to make them. Just remember: It's *your* business to know when you are in the business of selling.

23 / *Advertising Basics*

IT IS THE COMPANY'S JOB TO DELIVER ENOUGH LEADS OR PROSPECTIVE
CUSTOMERS TO GET THE SALESPERSON STARTED. BUT FROM THEN ON,
SALESPEOPLE WHO DO NOT HAVE ENOUGH PROSPECTIVE CUSTOMERS TO KEEP
THEM BUSY ALL OF THE HOURS THAT THEY WISH TO WORK ARE NOT REALLY
IN THE BUSINESS OF SELLING.

WORD OF MOUTH IS THE MOST POWERFUL FORM OF ADVERTISING.

No OTHER ADVERTISING CAN OUTSELL a satisfied customer, who costs the company nothing. The only
thing that can outsell a *satisfied* customer is a *dissatisfied*
customer. They feel cheated and they want revenge.
They will go to much greater lengths to convince people
not to buy from your company than a satisfied customer
will go to persuade people to buy from you.

Research has shown that when customers become dissatisfied with
their purchase over 75 percent of the time it was a salesperson who
caused that dissatisfaction. As a rule, no salesperson would do anything
knowingly that was going to cause a customer to become dissatisfied.
Most of the time, we can trace the cause of customer dissatisfaction to
the salesperson's incompetence.

Often, the source of that incompetence in companies whose
prospective customers are brought in by advertising can be traced to the
salesperson not being fully aware of the advertising and not having a
comprehensive understanding of what was said or implied.

It is unforgivable for salespeople not to know more about their company's advertising than their customer does. Nothing will more quickly
destroy a prospective customer's confidence and trust.

You must read and understand your company's materials and ads.
You should have viewed and heard radio and TV advertising before you
ever come in contact with prospective customers. Billboards and Yellow

Pages are included when I say you must know more about your advertising than your customers do.

Any prospective customer who has read, heard, or seen your advertising has read, seen, and heard the advertising of your competitors. Odds are the competitor's salespeople don't sell fifteen percent of the prospective customers who respond to their ads. That means for every fifteen sales that they made, 85 prospective customers left without buying. To some degree their shopping made them even hotter prospects than when they started out. Most of them will continue shopping. For that reason, professionally competent salespeople will know more about competitor advertising than most of the competitor's salespeople. It is not unusual for a salesperson to receive more prospective customers in their place of business because of a competitor's advertising than from their own.

In every case, whether a prospective customer came to you because of your advertising or a competitor's, that advertising has already started a sale. It has given the prospective customer some reason to take action. Salespeople are either prepared to pick up the sale at that point or they aren't.

Knowledgeable salespeople will tell you that the more specific a customer is in what they say they want, the harder they are to sell. Most prospective customers responding to advertising come to see something specific. Salespeople find these customers harder to sell than the browsers and lookers because they forget they have four objectives to be achieved before they start showing or demonstrating what they are going to sell — even when the prospective customer is specific in what he or she asks for. They take the prospective customer straight to the asked for item, then wonder why they failed to make the sale. You must not only know what was advertised, but you must know what you intend to do and say when you get a prospective customer who responds to your advertising. You must have a plan and you must follow it.

Your plan will assume that what was advertised is going to best meet the prospective customer's needs. What two things will you use to establish the comparison? What if the asked for item doesn't meet the prospective customer's needs?

This is not a one-time situation. This is a selling situation that most salespeople will face repeatedly. To handle it effectively requires productive skills. And those skills can only be developed by doing the same thing every time and doing it the same way. As you do, using the yardstick, you see what was productive and you repeat that. What was counterproductive, obviously you do not repeat.

In every case, remember you have four objectives to achieve before you ever arrive at the advertised or asked for product.

Assuming that product will best meet the prospective customer's needs, you will have made them as consciously aware of those needs as you could. You will have made them as consciously aware as you could of what they are using now and of their dissatisfaction with it. You must be prepared to take them by two other products on the way to the advertised item, which by comparison is going to best meet their needs.

While achieving your first three objectives, if you determined something other than the asked-for advertised product will best meet their needs, then the asked-for item becomes one of your comparison products.

The guided tour director always hopes his next prospective customer will be what he considers a "good one." To the tour director, the "good ones" are those prospective customers who think they know exactly what they want when they arrive. Problem is, that is the one kind of prospective customer they are least likely to sell. That would be funny if it weren't so tragic for the guided tour director's career.

The next mistake salespeople often make when they take the customer straight to the advertised product makes it even harder for them to get the sale.

If I told you I had some $100 bills I would sell you for $50 you would ask, "Why?" There are only two possible reasons I would do that. The bills are counterfeit or they are hot. Right? Wrong.

I bought my daughter, Amanda, a clear vinyl Bear-Bear stuffed with over $1,000 worth of genuine U.S. currency. I paid $50 for it. The money was shredded at the U.S. Mint and sold to the maker of the bears. So you see, there can be a good reason for selling anything at a discount.

Regardless how often ads are seen that claim huge savings and markdowns, if those savings or markdowns are not based on prices that the products normally sell for, they are fraudulent and violate state and federal laws. I have no advice that will help you overcome false advertising claims. They have nothing to do with the honest business of selling.

Whatever claims are made by your advertising, it is an absolute necessity that you be able to substantiate those claims. This is the law. Even if it wasn't, failing to support advertising claims is the biggest mistake made by salespeople whose prospective customers are responding to reduced price offers.

When something is advertised on sale showing a regular price of $1,000 and a sale price of $500, more often than not customers say, "I want to see that product you have for $500," or "I want to see that $500 product you had in your ad." When the salesperson says, "Right this way, just follow me" he or she is not only on a guided tour, but is also on the way to showing the customer a $500 product on sale for $500.

The first thing this salesperson should do is say, "Pardon me sir, but was it the $1,000 (product) that we have on sale that you can buy for $500?" Remember the prospective customer did not come to buy a $500 product for $500. He or she came in to buy a $1,000 product for $500. That point must be made. Then the question is, "Why?"

"Pardon me, but was it the $1,000 demonstrator you can buy on sale today for $500 that you wanted to see?"

These two points are critical to your relationship with a customer Salespeople must make customers consciously aware of three things:

- **THE REGULAR PRICE**

- **THE SALE PRICE**

- **THE REASON FOR IT**

If they do not, they lose the customers' trust and confidence. They will find it nearly impossible to convince the customer the product is worth $500. When they support the advertising claim that it was a $1,000 product, well worth a thousand dollars, and that the company had a valid reason for selling it for $500, the prospective customer may still not buy because the product doesn't meet his or her needs. But if it does, you'll have no trouble with the price.

Another cardinal sin commonly made by salespeople is not having as much or more knowledge of what the advertising said and meant than the prospective customer. Think about that. If you ran an ad offering $100 bills for $50 each, do you think the prospective customer would read every word of the ad, get excited and rush in to buy? Of course they would, provided you gave them a valid reason why your offer was being made. Then, suppose you had a customer hurrying in asking to see those $100 bills you had on sale, and you turned and yelled back to the office, "Hey, Joe, did we have some $100 bills on sale?" What do you think would happen to that prospective customer's enthusiasm and excitement?

It certainly was not the exciting offer the advertisement said it was if nobody in the company knew what it was or where it was. That is more often the rule today then the exception.

Whether it is a ten-dollar item on sale for five dollars or a million-dollar product on sale for five hundred thousand, the same rules apply.

Real estate agents will say a home has just been reduced by some huge amount and give the prospective home buyer the new reduced price without ever establishing the value of the home at the original price. Given the reason for the reduction, the home was worth the original asking price to someone or it wouldn't have been on the market at that price.

When the price has been reduced only because what was offered has not sold, it doesn't make it *worth* less. But, it does put it within the budget of a lot of prospective customers. They can now own something that will better meet their needs.

But wait! What if the price was reduced because the product was damaged or defective?

In 1963, before computers, I was walking through my upholstered furniture warehouse and discovered 128 Fairfield chairs stacked eight high, which had caused the back cushion of each chair to be crushed and the skirts to be badly wrinkled. At $99.95, they were one of the best selling chairs in the U.S. I had bought them at a special price in factory select covers to sell at $59.95. We were getting ready for our year-end clearance sale, so I had the crew select three chairs in the best condition, take them to the shop and steam the wrinkles out of the skirts and use long needles to work the crushed corners back into shape.

When I did my television commercial, I showed the three perfect chairs and said we had 128 of these nationally advertised $99 Fairfield chairs in your choice of fabrics in our clearance sale for $37 apiece. We did not get a single call. I thought about that and redid the commercials.

I had the warehouse pick out two of the chairs with the most wrinkled skirts and crushed backs along with eight other chairs. In the television studio, I put the eight chairs in a stack the same way they had been in the warehouse, with the worst two on the floor in front of the stack. The commercial started by showing the stack of chairs, then zoomed in and panned down to the corner showing the crushed back and skirts. The camera then cut to closeup shots of the back and skirts of the two worst ones. The commercial went like this.

"I found 128 of these $99.95 Fairfield chairs stacked eight high in our warehouse. When we unstacked them, we discovered the backs and skirts crushed like this. You will find all 128 as part of our clearance sale tomorrow. I am sure that most women watching could take a darning needle and work the corners back into the original shape and use a steam iron to take the wrinkles out of the skirts. If you did, you would own a brand new $99.95 Fairfield chair for $47. They are your choice, $47 each starting in the morning at nine AM when the doors open." (Note: I raised the price from $37 to $47.)

I was in Chicago when the commercial ran. About four o'clock that afternoon I called to see how the sale was going. The 128 chairs were gone before noon. And we had sold almost 400 chairs from our regular stock before the day ended.

When you offer anything at a reduced price, you'd better have a legitimate reason. That reason justifies your price-saving claim. In this case, I was literally saying, "I am selling $99.95 for $47 because anyone with $47 could buy a genuine $99.95 product." Note that I established the chairs' price and value at $99.95 and because the customers believed the offer, when the chairs offered didn't meet their needs, they selected and bought other chairs that did.

If you have a $3,000 rebate on the automobiles you are selling, you must establish your car as being worth the price and even more than you were asking before the rebate. When it has been proven to be the car that best meets the prospective customer's needs, it is worth more than its original price and the $3,000 is in genuine cash savings and it made the price fit many customers' budgets who couldn't have hoped to enjoy the luxuries of such a fine automobile.

If customers believed the half-price claims being made in advertising today, they would tear the walls down to get in. If you really believed you could buy a brand new Cadillac at half price, you would be first in line to buy one. Even if it was only so you could sell it and make a profit.

In 1975, the Cumberland River flooded in Nashville, Tennessee. It went 21 inches over the 100-year flood level. The new Opryland was eight feet under water. My 120,000-square-foot warehouse and showroom had six inches of water covering the floor for four days. Flood insurance was not available. We had gotten most things off the floor, so our inventory was undamaged, but the flood would have meant financial ruin for my young company. The minute the water receded, we went to work 24 hours a day. In four days, we had the carpets stripped and the building floor washed down, dried, and set up for a sale.

I ran a quarter-page ad in black reversed type that said, "Flood sale now going on 24 hours a day until the building is empty." I scheduled ten-second TV commercials saying the same thing. In four days, we sold the building to the bare walls and did almost three month's worth of normal business.

When customers believe savings claims, they come and they buy. Unfortunately today, they are so overwhelmed by unsupported claims they believe few of them. Everyone in the state of Tennessee knew about the flood, so they believed. It is your job as a salesperson to support what is said in your firm's advertising. To the degree that you do, that advertising becomes even more effective.

I worked that flood sale in Nashville around the clock for all four days. I asked hundreds of prospective customers—some had come more than a hundred miles—how they heard about the sale. Most said a friend or relative told them. My own experience over the years convinced me that more people shopped legitimate sales because someone else told them about it than those who had actually seen the ads.

Prospective customers who shop sales and do not buy are far more disappointed than those who are just shopping and don't buy. They tell other people about that disappointment. That causes the company that advertised to have a harder and harder time getting prospective customers to respond another time.

In a customer driven company, no claims are made in advertising that cannot be or are not supported by salespeople. The yardstick tells everyone in the company when something does not work, so it won't be repeated. The salespeople are ultimately responsible for the accuracy and integrity of the yardstick and it will cause everything being done in the company to improve. Salespeople have only one choice. Use the yardstick accurately and watch everything in the company improve or join the losers in the lounge to complain and watch things get worse.

Most salespeople whose prospective customers come to their place of business spend over 75 percent of their working hours waiting for someone to sell to. They will sell fewer than fifteen percent of those they wait on. That means they are productive only about three and a half percent of their working hours. Professionals in the same company often sell over 80 percent of their prospective customers and are booked up with appointments most of their working hours, which makes them productive about 80 percent of their working hours. It is mathematically possible for the competent professional in the same company to do more than 20 times the volume of long-term average salespeople working the same hours.

When salespeople complain about the hours they work, a close inspection shows it wasn't the hours they had worked that they were complaining about. It was the time they put in doing counterproductive negative things. An idle mind is the devil's workshop. These salespeople think it is the company's job to see that they have what they call "good" customers to wait on during their working hours. They assume no responsibility for doing anything when there are no customers.

When salespeople use the customer accounting card, they discover they have something to keep them productive every working hour. In the beginning, it is learning more of what the yardstick has shown that they need to know: working on the skills they need so they are better prepared when they have their next prospective customer contact. As they become more effective and productive, they will be achieving their goals more often, which means they will have more and more follow-up work to do and more satisfied customers to look to for prospective future customers. They will have their own advertising program working for them around the clock.

It is the company's job to deliver enough prospective customers to get you started. But, from then on, the salespeople who do not have enough prospective customers to keep them busy all the hours that they wish to work are not really in the business of selling.

24 / *Selling on Credit*

THE WORLD'S ECONOMY IS CREDIT DRIVEN.
ALMOST ALL MAJOR PURCHASES ARE MADE USING SOME FORM OF CREDIT.

AN ALL BUT FORGOTTEN ELEMENT OF SELLING

TIME WAS WHEN THE MERCHANTS put a lot of their efforts on their first time credit purchases. The merchants knew that once they had satisfied customers coming in every week or month to pay on their accounts they would be able to keep them buying from then on as long as the merchant kept that customer satisfied. Many retailers realized more net profit from the interest charged on their accounts than they did from the sales. The company that did this best was Sears and Roebuck. Their advertising focused on a few key products, and made every effort to sell everyone in the market for those few products.

Here are three of them:

• automatic washers

• custom-made draperies

• credit paint sales

They knew that prospective customers buying these three products on credit had settled down. They were prime prospective credit customers. They succeeded in selling almost 50 percent of the washers sold in America for many years, and had similar success with drapes and paint. Once they had their satisfied customers on their books, they kept them there; for two reasons:

1. They had a multitude of things their satisfied customers needed at all times.

2. They kept their customers satisfied because they serviced what they sold.

Most of the years when Sears was growing, their satisfied customers made payments in person, which put them in the store at least once a month.

Sears not only kept customers satisfied well enough to keep them on their books for life, but they got their children on the books—then their children's children—and even their children's children's children. These satisfied customers made Sears the largest retailer in the world.

At one time, furniture and appliance dealers considered the baby crib the most important sale they could make. If they could get a couple on the books when they had their first child, they could keep them so satisfied that these customers would stay on the books. The mother brought her daughter in to buy her baby bed and thus started her own account, and so on.

I hear it said in the business world that customer loyalty is a thing of the past, that it does not exist today.

If that is true, why is it true? Every element that kept customers loyal fifty years ago still exists. In fact, the customer's desire to continue doing business with the same company is greater today than ever.

One of the most extensive research programs ever done in the retail industry covered a four-year period during which customers who had just made a purchase were asked where they had made their last purchase of that product.

There were two factors that surprised everyone because retailers had been saying for years that customer loyalty was a thing of the past.

During those four years of the study, 46 percent of the thousands of customers who had just completed a purchase were asked where they had made their last purchase and said, "right here." In other words, 46 percent had remained loyal customers. But the other 54 percent put an entirely new light on customer loyalty when they were asked why they had not gone back to where they had made their last purchase. Over 75 percent gave the same answer: The attitude of the employees, specifically the salespeople and their *indifference* to the customer. The next largest percentage group said they hadn't gone back because they had moved.

It wasn't the quality of what they purchased nor the other services they had received. It wasn't a competitor's advertising, sales, prices, or services. It wasn't any of the thousands of reasons salespeople give for not making a sale. It was the incompetence and indifference of the salespeople.

Even so, 46 percent of the customers went right on doing business with the same company, and 75 percent of the 54 percent who did not said they wanted to come back, but they just could not put up with the incompetence and indifference of the salespeople.

Customers mail their payment checks today so they no longer come in weekly or monthly to make payments. They no longer have to be kept satisfied, because once the sale is made, the salesperson does not have to come face to face with them again. Consequently, the customer is blamed and accused of being disloyal when in pleading voices they are really saying: "Do you love me or do you not? You told me once, but I forgot." Oh, yes! Salespeople would tell them anything just to get the order.

When customers came in person to make payments, the salespeople got to know them They knew what they would be buying next and when they had paid their accounts down enough to be able to add on new sales. Having this customer base was money in the bank for the company and for the salespeople in those companies.

You have read a lot about fear and trust in this book. It is far, far easier for customers to buy where they have bought before. They will put up with many things and even pay higher prices to keep from having to change.

Over 80 percent of all big-ticket purchases made today by individuals or companies in America are made by using some form of credit. Whereas well into the '60s, there were only three basic sources of credit available to most people:

• Banks

• Loan companies

• Credit accounts carried by sellers

Today, there are thousands of sources of credit and a myriad of credit plans. If there is no credit plan to meet a buyer's needs, sellers have what they call Creative Credit Plans.

Buyers' ability and need to buy on credit is greater than ever before and the ways for them to do it have become a thousand times more complicated. That makes credit information and knowledge something salespeople must have a lot more of. They certainly need more up-to-date credit knowledge and information than their prospective customers have.

If you study what it is that all top professionally competent salespeople do who are in the business of selling, you will discover that they form the same bond with their satisfied customers that was formed with satisfied customers in simpler times, regardless what they sell and regardless whether they call on their prospective customers or their prospective customers come to them. They maintain their own satisfied customer file just as retailers used to. They know what the satisfied customer's budget allows, what he or she will be buying next, and when their budgets will permit them to buy. The professionals keep communications open with their satisfied customers to an even greater extent than they could in olden times because of modern communications.

Knowing your satisfied customer's ongoing needs and budgets is even more important today than in simpler times. This bond is your main source of new prospective customers. That relationship means you will never be standing around waiting for a prospective customer to wait on and you certainly won't be sitting in the outer office *hoping* to get in to see a prospective customer, if he or she has the time. You work with your prospective customers by appointment. That means that you have gotten together by mutual agreement. Think about that because that's what the business of selling is founded on. Buyer and seller have the same objective: for the buyer to wind up and remain a *satisfied* customer.

The key to this is often knowing your satisfied customer's budget and staying up to date with that information. Increased business can increase a company's budget. A promotion or pay raise can increase the prospective customer's budget. The professional who is on top of this information is there first. The ones who aren't, come too late.

Individual and family budgets can be stretched to buy needed products, but they can also be broken. This is just as true of the biggest corporations in the world. No professionally competent salesperson is going to let a satisfied or even prospective customer overextend, but will help that customer to get back within a realistic budget. Each satisfied customer is a valuable asset to the professional.

If you work with the people in your company's credit department for a few days, you will discover their job is to find ways to *approve* every application for credit that they possibly can. They are not looking for ways to turn down credit.

When credit is turned down on one of your sales you can blame it on the people in the credit department and bitch to the losers in the lounge, but the problem won't go away. It will get worse. *If you want to eliminate credit turn downs, stop doing the things that cause them.* If you go to the people in your credit office when you have a turn down and say, "I am sure you had good reasons for turning down that person's credit. If you would explain to me what those reasons are, I will be able to do a better job in the future." When you do that, it won't be long before you feel you have the best credit department people to be found anywhere, and your confidence in them will increase your own selling enthusiasm.

Note: This is a two-way street. The credit person who turned down the prospective customer's credit could go to the salesperson and do the same thing and get the same results.

All credit is based on a prospective customer's ability to pay. Those people in the business of selling credit have only one goal, like all others who succeed in business: "A *satisfied* customer." They cannot achieve that goal if their prospective customers do not achieve theirs. Credit departments aren't there to run off credit business. They are there to figure out how to best meet the credit needs of all prospective customers.

In many fields of selling, finding a source of credit for the prospective customer is part of making the sale. Certainly, those salespeople who call on their prospective customers should have predetermined as much about their credit capabilities as they could before the call was ever made. People and companies who don't pay their bills are always eager to buy, in good times and bad. Professionally competent salespeople never call on deadbeats.

Most salespeople make excuses. "I am not the credit department. I make the sale. It's up to them what they do with it. I will write up anybody for anything!"

Only rarely is a sale made by a professionally competent salesperson turned down for credit, because they don't "write it up" until the prospective customer can qualify for credit.

Note: Many a big sale has been made to companies with credit problems that permitted the company to recover and become an even more satisfied customer. What happened in those cases was that the salesperson knew enough about that company and its needs and financial capabilities to provide the information needed to help them work their way out of their financial problems.

There are more businesses in business today because suppliers were on the job with the expertise and help when it was needed than there are companies who never needed it.

The salesperson considering the baby bed the most important sale he or she could make, is no different from the one who goes out of his or her way to make the sale by helping find credit for a small company trying to get started. Whenever a professional is competent, that professional's prospective customer becomes a lifetime satisfied customer.

Knowing the price of what you sell is a basic. Knowing the payments is just as basic. I don't mean you have to know them to the penny, but you should know them in round numbers.

You must know what financing plans are available to your prospective customers. You should be able to say that if they carry a thousand-dollar balance for a given number of months or years, the payments would run about $100 or whatever. If it is a 30-year mortgage of $1,625,000, the salesperson should be able to quote round numbers for the monthly and yearly payments.

I have talked a lot about the fears people have, both buyer and seller. Nowhere are the buyer's fears greater than when dealing with credit. Nowhere can the salesperson's own confidence instill confidence and trust in the prospective customer as when the credit aspects of a sale are being faced. Those salespeople who really master their profession put their prospective customers' minds at ease quickly. They can do that because they have all the knowledge and information they need about credit availability and cost. With that knowledge and the use of the yardstick, these productive skills are easy to develop.

One lesson professionals of selling have taught me can be invaluable to everyone in the business of selling.

Most businesses have some form of credit plan, and many of these plans offer 30 to 90 days the same as cash. In other words, if the customer pays the account in full within that 30- to 90-day period, there is no interest.

The competent professional salesperson says to the prospective customer: "You may wish to finance your purchase through your bank, but I recommend to my customers that they let me go ahead and put it on our credit plan." Then he or she gives them three good reasons:

• First: They can complete their purchase now and drive their new car home (or take whatever they have purchased right then).

• Second: When they pay off their account within 30 or 90 days (whatever the time is) they will pay not one cent of interest. So they might as well get that extra time interest-free.

• Third: They can always make other arrangements at their bank at their convenience. Of course, they can just leave the account on the company's credit plan if they wish.

• • •
• • • That approach accomplishes several things for the salesperson and
• • • for the prospective customer. It gives prospective customers confidence when salespeople say they may run the account through *their* bank even though *they* may not have used their bank to finance anything before. It saves face because most people are uncomfortable when it comes to asking about credit. It makes it easier for these customers to say, "Yes."

Salespeople who follow this plan discover that once the credit account is established, most customers leave it on the account and pay it out over the specified period of time. Professionally competent salespeople would much rather have their satisfied customers in their company's credit plan than in anyone else's.

For your information: Everyone in the business of selling who sells things satisfied customers buy on an ongoing basis will continue to sell over 80 percent of them on average, and those satisfied customers will return to do business with them, even those who sell automobiles, boats, homes, and airplanes. When you allow for customers who die or move a long distance away, that proves customers have far more reasons for remaining loyal than ever. A good credit relationship is an even stronger reason for this loyalty.

In bygone days, when customers made payments monthly in person, if there was a problem, it was handled by the people in the company where they made their purchase. Today, problems are handled by a computer. When one arises, the customer is only a name or number to the computer.

The last thing all professionals say to their satisfied customers before they depart is, "If you have any reason to call our company, I want you to call me first." That customer is a valuable asset to that salesperson, personally. Professionals intend to sell that satisfied customer for the rest of their careers and to get a lot of new prospective customers, because they have made them *satisfied* customers. The salesperson not only wants to personally see to it that they remain satisfied, he or she wants full credit for that satisfaction.

None of this matters to those who are *not* in the business of selling, but credit is one of the groups of knowledge that is an absolute must for a successful career in the business of selling.

Learning as much as you can about your prospective customer's financial capabilities is every bit as important as learning as much as you can about their needs. Your ability to maintain an ongoing relationship with your satisfied customers will depend on your staying up to date on their financial capabilities. Buying decisions are always moved forward by customer pay increases or by improved business conditions.

If this process is to mean anything to your company, it will be because you and the other salespeople have this information and use it. Those salespeople without a satisfied customer file have no use for the information. But salespeople with well-maintained satisfied customer files have an annuity that can and will multiply their earnings many times over those who don't.

SECTION IV

Introduction to the Book of Skills

> "C'mon, Lawhon, sum it all up. With all your years of research, what one big thing have you learned about selling!?!"

> "There are no big things in selling."

Selling is a combination of knowing a lot of little things about what is being sold while developing the productive skills needed to achieve ten simple objectives in their proper sequence. How professionally competent salespeople achieve these objectives is revealed in this section.

There never have been nor ever will be any two selling situations exactly alike, therefore, it is critical to your success to keep in mind that the only goal of a professionally competent salesperson is to turn his or her prospective customers into satisfied customers. The impossibility of describing each selling situation as it pertains to each of the ten objectives makes an "easy out" for the losers ("What I sell is different!") but the goal and the objectives that lead to that goal are the same every time. The purpose of this section is to show the reader the basics of the skills needed to achieve each objective in all selling situations.

My research included months of interviewing salespeople. Long-term, average salespeople were asked the same questions and I got the same answers from them every time. Management often asked me how I could do that. I replied that I was learning what they do that caused their prospective customers not to buy.

Their reaction was always the same: "Lawhon, you know what they do! Nothing!"

My response was: "There is no such thing as doing nothing and no such thing as an *ineffective* skill."

The very nature of a skill comes from doing something repetitively. As the same act is repeated over and over, it gets easier because the person becomes more skillful at doing it.

The question is not whether a skill is effective or ineffective. The question is whether it is *productive* or *counterproductive!* Even a couch potato has effective skills, but they are counterproductive.

The problem in today's world is not a shortage of productive skills, but a surplus of counterproductive skills.

One of the few things that everyone who studies selling agrees on is that within moments of when a salesperson and a prospective customer come in contact, something happens that gives the salesperson a better than 80 percent chance of making a sale or a better than 80 percent chance of not making it.

In the chapter "The Best Kept Secret in Selling," we saw what it was that professionally competent salespeople did that turned even ice-cold prospective customers into red-hot prospects who bought most of the time. There is something the professionally competent salesperson does every time that causes most prospective customers to buy, while salespeople who don't do what the professionally competent salesperson does are doing something else that causes most of their prospective customers not to buy.

In that chapter, you saw examples of what caused customers to buy and what caused them not to. What we *didn't* learn there was what *caused* that to happen.

Remember, it is a well-established fact that something happens at the moment of contact with a prospective customer that results in a sale or it doesn't. The professionally competent salesperson is almost guaranteed a sale before he or she has done any of the other things I talk about in "Your Road to Selling Success."

Often, I am asked if I think a productive greeting is the "most important" of all selling skills. Here is my answer: The objective of the greeting is to establish *positive* communication between you and your prospective customer. So productive greeting skills are all you need until positive communications *are* established and your first objective has been achieved. But there are *nine* more objectives you must achieve if you are going to reach your goal: a *satisfied* customer. Therefore, not one of the skills you need to achieve each of those ten objectives can be considered *more* important than another.

Nevertheless, the question still remains, "What could possibly happen when two people come in contact that is so powerful it will cause a sale to be made or lost?"

Adding to this puzzle is that the skills you need to achieve an effective greeting are the most fundamental of all selling skills and the easiest to perfect into habits.

The word "basic" means "essential," according to Funk & Wagnall's. Essential means indispensable, an absolute requisite. A basic selling skill, then, is the foundation upon which all other selling skills rest.

Either you have this productive skill and can develop the other productive skills you need to make a sale almost every time or you don't. Period.

As you strive to perfect these skills into productive selling habits, read the instructions in the book, try to achieve each objective in its proper sequence; and measure your results. When something hasn't worked go back and read the instructions again. This continued interaction will guarantee your ultimate success. It will come quickly and easily for some —most will find it slower going, but it will work for all who accurately use the yardstick and faithfully follow the instructions.

25 / *The Greeting I*

THE GREATEST REWARD MY RESEARCH AND WRITING
BRINGS TO ME ARE THOSE PEOPLE WHO SAY,
"MR. LAWHON, YOU HAVE MADE ME PROUD
OF WHAT I DO FOR A LIVING FOR THE FIRST TIME!"
THOSE PEOPLE HAVE ACHIEVED A POSITIVE COUNTENANCE.

EVERY EFFECTIVE GREETING has three ingredients. With those ingredients present, your greeting will work 100 percent of the time and you will make the sale almost every time. If they are not, you have almost no chance to make a sale. The ingredients of this single skill predetermine your success or your failure in selling:

- **POSITIVE COUNTENANCE**

- **COURTESY**

- **POLITENESS**

Are you sure you understand fully the meaning of these three words? Don't bet too much that you do.

Let's take them one by one and see what Funk & Wagnall's standard dictionary says.

Countenance *n.* 1. The face or features. 2. Expression; appearance. 3. An encouraging aspect: hence it shows approval or support.
Out of countenance *adj.* 1. Disconcerted: without ease or composure: abashed.
Abash *v.* 1. To deprive another of self possession; disconcert; make ashamed or confuse.

Synonyms for out of countenance are: confound, confuse, daunt, discompose, disconcert, dishearten, embarrass, humble, humiliate, mortify, over-awe, shame. *Any sense of inferiority abashes with or without the person having done anything wrong.*

To some extent, everyone reacts to another person on contact. This reaction will be positive or negative. It will not and cannot be some of both. No one, absolutely no one, can control that reaction. What they can control is the cause of the reaction.

Salespeople with a positive countenance when they come in contact with a prospective customer will have an encouraging aspect about them; hence their countenance causes prospective customers to feel that the salesperson approves and supports them, causing them to feel encouraged and confident. All of those positive emotions are stirred up in the prospective customer when they come in contact with a salesperson who has a positive countenance. The more positive the salesperson's countenance, the stronger these positive reactions of the prospective customer will be. Think long and hard about how easy it will be to work with a prospective customer who reacts to you with those feelings.

When the prospective customer reacts to your positive countenance, that causes you to react to them with all of those same emotions. When that happens, we have two people who have the same goal. They are supportive and approving of each other, which means they both want to help each other achieve a common goal. That causes each of them to feel encouraged and confident. It is easy to see that if there is any way possible for them to find something that will meet that customer's needs, a sale is going to be made.

You may feel you already know these things about "countenance," but that's not the problem. The problem lies in the reactions that take place when you are out-of-countenance or when you react to a prospective customer who is out-of-countenance, which is what happens most of the time.

When a salesperson and prospective customer first come in contact, both the customer and the salesperson will be caused to have the same positive emotions when the salesperson is in countenance. They will have the same negative feelings when the salesperson or customer reacts to one or the other being out-of-countenance. What does that mean? They will both feel disconcerted, neither will feel at ease, which causes them to feel discouraged, even disheartened. *They will have a degree of embarrassment and a sense of inferiority even though neither one has done anything wrong.*

When you fully understand this, it is easy to see why the salesperson whose countenance on contact causes a positive reaction finds it easy to make a sale while those who are out of countenance will always find selling embarrassing, hard, and even *humiliating.* Once you fully understand the words countenance and out-of-countenance, then and only then can you see why countenance is an ingredient of the basic skill of selling. Having a countenance so positive that it will cause the prospective customer to react to you instead of your reacting to the customer guarantees your success in selling.

PEOPLE REACT TO PEOPLE

When a salesperson is out-of-countenance it puts the customer out-of-countenance and in turn causes negative emotions to be stirred up in the salesperson. Trying to work under these emotional conditions has to be the hardest work in the world. No wonder so many who try selling give it up so quickly.

If you doubt that all of these negative emotions are stirred up when a customer and salesperson reacts to one or the other while out-of-countenance, listen to what average salespeople say when they fail to make a sale.

First, they blame the customer. (However, to the losers, they were *not customers* because they had not supported or approved of anything the salesperson tried to do.) Then the salespeople blame their company because it did not have the services, prices, and things to sell to support them in their efforts. Listen to their words and you will hear them trying to excuse their failures in an effort to avoid humiliation. They have been deprived of their self confidence. They are disconcerted, discomposed, and certainly not at ease with themselves.

When in-depth research is done with prospective customers who have not bought, we dig out all of these same feelings and emotions. They left with their needs unmet, unsatisfied, if you please, and that means *disappointed.* They blame that disappointment on the salesperson and his or her company.

Remember, this is always a matter of degree. The stronger your negative or positive countenance, the stronger the reactions on the part of all parties, and to some degree even the weakest of reactions can stir up all of the emotions. If you are reading this for the first time, you will have gained only a limited comprehension of its full ramifications and its effect on your success or failure. I have written and rewritten most of this chapter at least a hundred times. The reason I have is because every time I reread what I wrote I gained more comprehension and felt I could write it so it could be more easily understood. This was the first chapter on skills I started writing and the last one I finished.

Countenance is the first basic element of the first basic skill of selling. It is essential, indispenable, and an absolute requisite. It is the foundation upon which all other selling skills are based.

Courtesy. I will bet that you have found out an awful lot about countenance that you didn't know before. But I will bet that you still believe you fully understand the meaning of the word "courtesy." Here's what a standard dictionary says:

Courtesy *n.* Polite behavior, habitual politeness.

Habitual politeness. In other words, courtesy is a skill you can perfect into a productive habit. Because courteous persons have practiced being courteous and perfected that skill into a productive habit they are not even consciously aware that they are being courteous.

Those who aren't habitually courteous and polite are not consciously aware that they are not showing courtesy. They wonder what they did that was so counterproductive it caused someone to get upset with them. They are like a salesperson with bad breath or body odor. The customer is put off, maybe even nauseated, but the offending salesperson doesn't know what is causing the customer to back away. It is all the same thing, only impolite and discourteous acts done unconsciously are perceived to be intentional by the customer and they are far worse than body odor or foul breath. Now look up the word "discourteous."

Discourteous *adj.* Lacking courtesy, impolite, rude.
Rude *adj.* 1. Offensively blunt or contemptuous: impudent.
2. Characterized by a lack of refinement: uncultivated: uncouth:
3. Unskillfully made or done: *lacking in skill or training:* crude: rough: rude workmanship. Barbarous: savage.

Courtesy is one of the *three basics* of selling. It is essential and indispensable to every salesperson's success. It too is a skill perfected into a productive habit, for the most part, unconsciously. It appears to the salespeople who lack this productive skill that those who have it were born with it. They think it comes naturally.

Listen well. All skills are practiced with little or no conscious effort. For the most part, the person is not even aware of what he or she is doing. Therefore, a skill cannot be put on and taken off. It's either there, or it isn't.

Those who don't have this essential productive skill are seen by their prospective customers as being untrained, unskillful, offensive, rude, crude, uncivil, uncultured, impudent, lacking refinement, uncouth, even barbarous and vulgar, making anything they do counterproductive.

By degree, all these negative feelings are stirred up in the prospective customer when the salesperson is not habitually courteous. Having and practicing this productive skill is essential and indispensable to a successful career in the business of selling. If you have any doubt how critically important it is to be habitually courteous, consider how much harder it will be to make a sale when you are seen as offensive, rude, and unskillful by your customers when you are not even consciously aware of your lack of skill or your rude and offensive acts.

It is an ancient adage, but it is more true in our world today than ever before: Courtesy costs nothing, but it sure pays big dividends in selling. I would like to add to that old adage these words: *"The lack of common courtesy in selling can cost you everything."*

Politeness is the third basic productive skill that is essential and indispensable to your success in the business of selling.

Here is the definition found in a standard dictionary:

Polite *n.* Exibiting in manner or speech a considerate regard for others: courteous: cultivated. Synonyms: accomplished, civil, complaisant, courteous, cultivated, cultured, elegant, genteel, gracious, obliging, polished, urbane, well-behaved, well-bred, well-mannered.

A person may be civil without being considerate of others simply because his or her own self respect forbids his being rude. But one who is polite has at least some care for the opinions of others, and if polite in the highest and truest sense, he or she cares for the comfort and happiness of others in even the smallest matters. Civil is a colder and more distant word than polite. Courteous is richer and fuller, dealing often with greater matters and it is used only in the good sense and has a *positive* meaning or effect.

"Genteel" refers to an external elegance that may be superficial and showy. This word is inferior to polite or courteous. "Urbane" refers to politeness that is genial and successful in giving others a sense of ease and cheer. "Polished" refers to external elegance without reference to spirit or purpose. A person can be a polished gentleman or a polished scoundrel.

Antonyms: awkward, bluff, discourteous, ill-behaved, ill-mannered, ill-bred, impertinent, impolite, impudent, insolent, insulting, raw, rude, rustic, uncivil, uncouth, unpolished, untaught, and untutored.

When you are *habitually* polite, most of your polite acts are done without conscious thought. Then you have a productive skill that you have perfected into a *habit*. One that causes every prospective customer to feel a sense of ease and good cheer.

When you are *not* habitually polite, most of your impolite, counterproductive acts are done with no conscious thought. You are not even aware you are doing them. Little, counterproductive acts you do unconsciously will cause your prospective customers to feel you are awkward, bluff, discourteous, ill-behaved, ill-bred, impertinent, impolite, impudent, insolent, insulting, raw, rude, rustic, uncivil, uncouth, unpolished, untaught, and untutored.

Is it any wonder those salespeople who greet every prospective customer with courtesy, politeness, and a positive countenance are going to make a sale easily almost every time? And it is not going to take them long to do it, either.

Is it any wonder that those who are *not* habitually courteous and polite, who greet their prospective customers out-of-countenance, even though unconsciously and unintentionally, find it counterproductive and very hard to make a sale?

DEVELOPING YOUR THREE BASIC SELLING SKILLS INTO EFFECTIVE PRODUCTIVE SELLING HABITS

Remember that something has happened at the moment of contact that causes your prospective customer to have a positive or negative reaction. If positive, there is a better than 80 percent chance that you will make the sale. If negative, there is a better than 80 percent chance you won't.

In the chapter "Who Can Succeed in Selling?" I said everyone who studies selling agrees that enthusiasm has sold more things than all other elements combined. I used little Mary in the first grade class as an example to show what causes us to react with enthusiasm and little Johnny to show what causes us to react with fear and trepidation.

Now, close your eyes and imagine the features or face of little Mary. Imagine the expression on her face. She was smiling from ear to ear. That had an encouraging aspect. She approved of the teacher and the question she asked because Mary had the answer. She was *competent*. Without question this is the best example of positive countenance you could find.

Imagine, if you can, little Johnny's face and features. He reflected no approval at all of the teacher or the question. He did not support her in any way. His features reflected fear, shame, doubt, and a lot of other negative emotions.

It is obvious from this example that the more competent people feel, the more positive and productive their countenance will be. The less competent they feel, the more out-of-countenance they will appear, causing what they do to be counterproductive.

This basic essential and indispensably productive selling skill can only be developed into a productive *habit* if you have the basic knowledge and information you need. There is that word "basic" again. It means knowledge and information that is essential and indispensable to you.

Without the basic knowledge and information salespeople need, they should *never* be allowed to approach or greet a prospective customer:

• Credit information

• Delivery and service information

• Advertising information

• Basic inventory and availability information

• Prices, basic features, and basic benefits of what they sell.

• How to present and demonstrate effectively at least the basic features and benefits of what they sell.

With only these basics, even beginning salespeople can be confident that they know far more about all of these things than most of the prospective customers they will come in contact with. Knowing the basic knowledge and information gives salespeople the confidence they need to have a positive countenance when they first come in contact with prospective customers. Without this basic knowledge and information, they would be like little Johnny. When they don't have the answers, they will react out-of-countenance.

My point. In order to perfect this skill into a productive habit, you must have a positive countenance every time you come in contact with a prospective customer. With that basic knowledge and information you should be able to approach, greet, or call on prospective customers with a positive countenance almost from your very first day. If you do, in less than 30 days this skill will have been perfected into a productive selling habit and you *will* have a positive countenance when you come in contact with prospective customers from then on. As you gain more knowledge and information while practicing this skill, your countenance will become more and more effective, making it easier and easier for you to make a sale.

Listen well. I don't care how much effort it takes, I don't care how embarrassing your failures may be, and I don't care how hard it is to learn the basic knowledge and information, this investment will be the best one you will ever make. It is an investment in yourself and no one can take it away from you. It will reward you thousands of times over during your selling career. It is essential and indispensable to your success.

Now, here is the catch. You will not know for sure that you have come in contact with a prospective customer until after contact has been made. If you did not have a positive countenance when contact took place, it is already too late for you. That means you must get in the habit of having a positive countenance when you come in contact with anyone, anytime, anywhere in the course of your business of selling.

That may seem impossible when you first start out, just like it may have seemed impossible to eat with chopsticks the first time. But when you have your customer accounting card out before contact is made it reminds you to do it every time. And in no time it has gotten so easy to do that you are doing it unconsciously. Believe me, there is nothing that gets easier than that.

Let's go back to the word "countenance" and its definition as it is found in the dictionary. Countenance: 1. The face or features. 2. Expression: appearance. 3. An encouraging aspect: hence it shows approval or support.

All you need to present a positive countenance and to experience how others will react to it is to put a big positive smile on your face and then look in a mirror. You will feel yourself reacting positively to your own smile. You will find it impossible to react negatively.

Have that smile on your face when you come in contact with prospective customers and they will have an even stronger more positive reaction than you had. You will see their faces light up and that will cause you to become even more positive as you respond to their reaction to you.

You cannot have your accounting card out before you approach, greet, or call on a customer without being reminded to have that same big positive smile on your face before contact is made. You can't even have it out to make a phone call without being reminded, because the whole center of the card on both sides is a big smiley face designed to remind you of this basic, essential, indispensable skill upon which hangs the success of your entire selling career.

If you have a place where you stand to greet customers entering your selling area, you should have a mirror you can look in to be sure you have your smile ready. You should even have a big smiley face on the mirror.

You should have a smiley face on the mirror in your compact (if you're a woman), on the mirrors in the restrooms at work, on the mirrors in the bathrooms at home, on the rearview mirror in your car.

When you always have that smile on your face when you come in contact with anyone, anywhere, it has become a productive habit, and you have also gained enough of the knowledge and information you need to be reasonably competent, then you are over the hump and your success in selling can be guaranteed as long as you continue to use your 5 x 7 accounting card.

Do you want to know something? When you have a positive countenance, you will discover it is impossible to be impolite and impossible to be discourteous. Do you want to know even more? When you are out-of-countenance, it is impossible to have a positive smile on your face, it is impossible to be polite, and it is impossible to be courteous.

Now, how important does that word "countenance" seem? More important than when you first read it and I said don't bet a lot of money that you really understood its meaning?

When a prospective customer has been greeted by a salesperson with a positive countenance, the greeting was effective and positive communications were established. The salesperson's first objective has been achieved and he or she can proceed immediately to achieve the second.

Let me show you how that works in selling situations when the customer comes to the salesperson:

With a positive countenance, the professional may say something like this: "Good afternoon, do you mind if I ask what brings you into our showroom today?" 'Do you mind if I ask?' is not a greeting, it is a qualifying question asked with courtesy.

A professional salesperson on a car lot may approach a customer with his positive countenance and a question like this: "I see you looking at our new pickups. Do you mind if I ask if you are driving a pickup now?" This salesperson's positive countenance was all the greeting needed to start communicating on a positive level.

Many a book on selling will say, "Greet these customers and when they say they are just looking as most do, tell them to just look around make themselves at home. Then when the customer has settled down, come back and approach them again," or they teach what is called the "common ground" approach to a greeting. That is find something else to talk about when the salesperson and the customer have a common interest such as sports or the weather.

But when a salesperson is out-of-countenance, he or she can't get into positive communications with a prospective customer on any subject. When salespeople have a positive countenance, they don't need to waste their time or the customer's on chitchat.

Here is what I have found out about the greetings of the highest-volume, highest-paid top professional salespeople: Whatever it is they say when they come in contact with prospective customers, *it will be in the same words each and every time.*

They might say something different on first contact with customers greeted at the entrance than they do when approaching a prospective customer who is browsing, but in each case salespeople who have a positive countenance will use the same words every time a prospective customer is greeted at the entrance and a different set of words every time they approach a browser. This is an effective selling skill that they have perfected into a productive selling habit, which means they are doing and saying the same thing the same way every time—because it *works.* The longer they continue doing it, the more effective it becomes, the easier it gets, and the more confidence they have, which means their countenance gets more and more positive. They are reacting more and more enthusiastically.

When you boil it all down, you discover that when you have a positive countenance on contact, although you may say "good afternoon" or some other welcoming words, in some cases even shaking hands and introducing yourself, you will discover yourself already in the qualifying stage of the sale.

I am sure you have heard how Thomas Edison tried over 1,000 experiments before he discovered a formula for the electric light bulb. He was often asked how he could have failed so many times and kept trying. He became very adamant when he said, "I have never failed. I had found over 1,000 ways that didn't work." By the way, when he finally did find a way that worked, it didn't work very well, but he quickly perfected it into the light bulb we are still using today.

My point: When Edison tried something that did not work he admitted it didn't and never, I mean never, repeated it again. He could have gone on forever trying to make something work that didn't and never would have perfected the things that did.

Your 5 x 7 customer accounting card will tell you if your greeting and what you did or said worked. If it didn't, you can blame it on the customer or the company or you can be like Edison. Admit it didn't work and try something else. Once you find something that works for you, keep doing it and you will be able to make it work even better. It will soon become a productive selling habit that guarantees your success.

What about shaking hands? In many selling situations where the customer comes to you, it is not customary to introduce yourself or to shake hands on contact. It is a good idea not to do it if the customer isn't expecting it. In other selling situations it is customary for salespeople to introduce themselves and to shake hands.

Zig Ziglar says the man who does his dry cleaning can tell if a customer is a salesman because there will be a worn spot around the right pocket of his trousers where he wipes his sweaty palm before shaking hands.

That dry cleaning man is wrong. When a professionally competent salesperson has a positive countenance, his prospective customer has a positive reaction to him instantly and he in turn has reacted positively to the customer. If it is his custom to shake hands, his palm and his prospective customer's are dry as a bone.

It is the order takers masquerading as salespeople who are out-of-countenance. They are caused to feel disconcerted and awkward. They don't know whether or not to shake. Their palms are sweaty and even though they wipe them dry, they will be sweaty again by the time they shake hands, and there is nothing they can do about it. How humiliating.

Shaking hands is a skill, too. It can be a productive skill or a counterproductive skill. It is a productive skill all salespeople must have because there will be times when all salespeople need this skill and most of their customers won't have the skill.

If you are not skillful at shaking hands and your customer is not skillful, your positive countenance can disappear as you grasp the end of their fingers with your sweaty palm or they grasp the end of your fingers. You or the customer may catch the other's hand so that the slightest pressure causes excruciating pain. This, like all other skills, can only be perfected by practicing until you get it right.

When you are skillful at shaking hands, you do it with confidence and enthusiasm. When you aren't, you don't. In order to perfect a productive skill, you should be looking at the customer's hand as you reach to shake. You should push your hand into theirs until the V between their thumb and forefinger is pressed against the V between your thumb and forefinger. Your grip should be gentle, but firm. At no time should it ever be firm enough to cause the other person discomfort.

One of the biggest problems with shaking hands is the macho customer who crushes your hand. No matter how slight, this pain destroys your positive countenance. You will discover that when you get the V's to meet firmly, *no one* can crush the bones in your hand. Practice with other salespeople, men and women. Try doing all the things wrong, including those things that hurt, so you know what not to do as well. Once this productive skill is perfected into a habit, you won't have sweaty palms because you won't even be consciously aware of what you are doing.

THE ACID TEST

You cannot possibly be polite and courteous and be aggressive or pushy at the same time. Holding a door for another and letting someone else go first, are two common acts of courtesy and politeness. This requires patience and practice if it is to become a habit and you must do it at every opportunity, not just some of the time. You can't be polite and courteous at work and not at home. It is either a skill you perfect into a habit, or it isn't. If it is, you are doing it without conscious effort.

If you aren't holding the door for your family and letting them go first, you aren't doing it for your customers. Your problem is that what you do for your family you do by habit, so you aren't aware of your discourtesy and lack of politeness. If you are not aware of it, then you are not aware of it at work, either. If so, these acts of courtesy and politeness that you try with your customers will be forced and counterproductive. You can't fool mother nature and you can't hide habits. You can be sure that they will find you out. Whether they are effective productive skills and habits or effective counterproductive habits is up to you.

26 / *The Greeting II*

SALESPEOPLE WHO CALL ON THEIR PROSPECTIVE CUSTOMERS FIND IT IS
EITHER MUCH EASIER FOR THEM TO MAKE A SALE (THAN SALESPEOPLE WHOSE
PROSPECTIVE CUSTOMERS COME TO THEM) OR IT IS ALMOST IMPOSSIBLE.

CALLING ON PROSPECTIVE CUSTOMERS

THE SALESPEOPLE WHOSE PROSPECTIVE CUSTOMERS come to them the first time know nothing about them and their needs when they meet, while salespeople who call on prospective customers should know who they are going to call on.

Knowing little or nothing about a customer's needs before you call and not having an appointment makes getting the order much harder. More often than not salespeople in this situation don't even get in to see their prospective customers, and when they do, it is usually after long waits or being told to come back. Under these circumstances it is impossible to keep a positive countenance.

For those who call on their customers it can be the easiest of all selling, or the hardest. Tragically, for most it is the hardest.

For most of my 35-year career, I was one of the largest buyers of home furnishings in the U.S. Thousands of salespeople called on me, but only a handful ever worked by appointment. Most showed up unannounced and hung around until someone could see them. It wasn't unusual for them to be there all of one day and sometimes the better part of the next.

When they did finally see someone, they *never* had a plan. They might ask if we needed anything or they would show us a picture, give us a price, and hope we would give them an order. If most retail salespeople get an order less than fifteen percent of the time, I would say these guys were lucky if they did that well, because most commitments for new product lines were placed at markets.

As these guys left without an order, after hours wasted just waiting to talk to someone, they almost always said, "I'll see you at the market."

Professionally competent salespeople who only called on me by appointment worked with me at the market by appointment, too, and they were busy full time at market. They never had several of their biggest buyers show up at the same time and they followed a plan with each prospective or satisfied customer when it was their appointed time.

When these professional salespeople arrived at our offices for an appointment, they showed up well ahead of time. They went first to the service department and made sure there were no pending problems. Then it was off to the warehouse and delivery departments to see if there was any problem getting their goods received or delivered. They learned about any service and handling problems we were having with competitor's products. Then they visited the advertising department, checking to see what was going to be advertised and what had been advertised. They always brought new ideas and materials to make it as easy as possible for us to advertise their products.

The next stop for these pros was the showroom, where they examined their company's floor samples to make sure they were all in salable condition. If they weren't, they saw to it that steps were taken to change them or to get them in salable condition before they left. They looked at all competing products and they visited with any salespeople who were not with customers. They made sure the salespeople were having no problems selling their products and at the same time picked up on problems salespeople were having with competitor's products. Their next stop was the inventory office, where they reviewed rates of sale, made sure orders were flowing smoothly, and got any information both good and bad that they could about the product of other companies and their services. They knew every competing merchandise weakness on our showroom floors before their appointment time ever rolled around.

When they finally walked into my office, they would know more about us and our needs for their goods than I and everyone else in our company combined.

Between markets, they were in and out of our company in no more than an hour or two while there was a lounge full of their competitors' salespeople without appointments, complaining about business and about how long they had been waiting to be seen. Most of those were there when the professionals arrived, were there when they left, and some would still be there the next day. When told what the professionals did, they all had the same answer: "If you think I am going to waste my time doing all those things, you are crazy. I don't get enough business out of this company to make even calling on them worth my time."

When I arrived for my appointment at market, the professionals were always ready. They knew every price and they knew production schedules. As they took me through the showroom they would even tell me about a product I carried on which sales had slowed down. It could be one of their products or one of their competitor's. They gave me rates of sales, profit margins, advertising results, and then showed me what they recommended as a replacement.

They not only kept that hard, fought-for floor space in our showrooms they already had, but they usually wound up getting some that had once belonged to one of those competitor salespeople who hoped I would stop in their space to get a guided tour. The guided tour directors rarely knew the prices of what they sold and I never had the time to waste while they got out their catalogs and price lists to look them up. It could take several hours to get through some of the larger spaces if you asked many prices, so whatever I stopped to look at on guided tours had to be really outstanding before I would even ask the price.

Never once do I remember receiving a letter from the company represented by one of these top salespeople informing me something was going to be discontinued. Whenever they were about to discontinue something, that salesperson showed up with an appointment, making me aware of falling sales on that item and of my current inventory. He told me exactly how many days' or weeks' stock I had on hand and told me how many fill-in items I might need based on my rate of sale.

If I had odds and ends, the pro was in touch with other dealers and in some cases even sent me a copy of every dealer's inventory so we could get anything we needed to satisfy an existing customer. The pro knew that the sooner a slow-selling item was out of my inventory the sooner it could be replaced with a faster-moving one he or she was prepared to supply.

Often professionally competent salespeople called on me because a competitor had discontinued a group and sent me a letter advising me of it. The professional was in my office ahead of the competitor. The other guy had no plan. By the time he did come to see me, he had already lost his space on my showroom floor.

Whenever customers' needs change, they are in the market for whatever it is that will help them best meet those new needs. That's where the professionals keep their eyes trained. They are ready to make their prospective customers react to these needs, while the losers in the lounge are waiting for the prospective customer to do something that will cause *the salesperson* to react.

There is no way that these salespeople waiting with the losers in the lounge could have a positive countenance if and when they did come in contact with the prospective customer.

It should be even more obvious that the salesperson with the advanced knowledge and information and a plan to follow would have a powerfully positive countenance and be bursting with enthusiasm.

These salespeople are factory representatives and what they sell is different from things other salespeople sell who call on prospective customers: things like jet airplanes, life insurance, industrial equipment, and so on. But their goals are the same and so are the ten objectives they must achieve to reach their goals.

It does not matter what is being sold. There is no way for salespeople who call on prospective customers with or without an appointment, who have no plan, to have a positive countenance; so there is no way they can develop an enthusiastic and effective greeting that works every time.

Getting an Appointment

Salespeople who call on their customers and lack the productive skills they need to get appointments are rarely successful. These skills are becoming more and more critical to a salesperson's success.

So, let's review the basics. Whenever you come in contact with prospective customers your *only* goal is to turn them into *satisfied* customers.

Most prospective customers for big-ticket products do not have a conscious, comprehensive understanding of their needs for the benefits of the features of what you sell.

Remember, the second objective of a professionally competent salesperson is to ask questions that make prospective customers consciously aware of their needs for the benefits of the features of what the salesperson is selling. As prospective customers become more and more consciously aware of more and more of their needs for these benefits, the hotter prospects they become.

When a salesperson's prospective customers are businesspeople or professionals and what you sell is going to far better meet their needs than what they are using, it is going to far better meet the needs of their competitors, too. If one customer buys it and his or her competitor doesn't, that customer has a leg up on that competitor.

All of this is what professional salespeople know that their prospective customers don't. Getting an appointment to make the sale means that in a sense the salesperson must be able to achieve on the phone enough of his or her first three objectives to get the appointment.

In the case of life insurance, the prospective customers have to be made aware of life insurance needs they had but were unaware of. If so, then they will allow salespeople to meet with them and show them how the salesperson's policy will best meet those needs. No salesperson can do that if he or she knows nothing about the life insurance the prospective customer has now. That information is a lot harder to get than it was for visiting salespeople to find out what was not selling well on my showroom floors. And that's why so many people who try to sell life insurance quit. But it's also the reason most salespeople who call on prospective customers don't get appointments.

Salespeople who called on me who normally never had an appointment would sometimes phone to say that they would be in town on a certain day with their sales managers and want an appointment. If at all possible I always gave them one. Why? Because they had a reason. The sales manager was coming because there was something important he or she wanted to discuss with me. Now, isn't it amazing that these same salespeople could call and get an appointment for someone else to sell for them, yet not be able to get an appointment for themselves to do the selling! The real reason the sales manager had for me to see him would have been all the reason the salesperson would have needed to get an appointment for himself if he or she had as much knowledge and information as the sales manager.

I can't remember one of those top professionals who called on me for years by appointment ever showing up with a sales manager. *They were competent to do the job themselves and their sales managers were too busy doing the jobs the guided tour directors were too incompetent to do.*

My point: If you don't have a good enough reason when you ask a prospective customer to give you an appointment, the odds are you won't get one, so don't bother making the phone call. If having a sales manager with you is a good enough reason, whatever the manager's reason for the appointment should be all the reason you would need to get one.

Here's the catch. I have had sales managers show up for an appointment who weren't one bit more competent than their salespeople. They came with nothing that would make me a more satisfied customer and they left without an order. In some cases they knew even less about me and my company's needs than their salespeople.

WHEN YOU CALL FOR THE APPOINTMENT

Just reaching the person you want the appointment with by telephone is getting harder every day. People in business are being harassed constantly by incompetent salespeople who know little or nothing about them or their needs. The more important they are, the greater their needs, but they must erect a phalanx of people around them just to keep pestering, incompetent salespeople away.

There is another side to that coin. I don't care how important anyone is, whether the president of IBM or the president of the United States, if you have something that will make them *satisfied* customers, even though they are not consciously aware of their need, they will be forever grateful to you if you get that appointment.

You start by having learned enough about the people you sell to and their needs to believe they really are prospective customers. You already have your customer accounting cards with names, phone numbers, and any information you have about them and their needs. If a person was referred to you by one of your satisfied customers, you have that information on the card, too. You have your schedule out and ready. You know what you intend to say when you get the prospect on the phone. You have a mirror handy so you know you look positive and are in countenance. Until you have turned the prospect into a *satisfied* customer, you will not have reached the goal you had when you placed that call.

Sometimes the person you are calling will answer the phone personally. If so, you must be ready with what you intend to say and with the questions you want to ask.

Often, an operator will answer. It is very important that you keep your positive countenance as you say, "May I speak with John F. Customer?"

You may also get put straight through and in that case you must have a positive countenance when you hear his voice and you must know what you are going to say. If not, you have not achieved your first objective.

Your countenance on the phone must have the same effect it would if that person were standing right in front of you. He or she is either going to have a positive reaction and there is a good chance you will get your appointment, or it will be a negative reaction and there is a good chance you won't.

Frequently, you will be put through to a secretary whose job is to screen all calls and let no sales calls through. When this person answers, you say, "This is John F. Salesperson (your name). Could you connect me with John F. Customer, please?" This may get you through if your countenance remains positive. The smiley face on your accounting card is a constant reminder.

The secretary may not put you through. Instead, he or she may say, "Is he expecting your call?" or something like that.

You must maintain your positive countenance as you say, "Would you let him know that John F. Salesperson with International Corporation (your firm) is on the phone? Is he in?" It's along about here you can lose your positive countenance if you don't stay ready. This may get you through to the prospect and you must keep that positive countenance, but if it doesn't, you have not achieved your objective. Hang up without an appointment and you have wasted your time.

The secretary may try to question you as to why you wish to speak to him. If you try to tell her, the odds are you can forget it. The secretary doesn't have the need. And anyway, she doesn't understand it. It is his or her job to keep guys like you from harassing the boss.

So, you repeat, "This is John F. Salesperson with International Corporation. May I ask with whom I am speaking?" When you get the name, write it on your accounting card and say, "Would you tell Mr. Customer I am on the line?"

The protector of Mr. Customer may be so rigid that no one can get through. Remember, most of the time when you have a plan and follow it, you will have gotten through early on. It is only as you perfect these skills that you will get through more and more often while taking less and less time to do it.

The harder you try to do anything even when you fail, the more you have learned. This is basic. Never quit trying until you have learned how to be effective and productive every time. Time spent perfecting this productive skill now will reward you thousands of times over during your career.

You may even reach a point where you explain to the person on the line that you understand how busy Mr. Customer is and that it is his or her job to keep people from bothering him. "But what I have to tell him is so important I am sure he will want the information. And he will appreciate your giving me a chance to speak with him. Would you please let him know I am on the line?"

Even then, the secretary may say, "I am sorry, but he is on the phone. If you will leave a message I will have him return your call." Any time that happens you say, "Thank you very much Mr. or Ms. Protector (her name). It is so important that I talk to him that I will hold."

You might ask, "You mean I should go that far just to get a prospective customer on the phone and still have to try to get an appointment?" Well you must be prepared to go that far. You may even have written down what you were going to say. When you fail and use the yardstick, it is easy to pinpoint what doesn't work.

There are two things you must keep in mind when you set out to perfect these skills. You will be awkward and find that most of what you try won't work the first time. If you are to succeed you must learn to make it work. As you do, it will get easier and easier while taking less and less time.

Remember, the person with whom you are trying to get an appointment wants to become a satisfied customer for what you are selling even more than you want to make him one. Only he or she doesn't know it.

Most top professionals write a letter making prospective customers aware of some of their needs, letting them know that they expect to be in their area and will be calling for an appointment at a time that would be most convenient for the prospect. The professionals constantly work on this letter to make it more and more effective. In no time, it does what they want it to do almost every time and then they send it out word for word every time. It will always be typed and addressed to the person they wish the appointment with. They will use a postage stamp not a meter.

It makes it even easier to get prospective customers on the phone if you are able to say you were asked to call by one of your satisfied customers, who is a friend of the person you are calling. Those who have become even more competent are able to get their satisfied customers to call prospective customers they know and tell them to expect the salesperson's call. Others are able to get satisfied customers to write a letter to the prospective customer telling them of their satisfaction and to expect the call. The professionals may go so far as to write the letter for the satisfied customer so all that person needs to do is sign it and mail it.

Developing the productive skill you need to get the person on the phone most of the time will really be quite easy when you use your yardstick. I carried this example to the absolute extreme.

If you are ever going to have the confidence to do these things, where are you going to get it? It will come as your competence improves. You will find yourself doing things with confidence that in your wildest dreams you would never have imagined yourself capable of. At first, you will only get through on the easier calls, but as you measure those results, reread your instructions, and try again, you will get through more and more, often in less and less time. You won't have to take my word for it. Your yardstick guarantees it and gives you a record of your improvement.

YOUR PROSPECTIVE CUSTOMER IS ON THE PHONE

Suppose you called for the head of the company and he or she answered the phone. I can guarantee you that if you sell life insurance and said, "Mr. President, this is John F. Salesman and I would like to get an appointment with you to talk about your life insurance," you will hear a loud crash as the receiver is slammed in your ear. We all know that. Most people who try selling life insurance learn that very quickly and because they never develop the skills needed to overcome that problem they hate to even try to make a call. "Can I help you?" doesn't work when the customer comes to you, so it certainly isn't going to work on prospective customers when you use their own telephones to intrude upon them.

If you expect to get an appointment you must be prepared with what you are going to say. Professionally competent salespeople who sell every conceivable thing that could be sold are making appointments by phone every day of their lives, and if you listen to what these professionals say when they place a call you will discover they sound like a broken record. What they say will be the same thing every time with every call. If what you sell requires you to get in to see someone before you can start your sale, your first objective is to get an appointment. It is the first skill you must perfect into an effective productive selling habit.

When you call on the telephone for an appointment, your prospect is not in the mood for chitchat. What you say must get you down to the business at hand at once. A positive countenance is basic—your countenance will be radiated down that phone line as surely as it would be if the customer was right there in front of you. The more positive it is, the stronger the radiation, and the better your chances of getting the appointment. If you are at all out of countenance when you get ready to make the call, forget it. All salespeople learn this quickly, so they start putting off calls, thinking they will do it later when they are more up to it. It isn't long until they have quit making calls altogether. Putting it off won't change a thing. It only makes things harder.

In the beginning, keep a mirror in front of you. I have found it is important for me to feel well dressed when I call on people. I have always had one suit in my wardrobe that I call my "banker's suit." I wear it for all meetings with bankers. I have found that when I fly for business I feel uncomfortable in the airport, on the plane, and at the hotel if I am not dressed for business. When I am on a pleasure trip, I don't feel that way.

You should be dressed so that you would feel comfortable if the person you are calling was in front of you. How you are dressed is a part of your countenance. It comes from the inside of you.

I even recommend for those starting out to develop this skill that they be in a posture that makes them feel confident when they phone. It may be standing behind your desk talking to the prospective customer who is usually seated at his desk.

When the prospective customer comes on the phone, you must say, "This is (your name) representing (your company name.)"

You must then establish your credentials. This is a busy person and a very important person in his or her own mind compared to this unknown on the phone. *What are the only credentials that anyone in the business of selling has? A satisfied* customer.

"I was talking to your friend (use the name of one of your satisfied customers) who was excited and satisfied that we had come up with the software that solved a problem that had his shipping department dead in their tracks. He told me that you were having this same problem with (describe the problem) and asked me to give you a ring. Have you gotten the problem worked out yet?" (You know he hasn't.) If you can ask more questions like, "Are you running into the same interchange breakdowns that Bill (his friend) was having? Is the lead time on the raw materials flow killing you?" It is obvious by now that you know more about his problem and his need than he does.

Please listen to me. I could give thousands of examples of what might be asked and never get close to the questions that you would ask to achieve this objective. The only thing for you to do is to look at the objective in each of these examples. Study the needs of the prospective customers for what you sell and figure out what you would have to ask to get them to tell you of their need for the benefits of what you sell.

In the beginning, you may not be able to use the name of a trusted friend of the person you are calling. You may only be able to name a company with a similar problem that had been caused to go away by what you sell.

The prospective customer is a busy man. Yes, very busy, but not as busy as you are.

"I am going to be in your city or area tomorrow (next week, next month or whenever) for a number of appointments. I have some time open on Tuesday morning or Thursday afternoon. If I could have a few minutes of your time, I can promise you that what I can show you will eliminate this problem with substantial savings to you."

If you have made this prospective customer consciously aware of enough of his or her needs and established your credentials, you have the appointment. If you don't, you need to ask a few more questions. They may not work, but they will teach you some of the things not to do. When you fail to get the appointment, if you can get your satisfied customer as a favor to you to call this person and ask him how it went, he or she can usually tell you why you didn't get the appointment and what you should have done.

Only a person who is in the business of selling can do that, but I can tell you that your sincere efforts to learn how to better meet the needs of customers like this will impress the person who refused the appointment. Do this every time you can and you will perfect the productive skills you need to get any appointment that you set out to get. In the process, you are going to have some of these people who turned you down reconsidering and calling you for an appointment. How very, very sweet that is!

The alternative is sitting in your hotel room putting off making any calls. Afraid to make a call. Hoping for something to happen that will keep you from having to make the call, while you fail in your selling career. I don't want you to have any doubt in your mind that in the business of selling, there is only one goal and one series of objectives that must be achieved to reach that goal.

KEEPING THE APPOINTMENT

When you enter the prospective customer's office for your appointment every rule is the same as those that apply to the greeting or approach, with all of the basics.

You could say, "Oh, yes, but I have an appointment. This man is expecting me." Is he? How excited is he to see you? You will not know until after contact has been made. You have a lot of time invested at this point. Can you afford to take a chance that the prospect will react negatively to your countenance and then waste all that effort?

Your positive countenance had better be there when first contact is made. It is customary for salespeople to shake hands as they introduce themselves and that makes it even more important that your countenance be up and running on contact. Shaking hands, like every skill, must be perfected into a productive skill.

"How's the problem with that interchange program?"

Wait. Slow down. Let's exchange a few civilities and courtesies first.

"Bill send his regards. I sure have come to respect that guy since I have gotten to know him. He tells me that you have a son who may make All-American. How's he coming?" You are there to get down to the business of selling, but you should still take every opportunity to show common courtesy.

You may have done a world of research and already know everything there is about this customer and his needs. That can make you a real smart alec, can't it? Or, it can make you a *real* expert.

Your second objective is still going to be to ask the same questions you must ask to learn enough about this customer's needs before you can demonstrate how the benefits of the features of what you sell will best meet these needs.

You may know it all about his needs, but *he* doesn't. If he did, he would not have his problem or his need, and you would not be there. Your questions make him aware of the needs and his answers tell you about them. Not *you* telling him. *That* is the business of selling.

The third and fourth objectives must be achieved. To whatever degree they have been achieved, it still leaves the need for your demonstration. You must continue your presentation and demonstration until you can just "write it up."

Every time you reread this chapter you are going to gain greater comprehension of what it teaches. The first time you read it, you may feel overwhelmed and think it tells you more than you could ever hope to understand and do. Just keep the simple basics of selling in mind. Reread the chapter "Who Can Succeed in Selling" any time you have doubts and then remember this: Even if you are brand new to selling you may already have a whole lot more of the knowledge and information you need than your customer.

You certainly know more about your credit plans, delivery, and services. Odds are that you know more about the benefits of the features of what you sell. You certainly know more about how to demonstrate the benefits of the features than your customers do.

When you have only the basic knowledge, it's far more than most of your prospective customers will have and that should give you all the confidence you need to greet them with a positive countenance.

There will only be one thing your customers will know more about than you and that is what their needs are, but please, please, remember this basic. Chances are they are not consciously aware of hardly any of their specific needs.

Your positive countenance makes it possible for you to ask a few simple questions such as, "Do you mind telling me what you are using now? How long have you had it? What do you like most about it? What has caused you to be most dissatisfied with it?" With those answers and others, you are more aware of their needs, while having made them more consciously aware of them than when you first came in contact with them.

Every time you do this and measure the results, you are going to learn more about what best satisfies your customers and makes them the most *dissatisfied*. This will permit you to ask not only more questions in your efforts to learn about them and their needs, but they will be more effective, productive questions. Every productive question you ask increases your knowledge, so your information base will increase, too.

I tell you this again to keep you aware of how simple selling is, provided you never lose sight of the basics.

Keep everything this simple and you will soon discover that selling truly can be the easiest, highest-paid profession there is.

27 / *Qualifying I*

QUALIFYING QUESTIONS ARE ASKED PROSPECTIVE CUSTOMERS ABOUT THEIR
NEEDS WITH NOTHING SAID ABOUT YOU OR WHAT YOU SELL. IT IS YOUR
INTEREST IN THEPROSPECTIVE CUSTOMERS THAT WILL CAUSE THEM TO BE
INTERESTED IN WHAT YOU SELL.

THE OBJECTIVE OF QUALIFYING is to learn enough about your prospective customers and their needs to determine what, among all the products you sell, is going to best meet those needs. When you do this you make the prospective customer consciously aware of those needs.

Your qualifying questions will be asked in the same sequence you use for your demonstration. You will make your prospective customers aware of their needs for the benefit of the features in the same sequence with which you demonstrate those benefits. This process will be clearer to you after you have read the chapters "The Presentation and Demonstration I, II, and III."

"How do I know in what sequence I will be making my demonstration if I don't know exactly what product I will be selling?" Regardless what you sell, the sequence you use for your demonstration should be exactly the same every time. If you are selling homes, you will always present every home in the same sequence and that is the sequence in which you ask your qualifying questions. The same is true of automobiles, life insurance, industrial equipment, and so on. It is true of anything sold by anyone.

Now you know why most salespeople never develop effective qualifying skills! They don't know enough about what they sell or the sequence of their demonstration to know what questions to ask or what sequence to ask them in.

Once you know the sequence you are using to demonstrate the benefits of the features of what you sell, then you have the sequence for your qualifying questions.

Just what are the questions you should be asking?

The objective of each question asked is to make prospective customers aware of the needs for the benefits of a feature of what you sell while you are learning whether they need the benefits of that feature, or not. That "or not" is a key to solving this problem.

If your prospective customer has no need and never expects to have a need for the benefits of a feature of what you are selling, the benefits of that feature would not add to its value if it were demonstrated. Chances are if this feature is demonstrated it could cause the customer to raise objections to buying what is being sold because the feature adds cost and the prospective customer has no need for it.

If important features are on some products even though a specific prospective customer doesn't need them, that could make that product worth less on trade-in or harder to resell without those features. In those cases, making the prospective customer aware of the benefits of the feature may not get you the sale, but won't cost it either. Remember, there is no perfect solution to any need.

I discovered this when I bought my first airplane. It was a Cessna 421-C eight-passenger, turbo-charged, twin-engine craft. Pressurized, it would fly at altitudes up to 28,000 feet and would fly at more than 300 miles per hour carrying enough fuel to travel 1,500 miles non-stop. It could carry luggage in the nose compartment, two wing compartments, and at the rear of the cabin. All of these things are what the salesperson told me the plane would do. What he didn't tell me was that it would not do them all at once.

With a full load of people, luggage, and fuel on the plane, you couldn't get it off the ground. If you took eight people, you had to take less luggage and less fuel. The plane would fly at over 300 miles per hour, but its cruising speed was 270 and a 100-mile headwind would cut its ground speed to 170. A 100-m.p.h. tailwind increased the ground speed to 370 m.p.h. and yet, it used the same amount of fuel per hour going 170 with the headwind or 370 with the tailwind. That fuel consumption with headwinds or tailwinds could cut the plane's non-stop range or add to it by more than a third.

My point is there is no such thing as a perfect airplane. Whichever one people buy will require that they give up some of one thing to get more of another. The prospective customers' objectives are to find the one craft that will best meet their needs and still fit within their budget. Nowhere do the prospective customers have to compromise more than when they buy an airplane, but this is true to some extent of anything you might be selling.

At all times, you must remember there is no *perfect* solution to any problem. Everything is a comparative. There are good and better solutions to all problems, but there can be only one *best* solution for that specific customer. That "best solution" is what you will be selling.

What makes your solution "best"?

It offers more benefits that meet more of your prospective customers' needs for the price than anything they have been shown elsewhere, or in the two comparisons you established when you achieved your fourth objective, or compared to what they are using now.

They could have looked at hundreds of other products on guided tours. Each of those products may have had a few features that offered benefits they liked and needed that weren't found on what you sell, but collectively, the benefits of the features on what you sell make it meet their needs so much better at the price you charge that you will still get the sale.

Once you have a list of the features of what you sell in the sequence of your presentation, it will be pretty easy for you to figure out which questions you are going to ask to make your prospective customers aware of their needs for the benefits of each one of those features. Your yardstick will tell you after the sale how productive each of those questions was and will help you improve the effectiveness of your questions.

Your goal when qualifying prospective customers is to have them tell *you* of their needs. Before you begin to demonstrate how the benefits of a feature make it meet those needs, you remind your prospective customers that it was a need they told you about, not one *you* told them they had. Believe me, there is a world of difference when you are selling prospective customers who have told you *all the reasons why they need to buy what you sell versus the guided tour director's telling them about features for which they feel they have no need.*

But—watch out! If you have *no* plan to follow when you first start selling, by the end of your first month you will have developed a complete set of all-too-effective counterproductive selling skills into *habits*.

The odds are good that you will *never* overcome those counterproductive habits.

Therefore, you *must* have a basic presentation plan that you will follow precisely when you begin selling. Your plan at that time might include only the key features, benefits, and prices. That much you must know about what you sell. You must also know how to demonstrate the *benefits* of those features. Of course, you would also know enough about credit terms and company services and warranties, and so on.

The word "basic" means essential and fundamental. You cannot sell if you don't have and know the basics.

This basic presentation plan will make it easy for you to prepare a list of the features and benefits in the sequence in which you will demonstrate them.

Now. Figure out questions to ask that will cause your prospective customers to tell you about their needs for the benefits of each feature. *If you don't have questions that establish the prospective customers' need for at least the basics of what you sell, you have no business trying to sell them anything.*

This list of features and benefits should grow almost daily when you first start selling, and the list of questions you ask should grow with each added feature of a benefit. You will never know this, if you don't actually write down the features and benefits in the same sequence as your presentation, adding more questions to that list as you learn more and more about what you sell.

If you think having a presentation checklist is a waste of time, consider this little known fact: No one has ever been killed taking off in an airplane that I know of. Fatalities occur on landing. No crash occurs until the plane comes down. It is a federal law that every commercial pilot must follow a detailed checklist before take off. Every item on that checklist must be dealt with before the pilot may take off. Pilots want to know before they start that they can not only get into the air, but far more important, whether or not they can get back on the ground safely.

It should be no different in any other profession, including *selling*. To get yourself into the habit of following the same sequence in your presentation every time, you, as the salesperson, should have a checklist of features and benefits in that same sequence. That will not only get you started at the right point, it will keep you from doing those things that cause prospective customers not to buy. That presentation checklist becomes your checklist for qualifying questions.

When you first start out, you are far better off if you actually *tell* your prospective customers that you want to check your list of questions in order to be more help to them, than you would by just winging it. I will guarantee you that your prospective customers will respect you far more for having done that than they will if you try to show them something they think won't meet their needs.

Of course, you *can* wing it, but the odds are your career will crash and burn. *Or, you can start with a plan, follow it, measure how effectively you are achieving the plan and you will be guaranteed success beyond your wildest dreams.*

All you need to do is to make a commitment to follow your plan and keep that commitment.

There is an old saying that tells you how to keep this commitment—if, at first, you don't succeed, try, try again—with one exception. Do *not* try the same thing a second time if it did not work the first time. Only your yardstick can keep that from happening.

How do you determine the sequence you will use in your presentation? In selling, your product is the basis for your script. Start with what the prospective customer can see. (Think about that: What they are looking at is what their attention is focused on.) What they will see first is what you present and demonstrate first. So you follow the script from that feature and its benefits on to the next in a logical and visible sequence.

Residential realtors have no problem knowing where to start their presentation every time. It will start with the location of the home and that means that they *must* have achieved their first four objectives before they ever arrive in that neighborhood. Otherwise, they can't point out things like schools, hospitals, shopping, and so on, showing prospective customers benefit after benefit of feature after feature of the location that makes the home they haven't even seen better and better meet the needs they said they had. As they stop in front of the home, visual features and benefits should be pointed out (remember "The Principle of Reflection"). The realtor should proceed in the same sequence right on through to the end every single time a demonstration and presentation is made.

Note: There will often be times when the importance of one feature and its benefits will take precedence over others. In these cases you may start with that feature or assure the customer that it will be demonstrated before you start. In either case, you then pick up your usual sequence of presentation.

These two questions were asked of me:

1. What would happen if we took twenty salespeople and gave each of them the same amount of time with the same customer with one specific objective, and at the end of a fixed amount of time each filled out a form describing the customer's needs?

Would we get a wide variation in the accuracy of the "need assessment" of the same customer? Some salespeople are very good and seem to have more talent for knowing, sensing, probing, feeling, interacting, empathizing, and finally understanding other people's needs. Others are not so good.

2. Is it possible for all salespeople to learn the skills they need to determine a customer's needs? Is it fair to say that what you teach will work with people scoring a C+ or better at this critical skill, or else they should seek a different career?

I started out by saying I believed almost everyone who could read this book could succeed in selling, and succeed beyond their wildest dreams. I put one qualifying exception on that statement. They must have an accurate way to *measure* what they are trying to do and they must *use* that measurement.

I have used spaced repetition, repeating points over and over, to make one point over and above all the others on selling: *No salesperson ever has or ever will lose a sale because he knew too much about a prospective customer's needs and about what he or she sells.*

Even the slow learners plodding along, persistent in their efforts to gain more and more information about each prospective customer that they have come in contact with, are eventually going to learn what they need to know while making their prospective customers consciously aware of enough of their needs. Even the slow learners will make a sale more and more often in less and less time.

I cannot put the words in your mouth that *you* must learn to say, nor can I tell you *what* you must know. I can tell you how to learn, what you must learn, and teach you to say what you must. No, I can do better than that. I can give you a way to measure how effectively you were able to learn what you needed to know and how effectively you said what you needed to say and that guarantees your success. Will it make you an "A" student? Oh, yes, if you stick with your yardstick like glue!

The yardstick not only guarantees you *can* be an "A" student, your tenacity and the yardstick guarantees you that you *will* be one.

I can hear right now what most salespeople are going to say when they read this. "Mr. Lawhon, I would starve to death if I did that with every prospective customer I came in contact with."

Yes, you would. And, you would starve to death if you had to make a living by assembling those simple products referred to in the chapter entitled "Habits" if every one of them was as sloppily done and took as long as the first one. But you could have been earning a living by the time you completed the third one. To some degree, that is the way all productive skills are developed. You may say you are not willing to make this effort to succeed in the business of selling. Sorry to have to tell you this, but you can make this effort in selling or you can make it in some other chosen field of endeavor. You will either develop the productive skills you need to succeed into productive habits or you will fail—your entire life will be a failure, too.

In the early fifties, I had a young man come to me with this story, asking for a job selling. "I am an ordained minister and I have a degree in teaching. I was given my first church and failed as a pastor because I could not preach. I would like to work for you long enough to get enough money to get me, my wife, and two children to Cuba. I can get a job teaching there that pays $4,000 a year and we can live on $2,000. With the other $2,000 I can support a missionary who can preach."

I said, "Young man, if you really are that sincere about wanting to learn to preach, I can teach you how and it won't take long."

"How?"

"Walk out on that street corner and start preaching. I guarantee that when you get hungry enough, you will learn to preach."

He didn't take my advice. Years later I ran into him in a J. C. Penney store. He was a clerk. He still couldn't preach. He hadn't gotten to Cuba and he looked starved to death mentally, physically, and spiritually.

My point: Yes, you may think you will starve to death if you follow these teachings with every prospective customer. But you won't, and I don't care what you sell. I guarantee that the more tenacious you are, the hungrier you get, the quicker you will learn to develop productive qualifying skills.

Once developed and perfected into habits you will own them forever. You will never know the true hunger and starvation that young man experienced. "Man doesn't live by bread alone" is an old adage because it is true. It is those things that build our confidence and make us unafraid that feed our spirits.

The knowledge, comprehension, and productive skills won't be gained by the third time you try them, but the yardstick will have already shown you some things to do that will make it work better. That should be all the assurance you need to know you can master this productive skill and succeed beyond your wildest dreams. Don't give up. Don't *ever* give up.

28 / *Qualifying II*

THE PROSPECTIVE CUSTOMERS' LEVEL OF DISSATISFACTION WITH WHAT THEY
ARE CURRENTLY USING MUST BE ELEVATED.

REVIEW "THE BEST KEPT SECRET IN SELLING" AS YOU READ THIS CHAPTER.

THERE ARE THREE BASIC STARTING POINTS for qualifying in all selling situations:

1. Prospective customers who do not own what you sell.

Your first objective is finding out everything you possibly can about what they are doing now and how they are doing it.

What questions should you ask? Any questions that will make them consciously aware of what they are doing now that the benefits of what you sell will permit them to do better.

How far do you walk to work every day? How long does it take you?

This bicycle will get you to and from work in five minutes. That saves you 25 minutes each way. That is almost one hour every working day. You could go on and tell them what they could do with that hour if they owned the bicycle.

Do you like to fish? Where do you fish? How long does it take you to get there? With your new bike, you would be home every evening in time to run down to your favorite fishing hole for a while. How many children do you have? If your son had a bike, too, he could go fishing with you.

I could follow this exploratory line of thought and wind up with a book bigger than this dealing only with a bicycle and the needs it might fill.

2. Prospective customers who already are using what you sell.

You will be making a comparison with what they are using now with what you are selling. The objective of your questions will still be the same.

Your questions will make your prospective customers consciously aware of what they are using now does for them and your demonstration will show them how what you are selling will do better.

NOTICE. NOTICE. THESE QUESTIONS ARE ASKED ABOUT THEM BEFORE ANYTHING IS SAID ABOUT YOU AND WHAT YOU SELL. IT IS YOUR INTEREST IN THEM THAT WILL CAUSE THEM TO BE INTERESTED IN WHAT YOU SELL.

Remember this example: Insurance salespeople fail because they ask the prospective customers if they can talk to them about insurance instead of asking questions about them that will make them aware of needs that will be met by the policies the salesperson has to offer. It is the same with the bicycle salesperson and it is the same with all selling no matter what is being sold or what the selling situation is.

Here again, the more you can learn about how what you sell can do better for your prospective customers than what they have now won't do or won't do as well, the more questions you will be able to ask. The more you can learn about their needs, the more you can make them consciously aware of those needs and the easier it will be to make the sale.

3. Prospective customers who are shopping for something specific or who are shopping price.

In both cases, they think they know what they want or they think they will know it when they see it. They won't. If they did, they would not be "shopping." It may be some time before you fully comprehend that. I don't often ask that something I say be taken on faith, but as you come to comprehend better and better what causes the prospective customer to buy, you will realize that these are the hardest customers for the guided tour director to sell and the easiest for the professional.

Remember the necktie customer in "Your Road to Selling Success?" The customer was sure he had found what he wanted at an incredibly low price. If the salesperson had said, "Sir, that is a beautiful necktie you have picked out. When they put it on sale, I wondered why. Do you mind if I ask what you intend to wear it with?" That question made the prospective customer aware of what he needed in the way of a necktie.

Now let me ask you *men* a question. Do you have any ties in your closet that you don't wear? I bet if you stop and think about it, the reason you have kept them is because you like them. The reason you don't wear them is because they don't go with anything you have so they don't meet your needs.

That salesman could have said, "Perhaps you would like to take the tie over to our suit and sport coat racks to hold it up to those that are the same color as what you have." As the salesperson saw what the young man held the tie up to, he would have learned what the young man needed and made him aware of it at the same time. He could have taken him back to the sale ties, picked out three for each suit or sport coat the young man had held the tie up to, and wound up selling several ties. He might have been able to sell him a new suit or sport coat to go with the tie he liked so well. I could continue this line of thought on a product as simple as a necktie until it became a large book, too.

When you look at this example, you will discover that the prospective customer knew everything he had in his wardrobe. He knew what he needed, but wasn't consciously aware of it at that time. What the professional did was make this prospective customer aware of needs he was not consciously aware of, needs that what the salesperson sold were going to meet, needs that competitors had not made the prospective customer aware of and because of that, had not stoked the fires of the prospective customer's desires.

In all three cases, the selling situations were different, but the objectives were the *same.*

A salesperson's ability to qualify will depend upon how many different questions he or she can ask in each type of selling situation. It is *your* career. It is your *business.*

Make a list and add each new question you come up with in its proper sequence to your list. Your objective will be to come up with every conceivable question you could ask that would make a prospective customer aware of a need for the benefits of the features of what you sell—as well as which feature caused them to become dissatisfied with what they are now using.

Aha! There's the catch! You can't ask a question about a need for a benefit (or a cause of dissatisfaction) that you yourself are not consciously aware of and have not experienced for yourself.

Years ago, I did a television commercial for a record storage cabinet with sliding doors. Inside were removable brass rods that could be insert-ed to hold the record albums upright. The sale price for one day only was nine dollars. We ran the commercial and waited for the mobs of cus-tomers to flood into our showrooms. No one responded in any of the ten large cities where I had locations.

I had one of the cabinets brought to my office and placed on my desk. I looked at it, thought about the commercial and decided to redo it. The new version went something like this: "When our doors open tomorrow morning at ten o'clock, these storage cabinets will go on sale. They are perfect for bedside tables, storage tables, sewing rooms, perfect for portable sewing machines, in the kid's room, for television stands, record storage, hall commodes, linen storage. At our sale price, they are even great for the work area in your garage. I'll bet you can find hundreds of uses for them in your home. Believe it or not, if you shop tomorrow between 10 AM and 10 PM, you can get as many as you want and need for your home for only nine dollars apiece. Yes, just nine dollars apiece if you shop tomorrow."

We ran this commercial on low-traffic weekdays periodically for sev-eral years. We sold an average of more than 300 cabinets per store every time it ran.

The more needs what you sell will meet, the more reasons your prospective customers will have for buying. But on one condition: they must be made aware of those needs. In this commercial, I not only thought of a use for one or more of these cabinets in every room in the house and the garage, but I encouraged people to think of other needs they might have.

Consider the thousands of sales I lost when I ran that first commer-cial, which had not made prospective customers aware of enough of their needs for the benefits of the cabinet. Those were sales that could have been made.

I should repeat this on every other line in this book. "You will never, never, never lose a sale because you know too much about your customer and his or her needs." You will never, never, never, lose a sale because you know too much about what you are selling.

Almost every sale you lose will be because you had not learned enough about your customer and his or her needs or you did not know enough about what you sell and how it would meet those needs.

When I called the cabinet a record cabinet in the first commercial, it caused the customer to see it only as a record cabinet and that caused them not to buy it. When the prospective customer does not buy it is the salesperson who causes them not to buy. What did we do that caused customers not to buy the record cabinets at first? The yardstick made me aware of the fact that our advertising caused them not to buy and made me look to see what we had done wrong.

In selling homes, the prospective customer can be made aware of the fact that an area of the yard would be the perfect place for a garden, swimming pool, and so on. The branch of a large tree could be just the place for a swing. A bedroom will convert to the perfect office, or private study, or hobby room. Needs and needs and needs that the prospective customer is not consciously aware of.

In qualifying prospective customers for a home, if the salesperson knows there's room for a garden, pool, or extra bedroom, he or she can ask if they might some day want to have a garden, pool, study, or home office. When the home is demonstrated, the salesperson can remind the prospective customer of the future needs that he or she had made them aware of and show the customer how this home is going to meet those needs when that customer is ready for them.

Residential real estate salespeople can make a list of every need that prospective customers say they have or think they might have for a home and continue to add to the list. When the salespeople check out new homes that have come on the market, they can review the list. The principle of reflection will cause them to see features and benefits they would not see if they were not consciously aware of what they were looking for.

It won't be long before these salespeople find themselves seeing places to put a garden, pool, or study. When they are looking at new homes coming on the market, they don't need the list to cause this to happen. It has become a skill they have perfected into a productive habit.

It's like the spot you get on a necktie or dress. Once you have seen it, you can't *not* see it from then on. Once your eye is trained to look at a lawn and see things it could be used for, you can't *not* see them. The more of these things your eye is trained to see, the more needs you will be able to make your prospective customer aware of that what you sell is going to meet.

Your goal is *satisfied* customers and the better what you sell meets their needs, the easier getting the sale will be and the more satisfied they will be. It should become more and more obvious that it is rare when prospective customers are consciously aware of very many of their needs for what you sell. When you ask them about a need, you make them consciously aware of it. The more of these needs you can ask them about that what you sell will meet, compared to what they are using now, the more sales you are going to make.

That is the business of selling in a nutshell.

29 / *The Comparison Selection*

There is nothing perfect on the face of this earth. But there are always some things being sold that will better meet a customer's needs than others. Customers buy when they are convinced what they are buying is the one thing that best meets their needs for the price they must pay.

THIS CHAPTER isn't about a new selling skill and it doesn't take a genius to figure it out. We know it was being used as far back as the Stone Age. It is the oldest recorded thing known about selling: "The wise merchant never shows all of his wares at once and he saves the best for last."

Arrowheads that were several thousand years old have been found as many as 3,000 miles from where they were quarried and made. They got there the same way silk got from China to Europe, on ancient trade routes. The merchandise passed through the hands of many traders before it reached Europe.

When a dealer in arrowheads arrived at the quarry where the arrowhead maker plied his trade, he would be shown a large assortment of good arrowheads laid out on the ground—all available, your choice, at one low price. The dealer would look them over and say, "They're pretty good, but I am going to look around to see if I can't find some that are better."

The arrowhead maker would look around to see that no one was watching and motion the dealer into his cave where he would say, "I keep my best arrowheads for my best customers in here," as he pulled animal pelts off a large assortment of obviously better arrowheads. "Of course these will cost you more," he says. The dealer would look them over saying they are much better, but he was still going to look around to be sure he couldn't find anything better.

The arrowhead maker would then reach under his pallet and pull out a large, soft leather bag of fine quality saying, "I save my very best arrowheads for my dear old daddy, but he's not well enough to hunt anymore. I will tell you what I am going to do: If you promise you won't tell other traders, I am going to let you have these arrowheads at the same price I normally charge for my better arrowheads." The comparison selection worked then and it works today. Not only did it get the sale, but made it easier to get and made it take less time. When the trader has left the arrowhead maker selected the best of his better arrowheads to fill his leather bag. Then he took the best of the good arrowheads to fill the gap. Now he was ready for the next trader. Good, better, best are always comparisons.

The greatest merchant empires in history were built on good, better, and best product lines. Needless to say, we all want the best and that led to another ancient saying: "Sell to the masses and you will live with the classes. Sell to the classes and you will live with the masses." That old adage remains true because there always has been and always will be far more people who make up the masses.

It matters not whether your prospective customer's budgets will permit them to buy the best and most expensive or limit them to the least expensive things on the market. The customers in both situations will have the same goal and that is to wind up having bought what was going to best meet their needs. Naturally, that means what they bought had to be priced within their means.

In every case, the professional salesperson is going to establish three comparisons, just like the arrowhead maker.

The first thing shown is going to be good and it is going to far better meet the prospective customers' needs than what they are using now. The second thing shown will be better because it will better meet their needs, but it will cost a lot more. The third will be best because it is not only going to best meet their needs, but it costs less than the second item shown.

If what you sell is the finest and most expensive of its kind, comparisons must still be made to establish it as the best. There are very few things in this world that are the finest and most expensive and that's why the comparison selection skill is used by every professionally competent salesperson in the world today.

More has been written and taught about how to overcome customers' objections to buying and closing the sale than all other things combined and none of it has caused any overall increase in the percentage of prospective customers being sold.

To most salespeople in the world today, price is the number one objection their customers give for not buying. Why? Yes, why is this seen as the only problem of any significance to the great majority of salespeople and absolutely no problem at all to those who are professionally competent?

No one ever has or ever will solve a problem in the purest sense of the word. People faced with a problem must find what is causing the problem, eliminate the cause, and the problem will cease to exist.

All problems are an effect. There can be no effect without a cause. We call that the Law of Cause and Effect.

WHEN A CUSTOMER OBJECTS TO BUYING ANYTHING, THAT PROBLEM WAS CAUSED BY THE SALESPERSON.

That is why the professionally competent salespeople who don't do those things that cause problems, feel insulted and indignant when asked how they overcome those problems.

THIS BOOK HAS ONLY ONE OBJECTIVE AND THAT IS TO HELP READERS LEARN TO DO THOSE PRODUCTIVE THINGS THAT WILL CAUSE THEIR PROSPECTIVE CUSTOMERS TO *BUY* RATHER THAN TEACH THEM HOW TO OVERCOME PROBLEMS THEIR COUNTERPRODUCTIVE ACTIONS CREATED THAT WOULD CAUSE THEIR CUSTOMERS *NOT TO BUY.*

One of those things that all top professionals will do every time that causes their customers to buy is to establish comparisons with what they have decided is going to best meet the prospective customer's needs before they start the presentation of what they intend to sell.

It requires two comparisons to achieve this objective. Professional salespeople will start by showing prospective customers a good product that will far better meet their needs than what they are using now. It will be priced at about the same price as what they intend to sell them, but it won 't meet the customers' needs as well.

The professional salespeople will then show them a second product that will better meet their needs than the first, but at a much higher price.

In both cases, the professionals let the customers examine what they show them. They might even point out a feature or two that can be used as a comparison. Then the professionals show their prospective customers what they intend to sell them. It will show that the product will far better meet their needs than the first one, with the price about the same. It will meet their needs as well as the second product shown, but at a considerably lower price.

As the salesperson makes his or her presentation and demonstration of what's going to best meet the customers' needs, it becomes more and more apparent that it better meets their needs than the first and even meets their needs as well as the second, which costs so much more, and *all of this is compared to what they are using now.*

Most guided tour directors' customers will leave without buying despite all the sneaky, tricky, high pressure, so-called closing techniques they might have been taught. The excuses they give for failure to buy can be boiled down to only two. The same two excuses that have been used since the Stone Age: 1. "We want to look around to see if we can find something we like better." And 2. "I am sure this is what we are going to buy, but we want to look around to see if we can get a better deal."

When professionals do a good job of achieving their first four objectives which includes the comparison selection, before they show their prospective customers what they intend to sell them, the customers' reaction is, "Oh! I like this one so much better than the first one we looked at." That overcomes or greatly reduces their wanting to look around to see if they can find something they will like better.

"Oh! I even like it as well as the second one we looked at and the price is so much less." This overcomes or reduces their desire to want to look for a better deal. It also makes them aware of the fact that if they did find something they liked better, the odds are it will cost a lot more.

Professional salespeople start their presentation by reminding customers of a need they had said they had when being qualified. Then they proceed to demonstrate how the benefits of a feature will make it better meet that need. This gives the customers a powerful reason to buy, and reduces their desire to shop further or to think they may find a better deal somewhere else. As they are reminded of one previously stated need after another and hear benefit after benefit of feature after feature demonstrated, making what is being sold better and better meet their needs, the demonstration will soon reach a point where all thought of finding anything the customer would like better or costing less has disappeared. Then, all the salesperson needs do to get the order is "write it up."

When asked why they use this productive comparison skill, the competent professionals one and all say:

"It makes the sale so much easier to get."

"It makes getting the sale take so much less time."

They go on to explain that they use the amount of time it took them to get the order after they had started their presentation as a yardstick to measure how effectively they had achieved their first four objectives, which include the comparison selection as Objective #4.

Nowhere can we see the effects of this productive skill more clearly than when selling residential real estate. Professionals sell circles around those who don't make comparisons. (I would call that being productive, wouldn't you?) When I ask guided tour directors why they don't use the skill, you guessed it—they say, "I tried that and it won't work for me."

I discovered an unusual thing happening to salespeople who were using the customer file card to measure how effectively they had achieved each of their objectives. Many salespeople told me they had tried to make this skill work for them for a year or more without success when all of a sudden it worked, and from then on it worked every time. It was some time before I figured out why it hadn't worked for them for so long, but once it had, from then on it did work. What caused it to start working all of a sudden?

I discovered it only worked when the salespeople knew ahead of time what they are going to use for the comparisons.

If real estate salespeople are qualifying prospective customers and have determined which home is going to best meet a customer's needs, it is almost impossible for the salesperson at that time to decide which two homes to use as a comparison. What the professionals do is determined by what homes they will think of as comparisons when they are looking for the first time at a home that has just come on the market. They say to themselves, "This home is so much better than such and such a home that costs about the same. It's every bit as good as such and such a home that costs quite a bit more." When the competent professional salesperson finds a prospective customer and has a home in mind that will best meet the customer's needs, he or she knows the answer to the two objections that could keep them from buying it. "Best meet this person's needs compared to what?"

In residential real estate these comparisons are easily found because many homes are put on the market at prices that are too high. Compared to what? Compared to other homes on the market. For a competent real estate salesperson, finding a home that is not near as much home as another home which priced the same is easy. Finding a home priced considerably above a home of equal value is not hard either. As a matter of fact, the professional will often use the same two overpriced homes over and over to sell other homes.

Regardless what you sell, if you want this productive skill to work for you, you must look at what you sell and ask yourself, "If I had a prospective customer and this was going to best meet their needs, what would I use to establish two comparisons?"

One of those comparisons would be priced about the same, but would not meet the customer's needs as well. The other comparison would be something costing more that wouldn't meet their needs any better.

When you have done that, you will discover that this productive skill will work for you the first time you use it and it will work every time from then on. Of course, you will find better, more effective comparisons, and more effective ways to make those comparisons as you continue to practice this productive skill.

Most salespeople are going to say, "I can see how those comparisons could be established if you were selling homes, furniture, jewelry and things like that, but what I sell is different."

It matters not what you are selling. If you wish to succeed, your only goal when you come in contact with prospective customers is to turn them into *satisfied* customers. You cannot achieve that goal if you have not learned enough about the customer and his or her needs to believe that you have something that will best meet those needs. Best compared to what? If you don't know you can't help your prospective customer know and the odds of your selling anything is zip. If you *do* know, I can guarantee you that in your own way you will use that knowledge.

A life insurance salesperson may have hundreds of different policies to offer, but only one is going to best meet the needs of any one prospective customer. Surely, that salesperson could find the two that would make the best comparison out of all those other policies.

What if you sell the only thing in the world like it. The only reason people will buy your product is because it will do something for them better than anything else for the price you are asking. What are those things people now use that what you sell does better? Make your customers consciously aware of those things before you start your presentation.

Nothing is perfect on the face of the earth. Everything is a comparison. When the first bicycle came on the market and the first rider passed someone who was walking, that person saw someone going much faster with a fraction of the energy. That comparison sold bicycles, and if what you sell gets sold, it will be because you can establish the comparisons you need to cause your customers to buy. If they object to buying, don't ever forget you caused their objections.

I've had two experiences I like to relate because they both show the need for this skill.

I was interviewing a 68-year-old salesman, a native Israeli who had been in the U.S. for eight years. Although his accent was very strong, he was one of the top volume professionals in his field. He had learned his profession selling in the ancient bazaars of the Near East. As I questioned him about making a sale, he said, "I always show my customers another product before I show them the one I intend to sell them."

When I asked him why, he gave the same answer of other top professionals. I said, "I do that too, but always show my customers two other products before I show them the one that I intend to sell them."

He was out of his chair like a shot, spouting words first in his native tongue, then in English. "Oh, yes! Oh, yes! I can't believe I have been so stupid all these years!" He saw at once that giving customers two comparisons would make getting the sale even easier than showing them only one. He could not believe that in fifty years of selling he had not discovered that for himself.

Interviewing what is to this day one of the highest-volume, highest-paid retail salespeople, I asked him about this skill. He said he used it because it made the sale go faster and made getting the order easier. I asked if he did it every time. He hesitated just a second before he replied, "Yes." After continuing through the rest of his productive skills, I returned to the subject of comparison selection. "You said you do this because it makes the sale go faster and it makes it easier to get the sale, but when I asked if you do it every time, you hesitated before you said yes. Do you do it every single time?"

"Well, he said, "when we get overrun with customers, I..." He too, shot out of his chair and yelled, "Don't say a word! I can't believe it! Don't you say a word."

But I did: "I am going to say it. You tell me that you do this because it makes the sale go so much faster and so much easier and just when you need to do it the most, you quit doing it."

He absolutely could not believe what he had been doing. I mean, he was stunned and mumbling to himself.

If you watch top professionals and guided tour directors when there are far more prospective customers to be waited on than there are salespeople, you will see the masters of selling at their best. They will be working one customer at a time as though they had all the time in the world. You will see those guided tour directors at their worst. They will either be hustling from prospective customer to prospective customer saying, "Can I help you?" and getting a "no" every time—or standing near the entrance of a showroom packed with prospective customers hoping to get what they call a "good one."

I wish I were wise enough and had the time to develop the comparisons needed for everything sold. I am not, but I do know this for a fact. The only goal of any salesperson is a *satisfied* customer. There are ten objectives that must be achieved to reach that goal and it matters not what is being sold. One of those objectives is a comparison of what will best meet the prospective customer's needs and nothing will make that go away.

If the salesperson doesn't know what those comparisons are in advance, he or she cannot use them and cannot develop this productive skill, one of the most valuable a salesperson can possess and one so simple a child could do it if he or she only knew what those comparisons were before they needed them. This productive skill, when perfected into a productive habit:

Makes it easier to get a sale.

Makes it take less time.

And that makes it worth the time and effort you need to get those comparisons organized *ahead of time* and be ready to use them.

30 / *All You Need to Know About Overcoming a Customer's Objections to Buying*

THIS BOOK HAS ONLY ONE OBJECTIVE: TO HELP THE READER LEARN TO DO THOSE PRODUCTIVE THINGS THAT WILL CAUSE PROSPECTIVE CUSTOMERS TO BUY—NOT TO TEACH HOW TO TRY TO OVERCOME PROBLEMS WHICH COUNTERPRODUCTIVE ACTIONS CREATE AND WHICH CAUSE PROSPECTIVE CUSTOMERS NOT TO BUY.

THIS SHORT CHAPTER NEGATES MOST OF WHAT HAS BEEN WRITTEN PURPORTING TO TEACH A PERSON HOW TO SELL.

AND, IT NEGATES MOST OF WHAT IS CURRENTLY BEING TAUGHT ABOUT SELLING.

MORE SALES ARE LOST because a salesperson did not know enough about the prospective customers and their needs than all other reasons combined. The second largest reason sales are lost is because the salesperson did not know enough about what he or she was selling. Almost all lost sales can be traced to one or both of these causes.

When any sale is lost, an offer has been made to sell something and the prospective customer has objected to buying. If this customer had no objection to buying, he or she would have bought. Hundreds of books have been written on overcoming customer objections to buying. When you look closely at those books covering "closing techniques," you will see they, too, are merely ploys for getting a prospective customer to buy who has objections to buying.

Every objection a prospective customer can come up with for not buying goes back to the salesperson's not knowing enough about the customer and his or her needs or enough about what the salesperson is trying to sell.

Example: A prospective customer objects to buying because what the salesperson shows them is the wrong size. Clearly, that salesperson did not know enough about what the prospective customer needed or not enough about what he or she was selling, which certainly would include the size.

If what a salesperson is trying to sell doesn't meet the prospective customer's needs, they are not prospective customers and all the sneaky, tricky, closing techniques and all the so-called skills for overcoming objections won't change that fact and if the customer is coerced, pressured or tricked into buying, what that customer buys is going to fail to meet his or her needs and that customer will be a *dissatisfied* customer who feels cheated because he or she *was* cheated. No other word will make that salesperson's action one bit more honorable. When customers have no need for the benefits of a product or service, they will not buy because they have no reason to. They are not prospective customers.

Once a salesperson's presentation of a product or service has begun, and the prospective customer raises an objection (at any time during the presentation) that the salesperson did not anticipate, that salesperson had not known enough about that particular customer and his or her needs, period.

Does that mean competent salespeople will never experience objections to anything they are demonstrating or presenting? Absolutely not! But the topic opens a Pandora's box containing all the evils of selling.

Every objection a prospective customer raises can become an excuse for a salesperson *not* to get the sale. Think about that, because it is those excuses you will hear as the losers in the lounge approve each other while blaming all lost sales on the prospective customer, the company, their competitors, or the product or service they sell.

There are only two kinds of objections to buying anything:

1. Valid
2. Invalid.

Most books on selling say that an *invalid* objection is not an objection to buying, but a request for more information. In most cases, the salesperson has not made the prospective customer consciously aware of his or her need for the benefits of the feature they are being shown, told about, or that is being demonstrated. When customers aren't aware of a need, they can't possibly see how what the salesperson is talking about has anything to do with them. Every book purporting to teach salespeople how to overcome objections says these kind of objections should be welcomed and seen as a sign that the customer wants to buy but just needs more information. Trouble is, 99.9 percent of all the salespeople who read that comment do not improve their ability to supply more information to overcome these objections. Why?

Simply supplying more information about how something is going to do something a prospective customer feels he has no need for (whether the information is supplied effectively or not) only annoys your customer. The harder the issue is pressed the more confused and irritated the customer becomes. More sales are lost for that reason than any others.

If you understand that point, you will also realize that most of what you read or hear about overcoming objections is very misleading.

If salespeople ask questions until they learn enough about their prospective customer and their needs to be able to show that what they sell is going to best meet those needs, the prospective customer will have been made just as aware of the need as the salesperson. The professionally competent salesperson has a lot more specialized knowledge than the prospective customer, so his or her comprehension of those needs is far greater than the prospective customer's.

For that reason, when you make your presentation, you will always restate what the prospective customer told you his or her need was—just to be sure the customer is *consciously* aware of that need before you start to tell, show, or demonstrate how the benefits of a feature of your product or service are going to meet that need. Any objections the prospective customer raises at this point are what we call "minor," which means you must both increase your prospective customer's comprehension of the need, then show how the need is met, or better, have the prospective customer *experience* to an even greater degree how it *is* met.

I have yet to meet a top professional who has not told me he or she makes the sale every time he or she has a qualified prospective customer, which means any time a competent professional starts a presentation or demonstration of anything, he or she makes the sale.

"That is too big." "That's not big enough." "That's too expensive."

"I can't use that color." Any one of these—and perhaps a hundred more—objections could be valid reasons not to buy, but professionals will not make a presentation of *anything* without first learning what they must know about the size or color or whatever feature is *needed* by their prospective customers; nor will they demonstrate something that cannot be made to fit within the prospective customer's budget.

It would be pointless for me to write chapter after chapter on this subject to teach you how to do something you would never face if you do what you are supposed to do. I refuse to support the losers in the lounge.

Remember, I said there were *two* kinds of objections to buying? So far, I have only dealt with invalid objections. But what about the prospective customers who have *valid* reasons for not buying? They are not prospective customers and that is the first thing the professional has learned when he or she sets out to achieve his second objective.

Remember what these professionals say? "Every time I have a *qualified* prospective customer, I make the sale." *Qualified* means the customer has told the salesperson enough about his or her needs for enough of the benefits from enough of the features of what the salesperson is selling to convince the salesperson he or she has a qualified prospective customer, and that what the salesperson is selling is going to meet those needs so well it makes the price insignificant. The salesperson knows these qualified prospective customers can be turned into satisfied customers.

If there is a valid reason for anyone not to buy what the salesperson sells, it should be learned before any effort is made to show, tell about, or demonstrate anything.

I repeat: Any time you have begun to show, tell about, or demonstrate anything and you do not make the sale, it was because you had not learned enough about your prospective customers and their needs, or you did not know enough about what you sell. *No professionally competent salesperson ever has or ever will make any effort to overcome a customer's valid objection.* Why?

A *valid* objection means the person does not have any need for the benefits of what is being sold or that the cost cannot be made to fit within his or her budget. Therefore, this person is *not* a prospective customer for what you sell. Don't forget: Your only goal is a satisfied customer. No customer with valid objections to buying what you sell can ever be turned into a *satisfied* customer.

The lesson the 9-Dot Puzzle taught was that when we know the solution to the puzzle or have the knowledge to solve it, then it ceases to be a puzzle, or ceases to be a problem.

Salespeople who try to figure out how to overcome objections that arise because they don't know enough about their prospective customer's needs for what they are selling will *never* find a solution to that problem. There is no sneaky, tricky way to get around these cold, hard facts. Managers who go on trying to teach salespeople how to overcome objections and develop closing techniques will *never* develop effective, productive, competent sales organizations.

When a close study is made of what the profession of selling really is and what the goal of every salesperson should be when he or she first comes in contact with a prospective customer, it negates almost every single word and all the implications in books, tapes, or sales training programs that deal with overcoming customers' objections to buying and to closing the sale.

When the salesperson's only goal is a *satisfied* customer, there is no closing of a sale. Writing the order, yes. Closing the sale, no. You will not find a chapter in this book on closing the sale.

Now, wait a minute, Mr. Lawhon. There is nothing perfect on this earth and that means there can be no perfect solution to the needs of anyone. All prospective customers, regardless of their needs, can find reasons why they should not buy and thus, have objections to buying. What do you have to say to that?

Now, let's go back to the first four objectives of the professionally competent salesperson. In the chapter "Your Road to Selling Success I," you saw that salespeople asked questions that made their prospective customers consciously aware of their needs while also making them consciously aware of their *dissatisfaction* with what they were now using. The salespeople established comparisons with their products that would far better meet the customers' needs than what they were using. This *good* solution to the prospective customers' needs would cost about the same as the *best* solution. The salesperson showed the prospective customer a better solution, but it cost almost twice as much. All this before the salesperson had shown or even started to tell them anything about the product that was going to *best* meet their needs.

Finally, the professionally competent salesperson shows the product that is going to best meet the prospective customers' needs. Compared to what the customers are using, they could see how the product better meets their needs (compared to the other products they had seen) and, most important, it was better than what they are using now. So they will sometimes say, "I will take it."

If prospective customers don't say they will take it right then, professional salespeople begin their presentation. They remind the prospective customers of one of the needs they said they have, point out a feature, then describe or demonstrate how its benefits meet that need. Their prospective customers don't object because they were the ones who said they *had* the need.

Notice the price does not go up as the benefit value of the product rises. Professional salespeople will continue to remind customers of their own stated needs, as they point out another feature, then describe and demonstrate how the benefit of the feature meets that need, until the reasons to buy become overwhelming. Those benefits have risen in value to the prospective customer way past the price of the product. They certainly offset the value of features and benefits found on other products.

But what about those things the customer may legitimately object to?

The competent professional will already have made the prospective customer aware of those things, even before the customer discovers them. *Notice:* Competent professionals will never sell a prospective customer anything with features they know customers will discover and object to once they start using the product. Professionals tell the prospective customer about these things because their only goal is a *satisfied* customer. They never do anything knowingly that would cause a prospective customer to wind up as a *dissatisfied* customer.

If a salesperson knows a prospective customer is going to see a feature the customer will object to, the salesperson will bring that up before he or she even shows the customer the feature or product.

The salesperson will say something like this: "Mr. and Mrs. Customer, I know you said you didn't like red. The product I am about to show you does have some red in it, but I feel sure that when you see how well it meets your needs and how well the other colors go with what you have, that little bit of red won't make any difference."

"Mr. Customer, I know you feel you don't need a lot of horsepower, but I feel sure that when you see how well this piece of equipment is going to meet your needs at the price for which you will be able to buy it, the extra horsepower will be a bonus. On those few occasions when you do need that power, you will have it."

Most problems arise when prospective customers ask the salespeople a question and the salespeople don't know why they asked it, even though they have the answer.

> WHEN PROSPECTIVE CUSTOMERS ASK A
> QUESTION FOR WHICH YOU DON'T HAVE THE
> ANSWER, SUCH AS, "HOW LONG IS THAT?" IF
> YOU HAVE TO MEASURE BEFORE YOU CAN TELL
> THEM, YOU ARE SHOWING THEM SOMETHING
> YOU COULD NOT HAVE BEEN SURE WOULD FIT
> THEIR NEEDS. YOU DID NOT KNOW ENOUGH
> ABOUT THE PROSPECTIVE CUSTOMER'S NEEDS
> AND YOU DID NOT KNOW ENOUGH ABOUT WHAT
> YOU ARE SELLING. WHEN THAT HAPPENS, YOU
> HAVE LEARNED ONE MORE THING ABOUT WHAT
> YOU ARE SELLING THAT YOU NEEDED TO KNOW
> AND YOU PROBABLY LOST THAT SALE BECAUSE
> YOU DIDN'T KNOW. THE YARDSTICK FORCES YOU
> TO LEARN THAT LESSON.

Okay, you made a mistake and lost the sale, and you paid a hefty price to learn about size, and you can study and review that lesson so you won't make that mistake again. Or you can blame the lost sale on the prospective customer and join the losers in the lounge.

Every time prospective customers ask you a question, whether you know the answer or not, always ask them *why* they asked the question. You will gain more of the specialized knowledge you need if you listen closely to what a prospective customer says, then make sure you remember what you have learned.

No, that knowledge won't have anything to do with overcoming a customer's valid objection to buying. I don't think anyone can teach a salesperson how to do that legally, but I guarantee that any salesperson who follows these suggestions will *eliminate* the cause of the objections their prospective customers give them for not buying. And *that* is the only way to guarantee that you can legitimately overcome those objections.

When the yardstick is used, there is no place to hide when prospective customers have objected to buying and turned down your offer. You can almost always trace the reasons to this fact: You did not know enough about them and their needs or enough about what you were selling and you left them not knowing enough about their needs. Oh, you can put band-aids on the problem, which won't eliminate it, and won't stop the infection. If the cause of the problem is not found and eliminated, the problem will only get worse.

But if you use your yardstick consistently, these incidents will occur less and less often until they disappear almost entirely.

If you show a defective sample or demonstrator of what you sell, you are making a mistake.

I could give thousands of examples, but the one that makes my point best happens when a man and his wife are shopping for dining room furniture. The legs on almost all dining tables are bolted on. The man instinctively will push the side of the table to see how sturdy it is. When this happens all day long to the floor sample, the bolts will loosen and the table will wobble. If you want to experience this for yourself and burn this important lesson into your brain, go shopping for dining furniture. Nudge the side of each table with your hand and you will not have shopped long before one wobbles, sometimes so badly you think the legs may fall off. Say something to a salesperson about it and this is the answer you will get almost every time: "Oh, that's our floor sample. You won't get that one. Yours will be brand new, still in the factory carton, perfect in every way. The nuts on the legs of this one have come loose from everyone shaking it." And that often costs the salesperson the sale.

If the salesperson showing this defective sample does succeed in overcoming the problem and makes the sale, two things will happen. One, it will take him or her far longer to get the sale. A lot more time than it would have taken to tighten those loose bolts before the customer discovered them. And two, when the table is delivered, it will be to a customer who is not all excited about getting new furniture, but apprehensive and bound to give that furniture an inspection that nothing could withstand because nothing on the face of the earth is perfect.

Even though the legs are tight when the table is delivered, the customer will go over every part of the table with a fine-tooth comb looking for the slightest reasons to object, and that customer will not stop looking until he or she finds them. Go with the delivery people when customers have seen a defective sample or demonstration unit and been told theirs would be perfect and you will see one of the main reasons customers cancel upon delivery. These customers might already have buyer remorse and all they need is the least excuse to cancel. When they know what they are looking for, they will find it. When they cancel upon delivery, who gets the blame? The delivery people, of course.

This is true of all things being sold. The computer with a faulty part, an automobile demonstrator with a small squeak or rattle, a diamond earring with a bent post, missing price tags—whatever it is, causes three things:

1. If you do make the sale it will take you longer.

2. It will increase the chance that the sale will be cancelled, but even if it isn't, the percentage of service problems coming from these customers will always be much higher. Not only does it put them on guard when delivery is made, but they stay on guard, finding insignificant things to complain about, making them more and more dissatisfied with their purchase and the person who sold it to them.

3. You and your company lose credibility—with that customer as well as everyone he or she talks to.

It is easy to blame others when what you are selling isn't ready to show. Whether it is demonstrators, floor samples, homes, building sites, mortgage papers and yes, even insurance policies and advertising campaigns. The fact is it is your job to create a *satisfied* customer out of a prospective customer. If you do overcome their objections to buying, it will take a lot of time and you will never have customers who will be as satisfied as they would have been had they had no reason to object.

Everywhere I go, I have average salespeople who say to me, "Mr. Lawhon, you wouldn't believe the things they make us do around this place. If we didn't have all those things to do we would have a lot more time to sell and that is what they hired us to do!"

It is as though they should not have to do anything to get ready to sell. At best they only do what they are ordered to do, and they resent having to do that. When you examine every objection customers will have to buying you will discover that the salespeople did not do the things they were supposed to have done. And the solution does not lie in teaching them how to overcome objections! Or, for that matter, even permitting them to try to overcome the objections!

The solution lies in teaching them how to do those things—whatever they are—that they must do to get ready to sell. Of course, they must have the knowledge and information they need. Of course, they must develop productive selling skills. And, of course, they must do anything else that must be done before they start to sell, even if it means picking up the trash around the front door before it creates a negative feeling about the company in the minds of prospective customers.

When a salesperson calls on a prospective customer and does not have the information that customer needs and can't seem to get it right away on the phone what kind of image does that put in the prospective customer's mind? It is the same thing. The first impression is the most important, whether it is your countenance, what you are selling, or your competence.

When you are in the business of selling, you are the owner. When customers object to doing business with you it is because of what you have done or not done. The buck stops with you! When you use the 5 x 7 accounting card it tells you what you should have known and what you should have done (or gotten done) before you came in contact with every prospective customer. Stop doing those things that cause prospective customers to object to doing business with you and you have eliminated their objections. Of course, in order for you to stop doing those things that cause those objections, you must instead do those things that cause prospective customers to buy. As far as I'm concerned, that is all you need to know about overcoming customer objections to buying when you are in the business of selling.

31 / *The Sale Begins:*
The Presentation

HE WHO HAS, GETS.
THE RICH GET RICHER AND THE POOR GET POORER.

BEFORE YOU READ THIS CHAPTER, reread the chapter "The Principle of Reflection," and "The Fear of Loss."

The objective of your presentation is to demonstrate how the benefits of the features of what you sell will make it best meet your prospective customer's needs.

The productive skills you need to accomplish that can only be developed and perfected by doing the same thing, the same way *every time.*

That means all salespeople must start at the same point and proceed in the same precise sequence from start to finish every time they make a presentation of what they sell—they are to perfect those skills into productive selling habits. But, wait! You just read in the last chapter that professionally competent salespeople measure how effectively they have achieved their first four objectives by how much demonstrating they had to do to get the order.

These top salespeople will make the most complete presentation and demonstration of what they are selling every single time. Of course, they interrupt their presentation and demonstration to write the order when the prospective customer is ready to buy, but once the order is written and signed they complete their presentation and demonstration.

Why? Because this concept is one of the least-understood aspects of selling. I will repeat it: The salesperson who is in the business of selling has only one goal—to turn prospective customers into *satisfied* customers.

How satisfied? The *most* satisfied customers he or she can make them. And what determines how satisfied they are?

> HOW MUCH BETTER WHAT THEY BUY MEETS
> THEIR NEEDS THAN WHAT THEY HAD BEEN LED
> TO EXPECT AT THE TIME THE ORDER WAS
> COMPLETED AND THE SALE WAS FINALIZED.

Sometimes salespeople will achieve their first four objectives so well their prospective customers will take one look at what is *best* going to meet their needs and say, "I will take it!" That's the principle of reflection in action. Because now your prospective customers can clearly see that compared with what they have now or were shown on guided tours, and the two options offered them, the benefit values of the "best" are overwhelming. They see enough of the benefit value of what is going to best meet their needs and make it worth a lot more than the price with one look.

Professional salespeople who understand what causes the "I will take it!" response to happen all strive to achieve the first four objectives so well that it happens every time. They measure how close they came when it doesn't by recording how much of their demonstration was made before they could write the order and complete the sale.

> IF THEY INTEND TO MAKE THE MOST COMPLETE
> AND THOROUGH PRESENTATION THEY POSSIBLY
> CAN EVERY TIME, THEN WHY WOULD THEY
> STRIVE TO WRITE THE ORDER AT THE EARLIEST
> POSSIBLE MOMENT?

Re-read "Learning How Things Get Done in Your Company." In that chapter you saw that the guided tour director promised more to get the order than the product and people in the company could possibly deliver. Because the customer had been led to expect more than he or she would ever get in benefits and services, the customer was bound to become dissatisfied. But the competent professionals promise as little as they can to get an order. As a result, their customers get a lot more than they were led to expect at the time of purchase, which makes them *more* satisfied.

When you have written an order with little or no demonstration you have promised almost nothing. Any benefits and services your customer receives over and above that, just makes them that much more satisfied.

Imagine how much more satisfied *you* would be if you found out *after* you had bought something that the company was going to *add* features to what you had bought that would make it meet your needs even *better* and at no additional cost. Would that make you even more satisfied? Of course it would!

Suppose the company added the features but never made you aware of them? If that happened, those features *did not exist* for you, because you would never be able to fully enjoy the added benefits of those features and they would not make you one bit more satisfied.

Let me remind you of some basics here. . .

Most prospective customers are not *consciously* aware of most of their needs for the benefits of most of the features on what you sell. When you have made them consciously aware of their needs for those benefits, they see these benefits instantly. It will take only a little more effort on your part to get the order.

Don't forget the lady who had the sofa for two years with a glaring defect in its pattern match that she never noticed. Once it was pointed out she could never look at the sofa and *not* see the defect. In fact, that defect was all she saw, yet she, her family, and her friends had seen that sofa constantly for over 700 days without having spotted the defect.

The feature/defect meant the sofa failed to meet her needs. If I had been unwilling to give her a new sofa she would have become a *dissatisfied* customer—so dissatisfied she could have sued and won. Which would have made her even *more* dissatisfied.

Suppose she had been told to be sure the pattern was well matched if she bought a floral patterned sofa. She would have seen the defect instantly the first time she saw the sofa. Suppose that instead of a defect there was a feature on that sofa that offered incredible benefits making it far better meet her needs. If she had owned it for two years before someone pointed out the feature and showed her its benefits—can you imagine how upset she would be with the salesperson for not having made her aware of those benefits?

Now, stay with me: *When you have gotten the order without complet-*

ing your presentation and demonstration, you have a very satisfied customer. The shorter the presentation and demonstration, you have made, the more satisfied you will now be able to make your customers. (Read this paragraph once more.)

Remember: You had made your prospective customers consciously aware of how their needs would be met when they own your product or service. You have written the order without pointing out many of the features or demonstrated many of the benefits. If you send them on their way without showing them many of those features, they will never enjoy many of the benefits. However, as they use your product they will remember those earlier stated needs and because you did not make them aware of the features that satisfies those needs, some remain unmet. The customer will become dissatisfied.

You may have to read this several times and hold discussions with a lot of other like-minded salespeople before you can acquire full comprehension of its importance.

But it boils down to this: The less you promise before you get the order and the more you can deliver than was promised, the *more satisfied* your customer will become.

Now here is the catch. Some of the time even the best professional salespeople have to complete a good bit of their presentation and demonstration to get the sale. Sometimes they have to make most of it. There will even be times when they will give their entire presentation and demonstration twice before the order is written. If they stay in selling long enough they may occasionally complete it a *third* time if that's what it takes to get the order.

Why do they repeat what has already been presented and demonstrated? (At this point, I am surprised you're asking.) *Spaced Repetition and The Principle of Reflection.* With the second and even third presentation, your prospective customers gain even greater conscious comprehension of how the benefits of the features make it better and better meet their needs. Your presentation and demonstration continues until prospective customers have experienced *ownership* of enough of the benefits to cause them to say, "I will take it."

The more competent you are when making your presentation and demonstration, the easier it is for you to get the order.

How do you become competent to do that? By making your presentation in the same sequence, from start to finish, every single time.

Guided tour directors never develop productive presentation and demonstration skills because they start showing or telling about what they sell at the first opportunity, which is rarely the same place twice. If you studied long-term average salespeople, as I have, you would see that the longer they have been selling the shorter the demonstration and the fewer the sales they make.

There are no short cuts in your developing productive skills. As you perfect each skill into a productive habit, it will take you less and less time to practice and selling will get easier and easier. This improved competence is the only shortcut to be found in selling.

WHAT IS THE SEQUENCE OF YOUR PRESENTATION?

If you're selling a life insurance policy that question could easily be answered. "With the beginning feature and its benefits and followed through in sequence to the end."

If you're selling a home the sequence would be just as simple. What you see first is where your demonstration starts. And that would be the location. When professional real estate salespeople are on the way to a house, they remind their prospective customers of their needs for shopping, schools, libraries, services, hospitals, and so on and point them out as they drive by. As they remind them of their stated needs they tell them or show them their proximity to the home that is going to *best* meet their needs.

As they approach the home, they stop to point out the features that can be seen and tell how they meet stated needs or satisfy a desire. This is done every time no matter what home is being sold. The professionals will follow a similar sequence as they approach the home, go through it, the grounds, the garage, and so on.

If they are selling automobiles they will start the demonstration with what the prospective customer first sees, moving them inside the car, under the hood, into the trunk, and on through the demonstration drive. Professionals will follow this same sequence every time, constantly alert for ways to make more effective each thing they do.

The yardstick tells them what works best and what *doesn't*.

The same principle applies to any of the thousands of things that you might sell, but now you must think in specific terms of what you do sell.

The skills you need to perfect a productive presentation and demonstration will follow the same sequence or path every time. To do that you must determine *where* you will begin your presentation and demonstration, where you will end it, and you must have a plan or route to follow from where you begin to your destination. Finally, you *must* follow that plan and measure your results *every single time*.

The only variation you will make is the point at which you interrupt your presentation and demonstration to write the order.

Note that I said "interrupt." Once you have written the order you have achieved your fifth objective. The sale is made, but you will not reach your goal *until the customer returns to do business with you and has sent others to do business with you.*

In the purest sense, your presentation and demonstration actually achieves *two* of your objectives. It is "interrupted" to write the order to achieve your fifth objective, and "completed" after the order has been written to achieve your sixth objective, which reinforces your customer's buying decision.

You must comprehend this completely.

Your presentation and demonstration skills achieve both of these objectives. To perfect them into productive habits you must practice them in the same sequence from start to finish every time.

To develop a plan to follow when you make your presentation and demonstration, make a list of every feature that *might* be found on what you sell. They must be listed in the order in which you will present them. (Note that I said every feature that *might* be on what you sell.) When more features are discovered, add them to your list.

Nothing is perfect, so no matter what you are selling there are some things that will better meet your customers' needs than others, but only one that will *best* meet their needs. That will be the one that meets *most* of their needs the *best* for the *price* they can afford to pay.

After you have completed your list of all the features found on what you sell in the sequence in which you are going to present them, then you have your plan—not only for your presentation and demonstration, but also the sequence of your qualifying questions. This plan enables you to develop effective qualifying, presentation, and demonstration skills into productive selling *habits*.

If I could send you a subliminal message on every page of this book it would contain this fact:

> ALMOST EVERY LOST SALE IS DUE TO ONE OF
> TWO THINGS —
>
> 1. EITHER THE SALESPERSON HAD NOT
> LEARNED ENOUGH ABOUT WHAT HE OR SHE IS
> SELLING; OR
>
> 2. THE SALESPERSON DID NOT KNOW ENOUGH
> ABOUT THE CUSTOMER(S) AND THEIR NEEDS.

To achieve your objective in the presentation and demonstration you must not only show or tell your prospective customers how what you sell is going to best meet their needs but ,every bit as important, you must have them experience as much of the benefits with as many of his senses as possible.

You *cannot* do this unless you and your customer are consciously aware of the customer's needs.

The more needs your prospective customer might have for the benefits of the features of what you are selling, the better it will meet those needs and the more reasons the customer will have to buy.

The more your prospective customer has been made consciously aware of each of the benefits, the stronger each of those reasons will be for him or her to buy.

Do not forget for a minute that it is the *customers* who describe to *you* what their needs are as you ask your qualifying questions.

Not one salesperson in 1,000 has effective, productive qualifying skills, yet without them no effective, productive presentation and demonstration skills can (or will) be perfected.

So much of selling is the old "which came first, the chicken or the egg?" But surely you can see that qualifying always comes before the presentation and the demonstration.

The objective of qualifying is to establish in the prospective customer's mind and in yours a conscious awareness of the customer's needs for the benefits of the features you are going to present and demonstrate.

The only way you can do this and perfect your productive qualifying skills/habits is to have a plan that you follow every single time when you ask your qualifying questions.

You must ask these questions in the same sequence in which they will appear in your presentation and demonstration. Therefore, you must know the sequence you will use in your presentation and demonstration before you can perfect productive qualifying skills.

Remember, I told you it is impossible for you to describe what you want your prospective customer to feel, see, hear, smell, or taste if you have not felt, seen, heard, smelled, or tasted it yourself. Even then, the more you had felt, seen, heard, smelled, and tasted of each feature's benefit, the more you could enhance your prospective customer's experience.

Simply, that means your productive selling skills are limited by how much you know about the benefits of the features of what you sell and to what extent you have emotionally experienced those benefits yourself.

Remember: Competing salespeople may have better products with more features offering more benefits for less money than what you sell. They may even have the same thing you are selling and priced *lower*. But when you have made your prospective customers *consciously* aware of their needs for more of the benefits of more of the features of what you sell than your competitor has, and then had your customers experience to a *greater degree* with more of their senses those benefits meeting their needs than your competitor did, you will get the sale even when your price is higher. And *you* will have a more *satisfied* customer than the competitor ever would.

Like all professions, selling is a service. The more skillful the sales professional is the more valuable his or her other services become and the more the client, patient, student, or customer is willing to pay, (but even more important) the more satisfied they will be.

Please note: Most of the benefits of most of the features of what you sell are basic. That means they are *essential and indispensable.*

Let's consider automobiles: All cars have a body, paint, wheels, engine, transmission, storage space, brakes, lights, ignition, and so on. Those are basic features. But what are the basic *benefits* of each of those basic *features?* How much of each of those benefits can you experience with your five senses? See if you can feel it, see it, hear it, smell it, or taste it. Try to *feel more* of it, *see more* of it, *hear more* of it, *smell more* of it, and even *taste more* of it. Discuss what you experience with other like-minded salespeople. (Ignore and *always* avoid the losers in the lounge.)

All houses have locations, lots, landscaping, neighbors, roofs, windows, doors, insulation, heating, plumbing, bathrooms, kitchens, closets, bedrooms, and so on. When real estate salespeople have a list of every basic item found on all homes, and they know how to feel, see, hear, smell, and taste more of the basic benefits of the basic features of the homes they are selling, then they can have their customers experience more of each benefit and the selling gets easier—a lot easier.

These same principles apply to everything that is sold. I can hear someone saying, "Yeah, but what I sell is different." These principles apply even when you sell intangibles like life insurance. They even apply to selling *ideas*.

When your customer leaves, your yardstick will tell you how productive your efforts were. You should constantly be looking for ways to improve your sequence and to get your customers to experience more of each benefit. As they do that, you will find your presentation and demonstration getting easier, taking less time, and becoming more productive. You will be interrupting your presentation earlier and earlier to write the order.

Remember, the professionals say that the point at which the order is written alone measures how effectively they achieved their first four objectives. When you first start out, much of your presentation and demonstration has to be made before you can write the order. As your presentation and demonstration skills become more productive it will take less time to get the order because you will discover that the skills you need to achieve your first four objectives have also been improving.

I am sure you have heard the adages: "He who has gets!" and "The rich get richer and the poor get poorer."

Those who have developed productive skills get even more productive skills, which causes them to achieve other productive skills, and those skills become even more productive causing them to get other productive skills. *That's* how he who has gets more, and *that's* why the rich get richer.

Those who have *counterproductive* skills/habits will become even more counterproductive, which will cause them to develop other counterproductive skills/habits. Those newly found counterproductive skills/habits will also improve, causing them to develop other counterproductive skills/habits. Yes, he who has, gets more of what he has. He who has counterproductive skills/habits is poor indeed, and he will get poorer even if he wins a lottery or inherits a fortune.

As you ask more and more prospective customers about their needs for the benefits of features of what you are selling and what they have liked or not liked about what they are using now, you will find yourself becoming more and more of an expert. Selling will get steadily easier for you.

One Step at a Time

You are reading a very lengthy book. But there is not a single thing taught in this book that would be hard for you to learn or hard for you to do in and of itself. However, if you look at one sitting at all of the things this book says you must learn and do, it seems impossible. If one time you looked at all the things you would need to know and do to be a competent ditch digger, that would seem impossible, too.

Everything we learn in life we learn bit by bit. Every skill (whether productive or counterproductive) is perfected over time. If you study harder and practice longer you will gain your knowledge faster and perfect your skills quicker, which means you will become more and more productive even sooner. In the business of selling, that means you are getting richer quicker, too. But quick or slow, once this knowledge is gained it causes you to get even more knowledge. The productive skills you develop cause more productive skills to be gained. So the rich do get richer—while the poor get poorer.

You must gain your basic knowledge before you can make even a modest presentation. And your initial presentation must be developed before you can develop your basic qualifying skills.

Most salespeople find it easier to develop productive skills if they begin with a list of the basic features they find on what they sell. You should prepare this list in the same sequence you will use in your presentation and demonstration. Then, practice presenting and demonstrating the benefits of each feature in its proper sequence to yourself. With each practice round, ask yourself to feel, see, hear, smell, and taste more.

Many sales training programs use role playing where one trainee acts the part of the salesperson and the other is the part of the customer. Sounds good, doesn't it? Doesn't work!

Instead, you must practice experiencing (in proper sequence) what you want your prospective customer to experience. Two or more of you can get together to discuss ways to experience more of any benefit. Never forget that you cannot describe what you want your customer to experience if you haven't experienced it yourself. To the degree you have experienced it with your senses, to that degree (and that degree only) you can have your prospective customer experience it.

With your checklist of basic features and benefits in the same sequence you will use in your presentation and demonstration, then you can ask yourself: "What question would I ask a prospective customer that would make him aware of his other needs for these benefits?" When you can do that, you've learned your basic qualifying questions.

Remember, if your customers are not consciously aware of their needs for the benefits of a feature, they don't have that need, and so they will have no interest in that feature or benefit. That will not only be a reason not to buy, it may well be a strong enough reason not to buy to cost you the sale. Unless you have a qualifying question that establishes the customer's need for every basic benefit of every basic feature of what you sell, *you are not ready to begin selling.*

Does that mean every customer needs every benefit of every feature of what you sell? Heavens, no! It only means you must determine which features offer benefits the customer does need and that there are no features offering benefits that make the product unusable. The more benefits of more features you can make the customer aware of the need for, the more reasons the customer will have for buying and the more you are assured of a sale.

If you find features that keep what you sell from meeting the customer's needs then this person is NOT a prospective customer for that product and you give no presentation.

Suppose you allow prospective customers to use a demonstrator or "loaner product" hoping they will like it well enough to buy it. Not one element in that "sale" has changed. If you let them use a new car for a day or a jet airplane for a month, you will have ten objectives to achieve to reach your only goal: a *satisfied customer.*

If the customers don't know what they are supposed to experience as they use that product, they are not going to *experience it.* You should always achieve at least your first four objectives and at a minimum the basics of your fifth before you leave customers on their own. To the extent you have succeeded, the customer has experienced owning that many more of the benefits while they are using the "loaner." Then—and only then—will they have more and more to lose if they *don't* buy.

32 / *The Presentation and Demonstration I*

REMEMBER, THERE ARE NO SHORTCUTS IN ANY PROFESSION.
THE ONLY SHORTCUT ON THE ROAD TO SUCCESS IN THE BUSINESS OF SELLING IS
YOUR IMPROVED COMPETENCE THAT MAKES IT EASIER TO GET THE ORDER.
AND IN LESS TIME, TOO.

AFTER HAVING READ THIS FAR, it should be apparent to you that making any buying decision is an emotional experience that can involve all five senses. The bigger and more complex the purchase, the more emotional the decision. The con artist understands that and can, as they say, sell refrigerators to Eskimos. But all buying decisions are made emotionally, regardless of whether the purchase is made from a con artist, an incompetent order taker, or the world's top professional salesperson.

Buyers must be able to support their decision with logic if they are to remain satisfied customers. If they cannot, the salesperson has created a *dissatisfied* customer whether or not he or she intended to.

I learned this lesson the hard way when I was about nine years old. To this day, I consider it my most painful and most important single lesson in selling.

Once a month, my mother sent me downtown to make the monthly household payments. This was in the mid-'30s during the Great Depression when payments were made in cash. She would give me envelopes with money in them for the gas and electric bill, water bill, house payment, and piano payment. For doing this chore, I got two trolley tokens and a quarter to spend at the dime store. Each month I looked forward to my trip with great excitement. Back then, a quarter was a fortune to a nine year old and it could keep me occupied in the dime store for several hours trying to decide what to spend it on.

For some reason I can't recall, on one particular Saturday I wound up with an extra dollar of my mother's money.

As I was shopping the dime store with my quarter, I spotted a pitch-man on the main aisle behind an elevated counter that was just about eye level to me. He started his pitch with "Ladies and gentlemen, step right over here and you can see a free demonstration of the latest man-made modern miracle—working utensils for your kitchen. You will see for the first time devices than can change some of your most wearisome kitchen chores into easy and exciting experiences. Everyone just gather around. Step up as close as you can to make room for the folks in the back."

Before his spiel was underway, my little nine year old chin was planted dead center on that counter.

His first demonstration caused my eyes to bug out. It was a gadget that when spiraled into a carrot, potato, or cucumber sliced it in corkscrew fashion leaving a single piece that could be stretched out like an accordion. One tap of a sharp knife would make it fall into a line of perfect slices.

What a miracle! And I was one of the first people in the state of Oklahoma to see this product in actual use! Although it had never been offered to the public, he said, when it went on sale in about two weeks, you would find them in the kitchen utensil department of every department and dime store in town, and they would sell for $2.50.

With that he tucked his man-made modern miracle worker in a small box that had "$2.50" printed in large letters on the end. Then he placed the box right in front of my eyes while he proceeded to his demonstration of the next miracle-working device, a utensil that would remove the core of an apple almost faster than the eye could follow.

If that wasn't enough to justify its three-dollar price when the public was finally permitted to buy it, he then performed right before my eyes another miraculous feat! With a twist, he stuck this device into an orange and juice flowed out as if from a faucet, filling a glass.

The demonstration went on until ten mind-boggling, miracle-working devices had been demonstrated, put in boxes with large retail prices on the end of each— ranging in price from $1.75 to $3.25— and when the last device had been demonstrated, boxed and stacked right in front of me, the total cost of the ten boxes came to over $25. That would be the total price of those ten miracle-working utensils when they were finally offered to the public. Then he said he knew that once word leaked out a stampede would ensue as the public raced to the nearest dealer to get these wonderful utensils into their homes. As his spiel continued, he quietly place nine more stacks of the ten items on the counter, making ten stacks in all.

When the stacks were all neatly arranged, he said that in order to spread the word, he was going to sell ten and only ten of these complete sets, knowing that just to see them in use, friends and neighbors would come from near and far, and through the placement of only ten sets in Oklahoma City, the demand would be so great, stores wouldn't be able to keep them in stock.

While he was saying this he was whisking each of the ten stacks into a paper bag. As the last stack was bagged, he said, "Now here is the most amazing part of this offer. Ten sets will be sold to the first ten people who lay one dollar on the counter. All $25-plus in merchandise will go to the first ten people lucky enough to get their dollar down, and no more will be offered at less than the regular prices, which will total over $25!"

Needless to say, my mother's dollar was the first one on the counter. I had my sack and was on my way out the door before the tenth dollar hit the counter. I was running as fast I could to catch the trolley. I couldn't wait to show my mother what a fantastic buy I had made.

To this day, I cannot remember a more emotionally charged or exciting buy. With my feelings running in a hundred different directions, I was completely out of breath as I found my seat on the trolley. I rode along, full of elation, peeking into the sack at the prices printed on the boxes. To this day, my mind can see them in technicolor: $3.25, $2.50, $2.75, $3.00, $3.25, $1.75, $2.25, $2.00, $2.25, $3.25—as I shook the bag to catch a glimpse of each price. I had bought it all—all $25.25 of it—for only one of my mother's dollars.

What a deal I had made, what a hero I would be! As I rode along I couldn't resist opening the box with the corkscrew device he had demonstrated first. I had to have one more look at it. When I pulled it out of the box my heart took a sickening dip.

It was nothing but a piece of a tin can cut into a strip about one-half inch by two inches with a wood screw through each end. Obviously, this was not the razor sharp device that had so miraculously made an accordion of that potato, carrot and cucumber.

Well, I consoled myself, maybe that one item isn't all he said it was, but I still have the other nine, which are worth a fortune without it. As the trolley wobbled along, a nagging doubt began to overtake me. With actual fear and much trepidation, I opened the second box. The orange juicer/apple corer. It, too, was cut with pinking shears from a coffee can with the printing still on it and curled into a one-inch tube.

My fears reached panic level as the full extent of the salesman's fraud dawned on me. I opened box after box, finally realizing with terrible dread that I had wasted an entire dollar bill that belonged to my family. I was frantic. I sneaked home and hid behind the garage until almost dark even knowing my parents would be alarmed that I was so late returning.

Finally, I went in and confessed to the terrible thing I had done. This experience was so traumatic that as I write about it today, I still feel the same dread, as if it had happened only moments ago.

So that was it. My first realization that we make our buying decisions based on our emotions and on how we feel.

Except later, we must be able to justify that buying decision with logic. When we can't, as I couldn't in that case, we all become *dissatisfied* customers. We feel cheated because we were cheated. The greater the fraud, the greater our dissatisfaction.

If those products had been as represented, with miraculous benefit values worth even more than $25.25, they would have delivered the benefits I had been promised. My story would have had an entirely different ending, an ending every bit as exciting and happy as it had been tragic and disappointing. My family and I would be telling the wonderful story to this day. As it happened, that was my last visit to that dime store, and almost 60 years later I still get depressed if I have to visit an old-fashioned dime store.

I wish I could teach every student of the business of selling this lesson as vividly as I learned it for only one dollar. Alas, the best I can hope for is that you learn from my embarrassing testimony.

Your customers will buy with their emotions based on how they feel about your offer, but after they have bought, your customer must be able to support that decision with logic if he or she is to remain satisfied.

When I read in a book or hear a sales trainer say, "When the cus-

tomer says, 'I will take it' just shut up and start writing, the sale is made,"
I cannot help cringing as I remember how I prayed that those gadgets
might somehow have the quality features I needed to support logically
my buying decision, so I could bask in the approval and praise of all
those whose approval was so important to me. My dismal failure to get
that praise scarred my brain indelibly and caused H.L. Green's 5 & 10 to
live always in infamy in my mind.

But wait. I said this experience was the most painful and yet important lesson I ever had in selling. It taught me well, but it taught me something more that may be even more important.

Give that devil his due. That con artist did one of the best presentations and demonstrations of what he was selling I have ever seen. He did
a better job of presenting and demonstrating the benefits of each one of
those gadgets to make a ten-cent sale (each gadget was only ten percent
of the dollar) than I have seen salespeople make who are trying to sell
thousand-dollar appliances, computers for thousands of dollars, and
$50,000 automobiles.

His presentation had made every person in that audience want the
benefits of each one of those gadgets before he ever let them know the
price. He had caused them to want those benefits so badly that they felt
each gadget was worth the price on the box even though they might not
be willing to pay that much for them.

My point is—he was not making *ten* offers. He was making *one*
offer that consisted of ten items or (and this is important) ten features, if
you can think of it that way. Each of those features offered many benefits. It was those benefits of the features of his offer that made prospective
customers feel it was worth the price on the box. Once that value exceed-
ed $25, and he offered to sell all ten features as one offer or product for
only one dollar, he didn't have to overcome a single objection to buying,
and he didn't need any sneaky, tricky—even pushy—closing techniques
to get the orders.

I remind you he was a fraud and a crook because he was knowingly
promising benefits that what he was selling would not deliver. Ignorance
is no excuse when you are arrested for breaking the law. If he had been
making his presentation and demonstration not knowing that what was
in the boxes was not what he had demonstrated, a court of law would
have convicted him of a criminal act anyway.

Emerson's essay "Compensation" says you cannot have the good without the bad.

Effective productive skills will be just as effective and just as productive when used to achieve illegal goals as they are when used to achieve legal goals. This man's goal was not a satisfied customer and a satisfied customer is the *only* goal of those in the business of selling.

Remember that this con artist showed one gadget at a time. He had perfected the productive skills he needed to demonstrate every conceivable benefit of each gadget. How did he do that? He started with the same greeting each and every time because it worked. He started with the same gadget every time and demonstrated each gadget in the same order every time to perfect those skills. He probably did that same pitch in that dime store three or four times a day every day for a week and then moved to another city before he was found out to do the same thing, which perfected his skills even more.

He never skipped a gadget nor did he ever try to shorten the demonstration of the gadget. As he became more and more effective doing what he did, it took him less and less time.

Now hear me. I have no doubt he could have stopped after demonstrating the first gadget, having established $2.50 worth of benefits and gotten some customer to buy it for a dollar. I am sure he could have stopped after the second gadget had been demonstrated and sold the two gadgets to at least ten people for one dollar. He could probably have sold most of those people some of the time when only five gadgets had been demonstrated, but he had found that if he wanted to sell ten people 100 percent of the time he had to demonstrate all the benefits of all ten gadgets every time.

Granted this man was a con artist. What he was selling would not deliver the benefits he was promising and there was no way he could possibly wind up with a satisfied customer. But suppose for a moment that he was honest and every one of those gadgets would do everything he said it would and do it even easier than he made it look? Don't you know that I (and everyone else lucky enough to have gotten them for a dollar) would have been some of the most satisfied customers ever created?

If you can imagine how excited and satisfied I would have been had what I bought done everything he promised, then imagine me becoming even more satisfied the next month when I visited that store again and saw all ten of those gadgets displayed at the prices as he had said they would be with people lined up to buy them.

This is a very important selling lesson that you can learn: This con artist was not offering ten different gadgets at ten cents apiece. He was making one offer that consisted of ten *different* gadgets.

- His demonstration made each one worth two or three times what he was selling all ten for.

- At regular prices, very few people would have bought even one of them, and certainly never all ten.

- Had they been ten cents apiece it is unlikely anyone would have bought all ten.

Everything you will ever sell winds up being *one* offer. But that offer is made up of many "gadgets." We call them "features." Each one of those features offers benefits in the same way each one of those gadgets in the con artist's offer was supposed to.

Look at what you sell, whether it's life insurance, telephone services, automobiles, homes, jewelery, or whatever. Your offer is always made up of many features.

Let's focus on the fact that what you are selling will consist of one offer. That offer is for something made up of many features just like the con artist's offer was made up of ten gadgets. Each of those features offers different benefits that will meet different needs. Some of those needs will be more important than others. No single prospective customer will have needs for all of the benefits of all of the features of what you sell.

Note: *Even though a person might not have had any need for the benefit of some of those gadgets, it did not lessen the value of the benefits of those gadgets for which they DID have needs.* In this case, had they felt they only needed the benefits of one gadget at one dollar, it was still a good buy and besides, they got the other nine free. I am trying to show how the prospective customer's mind sees what you are selling.

Had each of those gadgets in its individual box with the individual prices on the end been put inside one large box with a $25.25 price tag and no other information, no one would ever, and I mean *ever,* have taken the con artist up on his offer. Had he marked the box down to one dollar, very few would have bought it, either.

That may seem exaggerated, but, to some extent, that is how all your prospective customers will view whatever you are selling: as a box with a whole bunch of features inside it, most of which they cannot see. They can't see most of the benefits, either. Customers are unaware of most of the needs they have for most of the benefits you're offering, just as you would have been if you had seen all ten of those gadgets stacked together on the counter with no prices on them and no one to make you aware of your need for the benefits of each of the gadgets and no one to show you how they would meet those needs.

In your presentation and demonstration, you treat each feature as if it were a separate entity, just as the con artist treated each gadget. Imagine what would have happened if the con artist had asked me to try that turnscrew gadget myself to show everyone that even a child could use it? How much more do you think I would have wanted it if it had easily done for me what he said it would? What if he had had me take the core out of that apple and instantly extract a glass of juice from an orange and so on with each gadget? That would not happen unless the feature would do what he said it would, but the benefits of the features of what *you* sell will do what you say they will, and to some extent you can have your customer experience those man-made, miracle-working gadgets/features.

Forget the con man was a crook and imagine him making a legitimate offer. Study what he did. Find every feature of what you sell, no matter how insignificant, and treat it as though it was a separate gadget. Try to experience the benefits of that gadget/feature in every way you can. If what you sell is intangible, such as insurance or service programs, try to imagine as vividly as you can experiencing the benefits of each feature in your policy or offer so you can describe as vividly as possible what you want your prospective customers to see and experience with *their* imaginations.

When you do this you will discover it rarely takes much of your demonstration or presentation to get the order, because the collective value of the benefits quickly exceeds the price of your total offer.

Imagine the con artist having demonstrated the first gadget/feature then having had me try it out for myself. He puts it in the big box with the other gadgets/features concealed inside and says, "I only have one of these that will sell at this time, but the first person who puts one dollar bill on this counter, gets it." Don't you know my dollar would have been first?

Then picture what would have happened if he had said, "Young man, you don't have any idea what a fantastic buy you have made. I want all of these people to see what you actually got for your dollar." Then one at a time he pulls the other gadgets/features out of their boxes, demonstrates them, has me try them out for myself, puts each one in its own box with the price on the end and says, "Kid, I know you thought you only bought one gadget/feature and it was well worth more than you paid for it, but my offer included all ten gadgets/features! Take them, they're yours!"

Do you think that his demonstration and my experiencing the benefits of the other nine gadgets/features that I knew nothing of at the time I paid my dollar would have made me a more satisfied customer? A thousand times more satisfied? Of course, if his offer had actually done what he said it would.

What I have just described is exactly what happens when professionally competent salespeople make their presentations and demonstrations. They make them from start to finish every time, just as the con artist did. The only differences are that the features of what the competent professionals sell actually will do for the customer what they say they will.

Professionals will only interrupt their presentations to write the order, because long before it is over, the customers are so excited they want to buy. The salesperson writes it up, then says, "Folks, you have no idea just how good a buy you have made." The fifth objective has been achieved.

Now the competent professional is ready to achieve the sixth objective.

Thousands of times I have wished that man in Oklahoma City had not been a crook and that those gadgets had done what he said they would do. But if that had been the case I might never have learned some of my most important lessons about selling. We learn far, far more from our mistakes than we ever do from our successes.

33 / *The Presentation and Demonstration II*

Perceive: To become aware of something through the senses; see, hear, feel, taste, or smell. To come to understand or apprehend with the mind.

Funk & Wagnall's Dictionary

Need is a comparison so in fact it only exists as it is *perceived*. When we talk about a prospective customer's needs, we are really talking about *perceived* needs. (Many a sales meeting could be held on this subject.)

BEFORE YOU CAN MAKE A PRODUCTIVE PRESENTATION and demonstration, your prospective customers must be aware of their need for the benefits of each feature on what you sell. But it is even more important that it was the prospective customer that *told* you about those needs when you were asking your qualifying questions.

The guided tour director always jumps right in—trying to tell prospective customers why *they* need what he or she is selling when the tour director knows little or nothing about customers' needs, and the prospective customer is not consciously aware of most of them.

Imagine a customer arriving at the dinette set that will best meet her needs after the salesperson has achieved his first four objectives. She takes one look and says, "Oh, I like this set so much better than the first one we looked at. I like it even better than the second set and it costs over $500 less!"

Your reaction: "Mrs. Jones, you said there were two things you disliked about your present dinette. Number one was your chairs—they weighed a ton and when you moved them, they scratched your beautiful hardwood floors. On top of that, you said they felt like you were sitting on a rock. I want you to sit in one of these chairs. They are as comfortable as a fine occasional chair, wouldn't you agree? They have large, hard-rubber casters making them so easy to roll around that many of my customers like you who only need four chairs most of the time use two of them in other rooms. These casters will not damage your floors and they roll easily over rugs and carpet.

"One other thing. You said you hated your present table every time you had to try to get it open to put the leafs in. It took you and your two boys and your husband just to pull it open. Mrs. Jones, the slides under this table are made of steel. They will never warp. There are cog wheels in each slide. I have already released the locks that hold the table shut. I want you to take one finger and pull out on that end of the table. See how the cogs open the other end as you pull your end? It is so easy, your five year old could do it all by himself.

"Notice the wide trim around the underside of the table top? We call that an apron. Most table leafs are just flat boards. But this leaf has the same apron as the table top, and the table looks every bit as good with the leaf in as it does without the leaf. Mrs. Jones, the leaf is 24 inches wide and when it is in place you can not only seat six, but with a couple of folding chairs, you can comfortably seat eight."

At this point, the salesperson has dealt with only four features:

1. The comfort of the chairs
2. The hard-rubber casters
3. The 24-inch table leaf
4. The metal slides.

He reminded the customer of needs she said she had that the benefits of these four features will meet. He not only demonstrated and had her experience for herself how the benefits met those needs, but showed her how they will meet even more needs she was unaware of.

That is only four features, and with at least 24 more features on the dinette still undemonstrated, can you see how, after the demonstration of the benefits of these four features, she could say, "Oh, honey, we could use one of the chairs for your desk in the den and the other would be perfect in our bedroom. You know that when your folks and mine are both there we need to seat eight and we already have the folding chairs. I think it is perfect! Let's take it!"

After the order is completed, imagine how her excitement and satisfaction would increase as she is reminded of even more benefits from these four features that meet more of her needs. And you will then demonstrate the benefits of at least 24 more features. Each of these features offer many benefits that meet other needs, too.

Right now! Start reading this chapter again. If you expect to comprehend its full meaning, reread it sentence by sentence, paragraph by paragraph, substituting the benefits of features of what you sell. It is too easy to say, "What I sell is different." It is true that the features and benefits on all products are different, but your objectives are always the same, absolutely the *same* in every selling situation.

Here is another element of the presentation that is almost unknown.

Remember the lady in the chapter "The Principle of Reflection," who had the floral sofa with a badly mismatched pattern for two years? She'd never noticed it until a guest pointed it out. Once that happened, all that woman could see was the defect. Never again could she look and see the sofa—all she saw was that defect. Never again would the sofa meet her needs as she originally thought it did. Instantly, she had become a *dissatisfied* customer.

If you can, imagine that instead of a defect, that sofa had an unseen feature that offered benefits that would make it meet her needs far better. If she had remained unaware of the defect, the woman would never have become dissatisfied. But—if she were unaware of a feature and its benefits that made the sofa better meet her needs, she would never be as satisfied as she *could* have been.

Your only goal in the business of selling is turning prospective customers into satisfied customers. How satisfied? As satisfied as it is possible for them to be.

You know you must conduct your presentation and demonstration from start to finish in the same sequence every time if you want to perfect it into a productive skill/habit, interrupting it only to write the order when the customer is ready to buy. Obviously, every benefit of every feature you demonstrate after the customer has bought makes the purchase better meet his or her needs and makes them even more satisfied.

What more could a salesperson do during a presentation and demonstration that would result in even more satisfied customers?

Let's use another simple product. If you've ever watched men shopping for reclining chairs you no doubt found it funny. They go from chair to chair trying out those that look good to them, and two things happen most of the time when they sit in a chair. As they sit, their minds are occupied trying to figure out how to operate the reclining mechanism. When they don't know how some of their efforts and contortions are hilarious. They will not have given one thought to how the chair feels until they have it in the reclined position. When these guys get out of a chair, the total benefits they experienced were a hard-to-operate mechanism and the reclined position.

I don't remember ever failing to sell a reclining chair. As far back as I can recall, I always gave the same demonstration. After letting them sit and awkwardly recline in two reclining chairs for comparison, I took them to the one that was going to best meet their needs. I stood beside the chair and asked the prospective customer to sit. "But before you recline in this chair, I want you to sit as far back as you can and close your eyes. Can you feel that extra support in the small of your back?"

Because I told the customer's mind to feel that support, he or she felt it; I have never known one person who didn't say yes. Then I say, "It almost feels like a pair of hands massaging you, doesn't it?"

If you were watching, you would see the customers move a little side to side, pressing back in the chair farther, feeling as hard as they can for those massaging hands. "Yes, it really does."

Then I say, "This chair is engineered so the springs in the seat are softer at the back which means you sink a little deeper in the back of the seat. That causes more of your body weight to be carried by the back of the chair, which distributes it over a much larger area. This added comfort lets you sit in one position for a much longer period without ever feeling uncomfortable. You know how you sit in some chairs and in no time you have slipped down to the point you have to push yourself back into the chair to keep from sliding onto the floor?"

"Yes."

"I want you to try to slide out of this chair. . . . You can't do it, can you? Close your eyes again and feel how the chair actually seems to cradle you. Most people who buy a reclining chair only having reclined in it never give one thought to how good a chair it is. When they get it home, they discover they use it as a chair about as much as they do reclined. I think this is the most comfortable, best-engineered chair you will find anywhere, and you will have to admit that you could not have the best reclining chair if you didn't start with the best chair. Now, I want you to experience the finest reclining chair you can buy."

At that point, if it was a mechanism activated by pushing back in the chair I had my hand on the back as I asked them to just lean back in the chair and close their eyes. I reclined the chair smoothly and effortlessly for them. Had they tried to do it themselves not knowing how it worked they would have been clumsy and awkward. My chair reclined like magic. Once they had experienced its incredibly smooth reclining action they too could recline it with the same fluid motion.

Here is my point: The first impression is the most important each time and every time, no matter what you do. These customers' experiences in reclining chairs with guided tour directors had been one awkward experience after the other.

I encouraged these prospective customers to experience more of the same benefits in my chair than they had in the competitor's. Not only a few more benefits, but each benefit was made to supply far more comfort, support and durability than they had experienced in any chair anywhere else. What I have mentioned so far was only the beginning of my demonstration, because I had the customer experience far more of the benefits from every single feature before I was through.

Now hear me and hear me well. These customers, just like the lady with the defective sofa pattern, could own one of these reclining chairs for years and never, never, never experience the comfort they would experience during my demonstration. But, like the sofa lady, once having experienced seeing the defect or once having experienced the benefit, they could never sit in the chair again and not experience that incredible comfort. I cannot remember ever having failed to make a reclining chair sale. You can see why, can't you?

When I was considering new reclining chairs at the market, I would sit in each one and close my eyes, searching out every benefit of every feature. When two or more salespeople get together to see how much more of a benefit they can have their senses experience, they will be amazed. Then they can discuss how to tell the prospective customer to experience what they have. I don't care if it is the ease of touching the keys on a computer keyboard or driving a caterpillar tractor, the more of any benefit you can experience for yourself, the more your prospective customer can be led to experience it.

Those people who bought elsewhere the same reclining chairs I was selling, who had never been told what to experience or caused to experience it, could never enjoy the benefits as much as my customers. And because of that the others could never in a million years be as satisfied as mine. In the business of selling, your only objective is a *satisfied* customer. How satisfied? The most satisfied customer the benefits of what you sell can possibly make them.

And last, but far from least. . . . "Everybody has it. Everybody knows about it." I have heard that statement from thousands of average salespeople about thousands of things they sell. An automobile salesperson points to a sticker tag with several thousands of dollars worth of incredible features that offer unheard of benefits to the owner and says, "This one's loaded." Everyone knows what that means don't they? HOG-WASH!

All this may seem overwhelming now, but there is not a single big thing for you to learn nor are there any *hard* things to do. You do have a whole bunch of little things to learn and a whole bunch of *easy* things to do.

You will begin by acquiring basic knowledge of what you are selling and by creating a basic plan for your presentation and demonstration. That will be the framework or foundation for *all* the skills you need to achieve your first five objectives.

As you learn more about what you are selling and refine the sequence for your presentation and demonstration, you can determine the comparisons you will make to achieve your fourth objective.

The list of features and benefits in the sequence in which you present them is the basis for the questions you will be prepared to ask your customers when qualifying. Those questions will let you determine if they need the benefits of each feature or whether the feature would make it unusable. At the same time you are making them consciously aware of their needs and desires.

As soon as you begin your selling career you will ask all prospective customers what they are using now, what they like most about it, and what they like least. When you ask prospective customers these questions it will help you become more of an expert on what *satisfies* your customers most as well as what causes the most *dissatisfaction*.

As you gain more and more of this specialized knowledge and information your qualifying questions will become even more productive, your comparison selections will be more effective, your customers' level of *dissatisfaction* with what they have now will be elevated, and you will discover your countenance becoming more *positive* with each new prospective customer you contact. Your constant, accurate use of the yardstick guarantees your improvement in each measured area, which *guarantees* your success.

If you remember this overview as you learn more every day and perfect those easy-to-do productive skills, selling is going to be fun, not work.

34 / *Writing the Order*

IT IS FEAR THAT KEEPS CUSTOMERS FROM MAKING BUYING DECISIONS. IT IS
THEIR LACK OF CONFIDENCE THAT CAUSES THAT FEAR. IT IS THEIR LACK OF
COMPETENCE THAT CAUSES THEIR LACK OF CONFIDENCE.

IT IS FEAR THAT KEEPS THE SALESPERSON FROM ASKING FOR THE ORDER. IT IS A
LACK OF CONFIDENCE THAT CAUSES THAT FEAR.
IT IS A LACK OF COMPETENCE WHICH CAUSES THE LACK OF CONFIDENCE.

IN THE EARLY FIFTIES, I heard about an appliance sales-man who worked for what was then the highest-volume appliance dealer in the U.S. He never waited on a prospective customer in the showroom. He stood in an anteroom through which customers passed on their way out. He would ask each of these departing customers no more than five questions. For months at a time he would go without failing to sell 100 percent of the prospective customers who were leaving without having bought.

I was so intrigued I went to Chicago and watched him work for two days.

To put this in perspective, the selection of appliances and electronics was a fraction of what it is today. There were no televisions, stereos, VCRs, audio tapes, compact discs, microwaves, compactors, and so on. There were no double-door refrigerators, ice makers, frost-free features, and so on. For the most part, the selection consisted of radios, record players, gas or electric ranges (no built-ins), single-door refrigerators, automatic and wringer washers and dryers. This company did carry almost every model of every brand made at the time and they had as good or better prices, terms, and services as anyone. One other thing. In those days, husbands and wives almost always shopped together.

As the customers left, they passed through an anteroom, then out the doors. This man, in the most courteous manner, asked each couple his first question, "Did you folks find what you were looking for while you were in our showroom?" Because they had practically every known appliances there was, most said, "Yes." But during the two days I was there, three couples said, "No," and to them he asked his second question, "Oh, my goodness! What could you possibly be looking for in the way of an appliance that we don't have?" In each case, the prospective customers told him and in the most courtly manner he gently laid his hand on the lady's forearm, led her back into the showroom with her husband following, straight to the asked for appliance, and asked, "Is that it?" The lady nodded yes, and he wrote the order, took them to the counter, and went back to the anteroom.

That was the exception. Most people said they did find what they were looking for and of them he asked his third question, "Did you buy it?"

A lot of them said, "Yes," and he did a masterful job of reinforcing their buying decision before he sent them on their way. Well over half of these people when asked if they bought said, "No," and of them he asked his fourth question in the most positive manner. "When do you want me to have that delivered?" Over half of these prospective customers told him and he simply walked them back to the counter and wrote it up.

That still left a lot of people who had not bought and to the husband he always asked his fifth question, "Mr. Jones, I am sure you must have some very good reasons for putting off buying that new appliance that you and your family need so badly right now. Do you mind telling me what those reasons are?" Most often they simply did not have a reason for not buying and he would take them to the counter and write the order.

I am sure this exact situation may never exist again and that most people hearing about it for the first time find it hard to believe just like I did. As long as I can remember, companies have been doing customer surveys. They stop customers outside the showroom and ask if they will answer a few questions.

One of these questions is always the same as used by the man in Chicago: "Did you find what you were looking for?" When customers say, "Yes," they are asked if they bought. When they reply, "No," they are asked "Do you mind telling me why?" Over 75 percent of the time, they give the same answer: "Nobody asked me."

Wait a minute. People get in a car, risk their lives on the freeway, go to considerable cost in time and money to buy something they need. They find it; the price, terms, and delivery are fine; they leave with their needs unmet. And the only reason they can give is that nobody asked them to buy? That's *stupid,* and as we found in the 9-Dot Puzzle, people don't do stupid things.

It may come as a surprise to most salespeople, but very, very few salespeople ever *ask* for an order.

What I find inconceivable about these two examples is that in the case of the man in Chicago, every salesperson in that company knew he was out there. They all knew the questions he asked. They knew that every time they had failed to make the sale, they would not get one dime for their effort and yet, he would sell that prospective customer with his five questions almost every time.

Why didn't the losers ask those same five questions before they dropped the prospective customer?

When these thousands and thousands of customer surveys show that over 75 percent of the people had found what they wanted, but did not buy because no one asked them to, why weren't the customers asked right then to buy? Or better still, when the salespeople are told what their customers are saying, why don't they start asking every customer to buy before they leave? It could double or even triple their income. Why don't they do it?

This leaves two questions unanswered: Why do prospective customers have to be asked to buy? Why doesn't the salesperson ask them to buy?

Fear. That's right. *Fear.*

Prospective customers are afraid of making a buying mistake, and they need someone to give them the confidence they need to say "Yes." They are not competent to make that decision.

The salespeople are fearful of losing the sale. If they did ask for the sale, they asked fearfully and that caused the customer to be even more fearful. The salesperson has found a way never to lose a sale as long as he or she does not *ask* for the order.

If the boss asks why the prospective customer didn't buy, fearful salespeople can say they *made* the sale, but the prospective customer had to go measure or needed to bring in her husband. The prospective customer will be back, or the salesperson can say they were not customers at all, only lookers, browsers, tire kickers, and so on. Truth is, these fearful salespeople lack the confidence they need because they aren't *competent*.

The fearful salespeoples' third excuse will be that they did not have what the prospective customer wanted. As long as they have not asked for an order, they have not lost the sale, and believe me, most salespeople don't ask.

When new salespeople tried to ask prospective customers to buy, they asked fearfully, which caused the prospective customers to become even more fearful themselves at the very time that what they needed most was confidence. Because this didn't work, the salesperson quit asking. If you will go back right now and reread the chapter "Who Can Succeed in Selling," you will discover empathy and enthusiasm are *reactions*. It is the salesperson's competence and confidence that causes him or her to react to every prospective customer with empathy and enthusiasm. That is why, when professionally competent salespeople are asked what their closing techniques are, they say, "I just write it up, why?" Their confidence instilled confidence in the customer.

Here is the most important lesson to be learned about this problem from the salesman in the anteroom in Chicago: He did no *selling* at all. All of the selling had been done by the salespeople in the showroom. All he did was give the customers the confidence they needed to say "yes," then he wrote the order and collected his commission.

If you remember in the appliance salesperson's case, there were only three couples who left because they had not found what they needed. What we have overlooked in customer surveys is customers who left without having found what they needed, which in most cases is the majority. In most of these cases, as in the case of the three appliance customers, what they wanted and needed was inside the showroom. They simply hadn't understood enough about their needs to see it.

How did the man in Chicago become so competent that he was able to cause almost every customer to have the confidence to say yes?

Suppose you were taking customer surveys and each time customers said they had found what they wanted, but had not bought because nobody had asked them to, you said, "Would you like for me to get that on my next delivery or did you want to take it with you?" Each time one of them said yes, it would give you more confidence when you asked the question. As you gained more and more confidence, you would instill more and more of your confidence in the customer that they needed in order to say yes.

Suppose, when you asked that question and the customer still hesitated, you were to say, "I am sure you must have some very good reasons for putting off buying that product whose benefits you really need right now. Do you mind telling me what those reasons are?" Most of those customers would not have a solid reason for not buying and you could repeat your question, "When did you want it delivered?" and get the order.

I want you to remember, these are customers who have shopped and said they *found* what they needed. Their only reason for not buying: "Nobody asked me."

All I have done is show you that until the first four objectives have been achieved, it is very, very difficult to make any sale. To the degree that these four objectives have been achieved, the sale gets easier and easier to make. I hope you realize by now that had these simple things that we saw done as customers were leaving, been done as they entered, the sale would have been made by the first salesperson.

I can hear it now, "That may work for appliances and things like that, but what I sell is different."

These questions could be asked of those shopping for a home, whom other guided tour directors had tried to help and you would find the same results. The selling situation seen in the appliance company in Chicago is the same selling situation seen in the thousands of customer surveys for anything and everything.

Customers did not buy because they did not feel confident. They did not feel confident because they were not competent, and the salespeople were no more competent than the customers nor, were they any more confident.

As products and services become more and more complicated and as prices rise, the fear factors increase because the prospective customer is even less competent to make a buying decision. This is magnified even more when buyers making purchases for their companies that must also satisfy their bosses. That does not mean the fear factor in these simple selling situations wouldn't apply to computers, jet airplanes, life insurance, construction jobs, or even billion-dollar stock deals because they would, even *more so.*

In some cases, the fear factor based on the buyer's lack of competence could be increased a thousandfold.

If most salespeople don't ask for the order and top professionals in the world when asked about their closing techniques become offended and indignant as they answer, "I just write it up," then who is it who uses what my daughters call sneaky, tricky, closing techniques that we find written about so much in books on selling?

I refer the reader to the Britannica World Language edition of *Funk & Wagnall's Standard Dictionary.*

Sell *v.* To transfer (property) to another for a consideration, dispose of by sale: To deal in or offer for sale. To deliver; surrender or betray for a price or reward: To sell one's honor. *Colloquial:* To cause to accept or approve something; They sold him on a scheme. *Slang:* To deceive; cheat: a trick: a joke: To swindle.

There is no way anyone could read that definition of selling and still believe it is an honorable profession. The most important part of this definition can be seen in the colloquial and slang usages, because that is how selling is perceived by most people.

Listen again. To deliver; surrender or betray for a price or reward: To sell one's honor. They sold him on a scheme; to deceive: cheat: trick: a joke: to swindle.

I will bet you forgot that the first definition was: To transfer (property) to another for a consideration. Dispose of by sale: To deal in or offer for sale.

Everything people have come to believe about selling other than that has nothing to do with the honorable profession of selling any more than a quack is part of the definition in the medical profession or a shyster represents the legal profession.

And yet! You will find many, many books written to teach salespeople how to trick, deceive, cheat, and pressure people into buying something or doing something they don't want to do. When these salespeople succeed, they have swindled somebody out of something. When they don't succeed, the prospective customer feels the salesperson has tried to swindle them. The only thing sold is the salesperson's honor.

Any time what people have purchased meets their needs as well or even better than they had been led to believe at the time of the purchase, they will be *satisfied* customers and never begrudge the price they paid for it. The better it meets their needs, the more satisfied they become and the better the deal turned out to be.

Any time what people have purchased fails to meet their needs as well as they had been led to believe at the time of the purchase, they will become *dissatisfied,* and they will feel they were cheated because they really *were* cheated. As products fail to live up to customers' expectations and meet their needs, they become even more dissatisfied, feeling not only that they were cheated, but betrayed, deceived, tricked, and swindled as well.

It is the *only* job of everyone in the business of selling to see that that never happens to any prospective customers they come in contact with. They have one goal and only one when they come in contact with a prospective customer and that is to turn that prospect into a *satisfied* customer. They have not succeeded until that has happened.

Anything anyone does under the guise of selling that has any goal or objective other than a *satisfied* customer, has nothing to do with selling. It is either a fraud or a swindle, or both.

35 / *Reinforcing the Sale*

REINFORCING THE CUSTOMER'S BUYING DECISION IS THE MOST PRODUCTIVE OF ALL SELLING SKILLS—YET, IT IS ONE OF THE LEAST UNDERSTOOD OR USED.

REINFORCING your customer's buying decision is your most *productive* selling skill.

Every book I have read on selling teaches this skill, but the main reason given is to reduce "buyers' remorse" and cancellations. Even though the skill is widely taught I find very few average salespeople actually using it.

Over and over I have shown you how fearful a buying decision can be, and the bigger and more complicated the purchase the greater your buyers' fear. In the last chapter, "Writing the Order," you saw that because they lacked competence, most salespeople were just as afraid to ask for the order as the customer was to buy. When these incompetent salespeople asked fearfully instead of instilling in their customers the confidence they needed to say yes, customers became even more fearful. Most salespeople never do come right out and ask for the order.

When their customers do buy, there are almost always some elements of fear present. After the incompetent salesperson and his or her customers have parted, the customers' fears return. In the chapter "The Presentation and Demonstration II," you saw how my own fears returned when I was on the trolley with my ten gadgets and how those fears escalated when I examined each shoddy item. Now *that* was a classic example of buyers' remorse. If there had been any way for me to return those gadgets and get my dollar back, you can bet your life I would have tried it.

Maybe your customers don't have that same degree of fear and remorse, but they always have the fear to some extent, depending on your competence as a salesperson. The salesperson's incompetence is the *main* reason for customers canceling after they have bought. When they are pressured or coerced into buying, their fears are even greater.

Companies who use high-pressure hustlers in selling (note I did not call them "salespeople") are commonly fly-by-night operators; they often use every ruse in the book to keep a customer from canceling.

Today, federal laws give purchasers who have signed a contract a cooling-off period during which they are free to cancel the contract. Even so, some of these scam artists try to get their shaky buyers past the cooling-off period until they can no longer legally cancel. That is against the law, but it does happen. Fraud is illegal, too, but it happens as well.

When salespeople are taught that the main reason for reinforcing a customer's buying decision is to prevent buyers' remorse and thus reduce the possibility of cancellation, the reason most salespeople don't bother to reinforce is simple: When they are afraid to ask for an order and to get one despite their own fear, they are even more afraid that anything they might say could lose them the order so they make no effort to reinforce their customer's buying decision.

It is really amazing, but those customers who are most fearful after they have bought, due to the incompetence or integrity of the salesperson, are the ones who most need their buying decision reinforced and the very ones who receive the least of that reinforcement. The buyers with no need for reinforcement often get the most. How is that possible?

The competent professional never needs sneaky, tricky, or pressure tactics to get an order. Productive presentation skills are perfected as professionally competent salespeople make the presentation and demonstration of what they are selling in the same sequence from start to finish every time, interrupting the presentation only to write the order. After the first four objectives have been acheived, their customers are so confident that what they are selling will best meet their needs at a price they can afford, compared with anything they had seen on guided tours and that all the salesperson has to do is write it up. These are *satisfied* customers, far more satisfied than any customer a guided tour director or con artist will ever have.

What these *satisfied* customers have bought meets their needs every bit as well as they have been led to expect by their salesperson, and they are going to remain satisfied. But the professionally competent salespeople have not reached their goal until these customers return to do more business and send other prospective customers.

If you reread the story of my experience with the con artist in the dime store in the chapter "The Presentation and Demonstration II," you will see how I asked you to imagine how I would have felt if it had been a legitimate offer and after demonstrating the first corkscrew gadget the con artist had asked me to step up and perform those miraculous things myself. You could easily see how I would have been willing to pay one dollar at that point just for that one gadget. He could have taken my dollar, given me my gadget and sent me on my way, a satisfied customer who would remain satisfied.

Or, he could have said to me, "Young man, you have no idea how lucky you were to get your dollar down first, and what a fantastic buy you have made." (Remember, in this make-believe case each gadget would do everything he said it would.) He then proceeds to demonstrate every benefit of each of the other nine gadgets, having me then do the same thing with them myself. Then he puts them in the box with the price on it. Instead of having gotten only one gadget for which I gladly paid my dollar, I received the other nine and all of *their* benefits at no extra cost. Could you possibly imagine a more satisfied customer than that?

Note: All top professionals reinforce *every* customer's buying decision even though they may not need to for their customers to be satisfied. This skill may be the most *productive* of all selling skills because it brings customers back to the same salespeople—and they send more customers, who then become satisfied, and so on.

Reinforcing the sale is nothing more or less than the completion of the sales presentation and it sometimes includes a repeat of the salesperson's presentation and demonstration. Not only does this most productive of all selling skills get the competent professionals far more business than any other single skill, but if they aren't doing this, they won't be practicing their complete presentation and demonstration from start to finish every time. If they are not doing that, they will never, and I mean *never,* perfect productive presentation and demonstration skills.

Reinforcing your customer's buying decision is the *sixth* objective of all professionals on their road to success in the business of selling. It may not be the most important selling skill, but it *is* the most productive.

36 / *What's Next? The Seventh Objective*

THE EASIEST SALE YOU WILL EVER MAKE WILL BE TO A SATISFIED CUSTOMER. WHEN YOU ARE IN THE BUSINESS OF SELLING, MOST OF YOUR SALES ARE GOING TO BE MADE TO SATISFIED CUSTOMERS AND FRIENDS OF SATISFIED CUSTOMERS.

IN "YOUR ROAD TO SELLING SUCCESS II," when the customers bought the dinette and had their buying decision reinforced, the salesperson set out to determine what and when they would next be buying something that he was selling. In his case, this was easy to do because he had a lot of things the customer had ongoing needs for. It is not so easy for the automobile salesperson to do what the furniture salesperson does if, for no other reason, than it is apt to be two or three years before automobile customers are in the market again and the design and model they will buy then doesn't yet exist. This would be the case with many things people sell, but let's look at the dinette salesperson's goal and his seventh objective.

His goal was a *satisfied* customer. He would not have achieved that goal until the customers had returned and bought again and sent others to buy from him. His seventh objective is to find out as soon as possible what and when these customers will be buying again, and sell the next item to them even though it may be some time before the customers' budget will permit the salesperson to write the order.

Most industries know how much time elapses between purchases of what they sell, but these are averages. Customers aren't average. They are individuals. No two of them will ever be exactly alike. *Example:* The average pleasure boat buyers trade in their old boats about every three years. That means that some will trade their boat in within days or weeks after its purchase while some may never buy another. Everyone else does something in between, which results in people buying a new boat on the average of every three years. They call this an "itch cycle." When people have owned a boat for three years they are hot prospects for a new one. In theory, the buyer of a boat should be ready to buy another boat in three years, so that is when he should be contacted again!?! Hogwash.

Professionally competent boat salespeople maintain *ongoing* contact with their satisfied customers so they know when they will be in the market for a new boat, which will almost always mean knowing when the customer's budget will permit it. The professional's notes sent from time to time may include brochures showing new or improved features and models and a handwritten line or two: "Just wanted to keep you up to date."

When the satisfied customer's boat is a couple of years old and the salesperson has a new model with significant improvements or a larger boat that the salesperson knows this satisfied customer would really like, he or she will give a demonstration of the boat that stokes the fires of the customer's desires and establishes a powerful buying goal for this customer. What the salesperson has really done at this point is sell the customer the boat. The salesperson will write the order as soon as budget permits. Ongoing communications could include carefully selected cards sent at meaningful times with handwritten, personalized notes on them. Or the salesperson might call this satisfied customer to remind him or her that it is time for a service check-up and ask how well the boat is meeting that customer's needs.

There really is no end of reasons for the salesperson to keep in contact with a satisfied customer, but every one of these reasons must pass one acid test: Was his reason in the *customer's* best interest?

Now, picture in your mind's eye, the professional's satisfied customer when thoughtful notes or cards arrive with some useful information— short but helpful and needed. Would this satisfied customer have been made even more satisfied?

Would this satisfied customer be coming in contact with other boat owners who were dissatisfied? Would he or she be the best source of red hot prospective boat customers to be found anywhere?

Dissatisfied customers tell many times more people of their dissatisfaction than satisfied customers will tell of their satisfaction. When a dissatisfied customer tells a satisfied customer of that dissatisfaction, the satisfied customer is quick to tell where he found his satisfaction. It is wasted as far as the salesperson is concerned if the customer does not send the new customer to that specific salesperson.

Would you, as a satisfied customer, feel obligated and eager to do something for someone who had shown so much interest and performed services beyond the call of duty for you? Yes, yes, yes.

Contrast that with the salesperson who has not contacted a satisfied customer for three years, who shows up out of the blue wanting that customer to buy a new boat. That customer reacts like everyone else. "Unh-hunh. You only show up when you want something from me."

It does not matter what you sell and it does not matter how long it is between your customer's purchases, your goal is a satisfied customer. The closer your contact with those who have bought from you, the more benefits for them. Even if it is only a thoughtful card that makes them feel better, it will be easier for you to make the next sale—and the more prospective customers these satisfied customers are going to go out of their way to help you sell.

So, your seventh objective is to find out right then while your customers are still in your showroom (or as soon as possible) what they will be buying next and sell it to them as soon as possible, writing the order when budget permits. When that can't be done with the product you sell, your objective remains the same: Maintain positive communications so you can learn as soon as possible, before anyone else, what the customers will be buying next and when they will be buying it. The only way you can achieve this objective is by maintaining two-way communications. So this really connects your seventh and ninth objectives. Through your ongoing communications, you gain the information you need to achieve your seventh objective while at the same time achieving the ninth objective putting your satisfied customer's buying goal in writing.

KEEP IN MIND THE OPPORTUNITY THESE ONGOING
COMMUNICATIONS GIVE YOU TO STOKE THE FIRES
OF YOUR CUSTOMERS' DESIRES. TO SOME DEGREE,
EVERY CONTACT YOU HAVE WITH A SATISFIED
CUSTOMER SHOULD DO THIS.

The automobile and residential real estate sales professional will often have a buyer waiting for their satisfied customer's current automobile or home. This can greatly speed up the "itch cycle."

I was visiting a furniture store once when a prospective customer was telling the salesman that she and her husband were building a large new home on a lake. The house was almost completed and she was going to buy all new furniture, but wondered how she could dispose of the house full of furniture she had. She said that even though they had owned it for years, it was very good furniture when they bought it. The salesman said he had no idea other than running classified ads. I couldn't help myself. I said, "Pardon me, but in your tax bracket, you might consider giving the furniture to the Salvation Army. Their appraisal will permit you to take it as a tax deduction. The odds are that your tax savings would exceed what you can sell it for. You wouldn't have to do a thing. You could go right on using it until you move to your new home—they would pack it up at your convenience." This lady was so relieved. Her thanks were profuse.

When the salesperson has an acceptable solution for a prospective customer's problem, of what to do with what they have, that it can often be all it takes to make a sale. When salespeople are in ongoing contact with their customers, they know what they have and its condition. The principle of reflection causes professional salespeople to see or hear of prospective customers for what their satisfied customers own. That never happens to the guided tour directors.

Human relations and bonding does not change whether it is the bonding of a man and woman in marriage, parents with children, or salespeople with satisfied customers. The question will always be. . .

"Do you love me or do you not?
You told me once, but I forgot."

It is predicted that when the year 2000 rolls around, no company or salespeople will be able to stay in business that do not maintain strong ongoing relationships with their customers. Those whose only goal is a satisfied customer are in the business of selling and they won't have to worry about their job security. Everyone else will.

37 / *Till We Meet Again*

WHEN PEOPLE YOU HAVE NEVER MET IN YOUR LIFE ARE REGULARLY CALLING YOU ON THE PHONE TO SET AN APPOINTMENT WITH YOU TO LEARN ABOUT WHAT YOU SELL, YOU HAVE PERFECTED YOUR PRODUCTIVE SKILLS AND MASTERED THE PROFESSION. YOU CANNOT CONSIDER YOURSELF A TRUE MASTER OF YOUR TRADE UNTIL THAT IS HAPPENING TO YOU FREQUENTLY.

THE THING THAT MAKES SELLING EASIER and easier for those who are in the business of selling and who become masters of the profession is that what they do and what they say is productive and it is done repetitively. Many of those things are so easy. But like all things in selling, and that includes the simplest and even silliest, they are rarely done at first.

A magician will practice the simplest sleight-of-hand trick by the hour, doing it over and over until he has mastered it. Comedians will practice a punchline and a pause over and over to get the maximum effect. Once they have it down pat, they can milk that one bit for laughs throughout their careers. Jack Benny mastered the shrug of his shoulders and the hand to his cheek to the point that just these movements produced huge laughs every time. Such simple productive actions, even silly productive actions, when once mastered became productive tools in Benny's trade.

You might think saying good-bye is not a productive skill to be mastered like all the other productive selling skills. But, whether you like it or not, it is one of those things you will be doing every time you part with a customer for the rest of your selling career. You can take your chances on what's going to happen and you can bet that over a lifetime of selling, most of what you have done will have been effective and *counterproductive*. Which means it won't get you personally any more business from this customer and it may well cost you a ton of business. "Ho hum," you may say, but I say if you master a few productive skills and do them effectively and you will succeed beyond your wildest dreams. But it only takes one counterproductive skill to guarantee your failure.

Salespeople who have mastered their productive skills have a greeting that uses the same words, pauses and inflections every time. They will have also mastered the skill to use when saying, "Till we meet again," and they will do it in the same way every time.

In show business, there are two axioms for an exit:

- Always leave them laughing.
- Always leave them wanting more.

Entertainers whose careers last throughout their lifetimes and even become immortal did very, very few, very, very small things that became their trademarks. These little things that worked were done repeatedly, and that made them memorable. Memorable. What a productive asset for a salesperson! The only memory many salespeople leave in the minds of their customers is that the customers hope they never see them again.

I have picked up too many of my salespeople's cards discarded on the parking lot. They were usually handed to a departing unsatisfied customer with words like this: "If you change your mind, I'll be right here. Be sure you ask for me." That doesn't work. Ever. So why do it twice, let alone keep doing it until it has become a counterproductive habit you have gotten very effective at?

The professionally competent salespeople have an objective they wish to achieve when they part with their customer. That objective can be summed up with these words: "Till we meet again."

There are three things a good effective farewell should achieve for the salesperson:

1. It should give their customers one final reinforcement of their buying decisions, if they bought.

2. It should cause customers to look forward to doing more business with the salesperson whether they bought or not.

3. It should plant in the customers' minds the idea of sending friends, relatives, and business acquaintances to do business with the salesperson. I stress *salesperson*.

If you have any doubts about that being the one skill where sales-people on the whole are the weakest, all you need do is keep accurate records of how many prospective customers ever ask for a specific sales-person when they are shopping the same place for a second time. You will discover that the few who do are those who have not bought yet. It is rare in any field of selling when a specific salesperson who has never met the customer is asked for, even though that customer was sent to the company by a satisfied customer.

Word of mouth is the most effective form of advertising. No one can sell like a satisfied customer. Even in highly promotional companies, word-of-mouth endorsements of the company will create more prospective customers than advertising. It does not do a salesperson one bit of good to have created those word-of-mouth prospective customers if they don't ask for and insist upon him or her to help them find those things that are going to best meet their needs.

Let me repeat one point. More prospective customers are created by word-of-mouth than from any other source. This is usually because someone has bought something from a salesperson. They were satisfied with the product and services, but not satisfied with the salesperson enough to tell those prospective customers to insist on the services of that particular salesperson.

> WHEN PEOPLE YOU HAVE NEVER MET IN YOUR
> LIFE ARE REGULARLY CALLING YOU ON THE
> PHONE TO SET AN APPOINTMENT WITH YOU TO
> LEARN ABOUT WHAT YOU SELL, YOU HAVE
> PERFECTED YOUR PRODUCTIVE SKILLS AND
> MASTERED THE PROFESSION. YOU CANNOT
> CONSIDER YOURSELF A TRUE MASTER OF YOUR
> TRADE UNTIL THAT IS HAPPENING TO YOU
> FREQUENTLY.

There are some who teach that the time to get prospective customers from a satisfied customer is at the time the sale has been completed. I am sure there are some selling situations where that is true, but I am just as sure they are the exceptions.

Here's why: At the time customers buy, it is true they are *satisfied,* but whether they remain satisfied and become more satisfied depends entirely upon how well the purchase lives up to their expectations and meets their needs. The better the purchase has done these two things and the longer it continues to do these two things, the more satisfied the customers become and the more anxious they are to tell others. My experience and research convinces me that the most effective salespeople have ongoing ways to remind their satisfied customers to send them prospective customers. The longer this relationship continues, the more productive it is for the salesperson.

I used a variation of a very simple form of an effective way to say, "Till we meet again," in "Your Road to Selling Success." It consists of saying:

1. "I was so glad to see you go ahead and take the (product or service.) I know it is going to meet your needs so well that the longer you have it, the more satisfied you will become."

2. "I want you to have my card. If you have any reason at all to call our company, I want you to call me first so I can personally give you any help you may need."

At this point, I recommend the set of two business cards. However you may personalize your method of using them, I like the method shown in "Your Road to Selling Success" and feel that it will work for professionally competent salespeople. And they will make it work even better the more they develop their own personal techniques. It won't *ever* work for guided tour directors, but they won't continue doing it anyway.

Start with step one. The sale has been consummated and reinforced, making the customer even more satisfied with his or her buying decision. You have learned as much as you could about the customer and his or her future needs for what you sell. (If possible, you have even gone ahead and made the next sale, setting the date when it is to be written up.)

The customer is ready to leave. Remember to tell him or her again how much you enjoyed being able to help. Remind the customer again of your own confidence that he or she has made the best buying decision. Keep it short, sincere, and happy.

Whether you are seated, standing, or walking toward the door as you say this, is unimportant. What is important is that later you must remember what you did and how effective you were. If the sale had not gone as well as you felt it should, you want to think about what you would do differently. The time to think about what you will do the next time is right then, not when you are getting ready to meet the next customer.

You might complain, "That's too much work." Well, you don't have a choice. You will have to think about what you will say the next time you part with a customer. You can think about what didn't work and decide what you might do differently or you will find yourself repeating what did not work. Your yardstick reminds you and measures for you how effective each technique has been.

Your objective will be to show real appreciation and make your customers feel even more confident about their buying decisions. Focus on this one seemingly insignificant skill until you are satisfied that what you do has constantly been effective and productive. When that is happening, from then on it will take less and less time while becoming more and more productive.

If your customers come to you, what you do may vary, but the objectives remain the same. You have an opportunity to perform more services beyond the call of duty than the salesperson who calls on his customers. You can walk your customers to the door or to their cars. What I have observed with top professionals is that they never try to rush what they do. The more consistent they are, the better they become. If they walk their customers to their cars, they will do it every time, no matter how busy they are. The customer never feels rushed or pushed. The salesperson's decision to walk the customer to the car every time or not was based entirely upon how he or she feels about the sale. If the salesperson feels this added bit of courtesy was productive and had bonded the customer even more, he or she walked them to the car every time and neither rain, snow, nor sleet kept that salesperson from his or her appointed rounds. These seemingly insignificant investments of time and efforts are productive and pay giant dividends over a career, and I do mean *giant*.

I repeat: All salespeople either do these productive things or they don't. None fall in between. I have found that those who do these things are like kids with a new toy when they discover an added productive service to perform. The ongoing measurement of what professionally competent salespeople do that keeps them constantly aware of opportunities.

Step two probably has more variations depending on what is being sold than any other part of this skill. In the case of a home, the next purchase could be some years away. On the other hand, reselling the home for that satisfied customer could happen anytime. It often happens in this world that when people have no more than moved in, the husband or wife is promoted and transferred to another city. When they are bonded to the salesperson who sold them the home, that's who they call to re-sell it for them.

In the case of life insurance, the next sale could come at any time as new needs arise. The purchase of a new home creates plenty of need for enough life insurance to pay off the mortgage in the event of the death of either the husband or wife. I only give this as one example of thousands of situations that could arise. How much the salespeople know about their customers and their ongoing needs determines how much ongoing business they do.

The only thing you must keep in mind is this: You have the customer in front of you right *now*. Any opportunity you have to accomplish anything with that customer is now. Laying the ground work for future business is right now. If you have already done this as in the example in "Your Road to Selling Success," all you need to do is remind the customers that you will be calling to set the appointment when it's time to write the next order. With other products, your efforts to make the next sale to this satisfied customer will vary, but your objective is to be the one who gets that business. Do not forget that and do not forget the importance of measuring how effective you were each time you planted seeds to make future sales as you parted with a customer. Focus on this productive skill until what you do and say is productive, then do it every time.

Step two is the least used and the least perfected of all selling skills and yet, it is the one skill that can produce the greatest return on the investment of your selling time.

Example: As much as 90 percent of the time of salespeople whose prospective customers come to them is wasted waiting for prospective customers to try to sell. These salespeople typically sell fifteen percent or even fewer of their prospective customers. That means they are effective less than five percent of the hours they work.

Professionally competent salespeople work almost entirely by appointment. They set those appointments during slow traffic periods. They never wait in line for a prospective customer. They keep busy during slow traffic periods. If they have any free time, it is usually during peak traffic periods. Even then, they usually approach customers other salespeople have tried to sell and dropped. Those who have been selling five years or more tend to set their own schedules and are booked with appointments all of their working hours. They are productive 100 percent of their working hours in all cases. That is why they often make up to ten times more income than the average salespeople in their company.

No salesperson who measures the effective productivity of his or her working hours could knowingly go on doing what the guided tour directors do. Why should they work so hard to make so little and be in constant fear of losing their jobs? It is management's job to make everyone aware of this.

How you use your business card tells a lot about your selling objectives.

I like the two-card technique in "Your Road to Selling Success." Used properly, it gets a chuckle out of customers. The better you get at this simple skill and the more the customer is aware of what you are doing, the more customers seem to enjoy it. If you are uncomfortable with this I still recommend two cards even when dealing with bankers, heads of giant corporations and professional buyers who are buying for their companies.

Bankers know bankers, corporate heads know corporate heads, professional buyers know professional buyers and that's the best source in the world for prospective customers, if that's who buys what you sell. Yes! Yes! Yes! The *objective* is the same.

Those two cards of yours in their pockets are seeds of thought. When two cards arrived with your thank-you note and any ongoing correspondence, it fertilizes those seeds of thought. Sooner or later the crop will be ready to harvest. If you planted those seeds in a *satisfied* customer, it was fertile soil. It becomes even more fertile as they become more satisfied. The seed will grow and will bear fruit. I am sorry, but if you wish to enjoy that fruit, you will at least have to gather it. If you don't, it will get so ripe it will fall off the tree into someone else's hands. What a waste!

Almost all those who are hired and trained to sell fail because of their inability to prospect and/or to learn enough about their prospective customers and their needs. These failures come to know prospective customers as lookers, tire kickers, mooches, and browsers. In the life insurance field, they don't come to know their customers at all because they don't even know what a prospective customer looks like. It is rare for prospective life insurance customers to seek out a salesperson to announce that they are prospective customers.

One of the largest and fastest growing expenses in business today is advertising, all spent in an effort to attract or identify prospective customers. Yet, all the advertising in the world cannot offset a dissatisfied customer. Every dissatisfied customer forces the company to spend more money in advertising to try and offset the effects of *dissatisfied* customers. When I see an ad for a restaurant other than grand opening ads, I have to wonder what percentage of dissatisfied customers caused the need for that ad. The restaurant business has far and away the highest mortality rate of any business. The reason is very, very easy to understand. They succeed or fail based 100 percent upon satisfied and dissatisfied customers. It is the same with all businesses, it just happens faster in the restaurant business than any other because repeat buyers are greatly accelerated and dissatisfied customers tell far more people of their dissatisfaction than satisfied customers will.

When all is said and done, the only sure source of prospective customers is a *satisfied* customer. The sooner salespeople build customer files that assures them of a source of enough prospective customers to keep their appointment book filled up all the hours they want to work, the more assured they are of ongoing success in good times and bad. They need never fear for their job security. Those seeds are either planted, or not, whenever you say, "Till we meet again."

38 / *Maintaining Ongoing Relationships with Satisfied Customers*

DO YOU LOVE ME?
OR, DO YOU NOT?
YOU TOLD ME ONCE BUT I FORGOT.

PROSPECTIVE CUSTOMERS WANT TO BECOME SATISFIED customers far more than the salesperson wants to make them one.

When a salesperson has made prospective customers satisfied customers and they ever again have needs for what he or she sells, you can bet that they would rather buy from him or her than anyone else in the world.

OBJECTIVE #9: PUTTING YOUR SATISFIED CUSTOMER'S NEXT BUYING GOAL IN WRITING

The ninth objective is to *keep* satisfied customers, so that they buy from the salesperson on an ongoing basis. The professionally competent salesperson has a plan and he follows that plan. The objective of the plan is to keep the satisfied customer buying from him or her—no matter how long it is between sales. This will not happen if the salesperson has no plan to follow that will cause it to happen, even though the customer wants it to happen more than the salesperson does.

It was easy to show how this could be done with dinette customers, because they have current needs all the time for home furnishings. It was easy to show you the plan that the salesperson would follow to cause his satisfied dinette customer to continue to do business with him. It is not as easy to do in some fields of selling, but regardless of what you sell, a plan can be developed and followed to achieve this same objective. Like all plans it will begin with knowing where you are starting from and where you want to get.

Your plan will start when the sale has been completed and you and your satisfied customer have parted. The objective of your plan will be to maintain open and positive communications. When satisfied customers do not receive any word from the salesperson that shows honest ongoing interest in them and their needs they feel abandoned. It is exactly the same way a member of the family feels when children or parents don't write or call except on rare occasions. And, whey they do call, it's only because they want something.

There are literally hundreds of ways to maintain communications with your satisfied customers. You want to select those things to do that will work best for you. Then you establish a simple plan for doing those things that you can follow every time. This means that you will be doing the same things the same way in the same sequence with every satisfied customer, and that means that it is going to get easier and easier to do.

Example: Every salesperson should send a short note of thanks, written immediately upon parting with satisfied customers. The note should be written, addressed, and stamped by hand and should reflect a sincere interest in the satisfied customers and their continued satisfaction. If it was a business transaction it might be typed, but it should be personally signed with a short handwritten postscript that reflects this interest. Having a stamp on the envelope instead of being metered adds a small personal touch, showing even more of your interest in them.

Some top professionals like to send greeting cards for birthdays and special events. Each of these cards should be selected because they reflect a personal interest in the person for whom it is intended. This might sound like you would have to personally shop until you found just the right card for every person to whom you send a card. At first, that would be the case, but in no time you will have found a few of each type of card which will do what you want it to do. Your personal handwritten note or postscript on the card reflects even more interest in them.

Some salespeople clip articles of interest out of newspapers and magazines which may be of some use to their satisfied customers and enclose them with a note. If a company or person is written up for some achievement some salespeople have the article laminated or framed and send it with a short note.

Many salespeople find ways and reasons to call their satisfied customers on the phone. People browsing in showrooms don't like to be asked "Can I help you?" over and over by incompetent salespeople and they like it even less when the privacy of their home is invaded by phone calls from incompetent salespeople whose only purpose is to ask if they can help them.

No call should ever be made to the customer unless the salesperson has something to say that the satisfied customer wants to hear. When a salesperson calls satisfied customers immediately after a delivery has been completed to be sure that everything meets with their satisfaction it shows an ongoing interest in them and their satisfaction that is greatly appreciated. Even more important, if there was a problem the salesperson knows that if it is taken care of to the customers' satisfaction quickly, they will become an even more satisfied customer.

Automobile salespeople who call to see if they can pick up the customer's vehicle to bring it in for service and leave a new demonstrator for them to use accomplish a whole bunch of productive things:

1. He gets to visit with the customers and bring himself up to date on their needs.

2. He gets to drive their car and check it out so that he knows more about its condition than they do.

3. He has his satisfied customers actually experience owning all of the benefits that they could enjoy if they owned the new car. This makes the customer even more dissatisfied with what he or she currently has.

4. There is no time like right then to look to this customer for referrals. Why?

When services are performed that are above and beyond the call of duty in today's world they are so rare that when they do happen to someone the person will talk about it to everyone they know.

If you make the next sale to your satisfied customers, it will be after you achieve the same objective that you achieved to make the first sale.

You will have learned enough about their current needs and made them consciously aware of enough of those needs, then learned enough about what they are using now, making them consciously aware how dissatisfied they are with what they are using now. You can wait to do this until they come to you (if they come to you) or you can do this before their budget permits which is almost always sometime before they have become aware that it will. You can go ahead and make that next sale even though you won't be able to write it up until their budget does permit. You might even put their buying goal(s) in writing for them.

Don't ever forget that once they have become consciously aware of their needs of the benefits of what you sell compared to what they are using now they want to become your satisfied customer a lot more than you want to make them your satisfied customer.

I cannot tell you which of these things or all of the other things that you might do to keep ongoing positive communications with your satisfied customers. I can say that it will start with your thank-you note. If this is to become a productive selling skill, you must do it every time at the same time. Don't try doing a lot of things at once. When you are satisfied with your thank-you notes and that skill needed to write the notes has been perfected into a productive habit, select one more thing to do and stay with it until it, too, has become a productive selling habit.

Keep in mind that as each of these productive selling habits are perfected they have become so easy for you to do that you are not even consciously aware you are doing them most of the time. Within a year or two you will have powerful communications going on with every satisfied customer you have and you cannot imagine how successful that will make you.

Were you to ask anyone you know at any time if they could give you the name of five people who really do have a need right then for what you sell, the odds are that they can't come up with one name, let alone five. But, over the period of one year almost every satisfied customer you have is going to come in contact with a whole bunch of red hot prospective customers for what you sell. If your ongoing communications have been positive they have made your satisfied customers consciously aware of their satisfaction and who caused it. When one of these people tell your satisfied customer of their need, you can rest assured that your satisfied customer will tell them about you.

How strongly satisfied customers recommend you depends on how positive and consistent your interest in them, their satisfaction and needs have been. Having received a couple of your business cards with every communication you sent has made them so consciously aware of the cards and your reason for including them that a lot more of those red hot prospective customers are going to be given your card and even told to call you for an appointment. Until this is happening to you on a steady basis, you still have some work to do on these skills.

"I don't have time to do that" is the response I get from the losers in the lounge when I try to discuss the development of a new productive selling skill. Yet those professionally competent salespeople in the same company who sell ten times or more than they do are doing every one of the productive things needed to achieve all ten objectives and they often work fewer hours. It is never a question of having the time to perfect the productive skills needed to do these things. It is only a question of *taking* the time.

It is true that the counterproductive habits of the losers in the lounge consume all of what they call their working hours, leaving them no time to do anything else. I remind you of this again at this time because the most productive of all selling skills are those that keep the salesperson in positive communications with their satisfied customers and, sadly, those simple skills are what most salespeople lack.

The basic element of any productive skill is interest in the ongoing satisfaction of your customers. That is essential and indispensable if you are to perfect skills into productive selling habits.

Your Business Card

The most important tool the salesperson has when it comes to keeping customers satisfied, maintaining communications, and getting more prospective customers is a business card. Using a business card is like everything else the salesperson does. It will either be productive or it will be counterproductive.

It should be obvious that when a salesperson has left a *satisfied* customer their business card it will produce positive productive results. When an *unsatisfied* customer is left with his or her business card it will produce counterproductive results. When they left a customer *dissatisfied,* it can produce disastrous counterproductive results.

I realized this while still in my teens when I found one of my own business cards thrown on the sidewalk outside of my company by an unsatisfied customer. From that day to this, I have never given a business card to anyone who I felt did not want it nor have a need for it—a need that I had made them aware of.

During my thirty-five years in business, there is no telling how many of my salespeople's business cards I found discarded on the parking lots by unsatisfied customers. I always picked them up. I would ask the salesperson how they had made out with that prospective customer and they always assured me that they had made the sale—they were sure the customer would be back. I would give them their card, tell them where I found it, and in spite of this, they went right on doing what they were doing that was counterproductive. It was a deeply ingrained habit to which they were addicted. This kind of frustration caused me to do the twelve years of research that it took to complete this book.

Prospective customers who leave a business unsatisfied may not throw the salesperson's card on the parking lot, but it is almost always thrown in the trash. When this happens it isn't just because the prospective customer did or did not buy. It is because the salesperson had not shown a sincere interest in them and their needs so they had no reason to be interested in that salesperson much less what was offered for sale.

When professionally competent salespeople give one of their business cards, it is because they have given that person reasons to want and need it. They may have even written some important information on the card that the customer will need.

It is important for the salesperson's business card to have any information a prospective customer might need. Keep in mind when compiling information to have printed on your business card that it will often be given to a prospective customer by one of your satisfied customers.

Most professional salespeople do not have their home phone number on their business card, but they will often write it on the card by hand. You remember as they give their card to their satisfied customers, they say, "If you have any reason to call our company I want you to call me first so that I can personally see that your needs are taken care of." Then they might add, "My home number is unlisted, but I want you to have it in case you need it. Let me write it on the card." This is service beyond the call of duty. The customer may never call them at home, but the salesperson has shown special interest in them with this simple act.

Top professionals often have more than one version of their business card. For example, you have all seen distinctive small labels below the larger labels on fine clothing. The professionally competent apparel salesperson who has helped his or her prospective customers select only those things that are going to best meet their needs have these small tastefully embroidered labels made with just their name on them. They have the tailor sew them inside each garment. As the customer becomes more and more satisfied he or she is constantly reminded of the person who caused that satisfaction.

Other professionals have a smaller version of their business card made up on small, distinctive peel-off stickers. Remember, they have told their satisfied customers that if they have any reason to call their company to call them first. Salespeople who sell appliances, audio/video equipment, electronics, computers, automobiles, boats, airplanes, or who are service or building contractors, and in many other fields will apply this business card permanently in a convenient but inconspicuous place. It is a rare customer today who doesn't have questions after they have bought complex products. The frustration of trying to get answers can turn even the most satisfied customer into a disgruntled dissatisfied customer.

When this happens to you (as it often does to all of us) wouldn't it be great to have the phone number and person to call? The one who knows the most about us and our needs? And what we bought? How much more satisfied are you going to become? How much more anxious will you be to recommend not just the company where you bought, but the salesperson?

When you are in your new car with others, you are often asked how you like it. If you bought it from a top professional who has a form of his small business card stuck to the back of the sun visor or to the inside of the glove compartment door, the odds are that you are an extremely satisfied customer because he or she has seen to it. Not only do you brag about your satisfaction, but you are going to brag about the person who caused your satisfaction. Oh yes, and you just happen to have his or her phone number handy.

I recently saw some very thin magnets the size of a business card with peel-off stickum on one side. The salesperson can adhere his business card to the magnet. They cost about thirty cents (or less) apiece (depending on the quantity you buy). Imagine one of these magnets on the door of a new refrigerator when it is delivered. I bet most of them will stay there to hold notes. Better still, imagine a small decal on the side of a VCR or computer—products which are sure to cause the customer to call the salesperson for help.

Remember to keep both your satisfied and prospective customers' best interest in mind when designing your business card. The uses of this card are endless when the salesperson is professionally competent and his or her customers have bought those things that are going to best meet their needs.

The ninth objective is one that can be achieved in countless ways. Almost every professional salesperson with whom I have talked will have something they do a little differently than what others do. They are proud of how productive their skill is. As you see other salespeople doing all kinds of different things that work for them, you might be tempted to try doing them yourself. Just keep in mind: it is effective and productive for them because they have perfected the skills needed to make it work.

You are better off doing only one thing and doing it every time. As you start measuring the results the measurement will cause what you are doing to become more productive. It won't be long until what you are doing is distinctive, causing your satisfied customers to be constantly aware of your sincere interest in their continued satisfaction.

This will permit you to determine way in advance what you will next be selling your satisfied customers. You will be able to sell it to them even before their budget permits, setting the date to write it up when their budget does permit. Then you can put their buying goal in writing. Ongoing communications will keep a constant flow of prospective customers coming to you by your satisfied customers. The skills to achieve this are the most productive of all selling skills—productive skills which you need in the business of selling to assure your success.

39 / *Your Customer File*

YOUR GOAL IS EITHER A SATISFIED CUSTOMER OR IT ISN'T.
NO MATTER WHAT KIND OF LIP SERVICE YOU GIVE IT, IF YOU DON'T HAVE
AND MAINTAIN YOUR OWN CUSTOMER FILE AND PROTECT ITS INTEGRITY WITH
YOUR LIFE, A SATISFIED CUSTOMER IS NOT YOUR GOAL AND YOU ARE NOT IN
THE BUSINESS OF SELLING.

YOUR ONLY GOAL is to turn every prospective customer contact into a satisfied customer. You have not achieved this goal until those who bought have returned to you to buy again and/or sent others to buy from you.

When you started using a form of the 5 x 7 file card to measure how effective you had been every time you came in contact with a prospective customer, you did not set out to build a customer file. As you perfected the skills needed to achieve each of the ten objectives needed to turn a prospective customer into a satisfied customer, you wound up with a customer file card that had all the information needed to sell them on an ongoing basis as needs arose and to get them to send their friends, relatives and business aquaintances to do business with you.

Your customer file can be as comprehensive and complicated as you want to make it, or it can and should be kept as simple as possible with only that information you need to maintain your ongoing relationship with satisfied customers.

The more confident the salesperson, the simpler his or her system for keeping a customer file. In the chapter, "The Yardstick," I told you I thought keeping customer file cards and manila envelopes in file cabinets was the best way to maintain your files even though the company itself may keep a lot of the information in its computer.

The man who sells me my dress shirts uses 3 x 5 customer file cards. When he has used all the space on a card, he staples a new one to the back of it. He has some customers with several cards stapled together. His file cases are stacked on the back counter in his small shop. He is very proud to show them to anyone who asks. There is nothing fancy about what he does, but it works as well for him as any system in this space-age, computerized world.

Some salespeople need several four-drawer file cabinets for the records of their dealings with only one customer. Whatever you sell, your need for a systematic way to keep track of customer files will fall somewhere between those extremes. It is better to have a file that will hold more information than you need it to than one that won't hold enough.

Doctors' and lawyers' methods for filing are the best examples for you to look at when you are trying to decide what kind of records you want to keep on your customers. They record all information gained from every contact whether in person or by phone. If you call them or go to see them, they have your file out and they review it before they get down to business.

That is exactly what the highest-volume, highest-paid professional salespeople do, too. One of the few books I recommend on selling is *How to Make Big Money Selling* by Joe Gondolfo. Good, average life insurance salespeople will sell around six million dollars worth of policies a year. Joe has sold over 6 *billion* dollars worth in *one* year! That's 1,000 times what good, average salespeople do. Yes, he only sleeps four hours a night and puts in eighteen-hour days to do this. But there is only one Joe Gondolpho in the world.

Most people say, "I wouldn't work as hard as that man works no matter what you paid me." But wait. Joe Gondolpho could work *eight* hours a week and still sell over *100* times more life insurance than most good, average life insurance salespeople.

Think: Working harder has nothing to do with competence. The more competent salespeople are, the fewer hours they have to work to make more money. The more competent they are, the more information you will find in their customer files for every prospective customer they ever came in contact with. It is true that a salesperson must constantly clean out the files, eliminating those who have died, moved away, or who are no longer in business. But top professionals don't throw away those customer records. They just move them to inactive files, making it easier to stay on top of their active customers.

Top professionals keep an open file on every prospective customer they come in contact with who has *not* bought. This can only be understood by those who truly are in the business of selling. The professionals see these prospective customers as *challenges*. They know that anyone who has a goal knows where they are, has a plan to follow that will get them from where they are to where they want to go, and that those who follow that plan *will* reach their goal. To them, it's like climbing a mountain. The excitement comes from climbing higher and higher and steeper and steeper mountains.

All professionally competent salespeople need a form similar to an employment application with a space on it for everything they need to know about prospective customers to achieve their first five objectives. In the simplest of selling situations, this will usually fit on one side of a 5 x 7-inch file card.

Salespeople all need a form with space on it for everything they need to know about *satisfied* customers to achieve their second five objectives and reach their goal. Here again, when selling simple products or services, that could fit on the other side of a 5 x 7-inch file card.

It would be nice if the company you went to work for had one of these forms. Odds are that they won't. If they don't, design your own. The card is no more than a checklist of the questions you will ask all prospective customers you come in contact with and the sequence in which you want to ask them.

What you have learned about your customers and their needs will be what you want in their files. The more information in your file pertinent to them and their needs for what you sell, the easier it gets to continue doing business with them, and the easier it will be to get referrals from them.

It's never one big thing. Like everything else in the business of selling, it's always a bunch of little things.

Warning: When you start your customer file, begin with only the basics found on the 5 x 7-inch card illustration in the chapter entitled "Using the Yardstick." As you improve your ability to learn more and more about your customers and their needs, you will need more space. Don't limit yourself a single 5 x 7 card, but don't create a monster, either. Keep it as simple as you can with space only for the information you need on every sale. There will be thousands of exceptions. That information can be put on a separate piece of paper of a second card you attach to the main one.

Check with other top professionals who are selling what you sell, even if they don't work for your company, to see how they keep their records. You'll find most of them are usually glad to share their information.

Never discard information you learned about a *satisfied* customer.

If you have never had your own customer file, like all other things you will try for the first time, everything will seem to take forever. Much of what you do *will* be wasted effort. Many of the cards will be useless. Put a rubber band around them and date and store them at least for a while. Eventually, you will discover you are storing fewer and fewer useless file cards as you become more effective and productive. Visually seeing that bolsters your confidence. Little things, of course, but enormous benefits.

Treasure your customer file as it if were a mutual fund or a savings account. Every card you file for a satisfied customer is an investment. Ongoing sales to satisfied customers tend to get larger and those customers are likely to send you more prospective customers.

Think about this: Odds are their next purchase will be bigger. That means your commission will be, too. And, that means your "investment" pays over 100-percent interest every time a satisfied customer returns to do business with you. After three sales, it pay over 300 percent interest, ten sales over 1,000 percent, and so on. If you figure the commission on referral customers as a return on your investment, their potential alone makes each *satisfied* customer the best investment anyone ever made or could ever hope to make.

You don't need any encouragement to look at your savings account statements or at the status of your investments. When you realize the potential return you can derive from each satisfied customer, believe me, you will become one self-motivated person.

Getting your customer file started and maintaining it accurately will be the hardest thing for you to learn. You must do it daily, no matter how tired you are. And true, it could be months or even a year or more before you see any benefits. Look at it as a long-term investment. But when it does start paying off, your income will go up in a way that you never dreamed possible.

Some new salespeople have doubts and fears about whether they have chosen the right profession or the right company to sell for. That fear is all the excuse some salespeople need to neglect or even to fail to keep customer files. They will fail at selling because they will not have perfected this productive skill they needed to succeed in the business of selling.

Your goal is either a satisfied customer or it isn't. No matter what kind of lip service you give it, if you don't keep up your own customer file and protect its integrity with your life, a satisfied customer is not your goal and you are not in the business of selling.

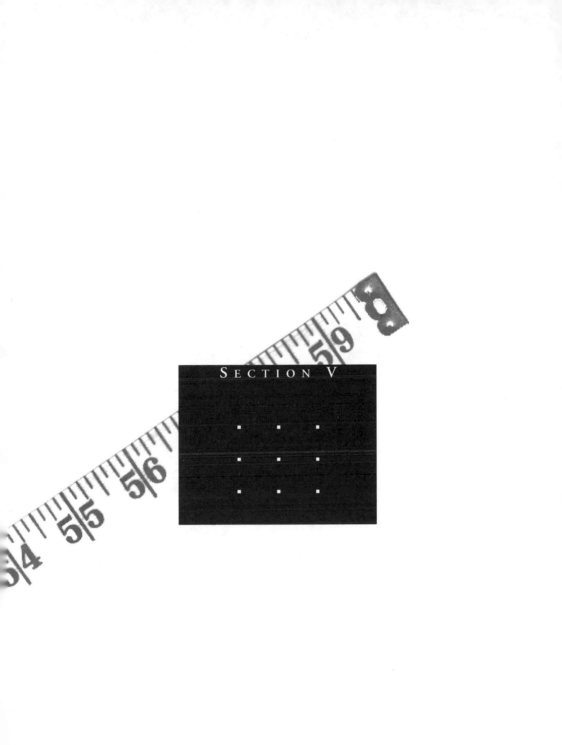

SECTION V

INTRODUCTION TO THE BOOK OF TRADE SECRETS

THERE ARE MANY THINGS TO LEARN AND PRODUCTIVE SKILLS TO BE DEVELOPED IF YOU WANT TO SUCCEED AT ANYTHING.

The middle school my daughters went to had an annual used book and art sale to raise money. Tens of thousands of books were donated and people drove from over a hundred miles away to browse and buy. One year, both daughters volunteered to work in the rooms where the books were sorted into categories.

When I picked them up after the first day one said, "Dad, you know how you are always talking about 'how-to' books? Well, we have more 'how-to' books than all the other nonfiction books combined."

"Would you like to know something about those 'how-to books?'" I asked her.

"Sure."

"They haven't even been read. And most of them are just like brand new!"

"How do you know that, Dad?" My daughter asked.

"You take a look at them tomorrow and see for yourself. When I pick you up, then I will tell you why they haven't been read."

The next evening as they climbed into the car they were both grinning. "Dad, you were right! Most of those 'how-to' books are almost brand new. How did you know that?"

"The people who bought those books thought the books would make them rich, thin, a better cook, a good salesperson, or whatever. As soon as they started to read the books they discovered that the books weren't going to *make* them anything. The books would only tell them what *they* would have to do if *they* wanted to be rich, thin, a better cook, a good salesperson, or whatever. So they stopped reading those books as fast as they could. They didn't even want them on their bookshelves. Mainly, they didn't want to be reminded of what they would have to do to achieve their goals. That's why they gave the books away.

"If it was a good book and the owner read it and did what it said to do, he or she became rich, thin, a better cook, a good salesperson, or whatever. You couldn't pry that book out of that person's hands with a crowbar."

There are many things you must learn and many productive skills you must develop if you are to succeed at anything in this life. We all know that. What most people don't know is that it requires no knowledge and no effort to develop counterproductive skills into counterproductive habits that guarantee failure. And no one has a choice as to whether they want or don't want counterproductive habits because their failure to opt for and develop productive skills guarantees that they will unconsciously develop counterproductive skills. But once they are perfected, the people with counterproductive habits they gained so easily will find their lives becoming harder and harder the longer they live. Getting a job will be harder and harder until they can no longer find any work at all.

But the people with *productive* skills will find *their* work getting easier and easier the longer they live. Their income will continue to rise as they become even more productive and they will never, never know job insecurity.

The chapters in this section are designed to help you get started along the productive road in your career, and to provide the course you must follow to stay on your personal road to success in the business of selling.

40 / *You Have No Bad Competitors*

THE NUMBER-ONE CAUSE OF CUSTOMER DISSATISFACTION HAS NOTHING TO DO WITH THE QUALITY OF THE PRODUCT SOLD OR THE SERVICE. IT HAS TO DO WITH THE CUSTOMER'S EXPECTATIONS.

PROFESSIONAL SALESPEOPLE learn very quickly that they never "knock" their competitors or their products or services. The competitors may be the biggest crooks in the world, but the competent professionals never call them that if they are dealing with prospective customers.

Most of the time, if the subject comes up at all, the master sellers will say, "That's a good company. Of course we feel ours is a lot better." They say that because they truly feel that way. Their positive confidence says far more than any accusations against the competitor or what they sell ever could.

The "best" of anything is that solution/product that will "best" meet a customer's needs. Just keep yourself focused on your ten objectives and you will reach your goal. Those ten objectives *produce satisfied customers.* Sometimes, you will be competing with frauds and people of questionable ethics, and whatever they sell may be of questionable value or quality.

When I was in business, I made a lot of mistakes, but I did some things very well. Handling competition was one of those things I managed to do well.

My company had operations in ten major cities. One of my rules was that any complaints from customers would be taken care of quickly to their satisfaction. To make sure that was done, I issued a simple statement to all branches: If a customer complaint was ever filed with the Better Business Bureau, the store manager where that happened no longer had a job. I *never* fired one manager because of that policy.

To oversee this policy, we knew the phone number of the Better Business Bureau office in each of our cities. We also knew the name and phone number of our ten largest competitors, as well as those of any companies we knew were of questionable character. Once a month, people from my office would call the Better Business Bureau in each city. They would say they were new in town and needed furniture. They had shopped three or four places and wanted to know if there was any reason why they shouldn't buy from any of them. Their list included my company's name and two or three competitors. From the time this policy was installed, we never had a customer complaint filed with the Better Business Bureau.

Our salespeople were told that if a question was raised about the integrity of our company or about a competitor's they were to reply, "As far as we know they are a good company and what they sell is good. Of course, we feel our company and what we sell is *better*. If you really have any doubts, here's a phone and the Better Business Bureau's number. Call them, tell them you are considering us and the other company. Ask if they have logged any complaints on either of us."

It was a rare competitor who didn't have some outstanding complaints on file at the Better Business Bureau—a few had a *lot* of them. Imagine how much confidence our policy produced in my salespeople, whether they ever used that information or not.

This policy proved to have been very wise on two occasions. In the seventies, the FTC (Federal Trade Commission) was very active. This agency cited the largest furniture retailer for false and misleading pricing and advertising. The company was required to sign a "cease and desist order," which means they admitted their guilt. They did demand that the FTC hold anyone else doing what they were doing just as culpable and they named several companies, including mine. When the FTC investigators showed up, I had them brought to my office.

"I assume you gentlemen are here to see that I am doing things right and want to help me in any way you can. I need all the help I can get and I do appreciate it. But if you came to nitpick, I don't have time for that and will see you in court."

One of the FTC agents said, "What do you mean?"

I told him their job was to protect the consumer. I handed them my list of Better Business Bureau numbers, along with the names of my ten biggest competitors in each city. I said, "You will not find a single complaint filed against my company. No one has complained about being misled by my advertising and no one has complained about what they bought or about my service. Every other company whose name is on those lists has outstanding complaints. Some of them have huge files of complaints that go back years. When you have cleaned up their files, then come see me. Otherwise, I will see you in court with those files."

They had walked through my showroom and listed six items before they came to my office. They wanted me to validate the comparison prices I had on those items to show that they were legitimate. I called in my head of merchandising and told him to call the factories that made those same six items and to get the name and location of the nearest dealer who carried them. Then I told him to buy one of each of those six items and have them in our building by that afternoon even if he had to take our jet airplane to another city to do it.

The FTC men said, "You don't have to do that."

I said, "You come back this afternoon, and after that, I don't expect to see you again."

They did and I didn't.

The second time this policy paid off actually saved my company. A major recession had hit and my company developed a serious cash flow problem, which, translated, meant deep financial trouble. As we were a public company, this bad news got a lot of publicity in the markets I was in. Competitors were quick to tell customers we wouldn't be around long. I kept the BBB up to date in each city. If I or my salespeople were faced with this problem by a customer, they simply had them call the BBB and ask about us and our accusers. It sure made getting those sales easier and helped us sell our way out of our problems.

There are many lessons to be learned from these experiences, but the most important is not to knock your competitors or what they sell. If they need knocking, let someone else do it. Just remember that if competitors are doing something wrong, sooner or later they will be out of business. Is it your job to make them quit doing the wrong thing so they can stay around ever longer? Of course not, but don't ever close your eyes to what's out there, either.

Two things combine to make a *satisfied* customer: customer-satisfying services and customer-satisfying products. When you provide those two elements to your customers and are professionally competent, you will get the sale almost every time, so it doesn't matter what your competitor sells or does.

Guided tour directors can have the best products, the best services, and the best prices, and they still won't wind up with satisfied customers for hundreds of reasons. The number one cause of dissatisfied customers has nothing to do with the quality of the product sold or the services. It has to do with the customer's *expectations*. The guided tour director leads the customer to believe that the product or people in the company will do something they wouldn't or couldn't, while the professionally competent salespeople's products are doing all they said they would do and a whole lot more. Their company's services live up to everything they promised and even more.

The longer you study selling and learn what almost all salespeople do compared to what a professionally competent salesperson does, the better you will comprehend what causes customer dissatisfaction.

You don't have to *knock* your competitors or what they sell to succeed in selling and to succeed beyond your wildest dreams. What you need to do is make yourself professionally competent, and if you use your yardstick habitually, it will guarantee your success.

41 / *Choosing the Best Sales Career for You*

No one can sell anything with enthusiasm and honesty that they don't believe will result in a *satisfied* customer. Nobody.

No one can ask prospective customers to buy from a company with enthusiasm and honesty when they don't like nor have confidence in the people who make up that company. Nobody.

No one can sell with enthusiasm and honesty to prospective customers that they do not basically like. Nobody.

MANY PEOPLE WILL AT SOME TIME TRY SELLING, but most will fail and change careers. Whenever I hear one of these people say they tried selling and didn't like it or it "wasn't for me," I always ask, "Why didn't you try brain surgery?" That would make about as much sense.

Like all professions, selling requires specialized knowledge and skills that no one was born with.

I don't want to discourage anyone who would like to try selling, but very few people succeed at what they have only *tried.* That is why the thousands of failing salespeople, when asked why they do not do those things done by the true masters of selling, say, "I tried that and it won't work for me." You might as well say you are going to "try" marriage. If there is any hope at all for a successful marriage today, it starts with two people who are not only in love, but totally committed to making their marriage succeed.

That is equally true of any career you choose. If you have not committed yourself to that career, you have little or no chance to succeed at it. If you remember in the chapter "Who Can Succeed in Selling?", I said my research and experience convinced me that almost everyone, even those with limited education, could succeed in selling. I can assure you, that if you have read this far, you can, too.

This chapter will help you select the field of selling where you will be happiest and have the best chance to achieve your greatest success.

Every book I have read on selling agrees that salespeople who achieve great success *love* what they sell. Most go further saying that to succeed in selling you *must* love what you sell. My research has shown there are three factors present in every person who achieves real success in the business of selling.

First, the professionals really do love what they sell. Or, at least, they have a strong affinity for what they sell. They feel very strongly that their prospective customers would be far better off owning and enjoying the benefits of what they are selling. It is impossible for anyone to get honestly excited or genuinely enthusiastic about what they sell who does not feel that way.

When you are considering a career in selling, your decision should not be based only on the jobs available in the help wanted ads. It should be based first and foremost on how you feel about what you will be selling.

The second factor we find in all who succeed in the business of selling is that they feel the same way about their companies and their people as they do about what they are selling. Their loyalty is rock solid. As a salesperson you cannot ask people to do business with the people you work for (and with) if you don't like or don't trust them. At least you cannot do that honestly and with genuine enthusiasm. Most of the world's top professionals are still with the company they started with. Many began in the "back end" of the company and worked their way up to selling.

The third element found consistently in those who succeed in the business of selling is that they feel the same way about their customers as they do about the people in their company and about what they sell. Feeling empathetic toward the needs of prospective customers is an absolute must for success in the business of selling. If you don't like the people you sell to, you can't have much empathy with them.

Now, I am not saying you *cannot* succeed if you do not feel positive about what you sell, about the people in your company, and your customers, but the more you like what you sell, who you are selling it for, and who you sell it to, the easier your success will come.

One other consideration: the longer you stay with your company, the more you have to lose if you change jobs. Your satisfied customer base is in that company. Sure, some of them might go with you to a new company, but their bond is with you, the people in your company, and with what you are selling in that company. If you change jobs, you will lose some and maybe all of those satisfied customers. Furthermore, most of your knowledge and information base is in that company, too, in what it sells, and in the services it performs. You lose most of that when you change companies. So, choose the company you want to sell for with care. It can have a great effect on your career.

When I was 21, I became manager of what was then known as a Grand Rapids Guild furniture company. That company sold the finest furniture in the world and I had the easiest, most prestigious position any young man could ever hope for. I *loved* what I was selling. I could not have been associated with more gracious people and for the first time in my life I was working five days a week from nine to five. I had only had one problem: I did not respect nor like the customers, who were for the most part the third and fourth generations of inherited wealth. They had never worked a day in their lives nor ever wanted for anything. If they purchased something it was solely to meet a need and they got no joy or excitement out of it. I was used to selling working people and when a husband told his wife to go ahead and buy a new sofa, I often saw a tear in her eye.

There is an adage, "Sell to the masses and live with the classes. Sell to the classes and live with the masses." That was often the way it was fifty years ago and to some extent it still is. A young man once made this point best for me. I was visiting my Kansas City operation when he came up to me and said, "Mr. Lawhon my uncle is a multimillionaire and he buys a lot of furniture. Are we ever going to carry any good furniture that I could sell him?"

"Son, we carry the finest furniture to be found anywhere in the world within the budgets of our customers. If you want to sell customers like your uncle, you will have to go somewhere else to work."

My point is not meant to denigrate the selling of anything. If it is a quality product with quality services that is going to best meet the customers' needs, which includes being within their budgets, selling is a needed and honorable profession. It drives the economy that supports the other professions. Your chances for success in the business of selling go up in direct proportion to how well you like (1) what you are selling, (2) who you are selling it for, and (3) who you are selling it to.

Your career in selling should be selected as you would any other career, not simply on the basis of what is available in help wanted ads. For instance, if you choose education for your career, you have to carefully decide which field of education. If you choose medicine, you have to carefully select the branch of medicine. So it is with selling. If you decide on a career in selling, you must judiciously select the field of selling where your career will be founded and built.

Once you have selected what you want to sell, who you want to sell it for, and to whom you want to sell it, then you are ready to start your career. If you are already in selling but haven't achieved any real success, you may have a tough decision to make.

If you like what you sell, who you sell it for, and who you sell it to, then the only question you must answer is: Are you willing to make the commitment you must make to learn what you must, develop the productive skills you must have and measure habitually what you are trying to improve? Following that program is going to be much harder for you than for those who have never sold anything in their lives, because they don't have any effective counterproductive habits to overcome while they perfect their productive selling skills. New salespeople are not yet members of the Losers in the Lounge Mutual Admiration Society. Not ever, hopefully.

To you, it may seem that the grass is greener on the other side of the fence. It really isn't. It doesn't matter where you go, you will discover the only person you must deal with is yourself. And you are the only person from whom you cannot escape. That is what is known as the "moment of truth."

If you decide you want to stay where you are and do what you must to learn and to perfect the productive skills you must have, then you have to make some major changes in your habits.

Talk to those family members whose lives will be affected. Explain to them that you are going to be working harder than you have ever worked for the next few months and you need and want their support. Make the same commitment to them you made to yourself. Draw up your own personal action plan, then follow it.

If you decide you would be more successful working for another company or selling a different product, then you must discuss that, too, with those who are important to you and whose lives will be affected. You are going to need their support.

Note: Never change jobs for the sake of change. Remember that old adage about the greener grass and select carefully the company you want to sell for. Apply for a sales position. If there are no openings, explain that you have read this book and chosen their company as the one you wish to be associated with. You are willing—even prefer—to work at any job in their company so you can learn as much as you can about how things get done there, who does them, and who gets them done. Explain that you are going to work harder at that job than anyone else because you want the first selling job that comes available.

This company is your prospective customer. If your objective is to make it a *satisfied* customer, you must make the sale and what you sold (yourself) must so well meet the company's needs that it becomes a *satisfied* customer when you are working for it.

If you did not make the sale the first time, you have probably learned an awful lot about the company and its needs, but obviously not enough. If you have only dealt with the personnel office, try getting an appointment with the sales manager. Explain to him or her why you want to sell for this company and why you are willing to take any job in the company to learn as much as you can until a sales position becomes available.

One of two things should happen: You will continue to learn more and more about the company's needs, which will enable you to show them how you could help them better and better meet those needs. The harder it is for you to get this job, the more you will have learned about the company, what it sells, and its customers—and the better your chances for success.

While trying to learn as much as you can about the company and its needs you may determine it is not the company you wish to work for. But you will have found out a lot more about what kind of company you do want to work for. And that makes a lot more sense to me than sticking a pin in the help wanted ads.

Choosing the right company for your first job is like choosing the right university. Serious students will read and learn everything they can about the universities that have the best programs for the fields they are interested in. Then they visit those universities and learn even more. They will spend weeks on their applications and supporting materials. Should you do less in your efforts to start your career?

BIG FROG, LITTLE POND?

We hear a lot about people who want to be big frogs in a little pond. But, legends are made when a little frog becomes the biggest frog in the biggest pond.

This book is not written for any one person, but to show people who want a career in selling that the most important thing in their lives is their personal goals, and that whatever they may be, if the individual can imagine them or dream them, they can be achieved with a career in the business of selling.

There is nothing wrong with wanting to be a big frog in a big pond. If you are looking for the greatest opportunity in sales or management, then you must look at companies with the biggest *problems.* The bigger the problem, the greater the need for selling competence and the more that competence will stand out, which means that is where the greatest opportunity lies. That may be in the company where you work right now. I must warn you that along with opportunity goes an equal degree of risk. Your desire for success must be so strong you are willing to take that risk or you should consider more stable companies.

Once you are professionally competent, you will discover your management will be willing to adjust your territory or schedule so you can enjoy some of your personal goals. We see this pattern with all great professionals. The starting golfers, tennis players, ballplayers or whatever, must play any time, every time, anywhere they can. As they become more and more competent, they can adjust their schedules to permit them to enjoy their success.

When you get the job working for the company that you want to sell for, and you go out of your way to do more than anyone else in the company while learning more than anyone else is learning, it will not be long before you are selling for that company.

What if you get the selling job to start with? (This applies to all salespeople starting out, whether it is in the company where they have been working for some time or they are just beginning.) The company you go to work for will have rules and policies. You must obey them to the letter. A good way to look at this is to say "Even though I don't agree with the way some things are done, I am going to do them that way and do them so much better than the others so that someone will some day ask me how I think things should be done." Until they do, don't try to tell them how to run the company. Leave it up to the losers in the lounge.

If a company is using this book as a basis for its sales training, that will make things much easier for you. If they are not you must succeed on your own. If the company is using the yardstick, that will make things much easier for you. If they're not, you must use one of your own and honestly account for every prospective customer contact. Do that, measure your improvement, and you'll guarantee your own success. Not using the yardstick guarantees your failure!

No matter where you start your selling career, the company will have some form of sales training. That can range from almost zero to study and learning programs that are ongoing and will take a lot of your time. You must attend those sessions and follow the programs with full attention. At the same time, study and follow the teachings in this book. If the company has no yardstick, develop your own and you will soon surpass your fellow trainees. When you go by them far enough someone up there is going to want to know why. Then you can explain what you are doing.

Do not ever join the losers in the lounge. *Never!* Not for any reason. Not for one minute! Do not listen to their negative conversation or socialize with them during or after work for any reason. Be polite, be pleasant and helpful, but do not waste your valuable time on counterproductive habits.

When you took a job you agreed to work for a certain number of hours every week. Once you are clocked in, those are working hours and every one of them is supposed to be productive. That means you must be engaged in some kind of *productive* activity at all times. In the beginning, learning what you need to know should consume most of the time when you are not with customers. Getting ready to sell and following up will consume more and more of your downtime. As you become more and more competent you become more productive.

Never forget: when you are clocked-in, those are supposed to be *productive* working hours. They can be productive hours that lead to your success or they can be counterproductive hours that guarantee failure. That choice is up to you at least as long as the company keeps you on. Whether you like it or not, you are only permitted one choice: Either you choose to develop productive skills or within 21 days you will have acquired counterproductive habits and your career will be doomed.

If you don't want to work long hours, you must make the hours you do work so much more productive than the others that soon you can set your own schedule.

The most important thing you must do is start with a plan—a personal action plan that determines where you are when you start and where you would personally like to be at the end of each month, after the first year, and after five years. Your only basis for that plan will be what the other salespeople are doing. If they are using the yardstick, too, doing this will be easy; if they aren't, you may have to guess at quotas, but within the first week or two of selling you will know where you are and can adjust your own quotas and goals. Keep your goals realistic. Remember, your ability to achieve your goals is based on customer contacts and what percentage of them you sell.

Whether the company's business is up or down has no effect on whether you do or don't improve. Your plan is based on your own individual improvement.

Your success or failure in any undertaking depends on the same factors you find in selling. Success begins with a commitment to make the extra effort from the start to learn what you need while you perfect the skills you must have. The big difference in choosing a career in selling and all other professions is that opportunities in the business of selling are the greatest—hundreds, maybe thousands, of times greater than in any other profession—because the need for competence is greater. The greater that need, the greater your opportunity. In an industry where most people have never shown any improvement at all, even a little bit stands out like a shooting star. With the instructions in this book and by using your yardstick, your improvement is guaranteed—and yes, you can succeed in selling—but make it easier on yourself by selecting the right things to sell and the right company to sell them for. Remember, you are running your own business when you are in the business of selling.

42 / *People Bond with People*

SUCCESS IN THE BUSINESS OF SELLING IS THE RESULT OF PEOPLE BONDING
WITH PEOPLE. WRITING AN ORDER IS ONLY ONE SMALL PART OF THIS
BONDING PROCESS.

IT IS PREDICTED THAT COMPANIES WHO DO NOT HAVE ONGOING
RELATIONSHIPS THAT BOND THEIR SATISFIED CUSTOMERS TO THE PEOPLE IN
THE COMPANY, AND TO WHAT THEY SELL, WILL BE UNABLE TO SURVIVE PAST
THE YEAR 2000.

PEOPLE DO NOT BOND TO A COMPANY. They are bonded to the people and products of a company. Surveys have long shown that consistently, over 75 percent of the customers who quit doing business with a company do so because of indifference by the people in that company, and most of the time those are salespeople. Products, services, prices, terms, competitors, and all the other reasons for which customers are lost, account for fewer than 25 percent of lost customers.

It is the same old story. Customers are saying, "Do you love me or do you not? You told me once, but I forgot."

When I discuss sales training with industry leaders, I often hear, "Sure, we get salespeople trained so they can go down the street to work for our competitors." In fact, what they are actually saying is, "We would rather have an untrained, incompetent force of salespeople that our competitors would not want working for them."

When managements feel that way, it is because most if not all of their salespeople are guided tour directors, hustling order takers, and losers in the lounge. Those people can ply their "trade" anywhere they go. They are not bonded to the people in the company, to what is being sold by the company, and most important of all, to the customers of the company. To convince yourself of this, just listen to the losers bitching, or interview them by the hundreds as I have.

I am convinced that one of the biggest mistakes management makes is hiring so-called "experienced" salespeople. "Experienced" at what? Salespeople with counterproductive selling skills cause most prospective customers with whom they come in contact not to buy—while the counterproductive activities of the losers in the lounge are cancers in the companies where they work.

When these so-called "experienced" salespeople are asked why they left their last sales job, they are quick to tell you every bad thing—real or imagined—about one of your competitors. The chorus goes on and on about how they tried to help in every way possible, but they could no longer stand the way their customers were treated. If you hire them it won't be 30 days before they are saying the same things about you and your company. The more jobs they've had, the more "experienced" they are—in counterproductive activities.

I often say to people in management, "I have many of the highest-volume, highest-paid top professional salespeople's names and phone numbers. I will give those numbers and names to you. Only, I doubt you could hire one, even if you gave him or her a piece of your company." What we so often forget is that employees, and that includes salespeople, are people, too. They don't bond to a company, they bond to people and to what is being sold by the company.

Professionally competent salespeople are bonded to the people in their companies and to what is sold by their companies. Their only goal is a *satisfied* customer. It is their job to create satisfied customers, but they know it will be the people in the company and what they are selling that keeps the customer satisfied and makes them *more* satisfied. A major share of the master sellers' specialized knowledge and information involves these people, their services, and what is being sold. If professionally competent salespeople change companies, they have an awful lot to lose. Never forget that fear of loss is far greater than the desire for gain. The one thing they fear losing the most is the most valuable asset they own: their satisfied customer base.

True, they created the satisfied customers and are bonded to them, but they had only begun the bonding process. The people in the company had to do to the customers' satisfaction what the customers were told would be done. What was sold had to live up to the customers' expectations and meet their needs. These three things created a *satisfied* customer who was bonded to the company and to the salesperson in the company.

Satisfied customers don't switch companies because the salespeople do. No one can fully comprehend this who does not know what a satisfied customer is and whose only goal is to make and keep *satisfied* customers.

Professionally competent salespeople *do* comprehend these factors. They are aware of what they stand to lose if they switch companies and, believe me, it is rare when a professionally competent salesperson does switch.

There are three exceptions that could cause professionally competent salespeople to change companies: (1) They cannot see themselves achieving their personal goals in the company where they work. (2) There is a change in the company that limits their ability to achieve personal goals. (3) They are entrepreneurs and want to start their own companies or to move into management.

When the salespeople are able to achieve their personal goals in a company, they have no reason to change. If they have been with the company any period of time and have built any customer file at all, they are achieving their career goals—and that will permit them to achieve their personal goals. Unless there is a change in the company that makes it impossible for that salesperson to continue to turn prospective customers into satisfied customers, they will not change companies.

Because professionally competent salespeople are able to achieve their personal goals through their career goals in selling, most do not aspire to management, for much of the same reasons that musicians who have perfected skills with their chosen instruments achieve their career goals playing rather than aspiring to be conductors.

I have found that most top sales professionals actually started working in the operational areas of their companies. They became bonded to the company, its satisfied customers, and its product(s) before they entered the business of selling. They learned first-hand what it took to satisfy a customer and they found they could react with empathy and enthusiasm when confronted with the needs of prospective customers, even though they had no selling experience. Therefore, their skills were developed as *productive* skills.

My recommendation to management searching for new sales

trainees would be to first look inside your own company! Secondly, look among your satisfied customers. You might need a minute to think about that suggestion, but like the young man in the convenience store, your satisfied customers can say, "I know! I know!" because they have had the same problems—and everyone knows no one can outsell a satisfied customer.

When I developed a retail sales education program it started with a three-week program that I called "level one." The trainees worked each day of the first week in an operational area of the company. The second week, they were given daily product learning assignments that required about ten hours each day. The third week consisted of five full days of classroom video-taped teaching sessions with subsequent discussion periods and a three-hour homework assignment each night.

The trainee moved on to "level two" at the end of the third week. At that time, regular sales schedules went into effect and all learning was done in downtime assignments, completed daily before leaving the building. The homework assignments continued.

One man whose company had phenomenal success with this program told me that he felt everyone hired for any job should go through "level one" because it was just as important for them to know what the salespeople were trying to do as it was for the salespeople to know what the operational people did.

He first discovered that the calibre of people he was able to attract and hire for his company was much better.

Then, he found that those who were hired to work in the warehouse, drivers and delivery people, office and service area personnel all were motivated to do a better job. Until then, he told me, all these workers were hired at starting wages. And if career opportunities were seen at all, they were usually restricted to their direct superiors. There had been very little incentive to excel.

These people could now see that if they did an outstanding job, learning all they could whatever their duty, they could get into sales and earn a lot more than they had ever dreamed possible. These people were soon bonded to the people and products in their company as well as the customers of their company. Within months, the top salespeople in this man's company were those who had been hired at starting wages for operational jobs.

Since then, hundreds of other company managments who were made aware of this man's success have begun to put all new-hires through "level one" and have enjoyed similar success.

If the people in a company are not bonded to the goals of the company, then there is no chance for the customer to be bonded to them.

Yes, I agree with current predictions that all companies who do not have ongoing relationships that bond their satisfied customers to the people and the product(s) of their companies will be unable to survive past the year 2000.

43 / *Selling Standards*

WHEN THERE ARE NO STANDARDS, THERE IS NO VISION.
WHERE THERE IS NO VISION, THE PEOPLE PERISH.
WHEN THERE ARE NO SELLING STANDARDS, THE BUSINESS WILL PERISH.

Standard *n.* Any established measure of extent, quantity, or value. Any type, model or example for comparison; a criterion of excellence; Test: A standard of conduct or taste. Synonyms - Example, ideal, rule. *(Funk & Wagnall's Britannica World Language Edition Dictionary)*

WHEN I STARTED TO WORK ON THIS BOOK there were no accepted standards in any field of selling. For two reasons:

Selling as a profession had never been fully defined. *A problem that has not been fully defined cannot be fully resolved.*

There was no standard by which the competence of a salesperson could be measured. *What is not measured cannot be improved.*

Results are the only standard for measuring any endeavor. What was the salesperson's objective or goal when he or she came in contact with a prospective customer? What were the results? Those results are the test and only test of the salesperson's competence.

One of the results of a salesperson's endeavor is easily measured: How many prospective customers did he or she come in contact with, and how many of them did he or she sell?

One result, and by far the most important, is not so easily measured. How *satisfied* the customers were with their purchases? There are only two standards by which this result can be measured: (1) Did the customer return to do more business with that salesperson and the company? (2) Did the customer send others to do business with that salesperson and the company?

It is fairly easy to find out if customers have returned or continued to do business with a company, but in some cases what is purchased will be the only one of its type the buyer will ever purchase or it may be several years between purchases. In those cases, the only real evidence of how satisfied they are with their purchase will be the number of customers they have sent to the salesperson and company to do business. This can be very difficult to determine, too. *Notice:* There are no tests that you can give a salesperson that will determine his or her competence. Only the measurement of the *results* of his or her endeavors will determine that.

If we define a salesperson's goal when he or she comes in contact with a prospective customer as his "destination," then we can determine the route that salesperson must take to reach that destination. If the salesperson has ten stops to make along the way it would be easy for us to measure how effectively he or she reached each of those stops. This measurement would cause the salesperson to improve each leg of the journey. As each leg improved, the salesperson would reach his or her goal more often in less time.

To do that, each stop must be fully defined and instructions must be given for getting from one stop to the next. If the salesperson did not reach a goal it would be easy for us to go back down the road to see which stop had not been reached and why it wasn't.

When a salesperson's goal is a *satisfied* customer and the objectives to reach that goal have been clearly defined then and only then would the salesperson be able to measure how effectively he or she had achieved each objective. As the salesperson improves his or her ability to achieve these objectives more effectively, he or she will reach the goals more often and sooner.

The customer accounting card (or a form of the customer accounting card) used every time the salesperson comes in contact with a prospective customer measures how effective the salesperson has been.

This establishes the standard and is the *only* accurate way to test competence. We could establish tests that would determine whether the salesperson had enough of the specialized knowledge and information, but these tests would have to be written for every product and service in the company. If this were possible it would only be the equivalent of a written test for a driver's license. It proves that the person knows what they need to know. But it is the result of the driving test that determines if they are competent to drive. Even then a person's total driving record is the only true test of competence.

We may never have an accurate way to measure what constitutes a satisfied customer because there are so many variables. But what we do have is a basic measure for selling competence. It is basic, fundamental, and essential and based on how many prospective customers the salesperson came in contact with each month and how many of them he or she sold.

I recommend that the recognition of selling competence in most fields of selling be established on six levels based on the basic measurement.

PHASE ONE

Bronze: Six consecutive months selling over 30 percent of the prospective customers that the salesperson comes in contact with.

Silver: Six consecutive months selling over 40 percent of prospective customer contacts.

Gold: Six consecutive months selling over 50 percent of prospective customer contacts.

PHASE TWO

A Single Diamond: One year selling over 60 percent of their prospective customer contacts.

Two Diamonds: One year selling over 70 percent of their prospective customer contacts.

Three Diamonds: One year selling over 80 percent of the prospective customer contacts.

These standards would be meaningless if there is no governing body to certify the applications and grant the awards. Only the accuracy of the statistics and the integrity of the audit will determine the value of any certification program.

All professions must have recognized standards if they are to have the confidence of patients, clients, or customers. Because the profession of selling has never had these standards, it is not recognized as a profession. So consumer confidence in salespeople as a whole is all but nonexistent. Any recognition of selling competence based on anything other than results will not gain customer confidence, it will damage it even more, if that is possible.

The only thing that builds consumer confidence in any profession is the overall results. To the degree that recipients of the services of any profession are satisfied, to that degree and only to that degree will people gain confidence in those who practice the profession. I believe that most of these percentages will fit most fields of selling. If they are adjusted up or down, it won't matter, as long as the standard used is based on an accurate record of the number of customer contacts each salesperson has.

Notice: To all salespeople who read this book—whether the industry or your company has established selling standards—your success will depend on you having selling standards. Without them, you have no career goals. Without career goals, you cannot achieve your personal goals.

No other profession offers greater opportunity for a person to achieve his personal goals through their career goals than the business of selling.

44 / *The Strangest Sales Story Ever Told*

WHEN WHAT IS BEING SOLD MEETS A CUSTOMER'S NEEDS AS WELL OR BETTER
THAN HE OR SHE WAS LED TO EXPECT, THAT CUSTOMER IS SATISFIED AND
NEVER BEGRUDGES THE PRICE THAT WAS PAID. HE OR SHE IS A SATISFIED
CUSTOMER AND THAT IS THE ONLY LEGITIMATE GOAL OF BUSINESS.

A STUDY IN SELLING

MY RESEARCH into what I call "the strangest sales story ever told" has taught me many of the most important things I've learned about selling. These insights created the breakthroughs that led to the creation of this book. For anyone who wants to gain even greater insight into selling, advertising, merchandising, marketing, display, and design, I believe an ongoing study of this incredible true story will teach him or her more than any book yet written.

Until now, I have talked mostly about selling things to an end user: cars, homes, boats, other products, to the person who will be buying it for his own use.

But when a manufacturer hires a salesperson to sell his products to a dealer who will sell it to the user, it is assumed the dealer is the customer and the one who must be kept satisfied. If what the dealer buys sells quickly, at a good profit, that dealer *will* be satisfied.

Well, not quite. If the *end user* who ultimately buys what the manufacturer makes does not wind up a *satisfied* customer, the dealer will cease to be a satisfied customer, too. You see, the dealer is only a middle man. And that makes it harder for you and everyone concerned to know for sure what a satisfied customer is (and especially those whose job is to see that all the buyers of your products wind up satisfied.)

This story begins with a product that was first offered back in the forties. People who bought new automobiles that cost under $1,000 back then almost always bought custom fitted seat covers at a cost of about $70. The covers came in ugly plaid patterns and were woven of twisted fibers that were hot in the summer and cold in the winter. Their only benefit was they kept new upholstery looking new longer. For this the customers gave up the beauty and comfort of upholstery and paid over seven percent more for their automobiles.

About three years later when they were ready to trade in the car, they removed the old, worn-out seat covers from upholstery that still looked brand new. The next buyer paid about $700 for the used car and the first thing he or she did was install new seat covers at a cost of about $70. Three years later, when the second owner traded it in, he or she took off the old, worn-out seat covers. The third owner paid about $300 for the car and you can bet the first thing that new owner did was have new seat covers installed at a cost of around $70, which was about 25 percent of what he or she had paid for the car. All that money just to keep the upholstery looking new! About three years later, when that car was hauled to the salvage yard with its old, worn-out seat covers, the upholstery still looked brand new.

Here's my point: Customers would put up with discomfort, give up the beauty of their new upholstery, and pay an enormous amount of money to keep from *losing* the beautiful new look of the upholstery in their car. That has to be a classic example of how powerful the fear of losing the *benefits* of something you own. No! No! No! That car was never fully paid for by any of the people who owned it. In the purest sense none of them ever owned the car, because it was financed, they only owned the benefits of the car. They paid all that money and gave up the very benefit they were trying to keep from losing in a car they didn't even own.

There is an awful lot to be learned about selling from this example and I haven't even gotten to the good stuff yet.

This was the most-wanted benefit of any feature that was ever offered on a car because in those days radios and heaters were optional at a cost of about $35 each on a new car. Many a car, even in the north, was bought without a radio or a heater, but it was a rare car that didn't have seat covers that cost as much as the radio and heater combined. Just consider those people in those cars at twenty below zero with no heater and seat covers that made it feel even colder, and you get some idea how great their fear of losing the new look of the upholstery really was.

Now, I want to make a very important point that will come up again later. No one ever bought seat covers *before* they bought the car. They had no need for the benefits of the seat covers until *after* they bought the car. Their need was created and they became fully qualified customers for seat covers when they bought the car, but not one minute before.

In the late fifties, when the price of most cars had risen to almost $1,500, a new set of custom-fitted, clear plastic seat covers was introduced at $150 or more, which was over ten percent of the price of the car. These would actually scald your bottom in the summer and freeze it solid in the winter, but at least you could see your beautiful new upholstery through the clear plastic. That is until the sun hit the plastic and turned it a muddy yellow. When the plastic froze in the winter, it would split wide open. To put this in perspective with today's car prices, the seat covers would cost over $2,000. That's a lot of money to pay just to keep your upholstery looking new longer.

They still make these fitted clear plastic covers for upholstered furniture. It's not uncommon for a customer to pay more for the fitted plastic covers than for the furniture, just to keep it looking new longer.

That brings us to the sixties and the true beginning of our story. A new product was introduced that *eliminated* the need for seat covers. It would keep the fabric looking new longer, repel all oil and water-born stains, and prevent anything from permanently staining the fabric. Liquid would bead up on the surface of the treated fabric and could be easily blotted up with tissue paper. It was developed by DuPont and 3M at about the same time. After it was applied to fabric, you could not see, smell, feel, hear, or taste this product. Unless someone made you aware it was there and demonstrated its miraculous benefits, you would not know it was there. This fabric protection was sold under the trade names of the chemical companies.

Nothing, absolutely no feature has ever been introduced on upholstered furniture that offered more exciting and wanted benefits to prospective customers. My company kept bottles of cola and coffee scattered around the showroom with boxes of tissue handy. When our sales-people spotted a prospective customer looking at a sofa, one of them would rush over and pour coffee or cola right in the middle of a cushion. The women customers would gasp out loud in horror, but the liquid just beaded into a ball. The salesperson tilted the cushion forward letting the liquid roll off on the tissue paper without leaving a trace. I am telling you that to women of that time, this was even more of a miracle and more exciting that seeing the first man walk on the moon. Selling upholstered furniture had never been more exciting or easier.

DuPont and 3M decided the easiest prospective customers to sell would be the fabric mills, and it wasn't long until even the most popular-ly priced upholstered furniture had fabric protection on it that was applied at the fabric mill. Needless to say, with this head-to-head compe-tition, the solution was sold at very competitive prices and added very lit-tle, if anything, to the retail price of the furniture.

Ah! But all good things must come to an end, mustn't they? When everybody had fabric protection on most of their furniture, as far as the salespeople were concerned everybody knew about it and most furniture had a tag on it saying the fabric was protected with Scotchgard or Teflon. It was old hat to the salespeople. All the original excitement was gone and they had one and all quit demonstrating the miraculous benefits. They no longer bothered even to mention that the furniture they were selling included a feature that offered the most-wanted benefit ever found on upholstered furniture.

Once fabric protection became a requirement on upholstery fabric for most upholstered furniture makers, it offered no benefit to the mill, to the furniture makers, or to the retailer, and added no visible profit to the sale for any of them. As a matter of fact, it became a nuisance. The manufacturers made no further issue of the fact that the fabric on their furniture had one of the protective agents on it. Most even quit putting the Scotchgard and Teflon tags on the furniture. As matter of fact, I doubt if there was any sure way for anyone (including DuPont and 3M themselves) to tell which fabric protection product had been used on the fabric when it reached the retailer.

I told you how much the customer was willing to pay to get the benefits of seat covers. That benefit was to keep their new upholstery looking new longer. Not only had they paid dearly to get that protection, but they had to give up the beauty and comfort of the upholstery fabric. Fabric protection gave them this same protection and they got to enjoy the beauty and comfort of the upholstery. Whatever the benefits of seat covers had been worth to customers, the benefits of fabric protection was worth many times more. Only those who have sold upholstered furniture can have any idea how much the customer wants to keep that furniture looking new as long as possible.

When speaking, I often use an example that furniture salespeople can relate to. I have had mothers in my showrooms with children who were permitted to run wild, totally undisciplined. It wasn't unusual for one of these mothers to buy a one-only floor sample sofa on sale. About the time they say they will take it, here comes one of their kids who dives onto the sofa going ninety-plus. I have seen these mothers scream at their children, "You get off of that sofa!" as they slap them and yank them off the furniture so hard you are sure they have disjointed the child's arm, saying, "Get off that sofa! That's *our* sofa. If you want to jump on sofas, you jump on *their* sofas."

Oh yes! They couldn't care less what happens to that sofa as long as it's *your* sofa, but the minute it's *their* sofa, they will say, "Could you cover it up with something and take it off the floor so no one can sit on it?"

When you say to one of these customers, "Would you really like to keep your sofa looking new longer and protect it against anything that might permanently soil or damage it?" they answer in an almost pleading voice, "Oh, could I? Could I?"

Now we come to the heart of the strangest sales story ever told. Around 1980, a young man with no chemical expertise and no capital to speak of remembered how badly customers had wanted the benefits of fabric protection when first introduced and how excited the prospective customers were when they saw it demonstrated. He concluded that they wanted and needed these benefits even more now than they did then. He knew no one had demonstrated the incredible benefits of fabric protection in years and that there probably wasn't a handful of people who had seen these benefits demonstrated. He knew that the people who had upholstered furniture with fabric protection on it couldn't see, smell, feel, hear, or taste it, and because no one had demonstrated its benefits, the customer did not know it was there. They owned the feature, but had never enjoyed the benefits.

This young man had a chemical company mix his own fabric protection solution that could be sprayed on the customer's furniture by the retail dealer. He developed a small 18" x 30" demonstration stand and got a retailer to let him set it up in his store. Salespeople who made upholstered furniture sales brought their customers to this young man.

He asked the customer a simple question like this. "How would you like to keep your beautiful new furniture looking new longer and protect it against any soil or stains that might permanently damage it?'

You can almost hear that mother with those undisciplined children saying in her pleading voice, "Oh, could I? Could I?"

He would give a short demonstration and write the order almost every time. The price was $70 for a sofa and similar prices for all other pieces. That was about 90 percent gross profit to the retailer. The salespeople who sold it were paid 20 percent commission on fabric protection instead of the regular five or six percent they were paid on the furniture sale.

When this program was installed in a retail store, the salespeople were far more excited than when fabric protection was first introduced. They, too, had never seen its miraculous benefits demonstrated. They quickly discovered they could take an upholstered furniture buyer to the demonstration center and in a minute or two they would sell a feature that paid them almost as much as they had made on the furniture sale. It had to be one of the easiest sales anyone ever made.

It quickly became the biggest selling, most profitable item in the company. Many large companies, small ones too, were making more net profit from fabric protection sales than they were on all of their furniture sales combined.

As word spread of the profits to be made, other companies were formed to market fabric protection programs. At that point, DuPont and 3M acted. They went to the mills and got them to refuse to warranty any fabric that had any chemical applied to it after it left the mill. They told manufacturers the same thing. I found this humorous because they were both selling their fabric protection themselves in spray cans for customers who wished to apply fabric protection to anything, including furniture and almost none of the fabric was warranted anyway. Needless to say, they didn't make any friends with the retailers who were realizing huge profits from their own programs. Hard to believe, but they were trying to block retailers from doing for their customers what their program had failed to do. That alone makes it a pretty strange sales story. The two giant chemical companies hadn't created any satisfied customers, but they would be darned if they would let someone else do so.

Ah, yes, but all good things must come to an end, mustn't they? As soon as competing retail companies had fabric protection programs, they started cutting prices and commissions. The cost of fabric protection on a sofa went from $70 to $60, $50, $40, $30, and commissions were cut to five and six percent until—miracle of miracles—it was *free!* Ads were run saying, "Buy your upholstered furniture from us and the fabric protection is free!"

Here was the first lesson to be learned from this study in selling. These ads proclaiming "free" did not produce prospective customers. You remember when I said people did not buy seat covers for a car until after they had bought the car because they had no need until then? People who have no *need* for the benefits of anything *will not buy.* The customer with no need for fabric protection was not interested in fabric protection even when it was free.

It was about this time I started my research and writing. Many of my lessons were learned as I studied this unusual selling situation and they led to many of my breakthroughs. One of these breakthroughs let me prove to every salesperson selling fabric protection that what gets measured, improves, and that is the most important thing anyone in selling can ever learn.

During the first two years of my research, I visited hundreds of retail furniture stores. By then, many if not most had a fabric protection program. The average price charged for a treated sofa had dropped below $40 and most had cut fabric protection commissions back to regular furniture levels. Salespeople who had been making $36 commissions when they sold fabric protection on a sofa, love seat, and chair now weren't making $5, which hardly made it worth the effort.

Every time I visited a store, I made it a practice to ask the salespeople and management about fabric protection. I still do. When I saw a fabric protection demonstration center I would say to a salesperson, "I see you carry fabric protection. What do you do, sell the customer upholstered furniture, then take them to the demonstration center to demonstrate and sell fabric protection?" Everywhere I went I got the same answer: "Oh, you don't have to do that. All you need to do is tell them about it and they will buy it."

"Why's that?"

"Everybody has it. Everybody knows about it."

Here are some more practices I found going on at that time. Every time I turned around someone had started a new fabric protection company offering the dealer a lower price for their chemical solution with fewer services and warranties. There was no assurance that the solutions even had enough protective chemicals in them to make them effective. Many retail companies with good effective fabric protection programs dropped them, bought cheaper bulk solutions and formed their own programs in an effort to squeeze out a few more dollars in profit.

By then, the attitude of most salespeople toward fabric protection could be summed up by three experiences I had on the West Coast. At a San Francisco furniture market, I ran into the owner of a chain of stores. I asked him what he charged for his fabric protection on a sofa and how it was going.

He said, "John, we got to where we were selling about 30 percent of the upholstered furniture buyers, but it's fallen off to where it's not even worth carrying. We even cut the price from $50 to $25, and when we did, we seemed to sell even less."

The next day, I was in one of his stores and I asked a salesperson how his fabric protection sales were going. He said, "Buddy, I put that gook on everything."

"You mean that no matter what I buy, you will put fabric protection on it?"

"Buddy, I just told you, I will put that gook on everything."

I pointed to some vinyl furniture and asked about it. He said, "I'll put that gook on that, too, if they want it."

What earlier had been the most exciting thing these salespeople had ever demonstrated had become "gook." Truth was, though, that salesperson put fabric protection on almost nothing because no customer wants "gook" on his new furniture.

Down the freeway a couple of miles, I stopped at one of the world's largest furniture retailer's showrooms. As I was leaving I asked a salesman how his fabric protection was selling.

He said, "Great, but it's a rip off."

"If it's a rip off, why do you sell it?"

"Because I want to keep my job."

How much confidence do you think this man could have in the integrity of what he was doing and in the management of his company?

To sum up my findings, by that time most salespeople felt fabric protection was a rip off. One reason for their opinion was that most furniture already had fabric protection applied at the mill and the salespeople just couldn't bring themselves to sell it again. By then, they knew that the cost of the solution to the company to treat a sofa was only a few dollars. Retailers were looking for the cheapest thing on the market and setting their prices based on what the competition was charging.

I found more companies had dropped fabric protection altogether or let their programs fall into disarray than those who were still trying to sell it. You might ask why I had continued my interest in this product, which cannot be seen, smelled, felt, tasted, or heard.

When customers have bought upholstered furniture, they have become fully qualified prospective customers for fabric protection, and we have an accurate record of that, which means we have a way to measure exactly how effective the salespeople were when they came in contact with a prospective customer for fabric protection. If what gets measured, improves, this product gives us a guaranteed way to prove that point.

During all this time, I was asking the managers and owners of these companies if they had any idea what percentage of their prospective customers for fabric protection were being sold. Most had no idea. Those who did only knew what percentage was sold overall, and none had been able to tell me exactly what percentage of their fabric protection prospects each individual salesperson was selling.

Even though they all had an accurate yardstick by which to measure how effective each salesperson was when it came to selling fabric protection, I did not find anyone using that yardstick. In every case, the percentage of fabric protection customers being sold was going down, down, down throughout the entire industry, and it was becoming less and less of a profit factor, so it was less and less important as far as management was concerned.

Let me ask you a question. Do you think that at any time since its first introduction that the customer's need for the benefits of fabric protection has gone down or diminished? Heavens no! But who cares about the customer, anyway? Certainly not those who don't even know what a customer is!

In 1986, I was speaking at a large company in Grand Rapids, Michigan. While there, I asked the president of the company how his fabric protection sales were going.

He got really excited. "John, we are selling fabric protection to over 70 percent of the people who buy upholstered furniture from us." He pulled out his computer printout to prove it.

Until then, I had found very few managers who knew what their sales force batting averages were. Of those who did, I had found none who sold more than 50 percent of their prospective customers. We went over the batting average of each salesperson on that long list. One was currently selling 68.1 percent, one was selling over 90 percent, the rest were in between.

He was the first person I had found using the yardstick to measure how effective each salesperson had been when he or she came in contact with a fully qualified prospective customer for fabric protection. That measurement had caused his salespeople to become the world's most effective and productive fabric protection salespeople. More effective than I had found in the hundreds of companies I visited. Unbelievably, that manager did not know it was his measurement that caused the improvement.

This was the first example I found that proved what gets measured, improves. Without doubt, this was the most important breakthrough of my research. But wait! I asked what they charged to put fabric protection on a sofa.

He said, "$75 for a sofa, $65 for a love seat, $55 for a chair if the sofa sells for under $1,000. $100 for a sofa, $90 for a love seat, $80 for a chair if the sofa sells for over $1,000." Those were the highest prices I had found being charged anywhere in the U.S., Canada, and the British Isles at the time. Most companies weren't charging half that. I asked what commission he was paying and he said, "Six percent for the furniture sale and 20 percent on fabric protection." He had some salespeople earning a thousand dollars and more a month just on their fabric protection sales.

There was one other factor that got my attention. The chemical company whose fabric protection program he carried was headquartered in Grand Rapids and it was the program being carried by most of the retailers in that city. I contacted twelve of them to see how they were doing with fabric protection. None charged over $50 on a sofa. Most were charging $35 or less. Most did not know what percentage of the customers were sold. Those few who did sold less than 40 percent and none knew the individual batting averages of their salespeople.

Here was a company charging two to three times what its competitors were charging for the same product and it was selling circles around every one of them. If you're finding this story hard to believe, read on.

Everywhere I went, I told company owners and managers this story. I told the story every time I made a speech. My objective was simple: The story proved conclusively that what gets measured, improves. Here was a company with a lot of salespeople, most of whom were not competent enough to sell ten percent of the prospective furniture customers they came in contact with. But when they did sell upholstered furniture they had become the most competent fabric protection salespeople to be found anywhere in the world. I say that because it is the only case of anyone selling anything at two and even three times the price that everyone else in their market was charging and who sold almost every prospective customer with whom they came in contact.

A few months later, I was speaking to a convention of over four hundred furniture store owners and managers. I was going to tell them this story, but before I did, I asked those who had a fabric protection program to hold up their hands. Almost all did. I then asked those who charged $30 or less to put protection on a sofa to raise their hands. Only one put up his hand. I said, "Sir, you are the only one here charging less than $30. Do you mind telling us what you charge?" He said, "$25, but we wind up giving it away most of the time. It's really more trouble than it's worth in my company."

I asked how many were charging $40 or less, and most of the hands went up. I asked $50 or less, and the rest went up. When I asked if anyone charged over $50, two hands went up: one in the far rear to the left and the other in the far rear right.

I asked the one on the left what she charged and she said, "$75."

"Ma'am, that sure blows the story I am about to tell." I turned to the person on the right asked what she charged.

She said, "$75."

"That's incredible," I said.

Then I asked only those who knew for sure what percentage of the customer who bought upholstered furniture were sold fabric protection to raise their hands. Less than half went up. I asked those selling less than 30 percent, about half the hands went up. I asked those selling less than 40 percent, and most of the rest went up. Under 50 percent, only a couple of hands were raised. I asked if anyone was selling over 50 percent, and two hands went up. You guessed it. They were the same two charging $75. I turned to the one at the rear left and asked what percentage of the customers they were selling.

She said, "Mr. Lawhon, we sell over 90 percent."

"Incredible. Here you are charging over double what most of those here charge, selling three or four times the percentage of customers. Do you mind telling us the name of your store?" She told me and I said, "Why, I have been to your company."

"I know," she said. "That's why we charge $75 and sell over 90 percent of the customers." I turned to the other lady and asked what percentage her company was selling.

She said, "Mr. Lawhon, we sell over 95 percent of the people who buy upholstered furniture from us fabric protection and we have gone for days at a time selling 100 percent."

"That's even more incredible," I said, "Do you mind telling us the name of your company?" She told us and I said, "I have been to your company, also."

She said, "I know, that's why we charge $75 and sell over 95 percent of our customers and sometimes go for days selling 100 percent."

I never marketed fabric protection nor endorsed or received commissions from anyone who did. What I did do over a three-year period was develop a fabric protection selling plan. There was a plan for management that told them what to charge and why, what commission to pay and why, and how to use the yardstick to cause improvement in the competence of their salespeople.

There was a set of audio tapes for the salespeople that taught them how to sell fabric protection. Remember, most of these salespeople could not sell fifteen percent of the prospective customers they came in contact with. The purpose of my plan was to have them selling over 80 percent of the customers who they did succeed in selling upholstered furniture fabric protection within thirty days and having them go for a week or longer without missing a single fabric protection sale within thirteen weeks.

That would make everyone who did that, even the weakest of salespeople in the industry, the greatest salespeople in the world when it came to selling fabric protection. After all, when you are selling 100 percent of your prospective customers a product at two or three times what your competitors charge, you can't get much better than that, can you?

To follow my plan, they had to use a reputable fabric protection program, they had to charge $75 for sofas costing under $1,000, $65 on love seats, $55 on a chair, and similar prices on everything else. They were to charge $100 on sofas costing over $1,000, $200 on sofas costing over $2,000, and $300 on everything that cost over $3,000, with similar prices on everything else. The salespeople were paid a 20 percent commission. There were awards and recognition based on the individual improvement of each salesperson's batting average, including framed certificates, for most improved, 100 percenters, and so on. I guaranteed any company following the plan that if it didn't work, all they had to do was call my 800 number toll-free and we would send them a full refund and they didn't even have to return the program materials.

Hundreds of companies have followed this simple plan. To date, I know of no company that has installed it whose salespeople weren't selling over 80 percent of the people who bought upholstered furniture fabric protection at premium prices in a short period of time.

At this point, I would like to show you how what I call the strangest sales story ever told taught two of the most valuable lessons to be learned about selling, lessons that very few in selling or management ever learn.

• What gets measured, improves.

• Nobody, absolutely nobody, wants the cheapest of anything. Even those whose budget forces them to buy the cheapest don't *want* the cheapest. We all want the very best that money can buy within our budget.

When I discuss this program and the prices for the first time with owners and managers of companies (now, numbering hundreds) they give me the same two arguments every single time: (1) "John, I can't get my salespeople to sell this stuff at $35, how in the world do you think I am going to get them to sell it for $75 or even more?" (2) "John, there isn't anyone in this city charging over $35 for that stuff. There is no way anyone is going to pay us $75 for it."

I have a stock answer. "I do not believe it matters one bit what you think about fabric protection, or what your competitors do. I think the only thing you should consider is your customers and their satisfaction. What they need and what they want. You have a good program right now. Keep it and keep the price at $35. Put in a second program following my guidelines at $75 on a sofa and pay 20 percent commission. Have your salespeople give customers their choice and I guarantee you the customers do not want the cheapest protection they can get for their new sofa even when it's the lowest-price sofas you have."

I have had many a company take me up on this and they have all discovered that when given a choice, the customer took the best protection money could buy. They had sold their last $35 fabric protection.

I want to repeat what happened when I asked long-term average salespeople in a company if they thought they would make any more sales if I lowered every price, even sale prices five percent, then ten percent, and finally 25 percent. Without exception, they said, of course they would make more sales if their prices were lowered five percent. They thought the second question was really dumb. "If we will make more sales when you lower our prices five percent, we are surely going to make more sales if you lower them ten percent." At 25 percent they said, "Why, if you lower the prices in this company 25 percent, you will have to call out the police to control the mob. They will tear the walls down to get in here."

In the same companies when I would ask one of the world's highest-volume, highest-paid top professional salespeople these three questions, their answers were, "No," at five percent, "No," at ten percent, "No," at 25 percent, and their answers came with no hesitation at all.

One man summed up best how the masters of selling felt when he said, "Mr. Lawhon, if you lowered the prices in this company 25 percent, I would probably quit. I work all the hours I want to work. I have customers coming in by appointment that keep me busy all my working hours. I sell every customer I can sell. If you cut our prices 25 percent, you might as well cut my pay 25 percent, but that's not why I think I might quit. *I believe that if you lowered the prices in this company 25 percent, most of the people who come to us for their furniture would think we had started carrying cheaper merchandise and stop coming.* That's why I would probably quit."

You can't turn anywhere in the market place without hearing, "Ours is just as good as theirs, but it costs less." You might as well say, "My $100 bills are just as good as anyone else's. I just sell them for less." It is the same thing.

Let me give you two examples and then you tell me which you are going to buy. Better department stores all carry a top-end line of men's better-quality, brand-name dress shirts. And most of them also carry their own private-label dress shirts. The connotation is that they are just as good as the brand-name shirts, but they cost about one-third less.

Suppose you were looking at brand-name shirts priced at $65 in a fine department store. When a salesperson approached saying, "Good afternoon, I see you looking at our brand-name dress shirts. Many people consider these the finest ready-made dress shirts you can buy. As you can see, we have an excellent selection and our price is the same as you will find in other fine stores. If you buy your shirts from us, we alter them to give you a better fit at no extra cost.

"If you are considering this brand of shirt, would you mind my telling you why I think you may want to consider our own private-label shirt? We use only bone or mother-of-pearl buttons. I don't know that they are better, but I do know they look better than plastic buttons and they do cost more. The most important thing about our buttons is that every hole has been reamed and buffed so there are no rough edges to cut the thread. The brand-name shirt uses a fine cotton lisle thread and there are seven stitches through all four button holes.

"We use a fine linen thread that has been waxed. It is so strong, it will cut your fingers before you can break it and we make eleven stitches through each hole. Our buttons will still be on this shirt when it's worn out. They use eleven stitches on each side of the button holes and that's more than you will find on most shirts. We use seventeen and you will never see one of our button holes lose its shape. If you look closely, you will see that there are eleven stitches to the inch of their fine needle work and detail. You will see that we use seventeen stitches to the inch.

"There is one other thing I wish to point out, and that's our fabrics.

They use 144 thread-counts in their cotton fabrics, ours has 210 thread-counts. Feel the difference for yourself. The longer you have one of our shirts, the finer the fabric will feel. Yes sir, their shirt is $65 and our shirt is $65. Which do you think you would prefer?"

You tell me. Of course it would not do a company any good at all to have their own label on a better shirt if there was no one there to show, demonstrate, and tell about the differences.

I bet you are thinking right now that there is no way you are going to get a salesperson to go to all that trouble to sell one shirt. You are right, but a professional shirt salesperson who is in the business of selling, whose only objective is a *satisfied* customer—one who will buy all of his shirts from him from then on—will go to even *greater* lengths than that to turn a prospective looker into a *satisfied* customer, even if it only means the sale of a single shirt the first time. He knows the shirt he sells that customer is going to meet his needs so well he will be able to keep him as a customer for life and get that man to send him others who will be his customers for life. He is starting a sale that could easily run up over $100,000.

There is more to be learned about merchandising and selling in these examples and in the strangest sales story ever told than is taught in most books.

It is getting harder and harder to find quality products today. And it isn't because customers don't want and prefer quality products over cheaper ones. But as long as there are no professionally competent sales-people in the business of selling who make customers consciously aware of their needs and then to show them how the quality product is going to far, far better meet those needs in the long run, making it cost a fraction of what the cheaper products cost, then most customers will buy based mainly on price. That's why discount stores with the lowest prices on the cheapest goods get more and more business.

The most dramatic experience I observed with my fabric protection sales plan occurred when it was implemented in the largest company in Canada, selling furniture, appliances, and electronics. At the time, this company was doing over 500 million dollars a year in sales. The company charged $49 to put fabric protection on a sofa and said their salespeople were selling 60 percent of the customers who bought upholstered furniture.

When an outside firm was retained to get an accurate count of what percentage of the customers were being sold furniture, management absolutely could not believe that it was about ten percent. The company installed my fabric protection sales program and raised the price to $79.95 on a sofa. Within days, the batting average companywide had gone above 80 percent on fabric protection.

About two months after it was installed, one of the owners called me to say that after the last full month's fabric protection sales had been tallied, the accounting office said it had added almost one million dollars net profit to the bottom line. They expected this program to add over eleven million dollars to the bottom line the first year.

A few months later, they installed a new president and I flew in for a meeting. I started off telling this same story I just told you. When I had completed it, the vice president of sales said, "Mr. Lawhon, that's not true."

Needless to say, I came close to heart failure before he hurried on to explain that previously, their management had the authority to give the customer fabric protection free if that's what it took to make the furniture sale. The 60 percent batting average was based on orders with fabric protection on them whether it had been paid for or not. The company had not been selling and collecting for fabric protection on 30 percent of upholstered furniture sales. The rest had been given away. When this program was installed and the accurate yardstick was used, the salespeople went from selling fewer than 30 percent of the upholstered furniture customers fabric protection to almost 100 percent at almost double the price in less than 60 days.

Two points: Management already knew what percentage of the upholstered furniture buyers were being sold fabric protection. Why didn't this measurement cause the salespeople to improve?

Salespeople cannot be improved collectively. They can only be improved individually. As they improve individually, the group as a whole improves. This company used the yardstick to measure the salespeople collectively. My plan required that it be used to measure how effective they were individually. *It recognized and rewarded that individual improvement.* This measurement caused the improvement.

What an important lesson we can learn from this study in selling if we only gain that one truth.

I introduced another element that almost guaranteed the salesperson a fabric protection sale every time. The company was to have a small square printed in red on the face of the order form that read, "Customer declines fabric protection" with a place for their signature. It was a rare person who would sign that square and *lose* the right to the benefits of fabric protection. I did not originate that idea. It has been used in many businesses for years.

This reverse strategy of making customers sign something in order to lose a benefit magnifies the customers' fear of loss. They sign away and lose their right to buy. They own that right. When they sign it away, they have lost that right.

Caution: Selling fabric protection is unique in that the need is not created until the furniture has been purchased. This type of product is called an after-market sale. It is the same as extended warranties, credit life insurance, and underseal for automobiles.

I had not seen such a dramatic improvement in sales competence take place in any other area of selling. The reason the improvement was so dramatic in this case was that once customers bought the furniture, that act alone created a new need. All I had to do was teach the salespeople a few questions to ask customers that would make them consciously aware of that need. Literally, that put salespeople in the same position the professionally competent salesperson is in when he or she has achieved the first four objectives.

I was visiting the owners of a 22-store chain that sold furniture, appliances, electronics, and carried their own credit accounts. They sold three after-market products.

- Fabric protection.
- Credit life insurance that would pay off the balance of the account upon the death of the customer.
- Extended warranties on appliances and electronics.

I asked how their extended warranties were going. They got so excited I had to slow them down. They told me their salespeople were selling over 80 percent of their prospective customers for extended warranties.

I said, "That truly is astounding. It's over double the national average. How do you do that?"

They proceeded to tell me how all incentives, contests, and awards were based on individual batting averages and improvement.

I asked, "How is your credit life selling?" They were even more anxious to tell me that they sold life insurance to literally 100 percent of their credit customers. When I asked how they did this they told of a program based on the individual batting averages of the salespeople.

When I asked about fabric protection, they looked stunned. They looked at each other and said, "I guess we really don't know about that, do we?"

I said, "I can't believe it. You have a yardstick that measures how effective each one of your salespeople has been when they get a prospective customer for extended warranties and credit life, and get incredible results but you aren't using it to measure fabric protection sales? I will tell you what. Why don't you call your office right now. Tell your people to call their managers and ask them to pull last month's sales tickets and tally how many people bought upholstered furniture in their store and how many of them bought fabric protection."

One store had sold about 30 percent, two had sold none, the rest averaged about eleven percent. They doubled the price, put the same incentive and recognition awards on individual batting averages for fabric protection sales, and within 60 days the company was selling fabric protection to over 80 percent of all upholstered furniture buyers.

My first objective when I developed the fabric protection program was to prove conclusively to anyone, including management and salespeople, that what gets measured, improves. The program has proven this beyond any doubt.

I wanted to prove that no salesperson was born with the knowledge or skills to do this. This was proved when salespeople unable to sell even fifteen percent of the people who came to their company needing upholstered furniture, and couldn't even give fabric protection away let alone sell it, within weeks were selling it at double and triple the price of competitors to over 80 percent of the prospects.

What I wanted to prove more than anything else was that no fabric protection sales program would have been needed, nor would it have worked, if this incredible feature had been used to sell more upholstered furniture, instead of using the upholstered furniture to sell fabric protection. *Think about that!* Think about it again!

This can all be traced to the fact that no one knew what a customer was, and in this case, no one was doing for the customer what needed doing.

Every benefit of every feature of what you sell is just exactly like fabric protection in the sense that you must assume all prospective customers you come in contact with are not consciously aware of their need for the benefits of any of those features. Even on those occasions when customers are aware, they don't have a comprehensive understanding of their needs for those benefits. The more the salesperson makes the customer aware of those needs for each benefit of the feature, the more the customer is willing to pay to get that benefit. As you saw in the case of fabric protection, customers could be made so consciously aware of their needs for the benefits of one feature, benefits the order takers couldn't give away could be turned into benefits worth more than the product being sold. To some extent you can do this with the benefits of every feature on what you sell. When you have learned to do that, you will have mastered the business of selling. Re-read how this is done in "The Presentation and Demonstration" chapters.

You now have the yardstick to measure everything you must learn to do. It guaranteed that salespeople would master the selling of fabric protection, and if you use it for measuring the selling of everything, it will guarantee that you can master the business of selling.

You have no place to hide. The decision to succeed or fail is in your hands. It is *your* business, the greatest business in the world because its only goal is a *satisfied* customer. You can succeed in the business of selling when you run it like a business. You can only succeed in business when you realize that the *only* business is the business of selling.

U S E   T H E   P R O D U C T   T O   S E L L   T H E   F E A T U R E

Use the product to sell the feature? What a waste!

For many, what you are about to read could be the most important study you will ever encounter in selling.

The need for the benefits of fabric protection was created when the customer bought upholstered furniture. They had no need for the benefits until they owned the furniture. That is true of most of the benefits of most of the features of whatever it is you sell.

When salespeople understand that one factor, for the first time they can comprehend the difference between what professionally competent salespeople do that causes almost every prospective customer they come in contact with to *buy* and what the guided tour directors do that causes most of their prospective customers *not* to buy.

When prospective customers look at a new sofa, they are not consciously aware of the fact that they are going to want to keep it looking new as long as possible and to protect it against stains or soil that might permanently damage the fabric.

When the fabric on a sofa has already been treated with fabric protection, professionally competent salespeople would have asked their customers questions during qualifying that would have made them consciously aware of the needs they would have once they owned a sofa. During the presentation, the professionals would have dramatically demonstrated how the miraculous benefits of the fabric protection met these needs. It is the most-wanted benefit of any feature ever found on upholstered furniture. And it was a benefit that every customer once they owned the furniture was willing to pay a whole lot more money to get once they owned the furniture .

When demonstrated by professionally competent salespeople, these benefits all by themselves could have made the furniture worth the asking price. They could have added so much value to the furniture being offered that the benefits would have caused most prospective upholstered furniture customers to buy.

We discovered it did no good at all as far as helping make the sale to have fabric protection on the furniture when the salespeople did not make prospective customers aware of their needs for the benefits of this feature, because it could not be seen.

That is just as true for every benefit of every feature on what you sell that prospective customers cannot see or do not see, because they are not consciously aware of their needs for those benefits once they own them

Go back over a salesperson's first four objectives once more. You see that those objectives must be achieved before you make any effort to show or sell customers anything. When they arrive at what you intend to sell them, they are consciously aware of their needs and you have established the comparisons that make the best choice obvious for them.

Now, as they are reminded of a need they told you they had and you have demonstrated the benefits of the feature that meets that need, each benefit makes what you are selling worth that much more. As it becomes worth more and more to the prospective customer, the value becomes overpowering. Each of the benefits of fabric protection on a sofa when demonstrated can make the sofa worth more to the prospective customer than the asking price. To a greater or lesser degree the benefits of every feature will do that same thing for competent professional salespeople.

You can see this proved graphically with fabric protection because it can be added on and charged for after the sale is made. The tragedy is that most salespeople only get to do that with fabric protection less than fifteen percent of the time because they sell fewer than fifteen percent of their prospective customers. But it could be the cause of them making an upholstered sale almost 100 percent of the time!

Incredibly, when salespeople tried to sell fabric protection for less, even to give it away to customers after they bought their furniture, the customers would not take it. They did not want cheap fabric protection on a fine sofa.

If you can see fabric protection as a feature and what it will do for customers that they need and want done, then substitute each of the features and its benefits of what you sell for fabric protection. Each feature and its benefits can to a greater or lesser degree accomplish the same goal for you.

If the benefits of one feature can make a sofa worth as much as the asking price, how much do you suppose *all* of the benefits of the *dozens* of features found on every sofa could make it worth? I think I am safe in saying many, many times its asking price. Now can you see why it takes the professional little or no demonstration to get the order without resorting to tricky or high-pressure tactics?

Look at every feature of what you sell and its benefits as though that feature were fabric protection and the customers could not see, hear, feel, smell, or taste. Because they can't if they are not aware of their need for those benefits once they own what you sell.

If you are the manufacturer who supplies parts that become features on a product that someone else manufactures, as in the case of DuPont and 3M, and if you want the benefits of that feature to help sell more of those products and cause customers to be even more satisfied with their purchase because of it, then you must develop a marketing plan that will cause what you sell to help sell the product it is part of. Because DuPont and 3M did not do that, fabric protection never became a feature that caused more furniture to be sold. The little bit of furniture that got sold was used to sell fabric protection and that is a shame. Shame on those chemical companies. Shame on the mills. Shame on the upholstered furniture manufacturer and shame on the retailers.

I don't care what you sell or who you sell it to, it will fit in that chain of business somewhere. If it does for end user customers what it is supposed to do, they are going to have to be made consciously aware of their needs for the benefits of the features, and they are going to have to have those benefits demonstrated to them. In almost all cases of big-ticket products, that can only be done by professionally competent salespeople. The reason is simple. No two products, customers, salespeople, or selling situations ever have or ever will be the same. It will take people whose only goal is to turn every prospective customer for what they sell into a *satisfied* customer. In order to do that, they will need the specialized knowledge and productive skills to achieve the same ten objectives every time. That defines a professionally competent salesperson. No selling experience ever made that more apparent than fabric protection.

You can see how this happens when the failure to use fabric protection as the most powerful reason ever found to sell more upholstered furniture caused less and less furniture to get sold. When the benefits of the feature were sold with professional competence, the sale was made almost 100 percent of the time. Until you understand why, you won't comprehend why most salespeople sell very few of the prospective customers with whom they come in contact while those few who are professionally competent will sell almost every prospective customer contact. If this, the strangest sales story ever told, teaches you only this one thing, it would be worth any study in selling a thousand times over during your selling career. The lesson it teaches about how what gets measured, improves, is worth all the study effort you put into it a *million* times over.

A Study in Management

Whose job is it to measure the effective competence of the salespeople? In my fabric protection sales plan, I told the salespeople over and over that my only objective for developing the plan was to prove to them that what gets measured, improves. That's why, when they saw the results and improvement that took place when they tallied their batting averages on fabric protection, it made them realize that if they accurately recorded every prospective customer contact and tallied those results, they would improve their batting averages overall.

I went on to point out that many of them would quickly find themselves making $400 to $800 more a month just on fabric protection sales, but once they were selling fabric protection to most of the customers who bought upholstered furniture, that would be all the added income they would earn from fabric protection sales unless they could find a way to sell more prospective customers for upholstered furniture than they were selling. I pointed out that most salespeople weren't selling fifteen percent of the upholstered furniture prospective customers they were waiting on, which meant 85 percent were leaving without buying. If they could sell only fifteen out of that 85 and sell those who bought upholstered furniture fabric protection, that would double their income and put most of them in the top ten percent income bracket in the U.S.

This is the lesson I learned: Left on their own, most salespeople would not tally their batting averages for fabric protection. If management didn't get it done, praise them, and recognize their improvement, no improvement took place. Of course, some did it on their own, but not one percent, maybe not 1/10th of one percent did so. But when management tallied the individual results of all of them, that measurement resulted in everyone improving.

I can tell managements right now that they must see that accurate measurements are kept and tallied or no accurate measurement will be used by most salespeople and no improvement in their salespeople's competence will happen. It never has and it never will.

In the case of fabric protection, management did not have to do one single thing to get an accurate measurement on how effective their salespeople were. A computer printout could be laid on their desks every morning showing the standing of each individual salesperson. As those salespeople improved, management took full credit for the results. They were often so excited about how much their salespeople had improved that they would call me. But more often they called a trade publication to tell them what success they were having.

I tell you this for only one reason: Over and over I said my purpose in developing this plan was *not* to sell fabric protection. It was to prove that what gets measured, improves. Once there was an absolutely accurate measurement available of each salesperson's batting averages, that measurement would prove conclusively that one and all would improve beyond their wildest dreams. I can submit hundreds, no thousands of case histories where that improvement took place, but the measurement was done for management.

When it came to managements, very few would do what they had to in order to assure themselves of an accurate yardstick by which to measure the effective competence of their salespeople with each and every customer contact. To the degree that they did, though, they saw consistent and ongoing measured improvement in the sales competence of their salespeople, and the turnover in their sales staffs dropped dramatically.

Why wouldn't the salespeople use this yardstick once they understood its objective? Fear. They were afraid of seeing and acknowledging failure. The old timers would fight the yardstick as if their lives were at stake. In one company, they issued an ultimatum to management. Either the yardstick went or they joined the union and the union would get it thrown out. That's the equivalent of saying to management that it can't take inventory or count the money. Management knuckled under in that case. Why?

Because management had the same fear the salespeople had. When there was no yardstick they had no customers, so their lack of sales could be blamed on customers who weren't customers at all. They were "lookers, tire kickers, mooches, and fronts, without a buyer in the bunch." It was the fault of the product, the company's buyer, advertising people, credit department, that they did not make sales. The yardstick put the lie to that, but only if it was used accurately. Only management could assure its accurate use, and management starts at the very top. In big corporations, until the board of directors directs the president and other officers to maintain as accurate an accounting of the salespeople's batting averages by use of the yardstick, no accurate yardstick is likely to be used in one of those companies.

The reason: Management's fear of the results of this accounting is far greater than their desire to gain the benefits they would derive from its use. The fabric protection accounting plan had to start with the top person in the company. When it did, it succeeded every time. No matter how successful it was, if any let up was permitted, the effectiveness started to slip at once. It had the same effect as if management were to say, "From now on, we are not going to take inventory or count the money as it comes in." It is the same principle. As simple as it sounds and as simple as it is, change is the hardest thing in this world to get people to make.

Using the yardstick is not an experiment. It is not something you think you might try. You either do it and do it every time from now on or you don't. Do it and that accurate measurement will cause improvement from then on. It must be company policy for those in the business of selling and it must become the only way you do business if the yardstick is to be effective.

Having installed a customer accounting system along with a sales education system in several hundred companies, I can assure you that the only resistance we ever encountered came from middle management and from the sales staff, and almost all of their resistance centered on the customer accounting plan. Sales training staffs and their management are supposed to be the ultimate authorities on selling in their companies. Anything that would undermine or threaten that authority will be resisted with fanatical vigor. Lip service you will get in abundance as their insidious efforts continue to undermine the effectiveness of the yardstick.

But it is always their opinion competing against a mathematical fact. What gets measured, improves. What doesn't, won't. If anyone is permitted to undermine the yardstick, that will negate everything.

I can tell you from experience that when my teachings are presented to those in charge of sales training the response is often, "We are already doing most of those things, most of the time." Truth is they aren't or this would not be the biggest problem facing all businesses today. What gets accurately measured, improves. All other arguments for what anyone is doing in sales training who have no accurate yardstick measuring each individual salesperson's improvement is null and void. With an accurate yardstick, improvement can be verified. Without one, it can't.

Improvement means change. The greatest fear we all have is our fear of fear itself. We fear what we don't understand. We don't understand what the consequences of change will mean to us, so we are afraid to do those things that will bring about change. The higher our positions, the more we have to lose, the greater our fear. We can become paralyzed by that fear.

Most change is based on someone else's opinion. There is legitimate cause for fear when that is the case. If that person's opinion is wrong, things could wind up much worse instead of better.

There is no opinion involved in measuring what you want to improve. None. The improvement is mathematically guaranteed. Ah, ha! Guaranteed for who? The individual salesperson, of course. Where does that leave the manager? The individual improvement of all the salespeople proves management has improved, too. Believe it or not, you will find that a lot, if not most, middle managers who see the failure of those under them as the main reason he or she is needed.

Everyone in business must realize that the success of everyone in any company depends on the satisfaction of the customer. When a customer buys what the company sells, that customer's satisfaction depends entirely upon how well that purchase met his or her needs.

It is the salespeople's job to help every prospective customer they come in contact with to become satisfied customers. The salesperson's effectiveness is measured by the customer's satisfaction.

Management's job is to help salespeople become more effective. Management's effectiveness is measured by the success of each salesperson.

The buck only stops when it reaches the top, usually the CEO. But courts are now holding boards of directors more and more accountable for company policies.

As people in the business world come to realize that the most valuable asset they have and that the only naturally appreciating asset is a satisfied customer, boards of directors will find themselves being held more and more accountable for the protection of those assets. And every company must be able to measure the steps being taken to improve the company's percentage of bottom-line satisfied customers.

That one step will cause the greatest change ever to hit the world of business. Something to fear? Not if you use a yardstick to measure how effectively the change is taking place in your company. That's guarantee

Something to fear? Oh, yes. If you're not using an accurate yardstick yet, you can rest assured that your job and your company are doomed. That's guaranteed, too. No one has a place to hide when competence is measured accurately: not at the top in an ivory tower, not at the bottom where common labor is performed, and nowhere in between.

45 / *Competence: Plan for It*

IT DOES NOT MATTER WHAT YOUR PRODUCT IS, IF YOU CANNOT GET IT SOLD WITH THE COMPETENCE NEEDED TO PRODUCE A SATISFIED CUSTOMER, YOU CAN FORGET ALL OTHER THINGS DONE IN YOUR COMPANY. YOU MAY HAVE THE MOST ADVANCED COMPUTER SYSTEM IN YOUR INDUSTRY AND RUN THE TIGHTEST SHIP, BUT IF YOU CAN'T GET YOUR PRODUCT SOLD WITH THE COMPETENCE TO PRODUCE SATISFIED CUSTOMERS, ALL THOSE OTHER THINGS MEAN IS THAT YOU CAN HAVE THE CLEANEST GOING OUT OF BUSINESS SALE IN HISTORY.

COMPETENCE: PLAN FOR IT or start planning your "going out of business" sale.

In a mass-produced upholstered furniture factory five people make each piece of furniture. They work as a team, each with a specific job. The quality of every piece of furniture turned out by each team must pass quality standards set by the company. The team members are paid a set amount for every piece of furniture they produce.

As the workers become more competent, they can do this job to company standards in less time, but there is a catch. Regardless how fast or how good each one is, their income is limited by the *team's* production.

If a factory runs ten production lines, there are ten teams. The first team is made up of the five most competent workers. They turn out the most production and are the highest paid. The second team is made up of the second best and so on down the ladder. It is each worker's desire to become more competent so he or she can move up to the next line and make more money per hour worked. Of course, the quality of what the workers do must be the same regardless which line they are on.

When these workers first start on a team, it takes them forever to complete one piece of furniture to an acceptable standard. If it weren't for minimum wage guarantees, they would starve to death. They are required to complete every step to an acceptable standard from the very first piece they work on, regardless how many times they must redo their work. It never takes long for them to be doing well enough to be earning minimum wage, but it may take a long time to reach the first team. Here's the catch. When orders slow down, the tenth team is the first one laid off. Then number nine, eight, seven, and so on.

The business of selling must be seen the same way. Salespeople have one goal and ten objectives they must achieve to reach that goal. If they do not hold themselves accountable for achieving each of those objectives in its proper sequence, they will never produce a quality product. The first five objectives are easily achieved, once the salesperson has tried to complete each in its sequence every single time he or she comes in contact with a prospective customer and has measured the results. *Every single time!*

It is important that management be close by just as it is in the upholstery factory. The foreman spends most of his time overseeing the starting team. Until it is producing a quality job every time, he must be right there. Once the starting team is over that hump, it is on its own.

Once salespeople can achieve the first five objectives every time, regardless how long it takes, they will need very little supervision. As long as they use their yardsticks, it will take less and less time to make each sale.

If people in management think that is going to happen accidentally, they should resign. If it *were* done accidentally, no management would be needed.

Mr. President, chairman, and CEO, if you expect to have a customer-driven company that will thrive and grow in the computerized world that is moving with space-age speed, it will all start with a customer-driven sales organization.

I can tell you right now that sales trainers and sales managers are no different from salespeople in one respect. They have effective skills. Those effective skills are habits to which they are addicted. The longer they have been doing what they do, the stronger the addiction. If those are effective counterproductive skills, they will prevent you from ever, and I mean *ever*, developing a customer-driven sales organization.

Mr. Chief Executive Officer, if you owned an upholstered furniture factory and knew exactly how many steps it took or how many objectives had to be achieved for each member of the team to produce a product that would pass your standards, you would not accept less than that of a worker, would you? That's *your* product. If it doesn't meet those standards, it is not going to best meet your customer's needs and keep them as satisfied customers. Then your days in business are numbered. You won't accept less than that out of the factory workers. Who do you hold accountable for those standards? The plant manager. Who does the manager hold accountable? The foreman.

We can blame workers for poor production and quality if it makes us feel better not to take our own responsibility seriously. But when those workers fail, it is a management failure. Period. The buck does not stop until it reaches the top.

You might have the most advanced computer programs in your industry and you might run the tightest ship, but if you can't get your product sold competently, all those other things mean is that you can have a very clean going-out-of-business sale. No matter what you produce or sell, getting it sold with the competence required to produce *satisfied customers* is the bottom line—for anyone, from the CEO to the salesperson on the floor, who is truly in the business of selling.

If you have read this book and wish to implement it in your company, I recommend you contact: "Customer-driven" 1-800-234-9384 for free literature. This is just as important for small start-up companies as it is for the world's largest.

THE BUSINESS OF SELLING IS THE ONLY BUSINESS

There really is only one business and that business is the business of selling. And in all business there really is only one goal: a satisfied customer.

I have heard people in all professions, not just selling, say, "I sure wish you could come talk to our people about selling. We have the same problems in our profession." I have heard this comment from educators, doctors, lawyers, bankers, and many others.

The success or failure of all businesses, including all services, depends upon how much the provider knows about the customers, clients, students, or patients, and how much the provider knows about what will best meet those customers' needs. Developing the productive skills to achieve those two things is the easiest part of selling, once you accept that what gets measured, improves.

The goal of every endeavor undertaken by anyone should be that the person or persons on the other side of that endeavor winds up equally satisfied with the benefits they enjoy from the transaction.

Everyone who sets out to reach any goal will discover he or she will have to follow the same sequence of objectives to achieve it as those who compete in the business of selling.

JOHN F. LAWHON is a seasoned professional. *The Selling Bible,* his second book, is the result of 35 years of selling, management, and ownership plus 15 years of additional research and diagnostic consulting — including hundreds of hours of personal interviews with both highly successful and long-term-average salespeople.

His first book, *Selling Retail,* opened the doors for his continued research into all fields of selling while becoming the basis of sales education for thousands of retail companies in the U.S. and Canada. It is credited with having done more to improve the competence of retail salespeople than all other such books combined. Most just say, "It works!"

The celebrated entrepreneur-marketer-educator and author employs a revolutionary approach to salesmanship and sales training with a proven, comprehensive plan that promises to be the salvation for the business of selling in the 21st century.

For more information about Mr. Lawhon's speaking programs and other sales aid materials, write:

The Business of Selling, Inc.
P. O. Box 14057
Tulsa, OK 74159
Or, call toll-free 1-800-234-9384